Cranford Library

JUL 2 5 1988

CRANFORD PUBLIC LIBRARY N.J.

3 9520 00099 0988

Cranford Public Library

L. N. J. 07016

W9-DDX-068

ETHEL
ROSENBERG

Ethel Rosenberg

BEYOND THE MYTHS

BY ILENE PHILIPSON

FRANKLIN WATTS | 1988
NEW YORK | TORONTO

Excerpts from Paul Lyons' *Philadelphia Communists:
1936–1956* © 1980 by Temple University are reprinted
by permission of Temple University Press.

Library of Congress Cataloging-in-Publication Data

Philipson, Ilene.   ROSENBERG, ETHEL
Ethel Rosenberg: beyond ..
Bibliography: p.
Includes index.
1. Rosenberg, Ethel, 1915–1953. 2. Communists—
United States—Biography. 3. Spies—United States—
Biography. I. Title.
HX84.R578P46   1988   364.1′31′0924   [B] 87-31634
ISBN 0-531-15057-7   Ros

Copyright © 1988 by Ilene J. Philipson
All rights reserved
Printed in the United States
6 5 4 3 2 1

CONTENTS

ETHEL
ROSENBERG

INTRODUCTION

AN UNEXCEPTIONAL LIFE

To most Americans she remains an "atom spy," a still-evocative symbol of a worldwide Communist conspiracy that threatens the democratic world. In the nineteen-fifties the government accused her of causing the Korean War and of jeopardizing "the lives of every man, woman and child in this country." President Dwight D. Eisenhower went further. In denying her last plea for clemency and assuring her death by electrocution, he charged that she "may have condemned to death tens of millions of innocent people all over the world." American public opinion generally agreed with the damning words of trial court judge, Irving Kaufman: she had committed a "crime worse than murder" that had forever "altered the course of history to the disadvantage of our country."

But, to many Western Europeans and liberal-minded people around the world, her imprisonment and death at the hands of the United States government lingers as a vivid reminder of much that is wrong with America: its fanatical anti-Communism, its disregard for world opinion. To people in Rome, Paris, and other European cities, the image of this little Jewish housewife from the Lower East Side of Manhattan is testimony to honesty, courage, and determination in the face of overwhelming odds.

2   For many political progressives and Communist party members, here and abroad, she is much more. Her actions while on trial, in prison, and at the scene of her execution transformed this "ordinary American" into a martyr. She "lifted the hearts and steeled the spirits of countless simple men and women like [herself] in every corner of the earth." "We are convinced," the Communist party's *Worker* wrote in 1953, that "America will enshrine [her] memory in the ranks of innocent martyrs who died in the cause of truth."

While her detractors maintained that for her "the defense of the Soviet Union . . . [was] the sole principle and criterion of all value," her defenders believed that she "saved America's name," and that she was one of the "noblest Americans who ever walked this land."

Her friends believed her to be a devoted mother who lavished affection and attention on her children. They describe her as sweet, warm, and loving. But she knowingly chose to orphan her sons and prevented them from visiting her for the first year of her incarceration. In her court appearances not a hint of human warmth radiated from her. In fact, her cold, virtually emotionless demeanor is thought to have hurt her chances with the jury that tried her and exacerbated the image of the heartless spy who "thought and felt whatever [her] political commitment required [her] to think and to feel."

Her stoicism on the witness stand, and when she heard the verdict of guilt and sentence of death shocked people at the time. It was so unlike a woman, and so peculiarly unlike a woman of her background. In part, it led President Eisenhower to write that "in this instance it is the woman who is the strong and recalcitrant character, the man who is the weak one. She has obviously been the leader in everything they did in the spy ring."

Yet this "recalcitrant" head of an atomic spy ring cried herself to sleep every night while in prison, considered *Parents' Magazine* to be her favorite periodical, and was in psychotherapy four times a week at the time of her arrest. Except for one summer, this master spy never lived more than five miles from the tenement where she was born, nor traveled further from New York than to New Jersey. Nevertheless, she was believed to have connections to the highest circles in Moscow.

The testimony that accounts for her being only the second woman in American history to be executed at the hands of the federal government was that of her younger brother upon whom she had doted in childhood. He and his wife were effectively responsible for sending her to the electric chair. No one else claimed to witness her involvement in any conspiracy or crime. The response of her Orthodox Jewish family, whose religion considered family ties more important than any other social relationships, was not merely to believe the brother's account, but to shun the sister, deny her any aid, turn its back on her children, and refuse to attend her funeral.

Who was this person who inspired the hate and condemnation of her own family, the vast majority of the American people, and the United States government? Who was this Jewish housewife revered by many here and throughout the world as a martyr and symbol of resistance, dignity, and hope? Was she the cold, domineering partner in an atomic spy ring? An innocent victim of a government frame-up? A devoted mother, or a soldier of Stalin who "placed her duty as a Communist above her country and even more, above her two children"?

What had she done to inspire the hatred of her own family? How was she able to withstand two years of solitary confinement, with the constant threat of death hanging over her, and not cooperate with the government? Why did she choose to orphan her two small sons who begged for her to come back to them? In truth, who was this woman who went to the electric chair proclaiming innocence to what J. Edgar Hoover called the "crime of the century"?

———

Photographs of Ethel Rosenberg show a pudgy little woman who often looks many years older than her actual age. Most of the photographs of her are from her arrest and trial when she was thirty-four and thirty-five years old respectively. In these photos she is usually pictured in matronly dresses and utterly ridiculous hats. Her thick waist and large hips are accentuated by a belted dress that hangs almost to her ankles. Her face in repose often has a look of disdainfulness or haughtiness. Partly this results from heavily lidded, wide-set eyes set under well-arched brows. Partly it stems from the tiny mouth whose lips seem naturally pinched or pursed. But, in the few pictures where she is smiling, the look of disdain completely melts away; instead we see a head cocked to one side, eyes crinkled, and round, ample cheeks. The lips part to reveal small, well-formed teeth. The grin is engaging; the countenance radiates a warmth and vitality we might not have imagined in such an otherwise aloof and disdainful visage.

To look at this woman it is difficult to imagine anyone either

4   as menacing or heroic as she has been portrayed. But then our fantasies of what female spies or political martyrs look like probably never come in the form of five-foot, one-and-one-half-inch, overweight, working-class Jewish housewives. Part of the problem of trying to reconcile photographs of the real Ethel Rosenberg with our fantasy images is that political symbols usually cannot be fully represented in the form of incarnate individuals. Somehow real people with all their inadequacies and flaws are not readily translatable into monuments and effigies. Thus it is hard to believe that someone who chose to wear hats with six-inch high artificial flowers sticking straight out from them—as Ethel did the day she was arrested— could fully represent the international Communist menace.

In the same sense, a woman whose facial expression so often seemed imperious is not the most likely representative of pure truth and innocence. This may account for the fact that when the Communist party's *Worker* ran a story on the Rosenbergs' lives entitled "The Two Immortals," it used drawings rather than photographs of the recently executed couple. While Julius appears quite similar to how he actually looked, Ethel is portrayed with her hair pulled straight back from her face (a style she never wore, but which conveys a bit more purity than her actual unruly curls), and any hint of haughtiness is absent. Perhaps no real human being could look the part of the "Saint on Earth" that *The Worker* assigned to this dowdy housewife, so an artist's rendering may have seemed more appropriate.

But more than Ethel Rosenberg's appearance is in question when we look at how her life has been used as a political symbol by people of vastly different ideological persuasions. From the beginning of "the Rosenberg case," each one of Ethel's actions and each part of her past that was uncovered was seen through a political prism and used to advance a particular point of view. Thus a single piece of behavior could have radically opposing meanings, depending on whether one was "pro" or "anti" Rosenberg.

A striking example is Ethel's choice to orphan her children by not cooperating with the government and thus dying in the electric chair. The mélange of political liberals, progressives, and radicals who believe the Rosenbergs were innocent and/or victims of a government frame-up take this act to represent an enormous sacrifice made by a devoted mother in the service of some of the highest human values. Through this act she demonstrated her ability to relinquish her most treasured possessions, her children, to prevent

the government from enlarging its witch-hunt, branding all progressive people spies, and assuming that ordinary Americans—like
herself—would forsake their standards and beliefs, if enough pressure were exerted.

The anti-Communist and neoconservative ideologues who believe the Rosenbergs were not only guilty as charged but deserved
the punishment they received, take a much different view of this
matter. To them, Ethel's actions reveal the workings of a heartless
political fanatic whose commitment to Communism outweighed
her capacity for maternal feeling. In the nineteen-fifties, when the
fear of domestic sabotage by cold-blooded Communist zealots was
at its peak, this view was particularly widespread.

What gets lost in this political tug-of-war over Ethel's legacy is
the actual woman, the motivation for her actions, and the meaning
such actions had for her. "Communist spy" and "innocent martyr"
are concepts so infused with prejudice and myth that they do not
allow a human being to emerge. And, since almost all of what has
been written about Ethel has been an attempt to prove whether or
not the Rosenbergs were guilty of spying, it is difficult to peel away
the layers of constructed meaning, interpretation, and myth in which
her personality and actions have been wrapped to discover anything
resembling a real human being.

In saying this, I am not trying to suggest that what you will read
here is the definitive truth untarnished by my own perspective. I
have brought to this study my own values and biases, which I believe
no author can completely overcome. But I have sought to understand Ethel Rosenberg on her own terms. I have tried to discover
why she behaved in certain ways and ventured on particular courses
in terms of her own psychological needs, her familial and social
background, and the times in which she lived. I do not believe we
can fully understand her through ahistoric or universal ideas of
martyrdom or political fanaticism or sainthood. I think that to appreciate the person who was Ethel Rosenberg, rather than the political symbol, is to acknowledge the familial, cultural, social, and
political context in which she grew up, lived, and died.

Ultimately, this is a precarious course to follow because the
terrain of debate in the Rosenberg case has made any commentary
on any of the principal actors ammunition in the battle over guilt
or innocence. Thus to suggest that Ethel was not always truthful or
self-sacrificing is likely to be interpreted by participants in the debate
as support of her guilt. Similarly, to assert that she acted nobly and

6 courageously is to brand one an unqualified advocate of her innocence. This all-or-nothing struggle over the ultimate "truth" in the Rosenberg case unfortunately makes open inquiry, honest confusion, and a willingness to set forth ambiguous information extremely difficult. Needless to say, it has also made the quest for Ethel Rosenberg problematic.

A case in point: In 1953, shortly before the Rosenbergs' execution, the Committee to Secure Justice for the Rosenbergs published an edited collection of the Rosenbergs' prison correspondence. The purpose of the collection was to raise money for their defense and their children's support, and to demonstrate their innocence to the world. A second edition, appearing after their death under the title *The Testament of Ethel and Julius Rosenberg*, was explicitly published to "trace the growth of the man and woman whose names are revered by millions of people around the world, who now believe them martyrs to world peace." The letters written by Ethel in the first and the expanded second editions reveal an incredibly brave, often angry, occasionally depressed woman. The style is often forced and pretentious, and she frequently sounds quite rhetorical. But, at the same time, the unbiased reader must be moved by the dignity, intelligence, and perspective that the writer displays while laboring under the most dehumanizing conditions, namely, solitary confinement and the constant threat of imminent death.

What is striking about Ethel's letters is how well she copes and how little she seems to let her personal worries—about her children, her family, her state of mind, and the like—preoccupy her. In part, it is this selflessness, which is displayed in both her and Julius's letters, that allows the editors of their correspondence to proclaim that the Rosenbergs' "words have already become world classics of democratic eloquence and inspiration." Clearly, authors who only spoke of their feelings and their individual concerns could not pretend to rise to such stature.

For their defenders, these letters are prima facie evidence of the Rosenbergs' ability to sacrifice the personal for the political, to elevate themselves from being ordinary people to "giants" and "martyrs in the cause of peace." For their detractors, the jailhouse correspondence buttresses the belief that a Communist cares more about ideology than human relationships. The fact that a wife and mother, particularly in the midst of the postwar celebration of family and motherhood, could speak as frequently about world issues as about her children, confirmed the worst anti-Communist assumptions. Leslie Fiedler, the noted literary critic, wrote that the letters revealed Ethel to be "incapable of telling treason from devotion, deceit from honesty" and that her relationship to everything, including herself, was false. Robert Warshow similarly concluded from her correspondence that she was a person of "no eloquence and little imagination," alienated "from truth and experience."

In some ways these different interpretations are simply one more example of how ideology constructs a person known as Ethel Rosenberg. But I think the issue of the Rosenbergs' prison correspondence raises something even more disturbing.

It is not widely known that the published letters represent only a small percentage of the Rosenbergs' prison correspondence. The editors, whose aim was to justify their image of the Rosenbergs as innocent martyrs, clearly chose letters and portions of letters to print that would support their image. Thus not only did a particular perspective on the Rosenberg case color interpretations made of Ethel's life, but it determined the very material the public has had on which to make its own judgments.

In some ways this selection backfired. In trying to show an innocent martyr, the editors of the letters tended to obscure the complexity, turmoil, and depth of Ethel Rosenberg while in prison. Through their attempts to make the Rosenbergs superhuman, the editors allowed them to be seen as subhuman by critics eager to point out pretension and falsity. Regrettably the Rosenbergs' sons, Michael and Robert Meeropol, have continued this tradition. As holders of the copyright on their parents' correspondence, they have been willing to grant authors permission to reprint portions of the letters, I believe, only if there is agreement with the Meeropols' view of their parents. Thus the Meeropols sued Louis Nizer for copyright infringement over his book, *The Implosion Conspiracy*, which quoted from only a handful of previously published letters, but argued that the Rosenbergs were guilty of conspiracy to commit espionage. Conversely, when Walter and Miriam Schneir brought out the second edition of their classic defense of the Rosenbergs, *Invitation to an Inquest*, the Meeropols offered no objection to their publishing twenty-three pages of excerpts from the Rosenbergs' letters—excerpts that only portrayed their parents in the most positive light.

Lacking access to the complete and unedited correspondence of Ethel Rosenberg, the public will have to continue to rely on authors' interpretations and selectively published letters to assess her as a person and historical figure. That this assessment has more often been critical than kind should prompt her protectors to allow her to speak for herself.

———

Shortly after the Rosenbergs' execution, a reporter for *The Worker* approached Emanuel Bloch, the Rosenbergs' attorney, about writing a series of articles on the Rosenbergs' lives. Bloch was discouraging. "I'm afraid you won't get much. You won't find many people who knew them, or if you do they will be afraid of you. And if you did get them to talk, what could they say? They were such—no, I'm not going to say ordinary people—but ordinary progressive people. Believe me, they led unexceptional lives."

That was in 1953. In 1987, thirty-four years later, the attempt to uncover an "unexceptional life" has been even more difficult. It has taken me to many blind alleys and a number of closed doors. It has taught me much about the sons and daughters of immigrant Jews, the American Communist party, and the lingering legacy of McCarthyism. It has shown me that family antagonisms die hard. Above all, it has illustrated that the emotions, passions, and fear surrounding the Rosenbergs in the early nineteen-fifties are very much alive today.

Most biographers take as their subjects people who, by virtue of their accomplishments, talent, birthright, or associations are public figures. In such cases the subjects leave behind work or artifacts that can be analyzed, or a career such as that of explorer, sports figure, criminal, stage performer, or the like that has been documented by others. Ethel Rosenberg left neither works nor a career. Prior to the last three years of her life, her existence seemed irrelevant in traditional biographical terms. She did not keep a diary. Like most people she knew, she almost never left New York City, so she had virtually no one with whom to maintain a correspondence. Her vocation was clerical worker and housewife, so she produced no work of art, engaged in no noteworthy career, left no unique imprint upon the world around her.

In 1950, however, this obscure, thirty-four-year-old mother of two was thrust before the public's eye, albeit against her will. Even then her observable actions were few: her two grand jury appearances, her arrest, pretrial hearings, twenty-three-day trial, sentencing, and removal to Sing Sing. There she was swallowed up in the bowels of the prison—never to be seen again. All told there were about thirty-five to forty days in which Ethel could be watched by the media and have her actions reported to the world. Beyond this were the few stories that came out of prison from former inmates, wardens, and visitors. There were the unsubstantiated reports of gossip columnists, and the letters Ethel wrote to her husband, lawyer, psychiatrist, children, and in-laws during her three-year incarceration. For a life spanning almost thirty-eight years, this is not very much. Like the lives of most working-class people, most of Ethel Rosenberg's life remains hidden from history.

Where, then, does one turn to discover an "unexceptional life," as Emanuel Bloch described it? First, it would seem that the immediate family could be the greatest help. But Ethel's husband died with her; her two sons were seven and three years old when she was arrested, and her own family abandoned her, forever refusing to speak about her in public.

Many of Ethel's friends and acquaintances, however, were extremely informative and helpful. I was fortunate enough to talk with both of Ethel's psychotherapists. The material and insights they provided have been invaluable. So, too, were the memories of her friends whose recollections gave dimension and color to facts and events. Ethel Appel, Julius Rosenberg's older sister, provided crucial information over the course of countless hours. As one of the only surviving family members, and the only person alive who regularly visited Ethel and Julius during their two-year imprisonment at Sing Sing, Mrs. Appel was always informative and compelling.

Michael and Robert Meeropol gave me permission to see and read all of their parents' unpublished correspondence. This allowed me rare access into Ethel's mind—her feelings, longings and needs while in prison. It also gave me greater insight into her relationships with her husband, children, family and psychoanalyst. Sadly, however, the Meeropols were not willing to permit me to publish or paraphrase any excerpts from this revealing unpublished correspondence. Although they are both now middle-aged men, Michael and Robert's investment in maintaining an idealized portrait of their mother—for themselves and for the public—seems as great as it was when they were tragically orphaned in 1953.

The Meeropols' attorney, Marshall Perlin, was helpful in guiding me through the voluminous FBI files on the Rosenbergs that have been released to him on behalf of the Meeropols under the Freedom of Information Act. Although not all of the files on the Rosenberg case have been released, and many of the ones Perlin

10   has received have been censored by the FBI, they represent an invaluable resource, to be used with caution.

But all of these sources do not provide us with the definitive portrait of Ethel Rosenberg. Memories fade, government-censored FBI files can distort, stories told over and over, or even for the first time, are colored by years of political battle over the meaning of a woman's life and the legacy she bequeathed.

Even if this were not so, we would still not grasp fully the "objective truth," the true richness and complexity of another human being's life. As author Edgar Johnson wrote, biography is "a psychological intersection between the personality of the biographer and that of his subject." In this sense then the following is one author's understanding of a woman who can no longer speak for herself, whose actions can only be interpreted and not definitively explained.

I believe the only way to make sense of another's life is through empathic understanding, the ability to put oneself in another's place, to try to imagine the constraints, compulsions, conflicts that another felt. Studying another human being is not akin to examining blood cells, molecules, earthquake faults, or stars. What distinguishes biography from physiology, physics, geology, astronomy, or any other "science" is that there are no laws or universals to act as guides. Psychology can and must inform how biographers conceptualize their subjects, but it cannot impose an "objective" methodology for comprehending a life. At best, it can provide theoretical tools to explore and analyze empathically.

Ultimately then what is left is one person staring at and listening to another through time. As much as I observe and as many theories as I come prepared with, I am experiencing my subject through my own senses. I can only listen carefully to what she tells me and to what others around her tell me, always mindful that behavior and actions typically have multiple causes and meanings.

In the course of studying a life, especially one as puzzling as Ethel Rosenberg's, the question of how to comprehend confusing or contradictory actions is salient. One method would be simply to gloss over them by actual omission or by merely referring to them without attention or analysis. A second means would be to interpret them according to a single theme. Biographers frequently come to perceive one particular event, fact, or relationship as the key to virtually all of their subject's behavior. When a perplexing bit of the subject's life comes up, this single theme is called upon to explain both motivation and meaning. Often this method is thought to be an objective form of analysis because it employs some universal category, such as Oedipal conflict, to explain behavior. The third, and I believe most fruitful and honest method for understanding a complex human being, is to offer a number of explanations for puzzling or contradictory material. This method of "overdetermination" helps guard against the pitfalls of unrestrained subjectivity. Of course, the *field* of explanation is delimited by an author's own knowledge, prejudices, and beliefs, but the reader is presented with possibilities that a single explanation would obscure.

To uncover Ethel Rosenberg means seeing not only behind the political legend but beyond her relationship to her husband. In the public's mind the identities of Ethel and Julius Rosenberg are virtually fused, linked forever in their criminality or martyrdom, depending on one's perspective. The "Rosenberg case" subsumes both as individuals and diminishes the uniqueness of each of their personalities. In most of the books written about this most celebrated case, Ethel and Julius's personal characteristics are lumped together and only trotted out to buttress larger claims about their guilt or innocence. *They* were political fanatics; *they* were rigid, self-righteous ideologues; *they* were innocent and honest, and so forth. In other words *they* were the same in feelings, actions, motivations. Because they took the same stance toward the government's attempt to make them talk and died together because of this stance, it is generally believed that in some basic way they were the same. As we shall see, however, even in their ultimate decision to refuse to cooperate with the government and go to their deaths, their reasons were not identical. Beneath the many interpretations made of "the Rosenbergs" lie two people with vastly different personalities who cannot be understood as equivalent.

If Ethel has been lost through aggregation with her husband, her identity has been equally obscured under the weight of "the Rosenberg case." When people refer to "the case" they may mean anything from the actual legal motions and maneuvers made on Ethel and Julius's behalf between their arrest and execution (1950–1953), to a whole series of events beginning in Los Alamos, New Mexico, in 1944 when Ethel's brother David Greenglass supposedly transmitted a sketch of the atom bomb and ending with the termination of the FBI's main investigation into the "Rosenberg spy ring" in 1957. Where the actual person of Ethel Rosenberg enters into this grand sweep of history is not always clear.

Because so much has already been written about "the case," so many volumes have examined every aspect from every possible perspective, I have chosen to place the case in the background and Ethel's experience of it in the foreground. For many followers of the case, this undoubtedly will be a disappointment. But, ultimately, I think they may discover that it is possible to gain insight into this momentous historical event by looking carefully at one of its principal actors. By exploring her background, her motivations, her values and needs, we all may come to know "the case" and its historical environment more fully. Her life can make history more understandable, just as history can illuminate her life.

Uncovering Ethel Rosenberg takes work and a willingness to suspend judgment. Only an open mind can retrieve her life from the political uses to which it has been put. To understand her and her actual achievement, it is necessary to peel off the layers of legend, piety, and defamation that have coated her identity in the years since her death. To do this makes her more human and perhaps less worthy of either hate or adoration, but I think that it will make her decisions more understandable, her actual life more compelling, and her place in history more secure.

Ethel
Greenglass

1915–1939

1

BEGINNINGS

Esther Ethel Greenglass was born on 28 September 1915 into a unique setting, the likes of which the world had never seen before and most likely will never know again. She arrived into an environment more crowded than anywhere in Europe, Asia, or Africa. The traffic, the noise, and the tumult were overwhelming. People were everywhere—on the streets, in the shops, crammed into small rooms where they worked and slept, ate and made love. Poverty was everywhere, disease rampant, hardship reflected on most faces. But in the midst of this want, a vitality stirred in the hundreds of places of worship, the live theaters, cafes, libraries and bookstores, the lecture halls and newspaper offices. Socialists and anarchists mingled with free thinkers, nationalists, and religious zealots.

Some 353,000 people were packed into that quarter of Manhattan from the Bowery on the west and 14th Street on the north to the East River on the east and south. New York City as a whole supported a high proportion of the world's Jewish population, a population that differed sharply from its Gentile neighbors who often lived only a few blocks away.

Most of the Jews in this ghetto were immigrants from Eastern Europe—Russia, Poland, Romania, and Austro-Hungary. Many had lived in the Pale, an area between the Baltic and Black Sea where

Jews were legally authorized to settle by the Russian government. They had resided in small towns, *shtetls*, where they had worked at petty trading, small crafts, and shopkeeping. Their lives had centered on religion and the family; their values revolved around the importance of learning, the observance of ritual, and the acceptance of suffering as a way of life until the anticipated coming of the Messiah. Although in their hearts they knew they were the "Chosen People," their everyday lives were deeply colored by extreme persecution at the hands of Christians who determined where and how they could live. With the accession of Tsar Alexander III to the Russian throne in 1881, this persecution accelerated dramatically. A succession of terrifying pogroms occurred across Russia from which many Jews fled by emigrating to the United States and settling in New York City.

By 1915, the almost entirely Jewish Lower East Side of New York was a vibrant and complex society within a society. It had its own institutions, language, and culture, although all of these were in flux as Jews were becoming increasingly Americanized. This New World ghetto presented a curious contrast of premodern *shtetl* existence and the apogee of competitive capitalism. The pushcarts lining the streets still provided most inhabitants with their daily needs, and shopping could easily take half a housewife's day as she went from cart to cart searching for the best bargains. But shops and still larger stores, owned by Jews who had been able to save up small amounts of capital, were increasingly replacing the carts throughout the neighborhoods. Synagogues, too, were virtually on every street, and most of the Lower East Side respected the Sabbath, or *shabbes*, on Saturday, by not working, shopping, or engaging in any worldly activity. But many did not, because they had broken with their religion, found *shabbes* inconvenient to honor, or were forced to work by an employer who followed the traditional American custom of not working on Sundays only.

Yiddish was still the language most commonly heard on the streets, but English was spoken almost exclusively by the children and adolescents, and many adults now spoke a Yiddish laced with American words and idioms. Yiddish newspapers were seen everywhere, but among the copies of the *Forward* and the *Day*, one could see, here and there, such English-language papers as the *Daily News* or the *Tribune*. The appearance of the people also was markedly different on the Lower East Side. Old men with long beards were seen everywhere, as were older women wearing wigs in the

Orthodox style. Many women—old and young alike—walked through the streets with shawls draped over their heads, looking more like Russian peasants than twentieth-century New Yorkers. But, many were also seen wearing the latest hobble skirts, if only in the cheapest reproductions.

The landscape of this ghetto was fairly uniform. Gray stone tenements lined almost every street. They presented solid fronts with no greenery, gardens, or vacant spaces between buildings. Certain structures, however, stood out—the *Jewish Daily Forward* building, the tallest in the quarter, Cooper Union with its domed roof, the brick facade of the Henry Street Settlement, and the splendor of the theaters like the Grand and the Thalia. But, in general, the environment was monotonous, cluttered, and dingy. Garbage—from the pushcarts, the horse-drawn wagons, the pedestrians, and the shops and tenements—strewed the streets in a profusion not seen in other parts of the city. Clotheslines with drying undergarments filled the wells and alleys between buildings, and in warmer weather quilts, mattresses, and featherbeds hung from windows to expose them to the sun and kill off the variety of insects that infested most tenement households.

Privacy was unheard of in this environment. Whole families often lived together in one room; boarders frequently shared rooms, even beds, with family members; toilets were almost always shared with neighbors. The streets, the alleyways, the libraries, cafes, and even the few parks were always crowded. People—family members, neighbors, friends, acquaintances and strangers—were ever present to hear and see one's every move and act. Even the crowded *shtetls* often had nearby forests or meadows to which one could escape, to think, to reflect, to daydream. But here people and their clamor were everywhere:

> *I can never forget the East Side . . . a tenement canyon hung with fire-escapes, bed-clothing, and faces.*
>
> *Always these faces at the tenement windows. The street never failed them. It was an immense excitement. It never slept. It roared like a sea. It exploded like fireworks.*
>
> *People pushed and wrangled in the street. There were armies of howling pushcart peddlers. Women screamed, dogs barked and copulated. Babies cried.*
>
> *A parrot cursed. Ragged kids played under truck-horses. Fat housewives fought from stoop to stoop. A beggar sang.*

Into this pandemonium of life, Esther Ethel Greenglass was born, the first child of Barnet Greenglass and Tessie Feit Greenglass. She was delivered at 64 Sheriff Street, a tenement house between Rivington and Delancey Streets. The trains traveling to and from Brooklyn over the Williamsburg Bridge, a half-block away, provided a loud and constant drone against which the street offered up its cacophony of voices and clatter.

Directly across the street from number 64, an old stable quartered the horses that pulled delivery trucks and vans throughout the Lower East Side. In the hot summers, the ever-present odor of overworked and underfed horses pervaded the rooms of the equally overworked and underfed human inhabitants of Sheriff Street. Flies swarmed through windows forced open by the heat. A few doors down, a pushcart barn housed the carts that lined Rivington and Essex streets during the day. At the end of the day, weary vendors wheeled home their pushcarts, laden with rotting fruits and vegetables, cheese and fish. Several neighboring fresh fish shops contributed their stench to the air, making this single block of Sheriff Street one of the filthiest on the whole Lower East Side.

A synagogue and several small machine shops were also on the block. Taken together, these various enterprises gave Sheriff Street a distinctly commercial cast, although the many tenements housed hundreds of people above the din and tumult of the street.

Number 64 was built sometime between 1880 and 1901. It was based on a "dumbbell" design, the most common architectural plan for tenements built during the last part of the nineteenth century. Four apartments were housed on each floor, with two water closets on each story to be shared among the four units. The tenement house itself stood four stories high on a lot twenty-five feet wide and about one-hundred-feet deep. The stairway connecting floors was in the center of the building. The only source of natural light was from windows at the front and rear of the structure. Narrow air shafts on the sides of the building provided no direct sunlight and only the poorest ventilation. The public hallways therefore were dark, and walking down them or through them to the toilet was often hazardous. Jacob Riis, the journalist and social reformer who spent much time on the Lower East Side, called the dumbbell design "the one hopeless form of tenement construction."

The Greenglasses occupied a ground-floor apartment directly behind Barnet Greenglass's sewing machine repair shop. Barnet, whom almost everyone called Barney, repaired machines for many of the hundreds of sweatshops dotting the East Side. He worked from early in the morning until after nightfall in his small room strewn with parts, tools, rags, and debris. Everything was covered with a thick layer of dust, and Barney often appeared as dusty as the machines and tools around him. Neighborhood cats roamed in and out of the shop, lounging lazily wherever it suited them, bringing with them the fleas that nested in every rug, bed, and cushion of the building.

Directly behind the shop was the narrow, windowless bedroom where Barney and Tessie slept. The few pieces of furniture in the bedroom were also covered with dust, and the papers and clothes strewn around the room gave it the small, dark, disorderly appearance that often accompanies poverty.

Behind the bedroom was the kitchen, the most used and best-kept room in the apartment. The room was dominated by a large, wood-burning stove, the center of Greenglass family life since it was used to cook the family's meals and to provide the only source of warmth in this cold-water flat. With almost no access to any direct sunlight, the apartment was quite cold and damp most of the year, with the only relief coming at the height of summer. Family members would sit around the oven, their feet propped up, soaking in the heat that quickly dissipated once one was outside the kitchen. In the depths of winter, the tenement sometimes became so frigid that ice formed in the toilets.

The other mainstay of the kitchen was the high-legged clothes-washing tub with an enamel top that could be removed only with great effort. Tessie used it not only to wash the clothes, but to wash the dishes and her children as well. For each washing, she had to light a wood fire and boil huge pots of water.

The last room of the flat was probably used by Sammy Greenglass, Barney's son from his first marriage, who was eight years old when Esther Ethel, soon to be known only by her middle name, was born. In addition to its fake mantelpiece, Sammy's room had the only window that faced outside, aside from the one in Barney's shop. The window looked out on a clapboard-fenced yard littered with trash. Roosters and the omnipresent cats roamed through the refuse; a single tree struggled for life amid the garbage.

This was the intimate environment into which Ethel Greenglass was born and where she spent all her childhood and adolescence.

Despite her dreams and hopes, she was never to move much beyond these meager beginnings. In some ways she was like the tree in the backyard, but in other very important ways she was not.

———

The frigid temperature of the Greenglasses' apartment was apparently equaled by the relationships among family members at 64 Sheriff Street. As an adult, Ethel spoke of her early life as one of "penury" and this apparently referred to more than just the material poverty and scarcity that enveloped her family.

In fact, little is known about the Greenglasses, given their refusal to be interviewed and the dearth of information that exists about them. What we do know is that Tessie and Barney were both Jews, she from Austria and he from Russia. Their native tongue was Yiddish and they were both reared in Orthodox Jewish homes. When Barney immigrated to the United States, he was already a skilled worker, a mechanic. He probably turned to repairing sewing machines because the needle trades in general were one of the very few industries monopolized by Jews. By 1900, over ninety percent of the garment industry in New York was controlled by Jews, so there was a market for a man able to turn his knowledge of machinery to the repair of sewing machines used by private tailors and in sweatshops throughout the Lower East Side. Although he earned only enough for his family to live an impoverished existence, Barney's repair shop made it possible for him to avoid the worst working conditions of the Lower East Side—the sweatshops and factories with their excessively long work hours, backbreaking labor, and the expectation of an early death.

Like most married women in the Jewish ghetto, Tessie was a full-time homemaker. While it was common for girls and unmarried women to work in stores, factories, and sweatshops, a Jewish wife usually tended her home. As one of the foremost authorities on Jewish life in America, Irving Howe, has pointed out:

> Not only tradition but practical sense enforced this choice: it was so hard to maintain any sort of decent life in the tenement, it took so much energy just to cook and clean and shop and bring up children, that the immigrant wives, who in any case seldom possessed marketable skills, had to stay home. . . . Nor did staying home mean leisure or indulgence for the wives. It meant carving out an area of

protection for their families, it meant toil and anxiety, which
all too often left them worn with fatigue, heavy and shape-
less, prematurely aged, their sexuality drained out.

As time went on, Tessie seemed more worn out than most. From almost all available accounts, she seems to have been a bitter woman who was disappointed by her station in life. Undoubtedly her lot was a hard one. After Ethel was born, she had Bernard two-and-a-half years later, and then David four years after that. Taking care of four children in a cold-water tenement flat meant that the most basic household tasks—feeding her family, washing clothes, keeping her children warm in the winter—were extremely difficult, leaving little time for any leisure, escape, or idleness.

Compounding this very real hardship was the disappointment Tessie seems to have felt about her marriage to Barney Greenglass. Most people who knew him describe Barney as a sweet man who was both shorter and smaller than his wife. Most have characterized him as passive or as a *nebechel*. For well over thirty years, he labored long hours in his little repair shop, grew bald and bent, but he was never able to move his family into a better section of town or into an apartment with steam heat, hot water, or a private toilet.

A life of material deprivation and little reward or comfort was probably not what Tessie had bargained for. During the late teens and twenties of this century, remaining at the poverty level on the Lower East Side for someone with ambition was particularly difficult. This was a time of enormous movement in the Jewish community, a time when thousands of Jews were able to escape their ghetto for better areas of the city and beyond—to the Upper West Side, Brooklyn, the Bronx, New Jersey, Connecticut, even California. By 1930 the Lower East Side had a Jewish population of only 121,000 in comparison to 353,000 only fourteen years before. The disappointment and perhaps even resentment at seeing neighbors, acquaintances, and friends doing better, approximating more closely the "American dream," must have weighed heavily on Tessie.

The interests and beliefs that sustained many contemporaries of the Greenglasses and allowed them to endure economic hardship apparently did not touch Tessie and Barney. Accounts of Jewish immigrant life in the first part of the twentieth century reveal a people who thirsted for education, for culture, for their children to succeed where they had failed. Jewish immigrants flocked to settlement houses, night schools, and public lectures to feed a craving to learn about the world, a world so many of them had been prevented from knowing before they arrived in America. Jewish socialists and anarchists dedicated their lives to social transformation, spending their few hours away from work debating political ideas and events. Religious zealots and Zionists directed their passions to the Talmud or to what they saw as the pressing need for the establishment of a Jewish state. This immigrant generation was a generation of dreamers, whose thoughts and ambitions focused on a better life for Jews in general and for their own children in particular. "The Jews who came to America were a people infatuated with ideas of the future, not so much for themselves as for their children. The future was their dream, their 'fix.' "

The Greenglasses did not share in the uproar of intellectual, political, and religious life that consumed much of the Lower East Side. They did not value learning, treasure books, or surround themselves with music or art of any kind. For them politics only got people in trouble and was just so much talk anyway. While they continued to observe the Jewish religion and conform to its dictates, it did not seem to inspire or uplift them. As a friend of Ethel's remembers, the God that Tessie pictured to her children "was always on the mother's side and the side of practicality." Although the Greenglasses undoubtedly wanted their children to succeed, they gave them little spiritual or economic material on which to build that success.

Thus Tessie did not have much to support her in her disappointment and frustration with her life. For her no higher religious beliefs made her deprivation understandable or provided justification for her sacrifice; no political vision enabled her to direct her anger at something or someone outside herself and her family; nothing compensated for the cruel life so many others around her seemed to be escaping. This was Tessie's burden and it seems to have enveloped her.

From all accounts, Barney was, at least outwardly, much more content with his lot. Everyone seems to remember him as smiling, "an adorable little man with high red cheeks." He did not seem to have much drive or ambition, or if he did, he did not act on it. He worked at his repair shop and used his little free time to indulge his one pleasure, attending the Yiddish theater. Not a dynamic or forceful man, Barney Greenglass trod lightly on the earth, leaving little by which to remember him.

Perhaps this added to Tessie's unhappiness. She not only lived in poverty because of her husband's lack of success, but she lived with a man who did not seem to care or care enough about his situation. She had married a *nebbish*. She seems to have dealt with her dissatisfactions by turning her interests and affection to the next closest males in her life, her sons. As a witness to the Greenglass family reported, Tessie was "a bitter woman, whose affection, such as it was, all went to the boys in the family."

This was by no means an unusual preference in a culture that, because of its religious convictions and economic realities, made such a choice seem both natural and necessary. Orthodox Judaism always has taught that the ideal life was that of a religious scholar and that such a scholar was always a man. Sons alone could study the Torah, assume all the major religious responsibilities of Judaism, and recite the memorial prayer for parents after they had departed. A son was an asset, a prize. His birth was cause for celebration, whereas that of a daughter merely was tolerated. As the Talmud puts it, "Woe to the father whose children are girls."

Due to the Diaspora, the universal oppression of Jews, and the lack of a Jewish state, Jewish sons carried on their shoulders the entire history of their forebears and were the only means of perpetuating Judaism. In America this task took on new and greater urgency and meaning. As Irving Howe states, "With gratifications postponed, the culture of the East Side became a culture utterly devoted to its sons." If one had to suffer in poverty and want, a son could rise above the squalor, beyond the Lower East Side, and provide a better life for himself, his own family, and perhaps his parents too.

Tessie Greenglass, however, seems to have gone beyond merely catering to her sons over her daughter. Ettie, as Ethel was known as a girl, was the particular object of her mother's anger. Tessie seemed to take quite literally the old *shtetl* maxim, "Many daughters, many troubles; many sons, many honors." She saw her daughter as a trouble, a source of pain. She denigrated her accomplishments, which were many, while praising those of her sons, which were few. Ettie excelled in school and was engrossed by books and ideas, but this did not impress her mother. Her brothers, on the other hand, were average students at best, but they received their mother's approbation for piddling achievements. Ettie succeeded in acting and singing, and yet her mother saw these as silly diversions, and felt no pride in her daughter's success. Tessie sided with her sons in sibling squabbles and left Ethel to her own resources in defending herself against her brothers. It seemed as if there were absolutely nothing her daughter could say or do that would elicit Tessie's love. As an adult, Ethel confided that she constantly felt "whipped" rather than loved by her mother. For most of her time at home she seemed to receive only her mother's begrudging tolerance and acceptance. Why this was so we will never know, but we can make some educated guesses.

As her mother's first born and only daughter, Ethel was in some unfortunate ways the child with whom her mother would identify most closely. Tessie may have displaced much of her anger and frustration onto her daughter. She may have felt a great deal of self-loathing over her situation—*she* had married Barney, *she* seemed powerless to alter her life—yet she may have been unwilling to admit that self-loathing to herself. It was easier to express her anger at her oldest child and only daughter than to express it toward herself, to lash out at the other female in the family rather than recognize how she herself was responsible for a life unfulfilled.

Another possibility is that Tessie envied her daughter, envied the possibilities, the life opportunities that she felt were no longer open to her. Ethel was an American, she would never know what true oppression or even persecution was. In America there was no denial of basic freedoms to Jews as there had been in the old country. Ethel could go to school—for free—and learn to read and write, unlike Tessie who was illiterate. Ethel had time and opportunities to do things that Tessie as a girl and young woman never had, in fact, that she did not now have time for and probably never would. We cannot know what had burned in Tessie's heart when she was younger, what passions and longings she felt. At the time of Ethel's birth, she was about thirty-three years old, and given the life she had undoubtedly experienced, this was an age far removed from youth and its yearnings. Thus Tessie could only envy Ethel's opportunities for self-betterment, for fun, for a life centered on something other than the daily struggle for existence.

Another perspective from which to view Tessie's bitterness toward her daughter is in light of Ethel's betrayal of her mother's very life and values. Lincoln Steffens wrote in 1931:

> The tales of the New York Ghetto were heartbreaking comedies of the tragic conflict between the old and the new, the very old and the very new, in many matters, all at once; religion, class, clothes, manners, customs, language, cul-

*ture. We all know the difference between youth and age,
but our experience is between two generations. Among the
Russian and other eastern Jewish families in New York it
was an abyss of many generations; it was between parents
out of the Middle Ages, sometimes out of the Old Testament
days hundreds of years B.C., and the children of the streets
of New York today.*

The chasm separating mothers and daughters was particularly great
and deeply painful. In the Old World, daughters stayed close to
home by their mothers' side. The family was woman's domain.
Mothers taught daughters all they needed to know; lines of authority
had been clearly established for hundreds of generations. But with
the immigration to America, all that had seemed ordained by God
was altered. Old World mothers lived by traditional values of stoicism in the face of recurrent suffering, and self-sacrifice for the good
of the family, especially for its male members. American-born
daughters, on the other hand, were stirred by ideas of personal
fulfillment, social mobility, and romantic love. The lives of their
mothers seemed grim in comparison to images reflected in magazine
stories, shop windows, and silent movies. What their mothers could
teach them scarcely prepared them for life in the highly industrial-
ized and continually changing world of New York City in the nineteen-twenties.

For immigrant mothers, the outside world was both frightening
and threatening. Excluded from access to most institutions of American society by reason of sex, education, religion, language, and
custom, most of these women stayed within the confines of the
known and accessible—their families and communities on the Lower
East Side. To venture further was to move into alien territory whose
language and social conventions were foreign, where they could
not help but feel awkward and backward because of their clothes,
their mannerisms, and their understanding of the world. Yet this
was an environment their daughters increasingly sought and inhabited.

Out of their fear and confusion, many immigrant mothers looked
up to their Americanized daughters, but others resented their children who appeared not to need them and their traditional values
and abilities. Their daughters' American ways mocked them and
made them feel foolish, throwbacks to a period of time that had
long since passed.

Ethel undoubtedly harbored contempt for her mother's ways. As a youngster, she spoke frequently to her friends of how she resented her mother's small-mindedness. She often said that she never wanted to grow up to be like her mother, that she would never be satisfied with her mother's lot.

Whatever the precise origins of Tessie's anger at Ethel, the Greenglass family was a place of little joy. Although she was significantly more appreciative and caring of her sons, Tessie was by no means a very warm and tender mother with any of her children. Barney, because of unwillingness or inability or both, did little to intervene in the relationship between Tessie and her offspring. Whatever feelings he might have had were apparently rarely expressed. He spent most of his time in his shop and loved it when his children visited him there. A friend of Ethel's remembers: "The kids ran in and out of his shop, asking for a penny or a nickel, and although he was always working he seemed to like their chatter." But Barney remained in the shadows once he stepped into the rooms behind his shop. For in the Greenglass home at 64 Sheriff Street, Tessie Greenglass dominated life.

2

A GATHERING
OF FANTASIES

By the time David Greenglass was born in 1922, Tessie was about forty years old, and a life of hard work was catching up with her. She turned to Ethel, then only six and a half, to assume some of the responsibilities of caring for her younger brothers. This was not an exceptional request in the culture of the Lower East Side, for it was considered natural that older sisters take care of younger siblings. Sammy, Ethel's half-brother, then fifteen years old, was expected to devote his energies to study as befitted a Jewish boy his age; girls assisted their mothers and prepared for their domestic responsibilities as future wives and mothers.

Ettie clearly must have been aware of how differently she and her brothers were treated, how everyone seemed to dote on little David, or Doovey, as he was called. Perhaps because he was a particularly cute baby and the youngest, Doovey was his mother's favorite child. Although she never received the positive attention given Doovey, Ettie obediently assumed the responsibility of second mother to Doovey, and to a lesser extent, Bernie.

Tessie was a strict parent and there is some indication that she used corporal punishment. All of the Greenglass children seem to have been obedient and a bit cowed by Tessie's ready ability to release her anger on them. But Ettie was also the butt of Sammy's anger, and as he got older, of Bernie's hostility and aggression. Perhaps this was because she was a girl, or possibly because her brothers resented her success in school. If they were not smarter than she was, they were certainly crueler. It is also possible, however, that they simply imitated Tessie's animosity toward Ettie and acted on her unspoken permission to maltreat their sister. In a sense, Ethel became the family scapegoat.

Sometime in the nineteen-twenties the family that had leased the apartment above the Greenglasses' moved. Because the rent was cheap and the sewing machine repair business was going relatively well, Tessie and Barney decided to rent these rooms as sleeping quarters for their oldest children. After years of having two adults plus three and then four children living in two small rooms, the family must have yearned for more space. With this move, Ethel, for the first time in her life, gained some privacy—her own room with two windows overlooking Sheriff Street that actually received sunlight. Ethel was probably given this room because it was smaller than the others and could not be shared. This was one of the few times that being a girl in the Greenglass family entailed any privilege.

Because the family could not afford to buy furniture, a bed stood alone in the otherwise barren interior of Ethel's room. The floor and window sills were usually dusty, if not altogether dirty. Tessie was not a tidy housekeeper, a trait she passed on to her daughter. Ethel seemed as oblivious to her surroundings as her mother was; making a room look pleasing to the eye was foreign to her.

Ethel spent much of her time in her room poring over her school work. She had an average intelligence, if IQ tests are accurate indicators. When she was given such tests in 1931, her overall score was 111. Ethel compensated by applying herself rigorously to studying, reading, and composing. She adhered to a rigid schedule of study that was so effective she was considered to be one of the two best students in her grade school and junior high. "Only one girl was ahead of Ethel in scholarship—a good friend of hers, a girl crippled from polio, who lived in the same block. They vied for scholarship, but were not competitive. Ethel worked hard, studied, but there was nothing snobbish in her approach to scholarship."

After skipping a grade, Ethel graduated from grammar school in 1926. She was then placed in "rapid advancement," which allowed exceptionally bright students to complete three years of junior high school in two.

Although she did well in all her subjects in junior high and then high school, Ethel excelled at English. She spent hours in the evenings writing and then rewriting compositions, and her effort usually was rewarded by receiving high marks and by having her essays read aloud in class. Ethel's "themes" were the ones most often read to students by the English teacher, who often praised Ethel for her use of sophisticated vocabulary.

Ethel's facility with words also helped her to succeed in foreign languages. In three years of French, her grade never fell below a 90; in two-and-a-half years of German, her marks ranged between 84 and 98. She had somewhat more difficulty with math and history, with her performance dependent upon the particular content of the course and the teacher. Her math grades gradually declined from As to Cs as the difficulty of algebra and geometry replaced the easier coursework of junior high school math. History was perhaps her weakest subject with only an occasional high mark distinguishing an average performance during her last four years of school. Yet, because of her ability to study and her determination to apply herself to her schoolwork, Ethel received a score of 81 in European history and 91 in American history on her New York State Regents Examinations.

Ethel loved school and was an exemplary student. She was rarely absent or tardy, and consistently was given As in "self control" and "personal habits." School provided her both with avenues of self-expression and a way to receive acceptance and praise—all of which she felt denied at home. By closing the door to her room and concentrating on a French lesson or English composition, Ethel could remove herself from the rancor she felt around her. Her high school, too, was particularly demanding, so that success did not come easily, but when it did, it was highly valued. Because school teaching was one of the few ways college graduates could make a living during the Depression, Seward Park High's "faculty comprised the cream of the crop of college graduates," a teacher from the time recalls. "And our students, poorer than in the [early] Twenties, saw their way out of poverty through education and ate up knowledge as if it were dessert. Teachers bore down on them and made requirements of them akin to those of the French Lycees or the German Gymnasiums, and the students met the requirements."

Out of her love for her English classes, Ethel became interested in plays and in drama. Sometimes she was taken to the Yiddish theater by her father. This was practically the only interest Barney evidenced outside of work, family life, and a desultory respect for religious observance. Probably in part because she shared it with her father alone (since apparently Tessie did not attend), the theater had sparkle, excitement, a thrilling attraction for the young Ettie Greenglass.

By 1918 New York City had nearly twenty Yiddish theaters. The productions they mounted were typically melodramas or broad comedies. In general they were expressive, sentimental, and over-drawn, designed to elicit either unrestrained tears or belly laughs. But, most importantly, they mirrored the audience's own experience in heightened form. Whether the play took place in biblical times, in a rural setting, or within Gentile society, the plot, theme, costumes, and dialogue were constructed or colored to reflect life as it was then known on the Lower East Side. Since the audiences were mostly uneducated or undereducated working-class people, the Yiddish theater pandered to simple tastes, to people who wanted escape from a harsh reality more than they wanted an evening of subtle and sophisticated art.

High melodrama enacted in brilliant costume and with relatively lavish sets must have awed and inspired a young girl whose everyday life seemed so gray. Seated by her father, who relished the plot and admired the actors, might easily have prompted Ethel to want to be an actress herself, to receive admiration and acclaim. But it was more than Yiddish theater that began to fuel Ettie's daydreams.

Moving pictures were quickly becoming the favorite pastime of Lower East Side Jews, particularly of the women and children. As early as 1909, New York City had over 340 movie houses and nickelodeons, many of them in the Jewish quarter. By the mid-nineteen-twenties, when Ethel must have first started attending them regularly, silent movies were the "craze" on the Lower East Side. They exposed their audiences to a life few had ever witnessed. Frequently focusing on the private lives of the rich and fashionable, these movies revealed "vamps" and gamines whose attitudes and behavior were both shocking and tantalizing to first-generation Americans. In daring clothes and sumptuous surroundings, movie actresses demonstrated an independence, sexuality, and joie de vivre that excited and spoke of previously unimagined possibilities.

"For second-generation immigrant women . . . these new movies were manuals of desire, wishes, and dreams. . . . Here was guidance their mothers could not offer. By presenting an illusory world where 'a shop girl can marry a millionaire,' these movies evoked a vision of the American dream for women and the means to its feminine realization."

While the Yiddish theater merely reflected back immigrant experience in heightened and more expressive form, motion pictures dramatized unknown experience. While the theater glamorized the familiar, film implicitly demonstrated just how unglamorous the familiar was. After emerging from darkened movie palaces into the clutter and noise of the Lower East Side, it must have been difficult to accept one's parents' ways as the only ways of living.

Ethel began her attempt to transform her growing fantasies into reality in the ninth grade, when she appeared in her first school play as a nurse in something called *Good Medicine*. Since no auditorium existed, sliding doors between classrooms opened so that several rooms of children could see the play while remaining seated at their desks. At this time Ethel also began to enroll in music and elocution classes. Because no drama courses were offered, these classes provided Ethel with the only formal means to prepare for the stage. For two years, she rigorously applied herself to these courses and continued to audition for virtually every school play. Gradually, she began to be cast in more substantial parts. By the time she was a senior in high school, at age fifteen, she "was the star of every dramatic program in assembly."

In many ways Ethel seemed one of the least likely candidates to be voted class actress, which is the distinction she eventually won upon graduation. By the time she was in high school she had matured into a rather short, unshapely teenager. At just over five-feet tall and weighing about one hundred pounds, Ethel was slim, yet her hips seemed disproportionately wide and her legs somewhat too short for her body. At the age of thirteen she had been diagnosed as having a severe spinal curvature or scoliosis. She had worn a cast to correct the problem for a year, but it was only partially successful. A friend recalls Ethel "sitting rather stiffly on our hard seats [in school], one shoulder raised slightly, trying to equalize her shoulders and make up for the curvature."

The only clothes she had were a few blouses and skirts that she interchanged and wore over and over. Although such a small wardrobe was quite common among girls at Seward Park, there were many who had nicer clothes than Ethel or who, at least, were able to look neater or more stylish in what they had. Ethel wore her wavy brown hair parted on the side and down past her shoulders. As she walked the eleven blocks between home and school, she looked like one of thousands of poor Jewish girls who inhabited New York's Lower East Side.

To people who did not know her well, Ethel's personality did little to distinguish her. Her classmates regarded her as quite shy, particularly around boys. Although she received high grades, she did not speak up much in class discussions, and was not known for being verbally adroit. As one classmate reported:

"She did have talent. But you'd never pick her as an actress. She was in my English class, and she wrote very well, got good marks in composition, but was too shy to shine in recitation. Somehow she overcame that on stage.

"She had none of the glamor we associated with Jean Harlow or Norma Shearer. Ethel never posed and wasn't even photogenic. . . . But she had a most expressive face."

"And," added another friend, "the saddest eyes I've ever seen. You never saw Ethel without a far-away look in her eyes. Someone once said her eyes gave her a 'malach's ponim,' a literal translation of which is 'angel face.' "

That face, which would become a familiar sight on political posters in the nineteen-fifties, was capable of conveying emotions and nuances of feeling that seemed far beyond the experience of most fifteen-year-olds. In repose her heavy-lidded hazel eyes made her face look much more mature than her actual age. Coupled with the "far-away look" her friend remembers, Ethel's eyes radiated a sense of mystery and depth that seemed out of place on this otherwise ordinary-looking Jewish adolescent. On stage, make-up and costume enhanced this aura. Ethel often applied dark eye shadow from her brows to her lashes that highlighted the heaviness of her eyelids and emphasized the sadness of her face. With deep red lipstick on her small, pursed lips, Ethel's countenance alone could convey mournfulness, pain, or utter tragedy. With costumes that frequently obscured her unshapely lines, Ethel seemed able to portray any protagonist however noble, however base.

When the curtain rose on the large stage at Seward Park High, this teenager, who rarely spoke in class, exuded confidence and mastery. Seemingly without effort, she conveyed joy and misery, tender love and raging anger. While an adult probably would have

found her performance too studied and melodramatic, her peers
were enthralled. A friend contends that her classmates all admired
"our wonderful little actress, Ethel." Under her photograph in the
1931 class yearbook is the inscription, "Can she act? And how!"
Further on, in a section entitled "Class Prophecy," an anonymous
author pretends that the year is 1950 and, through the new invention
of television, which the "general public could only read about" in
1931, is able to catch glimpses of class members midway through
the century. In a Paris night spot the author reports the following:

> Well, at one table, there seems to be quite a crowd making
> whoopee. That looks like Nathan H. Hausfather, the big
> capitalist, with Ethel Greenglass, America's leading actress.

America's leading actress of 1950—the thought is poignant when
we remember that television would be showing the world Ethel
Greenglass in that year, but under profoundly different circumstances.

What compelled Ethel to act and allowed her to be so effective in
her acting can only be a matter of speculation. Surely the fact that
her father loved the Yiddish theater must have affected her. Given
that Ethel felt unloved by the rest of her family, Barney's approval
and affection must have been quite important, even though he may
have appeared weak and ineffectual within the family and in comparison to his wife. According to one source, Barney went to see
Ethel perform but Tessie did not. If this is true, it would only serve
to confirm that acting may have been one means of directly or
indirectly pleasing her father and securing his approval.

Acting probably also served to boost her sense of self-esteem
and self-worth. Since her mother and brothers were more critical
than kind, Ethel may not only have felt unloved but unlovable as
a person. Being a successful actress could have undone such a self-
perception. To have hundreds of eyes approvingly riveted on every
gesture and every word, to hear applause at the end of a performance undoubtedly would have bolstered Ethel's self-esteem. As
the psychoanalyst Otto Fenichel noted, for an actor, "success on
the stage is needed in the same way as milk and affection are needed
by the infant." Acting might have elicited the approval Ethel missed
so much at home.

Alternatively, acting on stage may reflect Ethel's means of defending herself against her family's criticism and hostility. Over the years, Ethel developed a style of pretending she was untouched and unhurt by what she perceived as her family's rejection and meanness toward her. She learned to conceal her emotions and cloak her vulnerability to her family's barbs. This interpersonal maneuver must have constrained Ethel's expression at home and restricted what she allowed herself to feel. But it may have allowed her to experience some sense of control over a situation in which she felt continually victimized. One of Ethel's friends noted that "despite her yearning for warmth and affection, her relations with her family suffered from self-erected barriers." Ethel apparently did not allow herself to show need or hurt, for both would reveal her vulnerability and therefore perhaps make her more susceptible to greater pain.

Acting may have been a way to express the emotions she stifled at home. Through playing roles that allowed her to lash out in anger, shed hysterical tears, express mournful sorrow, or profess unrequited love, Ethel allowed herself to safely unburden her inner feelings. The range of her emotional expression was delimited by a script; the characters to whom she addressed herself were fictional. There was no reason to fear recrimination or experience guilt over hurting her family. She could both reveal pent-up feelings and conceal their true origins and objects at the same time.

Lastly, acting may have allowed Ethel to assume roles that probably seemed far more attractive than the possibilities to which she was exposed in her immediate environment. Just as in the movies, the parts in school plays offered ways of experiencing the world and acting in it that were somewhat foreign to Ethel's barren family life. Tessie and Barney's disinterest in the world around them, their lack of involvement in culture, politics, religion, art, or anything very meaningful outside of their daily routine provided Ethel with little with which to identify or to aspire toward. Acting, on the other hand, opened up new vistas where characters cared passionately about ideas, values, and other people. It suggested ways of being that were different from those Ethel observed in her circumscribed experience of life on the Lower East Side. The characters she played could be role models in a life that seemed to have comparatively few.

It was from acting that Ethel understood how things might be different, how her family's way of living was not the only way. At some point in her youth, Ethel decided she was going to escape poverty and a life centered only on making ends meet. But, according to Ethel's friend, "Not through some piddling little machine repair shop on the Lower East Side, but through the art world, . . . never having to live like her mother, forever going about the streets with a big shopping bag, searching for bargains, trading with the pushcart men. And never putting in endless hours in a tiny shop like her dad."

Life was going to be different and Ethel went about preparing for it. In addition to her immersion in the "art world" of Seward Park High's theatrical productions, Ethel began casually to practice singing. She had a very high soprano that has been described as thin and sweet. Despite the fact that no one in her family was musical and there is no evidence that music was heard in the Greenglass home, Ethel seemed to have quite a musical ear. She picked up tunes she heard quickly and had excellent pitch. She composed her own tunes and improvised satirical songs about life on the Lower East Side as she walked to and from school. She desperately wanted to take music lessons. Her mother, of course, was horrified by the idea. "If God had meant for Ethel to have music lessons," Ethel's friend characterized Tessie as saying, "he would have provided them. As he hadn't, there was something sinful about music lessons."

Ethel's interest and involvement in theater and music were mysterious and somewhat offensive to Tessie. It must have been painful for Tessie to have a daughter with her head in the clouds, who thought of singing lessons when the family did not have hot water. Art was for the rich, not for poor Jews who lived in tenements. Ethel's high ambition, her contempt for the way her mother lived, exacerbated the tensions between them. Already disappointed in her life, Tessie must have suffered her daughter's disdain and further denigrated her aspirations.

The smallness of her mother's vision seemed to fuel Ethel's motivation. Not only was she going to become an actress and singer (if she could only get singing lessons), but she was going to attend college as well. What college she would go to and where the money would come from did not seem uppermost in her mind. Thus, unlike many of her friends, she refused to take noncollege preparatory courses such as typing and stenography. For many, such classes offered the opportunity for a livelihood outside the factories and sweatshops in which their parents and relatives worked. They could become white-collar employees who worked shorter hours under better conditions. But Ethel would have none of this. Almost up until the day of graduation, she insisted that she would go to college and therefore continued with her college preparatory classes, eschewing typing for German.

———

By the time she graduated from high school, Ethel Greenglass had almost never been outside the Lower East Side, eaten in a restaurant, or ridden in a car. Most of her purchases still came from the slowly dwindling number of pushcart men lining Rivington and Essex Streets, and the food she ate differed little from the fare Jews in Eastern Europe had consumed for centuries. All but a handful of people she knew were either immigrants or their children. She had never directly experienced a life not dominated exclusively by Jewish people and their culture. Her greatest extravagance was buying ice cream sodas at Marchiony's ice cream parlor across from Seward Park High. For a girl who had such worldly dreams, she had lived a remarkably unworldly existence. Yet her dreams allowed her to survive and flourish in a family where she felt estranged and unloved. As a friend from a later period of her life remembers, "Ethel's family . . . was rooted in the ghetto, spiritually impoverished, content to stay there—with no love of culture apparent in any except Ethel, in whom it flowered as if to make up for the rest." Her dreams and ambitions centered on a life filled with passion, ideas, and art. She clung to those dreams as if to a lifeline. They were her salvation.

> *Actually I think she believed at the time that she could escape from the cold water flat on Sheriff Street, the poverty and slums on the East Side,* recalls the friend with whom she walked to school.
> *There were times, watching Ethel in a play, and after it was over, hearing all the lavish compliments given her, that I thought maybe she would escape from the squalor of the East Side tenements. After all, other bright kids from the East Side had hit Broadway. But then, as we'd walk home through the familiar streets, noisy and alive and full of vitality, I'd dismiss the whole idea. If it was evening, we'd go down Rivington, and if it was warm, families would be out on the sidewalk, some in chairs, some on fire escapes, the teenagers in groups or walking arm-in-arm.*
> *The idea of Ethel breaking away from it all, of any of us having a career, seemed crazy then. A 'career'—not in 1931! Not with men shivering on corners selling apples.*

The world in which Ethel sought to fulfill her ambitions had changed dramatically since the time she had entered high school. By 1931 the Great Depression had touched almost everyone and everything in New York City. Previously unimagined hardship and misery affected hundreds of thousands of people. Unemployment was rampant, evictions a common occurrence, the hungry were everywhere. Formerly hard-working people were reduced to begging; the suicide rate rapidly increased; and the Lower East Side seemed grayer and more destitute than ever. Despair replaced hopefulness and expectancy. Into this environment, Ethel Greenglass graduated, hoping to attend college and to find acclaim as an actress and singer.

3

FROM ART
TO POLITICS

The song, "Life Is Just a Bowl of Cherries" blared from radios in
the summer of 1931 as the last signs of prosperity cast their shadows
over the misery of New York City in that year. In 1931 the city saw
the opening of the world's finest luxury hotel, the Waldorf-Astoria,
and the tallest building, the Empire State. At the same time, New
York architects revealed their plans for a cluster of buildings to house
business offices, retail shops, ornate motion picture and music halls,
foreign trade syndicates, and broadcasting studios on a scale never
attempted before. This complex, Rockefeller Center, would dominate midtown Manhattan, and its initial construction over the next
two years would contrast markedly with the poverty and human
idleness surrounding it.

The skyline of Manhattan, with its increasingly vacant skyscrap-
ers, could be seen from the abandoned reservoir in Central Park,
which would be christened "Hoover Valley" by its inhabitants, in
honor of the incumbent president whom they blamed for their misfortunes. Hundreds of homeless people slept here and lived on stale
bread and the refuse from nearby markets. Many more people camped
in huts made out of cardboard cartons or scraps of tin and wood
along the Hudson River below Riverside Drive. Indigent men slept

nightly in the subway stations and huddled in the latrines of City Hall for warmth.

The Depression had hit New York City fast and hard. Within four months after the stock market crash of October 1929, breadlines in the Bowery were drawing 2,000 people daily. Within five months the number of families on relief had increased 200 percent, and stories of hungry men seizing truckloads of food were reported in the local papers. In one New York City health center, the percentage of malnourished patients increased from eighteen percent of total admissions before the Depression to sixty percent by 1931. By the Depression's second winter, the City was appropriating $1 million for direct relief to those in need, but this amounted to only $2.39 per week for an entire family.

In the fall of 1930, the International Apple Shippers Association decided to dispose of its surplus fruit by selling apples on credit to the jobless. In turn, the unemployed could sell apples on the street at five cents each. There were 6,000 apple sellers on the streets of New York City by early November. Both working-class and middle-class people were often reduced to this modified form of beggary. As if to add insult to injury, the Census Bureau classified these apple sellers as "employed," and President Hoover insisted that "[m]any persons left their jobs for the more profitable one of selling apples." Given that six apple sellers often lined a single block, each selling exactly the same fruit at the mandated nickel apiece, it is difficult to imagine any less profitable occupation.

The sight of previously well-employed men and women reduced to hawking apples on the crowded, wintery streets of Manhattan reflected the abrupt and disastrous downturn of the American economy. National income fell from $81 billion in 1929 to less than $68 billion in 1930, then plummeted to $53 billion in 1931, and finally dropped to $41 billion in 1932. Between 1929 and 1932, 85,000 businesses failed. Nationally, payrolls were cut by 40 percent between 1929 and September 1931, and annual per capita income—adjusted to the cost of living—sank from $681 in 1929 to $495 by 1933. Unemployment directly affected some thirty percent of the labor force in 1933, and this figure did not begin to reflect all of those whose wages and/or hours had been dramatically slashed or who "worked" at such pursuits as apple selling.

In the summer of 1931 there were no federal relief programs to stem this disaster. Food, shelter, and a dole were available only at charity kitchens, Salvation Army halls, and local relief agencies, all of which perpetually hovered near bankruptcy. People literally starved to death in New York City and died from illnesses exacerbated by malnutrition. Thousands of unemployed people—humiliated and hopeless—filled the city's parks daily, their clothes threadbare, their hair uncut, the soles of their shoes often reinforced with cardboard. Even for those who were still employed, wage or hour reductions frequently meant doing without the simple amenities of life—movies, new clothes, professional haircuts, newspapers, and not infrequently staples such as sugar, coffee, tea, or toilet paper. President Hoover remained firmly convinced that federal aid was unnecessary interference, that federal relief would encourage people to grow lazy and indolent, prompting workers to eschew gainful employment for the infamous "dole."

The Lower East Side was one of those sections of Manhattan hurt hardest by the Depression. Because so many people had earned only marginal incomes to begin with, it did not take much to push them over the brink into abject poverty. Since so many Jews were employed in the garment industry, the effects of the Depression were felt quite quickly. Consumers of all classes had rapidly cut back on such unessential purchases as new clothes. For all but the wealthiest, who did not buy mass-produced garments anyway, keeping up with the latest fashions now seemed absurd and beyond reach. In 1930 the output of men's suits dropped twenty-five percent below that of the previous year, and by 1931 had decreased by thirty-two percent. Clearly, clothing offered an obvious means of economizing for most people.

Large numbers of tailors, seamstresses, factory, and sweatshop workers were thrown out of work or had their hours and/or wages reduced as a result of the garment trades' decline, but the effect of the Depression on Barney Greenglass's sewing machine repair shop was mixed. Fewer sewing machines were in use throughout the clothing industry, but simultaneously manufacturers found it cheaper to repair them when they broke down than to buy replacements. In addition a general, albeit brief, return by many women to sewing their own clothes took place. Older machines came out of closets and often into Barney's repair shop. Thus the clients Barney lost through the slump in the apparel industry were replaced by both manufacturers and individuals forced to economize. As a result the Greenglass family survived the hard times of the early Depression years without much change in its financial situation. Perhaps this is one reason for Ethel's apparent obliviousness to the realities sur- **41** rounding her. Upon graduation in June 1931, she still clung to the idea of becoming a professional actress and singer. She seemed unaware or indifferent to the fact that two-thirds of Manhattan's playhouses had closed, that the Shubert organization was in receivership, and that thousands of actors faced penury. A committee had been formed to raise funds for idle musicians, an actors' dinner club had opened to feed hungry actors, and men who had been in the theater business, "who had responsible positions," could be seen selling apples in Times Square. At fifteen, Ethel had experienced most of the world through fantasy—fantasy fueled by plays, movies, and books. There was no reason the reality of the Depression should interfere with those fantasies.

A good friend said of herself and Ethel during this period:

> It's funny, how two kids from homes like ours, and in the midst of the Depression, could be like we were. If ever two girls had their heads in the clouds, it was Ethel and I.
>
> It was just that Ethel was in love with art, like I was. Not that we always knew art when we saw it. . . . But we were in love with the idea of art and hardly noticed the world around us.

Upon graduation, Ethel began to look for a theatrical group she could join. In September she discovered Clark House, a settlement house almost around the corner from 64 Sheriff Street, which sponsored a dramatic group for adolescents nine months out of the year. Most of the sixteen to twenty youths in the group were in their late teens, and they either worked full or part-time, or were looking for work. Clark House seemed safe and familiar, so Ethel joined its "Players."

Settlement houses had been crucial institutions in the Jewish community from before the turn of the century. Often founded and staffed by social reformers, social workers, nurses, or educators, these houses provided health care and classes on a variety of subjects, not the least of which was English for the foreign born. They organized sports and arts programs, offered instruction in crafts, household living, hygiene and baby care, supervised field trips, and sponsored a variety of social clubs.

As Jews became more assimilated, however, the usefulness of the settlement houses began to decline. When legal immigration was curtailed in the nineteen-twenties, and increasing numbers of Jews began to move out of the East Side, the settlement house found its natural constituency dwindling and many of its functions unneeded by the immigrants' children who felt increasingly at ease with American customs and ways. With the onset of the Depression, however, this trend was temporarily reversed. Youths turned to the houses looking for a way to pass time, meet people, or have fun without spending any money. Settlement houses frequently became the center of many young people's social lives during the nineteenthirties, serving as poor kids' college fraternities and sororities. Paula Berger, a member of the Clark Players, remembers the settlement house as "a home away from home—the second place friends and relatives would come to look for me if they didn't find me at home."

Clark House, and specifically the dramatic group it sponsored, became the focus of Ethel's life for the next few years. She spent many of her evenings inside the old brick building around the corner from home, rehearsing plays and chatting with new friends, most of whom were somewhat older than she was and many of whom worked in factories.

The actual dramatic training at Clark House was allegedly poor and the plays mounted mediocre, but Ethel threw herself into them with the same excitement and fervor she had displayed in high school. "She had a passion for theater, she was a wonderful actress. There was a flame in her," Maurice Blond, a fellow Player, recalled many years later. "When she took on a part she was very intense and empathic. She worked very hard."

The repertoire of the plays varied widely; it included both dramas and comedies, but all lacked social conscience or political meaning. This constituted a notable exception in a period when New York—particularly its Lower East Side—was suddenly and explosively alive with socially conscious theater to an extent never seen before and not yet repeated. Although it took a variety of forms, the new theater movement's fundamental assumption was that what appeared on Broadway, and was mimicked throughout the country, was escapist, uncreative claptrap. Art for art's sake was viewed as mindless and anachronistic. To present a piece offering little more than amusement, having no greater social meaning, at the very least was irresponsible.

The Clark Players, however, seemed totally immune to this growing movement. Tucked away in their settlement house, young and largely uneducated about the philosophy, meaning, and value of drama, these young actors seemed to idealize Broadway and mounted one sophomoric attempt after another to mimic it. For the Players, both youthful rebellion and desire for success entailed criticism of their immigrant parents, rather than of the traditional aspects of American life. To be rebellious and/or successful for many first-generation American Jews meant embracing American ways wholeheartedly to differentiate themselves from their parents. Thus to imitate Broadway plays seemed new and different enough. For these immigrants' children, to act like Americans was both rebellion and the supposed pathway to professional careers on the stage.

Ethel and her fellow Players performed *The Black Flamingo*, which criticizes the French Revolution from the aristocracy's point of view. They performed *Green Stockings*, which pokes fun at a woman for being a spinster and wearing green stockings. In the Players' rendition the spinster was contrasted with a younger, more fortunate sister, played by Ethel. The Players mounted dull productions of *Children of the Moon* and *A Pair of Sixes*, in which Ethel reportedly stole the show as the British nursemaid.

According to one of Ethel's friends and a fellow actor, "About the only play the Clark Players did which was any good" was *The Valiant*, a one-act drama previously made into a motion picture starring the former Lower East Side actor Paul Muni. The rather melodramatic plot centers on a man facing execution with remarkable calm and composure. Confusion exists as to the condemned man's true identity, which he attempts to conceal from his family, presumably in order to spare them any pain or humiliation over his plight. In the crucial scene, his younger sister, played by Ethel, comes to visit him shortly before his execution. He pretends not to recognize her, even when she recites their favorite line from Shakespeare, "parting is such sweet sorrow." He tells her to leave, to forget him and to inform her mother that he is not her son. She goes and, as he walks to his execution, he nobly recites a line from Shakespeare's *Julius Caesar*: "Cowards die many times before their death; The valiant never taste of death but once." While this play certainly did not fall under the rubric of socially conscious theater, it did uphold humility, heroism, bravery, and self-sacrifice as virtuous characteristics—apparently more than can be said for the majority of the Clark Players' offerings.

Ethel never seems to have questioned the merit or political meaning of the plays in which she performed. As one Clark Player noted, at the time "she wasn't even a liberal." She simply was enthralled with being an actress, with performing, with "art" however she may have understood it. After rehearsals, she and her girlfriend would walk back to their homes, reciting lines from various plays and particularly from Shakespeare. Their favorite lines, from *Romeo and Juliet*, must have sounded discordant, if not simply silly or callous, set against the dimly lit streets, abandoned buildings, garbage-filled alleys, and ambiance of despair that were the Lower East Side during the early Depression. But such self-absorption and naiveté also reveal an innocence that demonstrates how normal life can persevere in spite of the material impoverishment surrounding it.

Ethel's vision of the world at this time was reflected in a play the Clark Players studied but never produced, which her friend recalls "was about true artists who starved in a garret. This idea appealed to Ethel, who said she'd rather live that kind of life than live the way her family did."

In the fall of 1931, Ethel decided to push her "artistic" ambitions further by entering a talent contest as a singer. Such contests were quite common during the Depression as they gave people a quick way to earn money without much effort, and they also provided a source of home-grown entertainment that cost almost nothing to produce. Every Thursday night, Loew's Theater on Delancey Street sponsored an amateur competition. The audience determined the winner through its applause. The first prize was five dollars, the second two dollars—not inconsequential sums on the Lower East Side at the time.

What Ethel may have felt the Thursday night she stood before hundreds of people and sang in her high, sweet soprano for the first time in public is unknown, as is what song she sang or what, if any, was her accompaniment. We do know she won second prize, and partly because of this her ambition began turning toward a career as a singer rather than as an actress.

Jeanette MacDonald had recently introduced light operatic singing into mainstream culture through a series of motion pictures in which she starred during the early thirties. Between 1930 and 1932 she made nine movies that exposed her beautiful soprano to millions of filmgoers, and spawned countless imitators on the radio. The popularity of sopranos in movies and on the airwaves could only have propelled Ethel's interest and provided concrete role models for her ambition. But singing offered more too. After her initial roles with the Clark Players, Ethel must have recognized that she was a

very good actress but not the best. She did not stand out as she had
in high school, or star in every play, or "steal the show" most of
the time. This probably was a disappointment to the young woman
who had been Seward Park High's best actress of 1931. The clear
path to Broadway now may have seemed blocked by more than
just unemployment lines. Thus singing increasingly appeared as the
alternate route to life as a performer and perhaps as a star. A friend
from the Players remembers:

> *I think I know just when this desire [to pursue a singing
> career] was crystallized. She was playing around before
> rehearsal and the dramatic coach grew very excited and
> had her repeat a high note he'd heard her sing. He struck
> it on the piano and said, 'she hit high C; that's higher than
> Lily Pons.'*

This report clearly is inaccurate because high C can be hit by any
soprano, and Lily Pons, then a coloratura performing at the Metropolitan Opera House, could hit C above high C. But this woman's
memory does reflect that Tom Keenan, the Players' drama coach,
was excited by Ethel's vocal abilities and distinguished her from the
other actors because of it.

As Ethel's interest in singing increased, her involvement in dra-
matics decreased proportionately. After the Clark Players' fall 1933
season, Ethel began to drift away. She desperately wanted some
formal musical training, but her mother was consistent in her refusal.
Tessie Greenglass was not pleased with her daughter's preoccu-
pations; acting and singing seemed thoroughly impractical to her.
The more Tessie expressed this point of view, the more Ethel was
contemptuous of her mother's lack of appreciation of "art." A friend
remembers Ethel still maintaining "that she was not going to just
get married and worry about children and shopping and meals,"
like her mother, "she was going to be different."

Ethel was not about to let her mother's intransigence prevent
her from fulfilling her dreams. Lower East Side people frequently
sold their own furniture and household items to stave off total des-
titution, or they moved in with relatives or took in boarders to ease
their economic burdens and were desperate to sell furniture simply
to make additional living space. To get rid of a piano, some sellers
would let one go for what it cost to remove it. In this buyers' market
Ethel purchased a used, upright piano with money she probably

had saved from scrimping on lunches and bus rides. She had the piano installed in her bedroom and then spent countless hours trying to teach herself to play it to accompany herself while singing. Her determination was overwhelming. Eventually, she mastered the instrument through sheer willpower and the force of her desire.

Second, to further her career as a singer, Ethel decided to audition for a citywide chorus, the Schola Cantorum. Formed in 1908, the chorus had 250 members and devoted itself to the performance of serious choral music. Under the direction of Hugh Ross, the group performed regularly at Carnegie Hall and was frequently accompanied by the New York Philharmonic Orchestra. In 1934 Ethel attended an audition only to discover that Mr. Ross required his singers to read music by sight. He told *The New York Times* he was "very tough in accepting singers. When I audition . . . singers I give them 12-tone music to read. I need to know they can handle it."

Although Ethel had only minimal experience in sight-reading during her two years of music classes in high school, she was determined to develop this ability to audition for the Schola Cantorum. With the same resolve and self-discipline she had mustered to teach herself the piano, Ethel learned to sight-read. By 1935 she was able to audition for the chorus and was accepted as its youngest member at the age of nineteen.

––––––

Amateur acting and singing did not yet constitute a career, and Ethel's parents expected that their daughter would contribute financially to the household once she graduated from high school. Ethel, however, had made no plans for finding a job. Her college-oriented classes had left her ill-prepared to seek work; she had no real marketable skills. Being class actress at Seward Park High hardly provided her with a competitive advantage in the Depression labor market. Nevertheless, at her parents' urging, she began to thumb through the classified section of the newspaper.

In either late June or July 1931, Ethel came upon an advertisement for unskilled factory workers, listing an address on Bleecker Street, a part of Manhattan not far outside the narrow geographic world that constituted Ethel's universe. The following morning she found her way to the advertised location only to discover thousands of fellow job-seekers jammed in the block outside the factory. As she stood there, far from the factory doors, pressed against other bodies, more people continued to arrive. The appointed hour for the factory's opening and the acceptance of applications had come and gone, but still more unemployed people, hungry for work and tired of looking for it, poured into the now suffocating crowd. The air was thick and the summer sun beat down. The crowd began to vibrate with anger.

Ethel was stunned. She had never seen or heard anything like it. That so many people could want unskilled factory work and want it so desperately was astonishing. Without notice, a fire truck had quietly moved alongside the crowd and suddenly directed the full force of one of its water hoses directly into the mass of job-hungry people. The sheer force of the spray knocked many people over and its icy cold startled everyone it hit. Within seconds, the crowd was screaming and running in every direction as the hose fired at anyone in its range. Ethel ran too.

Probably in part as a response to this experience, Ethel immediately enrolled in a six-month course at the Public School 4 annex beginning in August to learn bookkeeping, stenography, and typing. Her determination to attend college, to avoid falling into a working-class job and the life-style it seemed to entail, quickly dissipated when she was exposed to the realities of the Depression. Although a college education would forever remain beyond reach, secretarial skills would at least enable her to work in an office, to be a white-collar employee—no small distinction for a young woman from her background.

In February 1932, Ethel completed her secretarial course and received a certificate indicating that she had successfully studied typing, bookkeeping, and stenography. She found a job immediately. How this sixteen-year-old, with no previous work history, was hired in the midst of New York's worst economic downturn remains a mystery. Although the job was no prize, any real employment brought with it some prestige in this, the grayest period of the Depression.

On February 24th, Ethel began work at National New York Packing and Shipping Company, located at 327 West 36th Street. She was hired as a part-time employee with the stipulation that she was willing to work full-time when the company needed her. Her pay rate was thirty-one and a half cents per hour. On the average she was to work about twenty-two hours a week, so her normal weekly pay amounted to roughly seven dollars. Although this was not a lot of money in 1932, it certainly was far better than what many were then earning. Some department stores were paying their

48 clerks as little as five to ten dollars a week for full-time work, and even some first-rate stenographers were earning as little as sixteen dollars a week full-time.

National was a freight brokerage house that consolidated packages of suits, dresses, skirts, blouses, shirts, and trousers from different manufacturers and sent them to stores throughout the country. Work was organized around conveyor belts. Men received the packages, sorted them, and tied them together. Women stood behind the men and wrote receipts for the packages. Speed was highly valued, so the employer hired only young people still in school or recently graduated. He would occasionally put them "under stop watch" to monitor their speed and eliminate anyone who was not working as quickly as the others. An employee at National and an acquaintance of Ethel's recalls, as "for the men, the only difference between us and horses was that we wore pants. The women had it a little easier. Ethel and the other girls . . . wrote receipts at top speed, until their hands and arms almost dropped off."

The company employed almost 150 people, most of them part-time. There were rarely more than 60 working at any one time however. No union existed at National, but, according to one of its employees, an "air of comradery" existed among the workers.

National New York Packing and Shipping was to be Ethel's employer for the next three-and-a-half years, yet it served a much greater function in her life. By the age of sixteen, Ethel had never had any reason to venture outside the Lower East Side. Now she had to work in a new neighborhood, alongside people from a variety of unfamiliar backgrounds. Although most of the workers were Jews, many of them came from the Bronx, Jersey City, and Coney Island. Even more unusual to her were the Italian Catholics and the few Protestants. The only non-Jews that Ethel had known before were teachers in school, some shop owners, bus drivers, and policemen on the streets. Working with a Brooklynite or an Italian Catholic every day, hearing about his or her life, listening to somewhat different views of the world, must have expanded Ethel's perspective and challenged some of her beliefs.

Life at National stood in sharp contrast to the cocoon of fantasy and escapism encouraged by the Clark Players and Ethel's involvement in "art." The workers were largely young people who had few illusions about life. Most of them came from homes hit hard by the Depression. Although they were young, many had been working at blue-collar jobs for years, and they had developed very

clear ideas about the causes of the economic situation in which 49
they found themselves. Many had left-wing political ideas and belonged to the Young Communist League.

During the Depression it was not difficult to be exposed to
radical political ideas in New York City. Both the Socialist and
Communist parties saw the Depression as capitalism's last agonized,
doomed gasp for life, and they vigorously attempted to recruit people to their views. The Socialist party, however, increasingly hand-
icapped by internal factionalism and dissent, progressively lost
members during the thirties. The Communist party, on the other
hand, grew at an astonishing rate. From being a small, sectarian
party of predominantly foreign-born Jews at the beginning of the
decade, it grew to be a sizable force in the United States with some
100,000 official members and a much larger number of followers
by 1939. The American Communist party had an enormous influence on young people in New York City, particularly on its Jews
and garment workers in such businesses as National New York
Packing and Shipping. Therefore when Ethel took her first job at
sixteen, she was exposed to more than the realities of working for
a living; she now came into daily contact with the Communist
party's perspective on the world.

The Communist Party–USA (CPUSA) had a mere 7,545 members
in 1930. It spent much of its energies and resources denouncing
other leftists—primarily socialists—as "social fascists." The Party
maintained that it alone was the true voice of the working class and
that other parties or organizations misled workers and diverted them
from the true revolutionary path that had been blazed in the Soviet
Union. Its response to the Depression was simple and unequivo-
cal—revolution. Nothing less than the establishment of a Soviet
America was worth demanding or fighting for.

This approach did not win many converts. To people hungry
for jobs and the means to feed themselves and their families, nothing
less than total revolution sounded foreign, too far in the future, and
probably simply ridiculous. Thus, at the beginning of the decade,
the Party found itself isolated from most American workers.

Gradually, however, the sectarianism of the American Communist party began to change, due both to an alteration of its leadership and a shift in the international Communist movement centered in Moscow. Earl Browder, a middle-aged Protestant, who had

been born in Wichita, Kansas, began to rise in the Party's leadership circles in 1929. The position he represented was reflected in the title of the report he made shortly after his elevation to the Party's governing body, "Fewer High-Falutin' Phrases, More Simple Every-Day Deeds," emphasizing the need "to get down to work." Around the same time, the Communist International, or Comintern, called on Communist parties throughout the world to carry out "mass revolutionary actions of the proletariat—strikes, demonstrations, etc." The American Party then began to organize demonstrations and marches to protest the high rate of joblessness and to demand unemployment relief. Party-led rent strikes, fights against evictions, and hunger marches became fairly common occurrences around Manhattan. The Communists formed Unemployed Councils, led by Party members or adherents and composed of jobless workers who demanded "work or wages." In Manhattan, the Down Town Council of the Unemployed conducted daily meetings of over 1,000 people in front of an employment agency.

The Party was able to more than double the number of votes it commanded for its presidential candidate from 48,770 in 1928 to 102,991 in 1932, despite the presence of liberal Franklin D. Roosevelt on the Democratic ticket. In New York City, the Communists increased their vote from 9,200 in 1928 to 24,000 in 1932. And in early 1933, the Party sponsored the first of many gatherings that filled Madison Square Garden. On 5 April, the Communists held an antifascist meeting that was one of its first attempts at demonstrating a "united front"; that is, it actively sought coalition with reformist political and trade union groups, even though its underlying purpose was to "take their followers away from them," as Earl Browder frankly admitted. However duplicitous this policy may have been, the Party successfully brought new followers into its fold under this program. It enabled people who agreed with the Party's call for unemployment insurance, or its commitment to championing the jobless and the working class, or its condemnation of fascism, to work under its auspices without necessarily embracing its continued call "For a Revolutionary Way Out of the Crisis, For a Dictatorship of the Proletariat and the Peasants."

By May Day 1933, the Party claimed that some 600,000 people marched under its banner across the United States. In addition to its 15,000 official members, the Party boasted a variety of "mass organizations" or "fronts" that had members who were non-Communists but whose leaders were Party members. In New York alone the Party controlled over 100 mass organizations, including such groups as the International Workers' Order, Unemployed Councils, John Reed Clubs, the National Committee for the Protection of the Foreign Born, Workers' International Relief, and the League of Struggle for Negro Rights. Although many of these were little more than paper organizations, others were active groups that spread the influence of the Communist party far beyond its official membership rolls.

It was not difficult for a progressively minded person to come across the Party in one of its many incarnations in the thirties, but in New York City it was almost unavoidable. Between 1930 and 1935, one-third of all American Communist party members lived within its borders. Their influence was varied and widespread. Communists and their "fellow travelers" appeared in places and roles that were unexpected and diverse. The Workers' Laboratory Theater, a part of the Communist dominated Workers' International Relief, often performed in Manhattan's subways, offering agitprop plays about the need for revolution to commuters. The Freiheit Singing Society—a Jewish-Communist group whose music focused on praise of the Soviet Union—performed about twice a year at Carnegie Hall or the Brooklyn Academy of Music accompanied by symphony orchestras. Party members made up the majority of employees at the City's Home Relief Bureaus, and controlled Manhattan's most popular fraternal benefit society, the International Workers' Order. It operated through the Workers' Cooperative Association, Camp Nitgedeiget (for Yiddish-speaking Jews) and Camp Unity (primarily frequented by American-born Jewish youth) outside the city.

Nowhere was the Communist party's influence greater than on the Lower East Side. Here there had long been an interest in left-wing causes. Jews from Russia and Eastern Europe had brought with them a sympathy toward socialist and even anarchist ideas. With the Bolshevik triumph in 1917, however, thousands of Lower East Side residents saw Jewish freedom from tsarist oppression as one of the indelible meanings of the newly born Communist movement. During the Russian civil war that followed the revolution (1918–1920), whatever area of Russia the Red Army entered, Jews were liberated from the control of the deeply anti-Semitic White Army. Lenin declared, "The Jewish bourgeoisie are our enemies not as Jews, but as bourgeoisie. The Jewish worker is our brother." Throughout the nineteen-twenties, the Soviet government genuinely attempted to treat Jews as an independent nationality with equal rights. The state financially supported a Jewish school system, a Jewish people's court, Jewish theaters, newspapers, magazines, and publishing houses—in other words, "a pro-Jewish policy unknown and hardly feasible in another country."

In 1922 the *Freiheit*, a Yiddish daily newspaper, began publishing on the Lower East Side, glorifying the triumphs of Jews under Soviet Communism. The Jewish Workers' Music Alliance and Workers' Cooperative Association were formed to blend Communist politics and Yiddish culture. In 1930 the CP-sponsored International Workers' Order (IWO) was organized with a primarily Jewish membership. In addition to its insurance and health benefits, the IWO grew to operate its own school system and summer camps, and to publish its own textbooks and a children's monthly. The example of Jews' progress in the Soviet Union provided a natural means for Communist recruitment on the already fertile soil of progressive Lower East Side politics.

Great disillusionment and disaffection appeared, however, when the iron grip of Stalinism took hold of the Soviet state in the late nineteen-twenties. Joseph Stalin maintained that Communist culture was "national in form and socialist in content" so that an independent Jewish nationality, culture, and history were contrary to the interests of socialism. The progressive Jewish policy of the previous few years was slowly dismantled, and independent Jewish concerns were negated under what were dubbed the all-encompassing interests of the homogeneous working class. Unfortunately, the leadership of the American Communist party accepted Stalin's reinterpretation of "the Jewish question" uncritically.

While Stalin's stance seriously damaged the Party's authority among Jews in the late twenties and early thirties, the ascent of the Third Reich in Germany in 1932 and the Communist party's emergence as fascism's most vocal opposition in the United States, again cemented the relationship between the Party and much of the progressive Jewish community. Nationally, by the thirties, forty to fifty percent of the Party was Jewish, but the percentage was much higher in New York City. In short, it was impossible to live in New York's Jewish ghetto and not be aware of the Party's presence. Although one may have disagreed with its line or its tactics, it was familiar, it was everywhere, and, for better or worse, it was largely Jewish.

With her daily work at National New York Packing and Shipping, Ethel Greenglass had more direct exposure to Party-inspired political thinking than ever before. In high school only a few of her

friends had been interested in political matters. Responding to the
effects of the Great Depression, some of Ethel's classmates were
moved by left-wing ideas, joined political groups, and helped to
organize meetings and rallies. Ethel, however, had remained aloof.
Her obsessions—acting and then singing—were her ticket out of
the poverty and deprivation of the Jewish ghetto. She believed politics were a waste of time for someone with her talent and ambition,
and although it was fine for others to be involved, she was just too
busy, too preoccupied with her own vision of the future. Ethel's
friend with whom she walked to and from high school was one of
the students who became politically involved. She remembers:

> Of course Ethel knew the facts of life. How could anyone
> live as we did and not know them? But in Seward Park
> High she'd read a leaflet, say we were right, but that she
> had her work to do and nothing was going to interfere with
> it. Her work then was dramatics, and there was no limit to
> her ambitions . . .

Ethel probably would have shown as little interest in left-wing politics at National as she had in high school had it not been for her
discovery of a number of Young Communist League coworkers who
shared her interest in art. Through them she discovered that the
Communist party celebrated more than just class warfare, although
this was its ultimate goal. It sponsored John Reed Clubs that gave
classes for workers in music, graphic arts, ballet, and theater. It had
established a Workers' Dance Theater Group, singing societies, and
the International Music Bureau, "an international union of revolutionary musicians." The Party's League of Workers' Theater claimed
300 affiliated drama groups throughout the United States by 1934,
and the Party had successfully established a cell within the highly
innovative and acclaimed Group Theater. As the Party moved further away from its sectarianism of the early thirties, its focus on
class struggle gradually gave way to the need to fight fascism and
preserve democratic rights. In this light, the Party increasingly valued the role of the artist-qua-artist.

It seems doubtful that merely knowing politics and art could
be complementary would have moved Ethel any closer to actual
political activity or involvement. But radical politics also offered
Ethel something much more concrete and immediate: the opportunity to sing. Through her coworkers at National, Ethel became

involved with a group of people in their late teens and twenties who gathered on evenings to make their own music. Since she had never been shy about displaying her vocal abilities, the group quickly learned how well she could sing and made her the group's premier songstress.

When they met in the evenings at a young man's apartment that had both a piano and steam heat, these young people shared more than music. They also had lively discussions of the political situation in Manhattan and the nation. The group seemed of one mind in its outrage at the callousness of big business, at the government's purported leanings toward the right, and by the plight of poor people who lived in their neighborhoods. Whether anyone was actually a card-carrying member of the Communist party, the Young Communist League's parent organization, is uncertain, but the Party's perspective was clearly endorsed.

This constituted Ethel Greenglass's formal introduction to a political life, one that fundamentally challenged her commitment to "art for art's sake." It spoke to the passion, commitment, and self-sacrifice that were integral to Ethel's theatrical ambitions, yet it appealed to much more altruistic, noble, and generous impulses. It ignited a spark that fired Ethel's imagination.

4

STRIKE!

Because so many of the employees at National New York Packing and Shipping were leftists, Ethel's workplace was fertile ground for labor organizing. Thus when Stanley Saposnick, a representative of the Ladies Apparel Shipping Clerks Union, began to recruit members there in August 1935, he met with some success. The union's leaders were considering calling a strike to demand that employers shorten the work week and raise the minimum wage for shipping clerks. Saposnick urged National's workers to join the union and also warned them to prepare to walk out on strike.

Although many of the politicized workers had only been *kibitzers* up to then, according to one employee, they needed little convincing to believe their work was the most poorly remunerated and among the most difficult in the largely well-organized garment industry. When packages piled up, usually on the late afternoon shift, the men were required to work at breakneck speed sorting, weighing, and tying bundles together, and then loading them into trucks. The women's work was less physically demanding but they had to endure the fast-paced monotony of writing one receipt after another. Their work was better suited to assembly-line machines than human beings. Both the women and the men were often required to work overtime, on holidays, and on Saturdays when business was brisk. When business slackened, however, some employees were told not to bother coming in at all, while others still worked a forty-four-hour week.

Ethel was one of the first to join the union. This probably occurred for a number of reasons. First, she had been angry with her employer since March when she and a number of other women workers had asked that wages be equalized among them. Ethel was being paid less than others who had worked at National for a shorter time and she felt this was unfair. Her request was denied because of alleged errors she had made in her work. She was informed that if her performance continued to be satisfactory, she would receive a raise in one or two months. This never happened, although her work was always satisfactory and often was praised by her immediate supervisor. Second, the many discussions she had had with her musical friends made her receptive to the idea of being a union member, a part of organized labor.

Third, the union representative probably spoke directly to the injustices of what Ethel saw around her. The need for a union, and perhaps even a strike, made sense to her after laboring for three-and-a-half years at a low-paying job that was little more than drudgery. When she had started working for National at the lowest ebb of the Depression, her wages were relatively good, particularly for an inexperienced sixteen-year-old. But this was 1935, and the economy had improved a good deal. Wages throughout the industry had increased, while those at National remained at early Depression levels.

On 19 August 1935, a general strike committee of the Shipping Clerks Union addressed a series of demands to eight manufacturers' associations. These included the demand for a thirty-five-hour, five-day week, a minimum wage of twenty-three dollars per week against the prevailing fifteen dollars, time-and-a-half for overtime, six legal holidays per year, equal distribution of work in the slack season, and a closed shop. The employers were warned that if they did not accede to these demands, the shipping clerks would go out on strike.

The following Monday, the union members at National met to discuss the situation. They decided to form a strike committee and to urge all their co-workers to walk out if the union called a strike.

No one seems to remember exactly how Ethel came to be part of the strike committee. Possibly no election actually was held and Ethel simply volunteered to be a member without contest. This would indicate how much she had begun to care about the issues at stake and how confident she felt in being able to represent other

employees. If she was elected, however, we learn something somewhat different. Apparently the men at National were slightly more
receptive to the union and the possibility of striking than were the
women. At this initial meeting Ethel was one of the few women
present, and her attractiveness as a potential committee member
may have been enhanced by the idea that she could organize other
women to go out on strike. In addition, as she moved further away
from her family, Ethel was blossoming into a warm and vivacious
woman. Her co-workers remember her as caring, always attentive
to others' problems and woes, and good natured. She rarely talked
about herself or any personal distress or unhappiness. The work did
not seem to exhaust, depress, or frustrate her as it did so many
others. Perhaps Ethel needed others to like her, and as her family
became less of a focus in her life, her relationships with her friends
and associates became increasingly important.

However she came to be part of the committee, Ethel warmed
to her new role quite readily and proceeded to walk about the
building for the remainder of the day speaking with female workers
about the necessity to strike. Since she faced a responsive audience,
she had only to repeat what the union representative had said and
embellish it with examples specific to the conditions at National.
The women may have been less eager to unionize and strike than
their male counterparts, but there is no evidence that Ethel encountered any hostility in her first day as a labor organizer.

That night the head of the Shipping Clerks Union, Philip Gosseen, actually called the strike. The next day somewhere between
9,000 and 14,000 employees from some 5,500 establishments
throughout the garment district responded to the strike call. Picket
lines were set up everywhere.

Ethel immediately immersed herself in strike activity. A member
of the strike committee recalls that "[y]ou couldn't forget Ethel, she
stood out from the rest. She was just as ready to do work in the
soup kitchen as she was to do picket duty or something more spectacular. She put her heart and soul in all she did."

Ethel must have been overwhelmed by the amount of work she
faced, but her attention was focused more on what she witnessed
in the streets that day and the next. Strikers traveled in groups
throughout the district attempting to prevent deliveries of clothes to
shipping houses and to thwart scabs from entering businesses to
work. Often they were attacked by scabs or men who would appear
seemingly out of nowhere. Strikers were clubbed to the ground with

58   iron pipes. Their heads were lacerated, their scalps bled. Noses and arms were broken. Philip Gosseen charged that "hired thugs engaged by employers" were attacking strikers and appealed to Mayor LaGuardia for protection. Christ Church, directly across the street from National, had been designated the strike headquarters, but by the fourth day of the strike it became an impromptu hospital for all the men who had been attacked and beaten in the streets.

Ethel was horrified at this brutality. On Friday, August 30th, many of the striking women decided to put their bodies on the line to demonstrate that they too would risk danger and attack in support of the strike. Silvia Barbanello, a twenty-one-year-old from the Bronx, led some 150 women, organized in squads, to lie down in the streets to prevent truck deliveries. At a mass meeting the day before at the Manhattan Opera House, she had urged striking women to wear raincoats over their dresses so lying on the asphalt would be easier. Ethel readily complied. In fact, she helped organize her squad to fill 36th Street outside National with its members' prostrate bodies. With many of their male coworkers standing by, the women effectively halted the trucks. They were so successful and enjoyed their tactic so much that they repeated it the next day with equal triumph. The sense of comradery and empowerment must have been enormous, for Ethel would recall it in the future as one of the happiest and most formative periods of her life.

That night, after a mass meeting of the strikers at Christ Church, Ethel set out for home on foot with a group of friends from National. Only a half-block from the church, six to ten men swinging iron pipes suddenly sprang at them. Within seconds there was the sound of pipes crushing flesh and then bone, and then, just as suddenly, the assailants were gone, disappearing into the blackness from which they had come. Dozens of strikers rushed to the writhing, screaming bodies on the street. Ethel watched in shock. These were not "the workers" who had been attacked, these were her friends. All that had been said about class warfare, about the evils of capitalism was true, was true in that very minute, on that very street. Years later, Ethel would tell people that it was the brutality she witnessed during this strike that "started her speaking up against injustice."

The strike continued, despite the violence that plagued it, and Ethel continued in her role as a member of the strike committee, which now met almost daily. Although Ethel had known all the members by sight before they came together as a group, these meetings provided the first time she actually spoke to many of them, almost all of whom were male and Jewish. She and a Catholic by the name of Hazel were the only women, and Ethel was far more outspoken and knowledgeable than Hazel. Ethel probably felt comfortable working closely with men, for she had been doing so since high school, first in Seward Park High drama performances, then in the Clark Players. But these meetings undoubtedly had an electricity and sense of purposefulness different from those centered on rehearsals and performing. The committee's decisions affected more than one hundred strikers from National who had entrusted it with the task of directing the strike in the company and negotiating with its president. But for the committee's members, the entire shipping clerks' strike, the ability to effectively organize labor, the trajectory of the Depression, even the eventual fate of capitalism seemed to hang in the balance of the committee's deliberations. These were volatile times; much that had seemed natural and immutable before the Depression now seemed open to change. For youths in their late teens and twenties, the possibilities and opportunities for transforming the world must have seemed endless. The cruelty and meanness they had witnessed and experienced only fired their determination to do something, to take a stand, to prevent the employers from so blatantly and brutally taking revenge in the future.

Ethel had the committee meet at her home, in her bedroom, two or three times during the strike. Members who were not from the Lower East Side were shocked to see the way she lived. One man had never known that people lived in such poverty, although he, too, was from a working-class background.

No evidence exists that Tessie and Barney objected to the strike committee meeting in their home. Their son, Bernie, had been working at National ever since Ethel found him a job there, so the Greenglass household was full of talk about the strike. Tessie and Barney, however, did not involve themselves very much in their children's lives by this time. Tessie once remarked, "You have a child under your arm until a certain age and then you don't butt in any more." Although the Greenglasses did not approve of unions and strikes since they believed involvement in them could only bring trouble, their protestations were not great, possibly for the kinds of reasons Irving Howe suggests:

> My parents objected to my politics, of course, and warned
> me about troublesome consequences, but both objections
> and warnings were weak. Why? Perhaps because life had

60   *been steadily wearing my parents down and they no longer had much energy for battle. . . . As immigrants they had already lost a good part of their authority over me. . . . The more we native born boys and girls made our way into American spheres of school and work, the more our immigrant parents grew uncertain about their right to command. They felt lost.*

By the second week of the strike, the International Ladies Garment Workers Union (ILGWU), with a membership of 100,000 in New York City, intervened, bringing pressure on the employers to settle. Other workers, such as the cloak- and dressmakers, began striking in sympathy with the shipping clerks. Gradually, however, individual employers started to sign agreements with the strikers, and a number of shipping clerks returned to work. Both because of the continued and effective use of scabs and these individual agreements, the strike started losing steam. David Dubinsky, president of the ILGWU at the time, attributed the strike's decline to a lack of "effective organization." By Wednesday, 11 September 1935, the strike was over. At a mass meeting at Christ Church in the afternoon, the strikers voted in favor of an agreement that included no formal recognition of the shipping clerks union, a forty-four-hour week, and a fifteen-dollar-a-week minimum wage.

Ethel returned to work that Friday. Although the strikers had effectively lost their ten-day strike, Ethel personally must have gained enormously. She probably possessed an expanded sense of her own abilities, for she had talked, strategized, and argued with men who had seemed much smarter and more experienced. She had convinced many individuals of the importance of the strike. She had met dozens of new people, made new friends, and discovered that her fellow employees were willing to trust her to make decisions that affected their lives.

———

These personal gains served Ethel well when Andrew Loebel, the president and active manager of National, called all the employees then at work into his office on 23 September. He had a hard time fitting everyone in; employees were wedged in between the furniture, on top of desks, and shoulder to shoulder throughout the room. The air was hot and stuffy; but as Loebel revealed his purpose for calling this extraordinary meeting, the temperature of the room seemed to rise even higher. Loebel began simply: he no longer wanted to negotiate with the committee that had engineered the strike, since he believed it was not representative of *all* employees. In other words, he wanted a new committee elected that represented supervisory personnel and clerical staff, as well as the workers who were directly involved in the shipping process.

Although he did not say it explicitly, his intent was clear. Loebel wanted a committee he could control. Secretaries and supervisors had a real allegiance to Loebel. Since they had sided with him during the strike, their presence on any committee would make it much more difficult for nonsupervisory employees to lobby effectively for their interests. In an attempt at mock democracy, Loebel asked the group for its reactions. The supervisors and secretaries spoke in favor of Loebel's proposal; members of the strike committee adamantly opposed it. According to a fellow strike committee member, Ethel "addressed the meeting, urging a large, strong, independent committee, democratically elected" which could not be dominated by Loebel. Although she was apparently "excited," she "brought out all the right points."

Loebel abruptly closed the debate and called for a vote by secret ballot. At this suggestion, Irving Goldberg, an outspoken member of the strike committee, demanded that before the ballots were distributed, the number of nonsupervisory employees be counted so that it would be impossible for Loebel to stuff the ballot box. National's secretary and treasurer, a Mr. Eisman, responded to this idea by firing Goldberg on the spot for what he deemed a brazen act of insubordination. Loebel then demanded that Goldberg leave the building and imperiously informed Goldberg's coworkers that if any of them chose to disagree with his handling of the vote, they could leave with Goldberg.

The stunned workers voted, along with the secretaries, supervisors, and even the officers of the company. A new committee was elected and this time Ethel was not on it, to no one's great surprise. Loebel may have won this round, but none of the former strike committee was about to concede defeat. The sides were drawn and they would pursue the fight whenever and wherever they could.

Their chance came three weeks later. On Friday, 11 October, one of the leaders of the strike at National and one of its best-liked employees was fired for insubordination. Since the strike, Paul Goldblatt had been increasingly harassed by his supervisor, a Mr. Morganstern, who deeply resented the union and felt betrayed by

Goldblatt's association with it. On this particular Friday, Morganstern contrived a situation in which Goldblatt faced an inordinate amount of work and then taunted him by saying that if he did not like the way things were run he could quit. When Goldblatt replied that he could not afford to quit, Morganstern fired him.

Word of Paul's dismissal spread quickly throughout the plant. Ethel was one of the first women to hear the news and immediately put down her book of receipts as she was told to spread the word among female employees. She rapidly moved from one woman to another to tell them what had happened to Paul and urged them to stop work immediately in protest. She argued that if they did not forcefully challenge Paul's firing, any one or all of them could be dismissed for similarly minor or trumped-up charges. Within an hour of Paul's dismissal, almost all the workers in the building, except those working under Morganstern, stopped work and assembled on the mezzanine outside Loebel's office. Although the president was out at the time, the crowd protested to his secretary, who assured them that her boss would meet with them the following morning.

Ethel arrived at work the next day ready for yet another confrontation with the man she had come to despise. But this was not to occur. As soon as Ethel walked in, she was informed that she was fired: she did not have the best interests of the company at heart. She was to leave immediately. Ethel protested vehemently: Miss Pace, the women's office manager, had praised her efficiency and had said she could not operate without her, she was so reliable. But this had no effect. One of the managers, a Mr. Weingarten, ordered her to leave. As she looked somewhat dazedly around her, Ethel realized that she was not the only one to have been dismissed. A member of the strike committee found her to tell her that he, other members of the committee, some strikers, and even her own brother had been summarily fired. Something had to be done. This was a sham and everyone knew it. They were *not* going to passively accept this.

Later that day, Ethel, Morris Fleissig, Hazel Darby, Alex Bernstein, and Victor Fleisher of the strike committee met with an official of the Shipping Clerks Union, Local 19953. They were told they could file suit against Loebel with the newly formed National Labor Relations Board (NLRB). The union official believed they had a strong case since Loebel had fired them for their attempt to organize fellow workers. The union would represent them and would also take up the illegal dismissals of Irving and Paul. Although the official was hopeful, he cautioned that it might take months before their case could be heard before the NLRB.

In fact, it was five months later, on 17 and 18 March 1936, that the National Labor Relations Board heard Ethel and her co-workers' case against Andrew Loebel. At the start of the hearing, Loebel's lawyer tried to have the case dismissed on the grounds that the National Labor Relations Act was unconstitutional. His motion was immediately denied, and the hearing proceeded. The employees told their story and answered the questions of the trial examiner. Then Loebel's counsel responded: all the employees who were fired were discharged for insubordination and nothing more. The situation was simple and clear; Loebel had the right as an employer to dismiss any of his workers as he saw fit. The attorney finished, and the Board took the testimony under advisement, announcing that the litigants would be informed of its decision.

Loebel apparently was incensed that the Board had heard the case and that its members seemed to be favorably persuaded by what his former workers told them. He had his attorney file a brief with the Board on 7 April and then again on 21 April. In addition to this, the Communist party *Worker* reports that Loebel

> . . . had no less than Attorney Morris Ernst, red-baiter extraordinary [sic] and a member of the American Civil Liberties Union board, appear for him in a behind-the-scenes operation, it was learned. Apparently Ernst himself was somewhat abashed at his anti-labor role, saying when he obtained a private audience with a board member, that he was not pleading for the employer for a fee, but was doing so out of personal friendship.

All of Loebel's maneuvers proved useless, however. On 29 June 1936, the Board found that Loebel was guilty of engaging in unfair labor practices and ordered that the employees be reinstated with back pay. Specifically, in regard to Ethel, the Board held that:

> There is no allegation or evidence that she was not an efficient employee. The respondent's antagonism to Ethel Greenglass undoubtedly arose by virtue of the fact that she was active in organizing the Union, was a member of the . . . [strike] committees, and had urged employees who

were working after Goldblatt's dismissal to cease working and protest against it.

We find that Ethel Greenglass was discharged because of her union membership and activities.

Thus Ethel Greenglass became one of the first American workers to effectively bring charges against an employer under the National Labor Relations Act.

The resolution of the shipping clerks' strike left Ethel, however, at a point where she had to decide what direction her life should follow. At the age of twenty, her desire to be a singer still burned, yet it was unclear how she might realistically connect this to her growing passion for politics. By the end of the year her course would be unalterably set.

5

"IL BACIO" AND
THE REVOLUTION

After Ethel was fired from National and was waiting for her NLRB hearing, she had begun to look for another job. In the fall of 1935, however, employment was not so easy to come by, so Ethel turned once more to singing with hopes of furthering her career. She had been attending rehearsals of the Schola Cantorum regularly, even during the strike, and now was able to indulge her passion for singing without worrying over struggles at National New York Packing and Shipping. At the end of November, the chorus performed Beethoven's Ninth Symphony at Carnegie Hall with the Boston Symphony Orchestra. In the middle of December, it appeared there with the New York Philharmonic under the direction of Otto Klemperer. In February it again appeared at Carnegie Hall performing works of Moussorgsky, Stravinsky, and Glinka.

Attired in the required black dress and standing among the 144 women and 78 men of the Schola Cantorum on the stage of Carnegie Hall, Ethel Greenglass must have felt closer to the fulfillment of her ambition than ever before. Her eyes also must have been fixed on the soprano who was the soloist in Beethoven's Ninth and Moussorgsky's *Joshua*, for this was the role Ethel desired and fully intended to assume, if only she could properly train her voice through formal instruction.

66   Her opportunity came in February or March 1936 when she was hired by the Bell Textile Company, located near Manhattan's City Hall, as a stenographer. Ethel had maintained her typing skills by practicing on a standard typewriter she had purchased from one of the men in the Clark Players. As a stenographer at Bell, Ethel earned more than she had at National, even though she was only working part-time with the promise of eventually going full-time. With more pay and a determination to save all the carfare and lunch money she did not turn over to her family, Ethel decided that she finally could afford the voice lessons for which she had yearned.

For two dollars a lesson, Ethel was able to study at Carnegie Hall Studios and work on both singing and piano. This necessitated careful economizing and diligent practice to get the most out of each lesson, but Ethel was prepared. Thus she began studying with "Madame"—the only name her friends can recall Ethel use when referring to her teacher. Madame taught the light operettas and concert pieces that Jeanette MacDonald and Grace Moore were then making so popular in movies and on the radio. The work of the composers Victor Herbert, Rudolf Friml, and Sigmund Romberg were staples and an Italian aria was occasionally thrown in.

Ethel was a devoted pupil. Since she had no standard by which to evaluate Madame, she accepted whatever her teacher told her as received truth. This was her one chance to become a performer and she was not about to let her long-awaited and treasured lessons serve no purpose through lack of practice. She wanted to impress Madame and advance rapidly. Ethel imposed a rigid schedule on herself, as a friend from the Clark Players recalled:

> This meant a very heavy program. Every night Ethel made out a little time chart for the next day. She is the only person I ever knew who wrote out an hour-by-hour, almost minute-by-minute program and stuck by it.
>
> One evening I went by and said, "Let's go for a walk, as we used to do—but not on Rivington Street." I had taken a look at her serious face and that's why I made the little joke. It was about Yom Kippur time, and we used to hate to walk on Rivington Street just before the holidays because they'd be preparing chickens kosher style and we couldn't stand to hear them squawk. But she pointed to her little chart on the wall and said no, her schedule called for practicing. I was sort of mad.

Ethel rigidly held to other self-imposed restrictions that her singing **67**
lessons demanded. At Bell Textile she joined Local 65 of the United
Wholesale and Retail Union. Lunch hour often was the time employees would go to a nearby coffee shop or cafeteria to eat their
meal and talk about the union. But Ethel was usually not among
the diners. In her effort to save money for lessons, she would bring
a lunch from home and, weather permitting, would eat it at one of
the two nearby parks. By walking five blocks down Broadway, Ethel
could lunch at City Hall Park. Or, if she felt less energetic, she
could go a mere two-and-a-half blocks to Thomas Paine Park facing
the U.S. Court House at Foley Square. Tessie always baked loaves
of *challa* on Fridays so that the house typically was well-stocked
with bread throughout the week. Ethel would often make a whole
stack of sandwiches and bring it to one of the parks at noon. In this
way she implicitly made a statement about what was most important
to her—the union or singing lessons, political activity or art—and
it is clear which continued to predominate. Still, when politics did
not directly obstruct her self-prescribed career path, Ethel was eager
to find some means of progressive political involvement. In 1936
in New York City this was not difficult.

> *We were living in New York and New York was said to be*
> *part of the United States. Yet, at least in our imagination,*
> *we were making New York over into another country, a*
> *place apart from the Old World and the New. . . . It was*
> *New York as both imperial city and center of action, the*
> *powerhouse of capitalism and crucible of socialism. . . .*
> *Years later, writing about the New York of his imagination,*
> *the critic Lionel Abel joked that in the thirties it "became*
> *the most interesting part of the Soviet Union . . . the one*
> *part of that country in which the struggle between Stalin*
> *and Trotsky could be openly expressed."*
>
> Irving Howe

At the very center of this "imaginary" New York stood the American
Communist party, freed from the fetters of sectarianism and in-
fighting that had characterized it in the late twenties and early
thirties. In a few short years the underlying creed of the Party had
changed from "all not for us are against us" to "all not against us
are for us." The movement of world events had forced the Party in
the United States to transform itself from a revolutionary party cham-

pioning the working class to a group involved in broad-based coalitions devoted to opposing fascism and preserving democratic
rights. The rise of fascist governments in Germany and Italy, the
fascist rebellion in Spain, and the appearance of pro-fascist parties
in a number of Western democracies had propelled this shift. The
leadership of the Soviet Union believed its country to be directly
threatened by an increasingly bellicose Nazi Germany and an indifference on the part of the governments of Britain and France to
Hitler's and Mussolini's territorial designs. In 1935, Mussolini invaded Ethiopia; in March 1936, German troops reoccupied the
Rhineland in direct violation of treaties; in July, the Spanish fascists
rebelled against their democratic government; in November, Germany and Japan signed an Anti-Comintern Pact; a year later Italy
joined them, and Hitler suggested that France might soon ally itself
with the fascist powers. Stalin believed these were the opening
salvos of a second world war and saw his country in an increasingly
isolated position. The only way to mitigate this isolation was to
court those countries that might ally themselves with the USSR
against fascism. The Soviets thus began to initiate friendlier relations
with the United States and Western Europe; what previously had
been the "imperialist powers," now were referred to as "the democracies." For the time being, defeat of fascism would eclipse the
Communists' struggle against capitalism.

Fascism, however, did not merely represent a threat to Russia.
The American Communist party increasingly saw signs of fascism
within its own country. No doubt these signs were sometimes exaggerated or perhaps created out of whole cloth to stir the com-
placent into action, strengthen the Party's position, or make things
seem so menacing that one just could not stint on contributions to
the Party's latest fund-raising drive. But much of what the Party said
reflected real fears and dangers, even though the language it used
to express itself could be alarmist or hyperbolic.

Not only the CP but many progressives and liberals believed
incipient fascist movements existed in the United States. The popularity of Senator Huey P. Long and Father Charles Coughlin was
pointed to as evidence. Both men used rhetoric similar to that of
European fascist leaders in the twenties: veneration of the traditional, of community, of the common people; hostility to industrial
growth, technological progress, and big bankers. Both were adamant anti-Communists and suspected anti-Semites. When Long was
assassinated in September 1935, the movement he inspired dissi-

pated. Father Coughlin, however, retained his popularity. Some forty million Americans listened to his Sunday radio broadcasts; he received more mail than any other American (including the President), and when he called for the formation of his own political organization in 1934, the National Union for Social Justice, more than five million listeners signed up within two months. In addition to his staunch anti-Communism and nationalism, Coughlin supported Mussolini against the Ethiopians and Franco against the Spanish Loyalists. By 1938 he was openly supporting fascism and anti-Semitism, although his popularity had by then begun to wane.

William Randolph Hearst, the nation's most powerful newspaper publisher, also fanned the flames of domestic fascism. As the nation's most powerful newspaper publisher, Hearst consistently railed against communism on his editorial pages. Day after day, boxed quotations from Lenin and Stalin and resolutions from the international Communist movement were carried in black-faced type in his newspapers. In this way, Hearst made the "communist menace" seem imminent. After a European trip in which he visited Hitler, Hearst wrote in 1934: "Fascism is definitely a movement to oppose and offset communism, and so prevent the least capable and least creditable class from getting control of the country. Fascism will only come into existence in the United States when such a movement becomes really necessary for the prevention of communism." Since Hearst was doing everything he could to make it seem that communism increasingly posed a threat to the American people, it was not illogical to believe he was setting the stage for a call for fascism.

All of this, too, must be seen against the background of anti-Semitism that pervaded the country before the war. According to public opinion surveys conducted in the late nineteen-thirties,

about one-third of all Americans thought Jews were less patriotic than other Americans; almost half felt there was good reason for anti-Jewish feeling; about half thought Jewish businessmen were less honest than others; and almost two-thirds found Jews to have some objectionable qualities. . . . In 1940, one survey found that while only 14% of the American people indicated that they would be influenced to vote for a congressional candidate because he declared himself to be against the Jews, 29% said it would not make any difference, and 12% said, 'Don't know.'

Although this level of anti-Jewish sentiment was nothing new, it took on new meaning in the thirties because of the events then taking place in Europe. If the Nazis could mobilize the anti-Semitism of their people into a national policy, could not the same thing happen in the United States?

When the CP became a leading voice in the United States denouncing fascism, it spoke to the real fears many Americans and particularly Jewish Americans were then experiencing. The Party did not just talk, it demonstrated and rallied and lobbied. While most Jewish organizations refused to demonstrate against what was happening in Germany, fearful that calling attention to themselves as Jews would exacerbate domestic anti-Semitism, the Communist Jewish People's Committee called for street demonstrations and a Madison Square Rally at which people had to be turned away. To be a Communist in 1936 was to be a fighter in an undeclared war against fascism and its attendant evils.

In order to encourage the United States government to ally with the Soviet Union against the fascist powers and to stem what it deemed the rising tide of domestic fascism, the Party recognized its need for far greater support from the American people. To most Americans, the Party remained a group of foreigners trying to bolshevize America at the behest of the Soviet Union. Being seen as having a greater allegiance to Soviet Russia than to the United States obviously lost the Party innumerable recruits, supporters, and the tolerance of the American people. Therefore, in consultation with Moscow, the CPUSA embarked on a program to demonstrate that Communist party membership was synonymous with loyalty to America and its heritage. The Ninth Convention of the Communist Party–USA became the showcase for the newly Americanized party.

The convention was held in New York City, where the national offices were located, from 24 to 28 June 1936. At the convention of 750 largely young, native-born Americans, the Party nominated Earl Browder as its candidate for that year's national presidential election.

Across the galleries, flaming red streamers with white letters carried slogans of faith in victory: The unity of labor can crush fascism and prevent war! For a free, happy and prosperous America! Keep America out of war by keeping war out of the world! High in the rear of the auditorium an

immense canvas showed the spirit of '76—drummer, fifer,
standard bearer—carrying red and American flags inter-
twined. Out of these emerged the faces of Washington,
Jefferson, John Brown, Lincoln, Frederick Douglass; be-
neath them the slogan: Communism is twentieth-century
Americanism.

At last there was a way to be simultaneously an American, and a patriotic one at that, as well as a part of an international movement tied to combating fascism, championing the working class, and building socialism. The last activity now seemed easier than ever, for the party's presidential candidate Browder reported to the convention that "a strong and consistent fight for democratic rights under conditions of decaying capitalism must ultimately lead the American people to the choice of a socialist path." In other words, Communists would no longer be required to do anything clandestine, dangerous, unpatriotic, or illegal. They could work in the same way that traditional American liberals would, fighting to protect and extend democratic rights. But what differentiated the Communists from the liberals was what went on in their heads. Liberals merely thought that what they fought for was an end in itself; Communists, on the other hand, knew that any particular fight cleared one more obstacle on the road toward an inevitable socialism. Communists and their allies could campaign for Roosevelt or other progressive Democrats; they could demand greater federal relief or extension of relief to larger groups of people; they could fight for Negro rights, denounce anti-Semitism, build the Congress of Industrial Organizations (CIO), support foreign peoples fighting against fascism, raise funds for political refugees, demonstrate against unfair labor practices, and all in the name of building socialism.

> *That was the tremendous thing about those times. The sense*
> *of history that you lived with daily. The sense of remaking*
> *the world. Every time I wrote a leaflet or marched on a*
> *picket line or went to a meeting I was remaking the world.*
> *. . . Because I was a Communist.*

This sense of affecting the course of history was reaffirmed over and over again, in small and large ways, in intimate conversations with fellow comrades and in rallies with tens of thousands of people. It was reflected in the *Daily Worker*, the *New Masses*, and the works of Malcolm Cowley, Lincoln Steffens, Granville Hicks, John Howard Lawson, Richard Wright, Mike Gold, and Joseph Freeman. It emanated from the stage in *Peace on Earth*, *Stevedore*, and *Waiting for Lefty*. It reverberated through one's very being every time the "Internationale" was played, or one marched triumphantly with thousands of others on May Day, or saw the Red flag and the American flag draped together. But, most importantly, the sense of affecting history was reaffirmed through the elaborate and dense web of social interactions that existed among Communist party members and sympathizers.

By 1936, the average, New York dues-paying Party members attended meetings every other week at their neighborhood branches, sold *Daily Workers*, occasionally ran off leaflets at Party headquarters, and perhaps attended a class at the Party's Jefferson School. These official activities were little compared to the "extracurricular" events and projects held under the Party's auspices. In addition to work in any one of the dozens of "mass organizations" or labor unions that the CP influenced or controlled, a New York Party adherent could attend parties, socials, fundraisers, musical performances, plays, art exhibits, lectures, nature walks, resorts, camps, or even restaurants that were sponsored by or affiliated with the American Communist party. On any given evening of the week, there were a variety of CP activities to choose from. On weekends, there were literally a dozen or more parties in Manhattan and Brooklyn one could attend. Party affiliation meant far more than a political identification; it meant friends, social life, community.

What was true of New York City in general, was particularly so true on the Lower East Side. With 3,000 actual members and probably many more "fellow travellers," the Lower East Side was "a city within a city, . . . a sovereign state, working-class and radical to the core, . . . politically *sui generis* in America: there were practically no conservatives. The right-wingers were the New Dealers. . . ."

In this environment Communists could live within a self-contained world that satisfied all their needs—from the most mundane, daily essentials to the most broad, existential quests for identity, community, and the meaning of life.

> [I]t was a total world, from the schools to which I sent my children to family mores to social life to the quality of our friendships to the doctor, the dentists, and the cleaner. There

*was an underpinning to everything in our lives that affected
the entire variety of daily decision, reference, observation,
everything! No one who didn't live through it can understand what it was like or why it was so hard to give up
. . . Right, wrong, errors, blind pro-Sovietism, democratic
centralism, the lot notwithstanding. In our lives as Communists, we had community.*

It was to this community that Ethel Greenglass turned her attention
in 1936 as she looked around her for some form of political involvement. As the experience of the shipping clerks' strike still
ignited her passions, she gravitated to something that would perhaps
rekindle those feelings of comradery, exuberance, and self-satisfaction generated by fighting for the underdog. The Workers' Alliance presented itself as the most likely means of achieving this.

Formed in March 1935 under the leadership of the Socialist
party, the Workers' Alliance of America was an effective representative of the unemployed during the Depression. In April 1936,
the Workers' Alliance and the Communist-led Unemployed Councils officially merged in the Party's attempt to form large coalitions
under the banner of the Popular Front. By October 1936, the CP
had gained control of most of the state organizations of the Alliance,
and claimed that 75 percent of the national membership, which
totaled around 30,000, was led by the Party.

In New York, the CP dominated Alliance was quite vocal and
visible in its work on behalf of the unemployed. In 1936, it had a
twofold strategy: to maintain relief for those who needed it, and to
fight against layoffs of Works Project Administration (WPA) workers.
During the previous year, President Roosevelt had terminated direct
federal relief to the jobless and instead created the WPA to provide
public-works jobs for every able-bodied adult. While the WPA furnished millions of jobs, at its peak it provided only for about one
in four of the estimated unemployed. Thus, with direct federal relief
abolished, the majority of the unemployed had to turn once more
to local and state agencies for financial assistance.

The Workers' Alliance staged demonstrations in front of Home
Relief Bureau offices and City Hall demanding greater relief for the
needy. In the latter half of 1936, about 1,000 of its members were
arrested in and outside Home Relief Bureau offices alone. There
were Workers' Alliance rallies at Union Square and parades to City
Hall. Continual threats by the federal government to slash appro-

priations for the WPA were protested by the Alliance, and it actually became the official collective bargaining agent for WPA workers. In the winter, the Workers' Alliance demanded warm clothing for relief clients; at other times its members demanded food for those in need. There was nothing ambiguous or confusing about its position: the Alliance clearly championed the underdog. It fought for those on the very bottom of the class hierarchy and continually argued for the government to care for those who could no longer help themselves.

It is unclear exactly how involved Ethel was in the Alliance during most of 1936. She apparently attended some of the rallies or demonstrations it sponsored, but by the end of the year she had found her niche in the organization and, of course, it involved singing.

The first memory of Ethel singing at a political event was in July 1936 in front of Ohrbach's department store on East 14th Street, across from Union Square. Here, every Saturday afternoon since March 1928, pickets had gathered to protest the unfair labor practices of N.M. Ohrbach and his lockout of a number of employees. These Party-endorsed gatherings often had been raucous affairs as police arrested pickets for blocking pedestrian traffic, for chaining themselves to guard railings around the store, and for verbally harassing customers. On one Saturday afternoon, Ethel appeared on the sidewalk outside Ohrbach's and sang for the pickets with a number of other entertainers.

A few months later, Ethel began singing at various Lower East Side events that were organized for what was fast becoming the Party's most popular and emotionally charged issue: the defense of Loyalist Spain. The Franco rebellion against the democratically elected government of the Spanish Republic began in July 1936. In August the CPUSA held a meeting of some 15,000 people in Madison Square Garden "to support the Spanish people and their struggle against Fascist reaction and barbarism in every possible way by adopting resolutions in our unions, by demonstrating in front of Italian and German Consulates, demanding that they stop their intervention in behalf of the Fascists, and by raising funds to be sent to the Spanish people." Fundraising events and informational meetings quickly sprang up throughout the city to implement the Party's agenda. Providing entertainment was a good means of raising funds, so there were numerous opportunities for Ethel to perform.

The Workers' Alliance staged one of its more dramatic demonstrations in December in New York City and Ethel's vocal talents were called upon again. The Alliance was protesting the current drive to reduce relief rolls throughout the city and decided to mimic a new tactic that industrial workers were just then pioneering—the sit-down strike. Instead of walking out to go on strike, workers simply laid down their tools and refused to work or leave the factory.

The Workers' Alliance called for a sit-in at five Home Relief Bureau offices in Manhattan and Brooklyn to begin the week of 7 December. Hundreds of Alliance members, dismissed WPA workers, and relief clients who had recently been dropped from the rolls entered Home Relief Bureau offices and announced they would not leave until their demands were met.

On Friday night, 11 December and in the early hours of Saturday morning, a representative from the Alliance brought Ethel around to each of the sit-in sites to entertain the hundreds of people who were undoubtedly growing restless in their cramped quarters. At 2:00 A.M. at the office on the Lower East Side, Avenue D between Second and Third streets, Ethel was ushered into a room with 200 women and men and 18 children who had entered the office at 4:00 the previous afternoon. "Because you're suffering through the night, we've brought a little entertainment for you," announced the Workers' Alliance representative, and Ethel sang Arditi's "Il Bacio." She sang one or two more concert pieces and was then shuttled off to another Home Relief Bureau office. Before the night was over she had sung at two offices in Brooklyn, one in Harlem, and another on East 32nd Street.

Ethel clearly was gaining a certain kind of stardom, or at least recognition, in left-wing circles. She had discovered her own way of blending her life's ambition with her commitment to fighting injustice. This did not mean she had relinquished her desire to be a professional singer, for she continued her lessons at Carnegie Hall Studios and practiced as diligently as ever. But she had withdrawn from the Schola Cantorum after only a year's participation, perhaps because the chorus went on tour and she was unable to leave her job. Political singing engagements now provided her with her only audience, thus sustaining her identity as a singer and feeding her commitment to her studies with Madame.

———

By the close of 1936, Ethel frequently was asked to sing at local political events; thus, she readily accepted a request to perform at a holiday benefit for a strike then in progress within the International Seamen's Union.

The strike had been called in October, led largely by CP members in the union. It had been a violently contested strike that eventually claimed twenty-seven lives, so in the last week of December many Party groups were attempting to raise funds for their embattled comrades.

Ethel came alone to the hall that had been rented on the Lower East Side for the benefit. At twenty-one she was used to attending social events without a partner. She had practically never dated and had professed a lack of interest in the subject since high school. A friend from Seward Park High recalls that Ethel "never went out with boys. . . . [T]o most of our gang of girl friends, who used to tell each other everything, and talk endlessly about our boyfriends, Ethel seemed to think she was too good for the boys we dated. Ethel kept aloof."

As a fifteen-year-old senior in high school, Ethel had been younger than most of her classmates and may have felt awkward and naive around boys. Perhaps because she felt ugly or unlovable, perhaps because she always had been teased and mocked by her brothers, she may have harbored deep fears that no boy would be interested in her. She probably turned her fear into feigned indifference.

Once she had graduated from high school and began to spend most of her free time with the Clark Players, new fears arose out of expanded possibilities. Her best friend from the Players recalled:

> We were very immature. And both of us were conscious of not having 'been out' and not having the right manners. All the Players gang went regularly to the Paramount Cafeteria on Delancey Street, near Loew's, after rehearsal. For a long time Ethel and I were afraid to go. It seemed to us quite a dazzling place. We were afraid we wouldn't know whether to use a fork or spoon. Here it was, just a cafeteria, but to us it was about like going to the Astor roof.

As time passed, Ethel was emboldened and not only mastered the cafeteria, but began to participate in social events that the Players organized during the summers. After a year in the group, she participated in daytime trips to the Palisades and to the Steeplechase at Coney Island, and once even sailed at night up the Hudson River.

Traveling beyond the Lower East Side and in the company of young men was beyond anything Ethel had previously experienced, but she still avowed complete indifference toward the opposite sex. She "simply had no interest in boys; . . . she had her sights on bigger and better things," her friend from the Players recalls.

It was her participation in the shipping clerks' strike that brought Ethel her first date at the age of twenty. Morris Fleissig, a member of the strike committee, was about three years older than Ethel and had worked at National New York Packing and Shipping full-time since 1931. Short, slight, and bespectacled, he had grown up in the same poverty as she and, in fact, lived only three blocks from her on Lewis Street. Their first date was similar to the others that followed: Morris called for Ethel at her home and they then strolled around the neighborhood. Once they crossed the Williamsburg Bridge and another time they walked to a street fair at the Lavanburg Homes, a nearby housing project. They never did more than this for lack of money, and it never occurred to either of them to ask the other over to her or his home. Perhaps, as Irving Howe has suggested, this was because of "feelings of embarrassment":

> One's mother spoke English, if she spoke it at all, with a grating accent; one's father shuffled about in slippers and suspenders when company came, hardly as gallant in manner or as nicely groomed as he ought to be. . . . The sense of embarrassment derived from a half-acknowledged shame before the perceived failings of one's parents, and both embarrassment and shame mounted insofar as one began to acquire the tastes of the world.

Thus by the time Morris moved away from New York City in April 1936, he had only briefly met Tessie, Barney, and Doovey, then fourteen years old, and had received no impression of the Greenglass family.

Although there is no record of whether Ethel dated anyone after her walks with Morris in 1935, no one remembers her being seriously interested in any man. Ethel had male acquaintances and friends whom she saw through the political circles in which she now traveled, but she never had a regular boyfriend. For reasons that are not entirely clear, men did not seem to be attracted to her, nor she to them. Perhaps she still feigned a certain amount of indifference around potential dates because she felt vulnerable and sought to reject them before they rejected her. Maybe she genuinely had not found anyone with whom she wished to go out. Perhaps she felt that dating a man would lead her down the path to marriage, children, and a reenactment of her mother's life, something she still eschewed. She may have felt that involvement with someone might interfere with her ambition to be a performer.

At the benefit for the International Seamen's Union in December 1936, however, Ethel came by herself in typical fashion, but she did not remain alone for long. After a while a man approached her. He was tall, slim, and had an endearing smile. His gray-green eyes fixed on her and he apparently refused to leave her throughout the evening. He told her that he was a sophomore at City College and he may even have let her know he was a member of its Young Communist League chapter.

This must have impressed Ethel a great deal. She knew almost no one who attended college, and he seemed so interested in her! After talking for awhile, she mounted the stage and sang her selection for the evening, Pestalozza's "Ciribiribin," ending with the refrain:

> Ciribiribin, Your glowing eyes shed rays of hope upon my heart,
> Ciribiribin, And though time flies I pray this love will ne'er depart.
> Ciribiribin, Come to my arms, love me alone. From doubt, refrain,
> Ciribiribin, Ciribiribin, Ciribiribin, kiss me again!

When Ethel stepped off the stage, her new admirer was there waiting for her, and his appreciation for her voice abounded. This sort of attention was something new to Ethel and particularly from someone well mannered and good looking. He was so unlike her brothers who were turning into short, stocky men with little sensitivity or brains. The Greenglass boys could not dream of going to college, even if they had wanted to. Here, however, was a man who spoke thoughtfully and seemed smart. He loved her singing, thought she had the most beautiful voice he had ever heard, and he could not take his eyes off her.

When Ethel left the party that evening and stepped into the biting December air, she did not leave alone. At her side for the first time was Julius Rosenberg.

6

JULIUS ROSENBERG

Their paths actually had crossed many times, yet they had never before spoken. Perhaps he had seen her before but the moment had not been right; his insecurity betrayed him, she had seemed unapproachable. In any case, they had grown up in close proximity to each other and under circumstances familiar to them both.

Julius Rosenberg was the youngest child of Harry Rosenberg and Sophie Cohen Rosenberg. Harry and Sophie both had lived in the same *shtetl* in Poland, yet they met for the first time only after both had come to New York City. Sophie arrived in the United States in about 1902 and Harry came some four years later. When they met, she was working in a garment factory sewing buttons and tags on shirts and he was a garment worker striving to become a tailor. When they married in about 1908, Sophie immediately quit her factory work to make a home for herself and her new husband.

In 1909 the Rosenbergs' first child, David, was born. Three years later Lena came, in 1914, the twins, Ethel and Ida, and lastly Julius on 12 May 1918.

At the time of Julius's birth, the Rosenbergs were struggling financially. Harry was trying his hand as a small businessman, operating a clothes cleaning establishment at 269 Audubon Avenue, some six blocks from Yeshiva University. His family lived in a cold-water flat in Harlem, and enough money was not coming in to support his family with its five small children. After some years of trying to make it as a shopowner, Harry had to admit defeat and moved his family back to the Lower East Side to take up work once more as a tailor.

The flat the Rosenbergs moved to was located at 127 Broome Street, about three blocks from the Greenglass's apartment. Here the family lived on the top floor of a five-story building that lacked heat and decent lighting. In the winter, rain and melted snow dripped through the ceiling and chill winds blew through the rotted window frames. There was frequently not enough food to eat, since Harry was often on strike as a staunch member of the ILGWU. Since strike benefits often were nonexistent, Sophie remained dependent on the free milk or bread the union would hand out to strikers' families. "I remember," recalls Ethel Appel, Julius's older sister, "we were so poor my mother hard-boiled the eggs, so she could divide one among us."

Unlike the Greenglasses, Harry Rosenberg was strongly committed to labor unions and understood the hardships he and his family suffered in life as the result of their class position. Because he was already a young adult when he came to this country at the age of eighteen, Harry had had time to learn the meaning of class hierarchy while living under the rule of Tsar Nicholas II. Like so many other immigrant Jewish garment workers, Harry Rosenberg saw his future intimately tied to the betterment of workers as a group. He understood why he lived in poverty and believed the only means of escape was to fight alongside other men like himself for better wages and working conditions.

Although Harry had no formal education as the youngest of thirteen children raised in abject poverty, he had taught himself to read and write Yiddish. This allowed him to read the most lively and popular newspaper on the Lower East Side at the time, the *Jewish Daily Forward*, which was published by a group of men affiliated with the Socialist party. While he was not a member of any formal political organization, Harry's social philosophy was not dissimilar to that reflected in the pages of the *Forward*: the working class had the power and the right to transform society so that it was more equitable and humane; only the masses of working people could bring this about, not some sectarian party; labor unions and electoral politics were excellent vehicles for building a more just social world; any social transformation necessarily had to respect Jewish religion, customs, and tradition.

Although Harry did not often speak about political matters at home and became increasingly conservative as he grew older, he did instill in his children a sympathy toward those at the bottom of society and in need, a respect for one's fellow workers, a commitment to the virtues of equality and justice, and a belief in working in common to achieve certain goals.

Harry's involvement in strikes made life very difficult for his family in the short run, but once the strikes were settled, the Rosenbergs usually benefited through the higher wages Harry earned. By the mid-twenties, they were able to move to 64 Columbia Street, exactly one block away from the Greenglass apartment at 64 Sheriff. Although this was a tenement as bad as any on the Lower East Side (and not dissimilar to the one Ethel's family occupied), the Rosenbergs' apartment was on the first floor, and thus was a move upward on the hierarchy of tenement living from their previous flat. Here the family crowded into four rooms. Julie was forced to share a narrow bed with his brother, while the girls in the family all slept together.

By the time Julie was ten in 1928, his family was able to make their greatest leap yet into domestic luxury. They moved into Lavanburg Homes, a modern housing project. Here, for the first time, they had steam heat, electric lights, and their own bathroom. Sophie's sister also lived in Lavanburg and her brother-in-law was the superintendent. Harry's salary as a sample maker for Turner and Company allowed the family not only the comparative luxuries of one of the city's first housing projects, but also enough so that Sophie could serve stuffed cabbage, gefilte fish and plenty of cream and cheese. The Rosenbergs were so comfortable now that their oldest child, David, could attend Columbia University on scholarship and thus not contribute to the family's income as did so many other nineteen-year-old boys.

These years before the Depression were good years for the Rosenbergs. Sophie was an immaculate housekeeper and a very good cook. She kept her family strictly kosher and made sure that *shabbes* was faithfully observed. Sophie had been reared in an Orthodox manner herself. Men's roles and women's roles had been clear and distinct. Therefore Sophie had learned only household work and remained completely illiterate throughout her life.

"In Europe we had to pay the teacher to come to the home—and feed him, too," she reported in an interview in 1953. "I had four brothers, and my mother said, 'You are a girl, you don't need education, you learn to cook.' " Although she never read a book, Sophie valued reading and learning as did a great many immigrant Jews. Both she and her husband passed on to their children, and especially their sons, a respect for education. This had a particular impact on Julie, perhaps due to his special relationship to his mother and the many illnesses he suffered as a youth.

As the youngest of five children and a boy, Julie occupied a role ripe for garnering his mother's affection. He was also a particularly cute baby: "He had blond curls and blue eyes and a smile that would melt a heart of stone." In addition to this, Julie had a series of illnesses that bonded him closely with his mother. During a particularly cold winter when Harry was on strike and the family was living in the unheated apartment on Broome Street, Julie, age three, contracted the measles. With virtually no food to eat and not one to hide her emotions, Sophie became nearly hysterical with fear that her youngest child would die. She stayed with him constantly and only left his side to stand in line for the free milk the union was handing out. Julie survived the measles, but a year or two later he was hit by a taxi near his grandmother's house on East Third Street and Avenue C. Sophie witnessed this and immediately lifted him into her arms and carried her young son, blood covering his face, to Gouverneur Hospital, some twelve blocks away. Julie recovered after a convalescence, but Sophie who had been eight months pregnant with her sixth child at the time of the accident, lost her baby because of the trauma and exertion she suffered that day. Again, when Julie was ten, Sophie was forced to take her son to the hospital in an emergency. This time he had a burst appendix and, upon arrival at the emergency room, the doctors informed her that it would be difficult to save her son. As he was wheeled away into the operating room, Julie saw his mother sobbing and told her not to worry. Again Julie survived.

All these brushes with death bound Julie closely to his mother. Sophie Rosenberg dearly loved her little "Yoyni" and doted on him a bit more than her other children.

Julie's convalescences also enabled him to pursue his favorite pastime, reading. Whenever he had the opportunity he would read and then reread boyhood adventure stories, thrillers, and mysteries. He read the Horatio Alger books, the Tom Swift adventures, and volumes by Deering, Burroughs, and Captain Wilbur Lawton. His choice of literature remained fairly commonplace and undisciplined until he discovered what would become his boyhood passion—the Talmud.

Julie began attending the Downtown Talmud Torah school when he was about nine or ten. Enrollment in Hebrew school was the norm for the majority of boys on the Lower East Side in this period. They would dutifully study the Hebrew language and religion, have their Bar Mitzvah, and then rarely step into a Jewish religious institution again in their lives, except perhaps on High Holy Days, weddings, or for others' Bar Mitzvah. Julie was different however; for him studying the Torah was a passion rather than a duty, an extreme pleasure rather than a chore. Everyday after school, he would walk to Downtown Talmud Torah on East Houston Street, and study for four or more hours; on Fridays he spent the whole evening, and on Saturdays the entire day. One of his teachers there recalled:

> He loved it. Most of the children would stay at the School an hour and a half, but Julie would spend four and five hours at a time in reading and prayer. He went at it so wholeheartedly he became lost to everything else. You could have thrown a stick of dynamite and he would have kept on. At times I would tell him, 'you are overdoing it.'

Although Sophie was always observant of Jewish custom, neither she nor her husband were keenly religious in the sense of frequently attending temple, reading the Talmud, or refusing to engage in secular activities. Since neither of them could read or understand Hebrew, they were at a disadvantage in their ability to worship anyway. Harry and Sophie took pride in Julie's achievements at Hebrew school, but they were somewhat amazed at their son's complete devotion to religious scripture.

Julie studied for his Bar Mitzvah during the depths of the Depression. By the early nineteen-thirties, the Rosenbergs' prosperity had declined due to the economic downturn in the garment industry. Life within the family had also degenerated to some degree. As Harry's work was now intermittent, the Rosenbergs needed more income, so Ethel had to drop out of high school to work and help support the family. Relations with her twin sister Ida had reached a new level of difficulty too. Ida had been deprived of oxygen at birth at a time when delivering twins was still a complicated medical procedure. She suffered some brain damage, although how much is unclear from listening to her surviving siblings. In addition to cognitive problems, Ida also had a number of psychological problems that made her difficult to control. Because of her mental retardation, her brothers and sisters often mocked her and laughed at her. This undoubtedly humiliated Ida and made life quite painful. "She screamed and shouted; you couldn't control her; she revolted against the way she was treated by others."

Living with Ida in crowded apartments, in accord with the then commonly accepted idea that the mentally retarded were a source of shame and should be confined within the family, must have been difficult under any circumstances. But this was the Depression: tension, fear, and anxiety consumed people's lives. Harry Rosenberg, who was particularly hard hit, one day exploded at Ida, who did not comprehend the meaning of the Depression or the effect it was having on her father. Her twin sister, Ethel, recalls: "My father lost his head and had her sent away because she was very disturbing." Harry had Ida placed in a New York City home. Ida remained institutionalized until her death in 1976, and there is no evidence that Julius Rosenberg ever saw her after she was removed from the family.

In the midst of this family upheaval and societal catastrophe Julie was Bar Mitzvahed on 30 May 1931 at the Downtown Talmud Torah. His parents did what was considered proper among Jews of the Lower East Side: they scrimped and went without so their son could have a fine Bar Mitzvah reception. Thus, on thick white card stock with gold lettering, Harry and Sophie announced Julie's Bar Mitzvah reception at Goldfein's Dining Room, 10–12 Avenue A, at 9:00 P.M. and asked their family and friends to attend.

At the conclusion of the celebration, the Rosenbergs told Julie they wanted him to quit his Hebrew studies, but he quickly and adamantly refused. Religious studies had become the center of his life, the core of his identity. The intensity of his religious interests distinguished him from his classmates and neighbors and is what still stands out in acquaintances' memory of the young Julius Rosenberg. One man recalls the time that he and a number of other boys were playing ball in front of Lavanburg Homes on a Saturday. Julie walked by just as the ball was hit too far and rolled in front of his feet. Because it was the Sabbath, Julie would not pick it up, because observant Jews are not to do any work, however trivial, in

honor of the holy day. The ball fell into a sewer and was lost forever. **85**
"We started to get mad, but we couldn't, because we were so impressed that anyone could be that religious."

Everything Julie read and was taught in Hebrew school, he believed completely, without reservation.

"I can see Julie's face now before me as I taught the Prophets, drinking in all I said," his Hebrew teacher remembered in a 1953 interview. "But when I taught the Prophets it was not just to speak of what happened 2,000 years ago, but what was happening around us."

> *A strike was in progress at Ohrbach's. I spoke of it in connection with a chapter in Isaiah . . . I said, "Ohrbach is sitting in the temple now, but who wants his contributions? Let him pay his workers a living wage, then his contributions will be welcome." . . . I saw Julie's eyes glowing. That boy Jonah, as we called him, took it literally. He believed. He took all we taught him literally. . . . I always stressed the theme of service. And my teaching that to serve was the greatest joy in life—well, the boy Jonah believed it . . . Jonah believed everything we taught him—literally. He took it very seriously. I felt he was becoming over-religious, more than I liked.*

For a full-time Hebrew and religious studies teacher in an Orthodox school to admit that he felt one of his students was becoming "over-religious" speaks to the intensity of Julius's religious fervor. His teacher attributed his zeal to his being "too gullible, too sincere," and this perhaps was true. Coming from a family that esteemed social responsibility and highly valued what could be learned from books, Julie had a foundation for accepting what he learned in Hebrew school. But certainly what we know of his family and its attitudes and beliefs does little to explain why its youngest member would become so immersed in Talmudic study and so pious in his beliefs.

Despite Julius's devotion to Judaism, he did not try to proselytize among his friends or remain aloof from his less devout neighbors and classmates. Childhood acquaintances remember him as friendly, thoughtful, shy, studious, and as a very neat dresser (probably because his father made all his clothes). His religious devotion did not make Julie unduly serious or morose. He had a good sense of humor and often liked playfully to tease his sisters Lena and Ethel and his friends. His sister, Ethel, remembers how he and his best friend, Milty Manes, whom he met in Hebrew school, would joyfully recite: "What is a belch? A belch is but a gust of air coming from the heart. If it should take a downward course, it would be called a fart," and then they would explode into laughter.

Julie graduated from Downtown Talmud Torah in June 1932 and was given highest honors. Without hesitation, he decided to continue his Hebrew studies by enrolling at Hebrew High School on East Broadway. Although this school occupied many of Julie's hours after public school ended, he did not become as deeply involved in it as he had with Downtown Talmud Torah. This may have been due to a less compelling curriculum or less interesting teaching staff, or to Julie's increasing awareness of life around him as opposed to life experienced through centuries-old scriptures. As he grew older, Julie seemed to be more sensitive to the inequities and injustices that were so blatantly apparent on the Lower East Side. Although all Americans were supposed to be suffering due to the Depression, some clearly were suffering far more than others. What he had learned at Downtown Talmud Torah did not sufficiently answer why there was so much hatred, unfairness, and mean-spiritness around him. His religious training did not speak in a way that made sense of a world filled with fascists, anti-Semites, and union busters. Julie looked for someone or something that could explain the realities of Depression America to him in a way the Prophets could not. He did not have to look far or for long.

In 1933, the Communist party had taken its first, hesitant steps in allying with non-Communists in coalition organizations. Although not yet in its Popular Front phase during which alliances with liberal and even moderate groups were the norm, the Party sought "to make yet another attempt to set up the united front of struggle with the Social-Democratic Parties," to "win over the social-democratic workers for active revolutionary struggle under the leadership of the Communist Parties."

The first new united front organization the American CP attempted to set up under this revived policy was a Free Tom Mooney Congress, which met at the end of April 1933 in Chicago. There were 1,073 delegates at the Congress, including representatives from the Socialist party, American Federation of Labor locals, and other non-Communist groups. Their aim was to free the West Coast labor leader whom many people believed to have been falsely

imprisoned on the basis of perjured testimony. It was this united
front organization that Julius Rosenberg encountered in his search
for answers the Prophets were not providing.

As a senior at Seward Park High in 1933, Julius heard a street
corner speaker on Delancey Street one day on his way home from
school. The speaker passionately told of the great injustice that had
been perpetrated against Tom Mooney. Julie bought a pamphlet
from the speaker which described the case and outlined how the
reader could help this "innocent victim." The fifteen-year-old boy
was instantly persuaded: he contributed his savings of fifty cents to
the Free Tom Mooney campaign, and began distributing CP literature on the case and collecting signatures on a petition to free the
imprisoned labor leader.

According to Milty, his best friend at the time, Julie then began
going to a CP "social center" a few blocks from the Lavanburg
Homes to find out more about what he could do to fight injustice.
This was probably part of the "elaborate system of cellar clubs for
teenagers" that the Party organized for fourteen- to seventeen-year
olds. These clubs offered a place to hang out, to meet people on
the Lower East Side. They were tenement cellars that had been
painted and brightened up a bit by local youths affiliated with the
Young Communist League (YCL). Open daily from ten in the morning to four in the afternoon, and two evenings a week, the clubs
had certain rules: "you can kiss, but you don't fuck; drink beer but
you don't drink hard liquor; you gamble but for pennies." Although
they occasionally sponsored dances, these clubs were used primarily as places for teenagers to sit around and talk. Julie undoubtedly had the opportunity to hear a good deal about the YCL at the
club he frequented because he soon was attending YCL meetings
on the Lower East Side.

As he became more involved in Communist politics, Julie decided to enlist the support of several local rabbis in one of the
causes the Party was then championing. At this time the CP was
trying to overturn not only the conviction of Tom Mooney, but that
of the Scottsboro boys as well. As in the Mooney case, the nine
black Scottsboro boys had been convicted on the basis of perjured
testimony. Julie asked for the support of the rabbis in trying to
overturn one of these cases. All of the rabbis refused. According to
Julius's sister, Ethel, their refusal had a devastating effect on her
brother. For years he had believed that the Jewish religion stood for
humaneness, equality, and service to those in need. He was taught

this and believed it without reservation. Here now were that religion's most venerated representatives turning their backs on what must have seemed a clear-cut issue of right versus wrong, justice versus prejudice. This one act, this refusal to lend their names or support to rectify a real-life problem, was a serious blow to Julie's religious conviction. Perhaps the rabbis' rebuff would not have symbolized so much, nor made such a lasting impression on him, if he had not already been exposed to a system of thought, a world view that rivaled Judaism in its explanatory abilities, its logic, and its systematic analysis. But Marxism had already reached Julie's ears and eyes through the YCL and the pamphlets and books he had been given to read. It spoke with as much authority and certainty as the Prophets, and it explained much more of everyday reality than anything in the Talmud.

Julie graduated from Seward Park High in June 1934. He had taken an entrance exam to attend Cooper Union but had failed it. It looked as though he would go to the Hoboken School of Technology, because under his name in the Seward Park High *Almanac*, it says, "He'll never be broken, By Yale or Hoboken." At the last moment, however, he enrolled in the School of Technology at the City College of New York (CCNY) intending to major in engineering. Why he chose this field remains unclear, but a classmate at CCNY, Morton Sobell, offers this explanation:

> *I suppose he chose engineering because, despite the remote employment possibilities, it seemed the most 'practical' course of studies available at City. He might more suitably have become a Greek scholar, but this offered no means of earning a living. Since his family was even poorer than my own, and lived in the slums of the Lower East Side, the need to earn a living undoubtedly loomed even larger in his calculations than it did in mine.*

In 1934, CCNY was a tuition-free college, so that Julie's only expense was the cost of the subway ride up to 137th Street. CCNY boasted a student enrollment of 6,000 and, since the close of World War I, had had the largest Jewish student body of any college in the nation. A study conducted in 1938 showed that 80 percent of the parents of the freshman class at CCNY were foreign born, with the majority coming from what had been the Tsarist empire. Furthermore, City probably had the largest number of Jewish faculty of any nondenominational college in the country, although even at CCNY they were concentrated at the bottom of the academic ladder. In all, CCNY during the thirties provided a college education taught by Jews for Jews from a working-class background. It catered to a people who by reason of their common religion, culture, residential patterns, and oppression clung together through every stage of their lives.

CCNY was more than an enclave of higher education for Jewish youth, however. It was also very much a center of radical political activity. According to the research of author Arthur Liebman, "Jewish students from CCNY formed a significant segment of the leadership and cadres of the YCL, which had its headquarters in New York City." The Young Communist League controlled the student newspaper and used the paper to advance its perspective. When a straw poll was taken on campus during the 1936 presidential race, 2,206 students responded. Of these twenty-three percent voted for the Communist party candidate, Earl Browder; twelve percent voted for Socialist Norman Thomas, and twenty percent voted for Franklin Roosevelt on the American Labor Party ticket, a New York-based party to the left of the Democrats. In other words, over half of the students had at least some identification with left-wing politics, a percentage "significantly higher than at any other campus in America." The faculty also was reputed to have "one of the largest and most influential Communist Party collegiate units in the United States," although Irving Howe, a student from 1936 to 1940, contends that this only amounted to "perhaps a dozen party members."

When Julie arrived on campus he found the most stimulating and relevant discussion not in the classrooms, but rather in the alcoves of the campus buildings where students stopped to buy cups of coffee or eat their lunches. Here radical male students analyzed world events, talked over competing political strategies, and debated with those who had varying interpretations of Marxist theory and practice.

You could walk into the thick brown darkness of Alcove 1 at almost any time of day or evening and find a convenient argument about the Popular Front in France, the New Deal in America, the civil war in Spain, the Five-Year Plan in Russia, the theory of permanent revolution, and 'what Marx really meant.' Anyone could join in an argument, there was no external snobbism; but whoever joined did so at his own risk, fools and ignoramuses not being suffered gladly. Each political group spread some of its pamphlets and papers on the alcove table. Here ideas simulated the colors of reality, here we defended the 'correct line,' that mystic pride of Marxism. I can remember getting into an argument at ten in the morning, going off to some classes, and then returning at two in the afternoon to find the argument still going on, but with an entirely fresh cast of characters.

Julie gravitated to Alcove 2 where the men from the YCL spent their time outside of classes. Here he received more of an education than he did in classrooms where, by almost everyone's account, the training was mediocre and the professors seemed "disinterested or incompetent." Julie began to attend the Friday night meetings of City's YCL chapter where world events were discussed at length. The meetings were informal, widely advertised on campus, and open to everyone. There was nothing clandestine or nefarious about being in the YCL at City College; in fact, quite the opposite was true. Since the group controlled the student newspaper, boasted about 400 members on campus, and had some of CCNY's most intelligent and articulate students in its ranks, Communist affiliation could seem prestigious and enviable. Even among students who were disinterested in politics or anti-Communist in outlook, the presence of the YCLers on campus seemed natural, a normal part of the political landscape. Thus, in the mid-thirties, living on the Lower East Side, which former Communist party official Carl Marzani has termed "Communist territory," and going to school at CCNY, with the most radical student body in the nation, must have made the world seem poised for revolution. To the sixteen-year old Julius Rosenberg, New York truly must have seemed "the most interesting part of the Soviet Union."

Julie's first two years at City College were devoted to taking the required liberal arts classes—English, calculus, history, economics, philosophy, Spanish, and other courses. It was difficult for him to attend to his studies, however, since life outside the classroom was so much more interesting. "Who could bother to study when next month the world was going to blow up?" Consequently, Julie devoted his time to discussions in the alcoves, political meetings, rallies, and leaflet production and distribution around all the issues that preoccupied the YCL during these years—fighting fascism, freeing the Scottsboro boys, supporting various labor struggles, and denouncing the Trotskyists, Socialists, and other opponents of the Marxist-Leninist line.

When Julie began to take courses in the Engineering School across the street from the main campus for the first time in 1936, the mood was somewhat different. Students were more conservative, careerist, and devoted to their studies. On Thursday afternoons, from twelve to two, the Engineering Society met. These meetings were devoted to the discussion of technical subjects; political talk of any kind was prohibited. Although decidedly uninteresting to someone so preoccupied with politics, these meetings allowed Julie to acquaint himself fairly well with a number of students from different years. As they talked outside of Society meetings, they discovered many of them shared a similar political perspective as well as an interest in engineering. With some of them Julie set up a small study group for the systematic study of the basic Marxist texts, something he had never done before and which probably made him feel somewhat deficient.

The year 1936 also saw an expansion of YCL's role on campus and a corresponding increase in Julie's political participation. In December 1935, representatives of the National Student League, a Party-affiliated college organization, and the Socialist Student League for Industrial Democracy met to form a joint organization, the American Student Union (ASU). This newly formed group was the first merger of Communist and Socialist organizations in the United States and represented the opening of the Popular Front on college campuses. Through the ASU, campus Communists were able to reach many students who had been hostile to or scared by a Communist identification. The ASU could mobilize far more people to sign petitions, donate money, and attend rallies than they could through either the explicitly Communist YCL or the reputedly Communist National Student League.

Julie promptly joined the ASU and worked diligently on the Student Strike Against War that it sponsored in April. He marched in its contingent for the May Day Parade and picketed at Ohrbach's in response to the YCL's glorification of that struggle between locked-out workers and their unyielding "capitalist boss." In fact, during the summer, Julie apparently was arrested for disorderly conduct during one of the picketing sessions outside Ohrbach's. It had become common practice for the New York City Police Department to arrest pickets for blocking pedestrian traffic, using abusive language, or in some way making it difficult for customers to patronize Ohrbach's. Julie was one of hundreds arrested in the last few months of picketing at the store. He gave an alias when police asked his name and spent two days in jail rather than pay the five-dollar fine that was imposed on him. By using a fictitious name, the arrest never appeared on his record, and no one in his family ever learned anything about it.

Julie also took a part-time job in order to cover his expenses, which his brother Dave, now a practicing pharmacist, had been paying for in part. He worked as a drugstore clerk on Lenox Avenue near 125th Street. In this largely black neighborhood, he was astounded at the overcrowding, the high rents and the exorbitant prices charged in the local stores that were owned and operated by whites.

One evening while he was at work, a speeding bus ran over a middle-aged black man, who was brought into the drugstore bleeding profusely. It took an ambulance nearly an hour to respond to an emergency call, and by the time it arrived the man had died. Julie was forced to mop up the man's blood. He swore he would never forget this "crime."

The impact of witnessing such an incident cannot be overestimated. This act of inhumanity offered living proof that what he read and studied about how working people were exploited by the ruling class was absolutely correct. The Communist party also was one of the only voices that spoke out consistently and forcefully against racial intolerance. Outside the black community, it was the strongest organized proponent of Negro rights, and was the only advocate of complete equality for blacks that many New York Jews encountered. For Julius to experience such a cruel, racist act and to feel so helpless in its wake, could only have stiffened his resolve to fight against the system that encouraged such atrocities.

When Julie returned to school, he threw himself completely into what was becoming the Party's most critical issue, the defeat of the rebel fascists in Spain. He talked with classmates of possibly going to fight with the Loyalists, as the Party was organizing brigades to join in the Spanish Civil War. While he considered and then discarded this both thrilling and frightening opportunity, he worked at planning ways to raise funds for the Loyalist cause.

After having read a good deal of Marxist literature, Julie now felt far more competent in alcove debates and discussions. He read the *Daily Worker* regularly and looked to it as a source of truth and

analysis. He literally and completely believed virtually every piece
of Party literature he read and looked to Party leaders as the primary
source of perspective on world events. In any debate, Julie typically
defended the Party line—intelligently and articulately, but nonetheless unquestioningly. "Before he gave an opinion he would read
his *Daily Worker*," a friend reports.

Julie truly believed in socialism as the answer to the world's
problems. He believed in it with a fervor that apparently inspired
some who knew him at the time:

> *Julie loved to talk of "the new world, the future, Socialism.
> And he talked of it not as an abstraction or some world far
> removed, or as if it were any matter for speculation. It was
> always in immediate terms, living and vital, as if it were
> just over the horizon. When you were with him, you thought
> of it in the same way. . . . I never knew anyone who had
> more boundless faith than Julie. . . . [I]t was his humane-
> ness, his devotion and his singleness of purpose which
> marked him."*

These very qualities had distinguished Julius Rosenberg earlier in
his absolute religious devotion. The "singleness of his purpose" was
now completely transferred from religion to politics, and this transformation had taken place in less than three years. The careful
attention Julie previously had paid to the Torah and the Prophets
was turned to the works of Marx, Lenin, and Stalin. His belief in a
better world through the coming of the Messiah was replaced by a
belief in the historical inevitability of socialism. When he spoke of
socialism, it was with the same ardor and piety that one could
imagine him formerly using to describe the return to Zion.

Julie probably could make the transition from Judaism to Marxism so quickly and so completely in part because there are many
structural similarities between the two systems. The former holds
that through a close reading of the holy texts one can understand
God's will and interpret it for others. Traditionally, the most highly
valued person in Jewish culture is the Hebrew scholar who studies
the Torah so as to be able to elucidate Divine Will. This emphasis
on exegetical study and the belief that moral truth can be arrived
at through devotion to written works imparts an almost magical
belief in the power of the written word. Those who can master the
Torah and its commentaries have a certain moral advantage, if not

94 superiority, over others and thus are venerated within the community. They alone can judge and arbitrate conflict, not due to physical prowess or political power, but because of their intellectual abilities revealed through their skill in interpreting the sacred texts. This glorification of the written word may lend itself to an inflated belief in the role of ideas in the moral transformation of society.

In Communist circles, and particularly among Communist intellectuals and academics, a similar devotion to ideas, their power, and their interpreters existed. In the nineteen-thirties, the writings of Marx, Lenin, and Stalin constituted the sacred texts, and it was believed that their "correct" interpretation could mean the difference between revolutionary success or defeat. The Party's favorite ideological opponents of the time were the Trotskyists. Their failure rested in their allegiance to a misinterpretation of Marx. The only correct line of thought, according to the Party, descended directly from Marx through Lenin to Stalin. Leon Trotsky was not merely a sophistic theoretician, he was a false Messiah for the working class. The YCL Marxist-Leninists of City College, who took these differences of interpretation as seriously as their Party's leaders, spent an enormous amount of time and energy denouncing and arguing against their local false Messiahs. Julie's friend who was so impressed by his love of "the new world, Socialism" proudly recounted that Julie "could be hard when it came to a matter of principle, of political responsibility. I once saw him expose a trouble-maker, a Trotskyite, without any hesitation, with complete firmness." Morton Sobell remembers that "most of his [Julie's] time was spent in the alcoves arguing with the Trotskyites there."

Why was the debate with and denunciation of Trotskyists so important? Because words mattered; ideas—at least the correct ones— could change the world and bring about socialism. A persistent line of thought that runs through Marxist-Leninism holds that if only workers could be adequately exposed to the right ideas, to the correct explanation of why they have to live and work as they do, they would rise against their exploiters and create a socialist revolution. In this revolution, the proletariat would be rewarded for its long suffering, just as the Jews would be with the coming of the Messiah and the return to Zion. Just as their belief in themselves as the Chosen People allowed Jews to survive the Diaspora and oppression until the inevitable coming of the Messiah, the historical certainty of a socialist transformation permits the working class to suffer its exploitation under capitalism. Julie's friend from City College recalls that "Julie had that sense of history which never left him and which allowed him to be cheerful when others were full of gloom."

These similarities may explain why Julie was receptive to a Marxist-Leninist mode of thinking and why the transition from Judaism to the Party was not particularly abrupt for him. Talmudic reading; immersion in the study of the "Law" (whether it describes how to honor one's parents or the falling rate of profits); sharp debate over questions of interpretation; acceptance of a world view that colors much of one's assessment of human nature; the meaning of life and how one should live in the world, characterize both Judaism and Marxism. But these similarities do not explain why he relinquished one so completely for the other. For this we can only look at how he had been taught to detest social injustice in Hebrew school and to some degree at home, and how religion had not been able to respond adequately or directly to the innumerable injustices to which the Communist party had opened his eyes during his adolescence. Julie was a sensitive youth who, for reasons that are not entirely clear, had a need to believe in something wholeheartedly and to submit himself to a higher authority whom he could idealize as the source of all truth. That he chose the Communist party to idealize and vow allegiance to was not an arbitrary or capricious choice.

The CP was the strongest voice he encountered arguing for equality and against social injustice. It argued louder against fascism, racism, and anti-Semitism than any other political party in the United States; it offered a systemic solution to the enormous problems of the Depression, and it was supported by the only country on earth that had had a "successful" socialist revolution. In the midst of the Depression, the Soviet Union looked very attractive. Soviet leaders declared that they had eliminated unemployment, that they were establishing an autonomous Jewish homeland in an underdeveloped area of the USSR, and that theirs was the only nation legally to ban anti-Semitism and actively fight fascism. Since the Soviet Union alone chose to support the Spanish Loyalists through the shipment of arms and supplies and the organization of international brigades, this latter claim seemed unquestionably true and served to elevate respect for Moscow and Communism among a relatively wide segment of liberal Americans. Thus Julie's involvement in the CP was a rational response to the social injustices he hated, and an outgrowth of what he had learned in Hebrew school, "that to serve was the greatest joy in life." The extent of his involvement, his boundless faith, his "singleness of purpose," however, probably stemmed both from youthful exuberance and what appears to have been an overwhelming need to immerse himself in an authoritative and all-encompassing belief system.

By the close of 1936 Julius, then eighteen years old, was thoroughly involved in YCL activities. Aside from the endless alcove debates at school, he attended meetings, fundraisers, and study groups. All of his friends from college shared his political sympathies and spent much of their free time talking about world events, local strikes, *Daily Worker* articles and books they had read. They spoke of Spain and followed the developments in its civil war closely. Spain was the crucible of fascism. If it fell, the likelihood of war between fascist powers and the USSR seemed great. So much was in motion; to Julius and his YCL friends, political stability never seemed more tenuous, more open to change. The correct political analysis was more crucial than ever, and how fortunate that they were there! Their adolescent grandiosity combined with the truly precarious national and international conditions to make them feel as though the outcome of their thoughts and actions could truly change the world. Irving Howe's reminiscence of his life as a Marxist youth during the Depression describes the experience:

> *Never before, and surely never since, have I lived at so high, so intense a pitch, or been so absorbed in ideas beyond the smallness of self. It began to seem as if the very shape of reality could be molded by our will, as if those really attuned to the inner rhythms of History might bend it to submission. I kept going through the motions of ordinary days: I went to college, had a few odd jobs, dated girls occasionally, lived or at least slept at home. But what mattered—burningly—was the movement, claiming my energies, releasing my fantasies, shielding me day and night from commonplace boredom.*

This passage describes Julius Rosenberg's experience quite well, with one exception: at eighteen he had not yet "dated girls occasionally." None of his friends remember Julie dating, and his sister clearly recalls no girlfriend in his life up to this point. Therefore, when he went to the holiday benefit for the striking seamen in December 1936, he did not go with a date.

When he looked across the room and saw Ethel Greenglass,
he recognized her. Had he seen her at a rally, at Lavanburg Homes,
or just around the neighborhood? Had he heard her sing when he
picketed Ohrbach's? Where he may have seen her remained unclear, but that he was attracted to her was unquestionable.

Ethel Greenglass was twenty-one, Julius Rosenberg, eighteen.
Neither had ever really dated, nor knew very much about hetero-
sexual love. In terms of male-female relationships, they were both
incredibly naive and probably quite awkward. Acting and singing
had filled her life, and religion and politics his. But once they met,
romantic love entered their lives and altered them in ways neither
could have possibly predicted that evening at the International Sea-
mens' Union benefit.

7

LOVE, AT LAST

Ethel and Julie became very close very quickly. Something clicked. It was as though the feelings and longings each had harbored for years could now be released. Julie later recalled that he had fallen in love with her soon after they met. A friend of Ethel's remembers that Julie "was a tall, good-looking boy, really a darling. Any girl would have been proud to go out with him. When our Ethel fell, she really fell. But who could blame her? . . . And from the time they met, Julie practically never left her side." They began to be seen together at many of the political events the Party sponsored throughout the city. "You'd see them together at anti-Hitler rallies and meetings to aid Loyalist Spain; they'd come in together and leave arm in arm."

For Ethel, Julie was the answer to wishes probably never spoken, desires so long denied that their fulfillment had been unexpected. For so much of her life Ethel had felt unloved and unappreciated. The coldness and bitterness of her family, of her mother's chronic disappointment with her own life had enveloped Ethel, seeped into her bones and left a core belief in her own unlovableness. To be a performer, a singer, was a way to garner the attention and approval she desired. But it was ephemeral. She sang; people applauded and praised her, and her brush with acceptance and warmth was over.

Now here was a man, albeit only eighteen years old, who loved her and appreciated her. She, who perhaps had thought no one would ever really love her, was spending every free minute with Julie, her wonderful Julie. Later in her life, she confided that Julie was her "savior" who rescued her from the emotional abyss of her family. "He was the antithesis of her brothers, and loved her for who she was, as a person in her own right."

For Julie, Ethel was just what he needed in his life at the moment. She agreed with him about politics and felt passionately about the same issues. They shared a great deal in their worldviews and this, of course, was prerequisite for him in his personal relationships. Ethel had backbone too, and Julie found this attractive. She had her own drive and ambition. He admired her ambition to be a singer and her sacrifices so she could take music lessons. And, she had ideas about what he should do with his life. Admittedly, he had been doing poorly in college. He had never been enamored with engineering, but now the courses had become difficult, the homework assignments long, and his interest had never been lower. So much was going on in the world, there was so much to think about and to be involved with that college seemed just a waste of time. Everyone knew that engineering graduates from CCNY were not hired because they were Jews and were considered too radical. His parents certainly could benefit by some added income if he went out and found a job. So why continue? Ethel believed he should stay in college. She appealed to his intelligence and his future, both of which might be wasted if he dropped out of City College. She would help him; she would type and edit all his lab reports and homework assignments, and they would work together on getting him through college. He found this plan attractive; it made sense. At times she seemed to have more faith in him than he had himself.

Thus, on most weekday evenings, Julie would climb the stairs to the flat at 64 Sheriff Street where Ethel had her room. Here he would sit and study or write while she typed out his reports. As he sat in a chair reading and smoking cigarettes and she typed at a small desk, they were so content they did not even seem to mind the cold of the unheated apartment.

Their contentment with each other was so complete and their need to be with each other so great that they began to exclude others from their lives. Ethel's friend from the Clark Players explains why she and Ethel ceased to be friends: "Every time I went over to Ethel's he was there studying and she was typing his homework, and that wasn't my idea of a good time, so I sort of lost interest." Another friend recalls that Ethel "was very much involved with Julius to the exclusion of others." Although Julie maintained his friendships with classmates from CCNY, his closest friend since junior high school days, Milty Manes, reports that after Julie met Ethel, he began spending most of his time at the Greenglasses', so that Milty's "former intimate association with him diminished rapidly. . . ."

When they did see friends, they were always Julie's. His favorite classmates at the time were Mark Pogarsky, whom he had known since high school, and Nat Sussman. Mark was living with Stella, a City College student, in her apartment near CCNY. Although living together outside of marriage was unusual among young people on the Communist left, it was neither unknown nor was it frowned upon. Paul Lyons, who studied nineteen-thirties Philadelphia CP members, states that "Communist morality upheld such arrangements. Monogamy was primary in and out of marriage. There was a slight touch of the bohemian in some young Communists; they enjoyed life and all its pleasures, including sex, but, on the other hand, they were decidedly wary of hedonism."

Julie and Ethel would often join Mark, Stella, Nat, and perhaps a girlfriend of Nat's on Saturday night or Sunday. In warm weather, they would take long walks and occasionally go to Lewisohn Stadium, paying twenty-five cents to hear such artists as Jascha Heifetz play a violin concerto to the accompaniment of airplanes passing over the outdoor arena. In colder weather, they would spend the evening at Stella and Mark's, see a movie, or attend one of the many parties or fundraisers the CP or one of its affiliates was sponsoring.

Whenever the couples got together, the men would do most of the talking. They discussed politics nonstop and were quite full of themselves. They "had a solution to all the world's problems" and vied to impress the women who were reduced to nothing more than asking questions, laughing at jokes, and remaining attentive but silent listeners.

Although the group of friends freely spoke of politics, current events, life at City College, and what appeared within the Party press, they virtually never spoke of anything personal, nor did they ask anything personal of each other. This was by no means unique to this group. It was the norm in Party circles to respect, or, as some might say, disregard personal life and feelings. There was a revolution to be made, masses to be organized, strategies to be mapped. CP circles were no place to dwell on the intimacies of everyday life. Communists were expected to "withhold personal feelings, especially in public; failure to do so was not considered to be proper and indicated a certain lack of character. Within the subculture, respect for privacy was the rule."

A number of reasons can be offered to explain this tacit prohibition of the personal. Sylvia Steingart, a friend of Ethel and Julie's from this period, suggests that "people were so involved with the political urgency of the moment that they didn't talk much about personal matters," making it seem as though time and priorities prevented people from speaking about private concerns. Betty Birnbaum, who dated Nat Sussman, argues that the Party discouraged personal revelation for the simple reason that "the less you knew, the less trouble you could make for somebody." This strategic response to the climate of anti-Communism in which the Party functioned even prevented Betty from asking Ethel if and where she worked at the time, despite the fact that in addition to their "triple dates," the two spent many hours singing together at Ethel's home. Another explanation is offered by social historian Paul Lyons, who writes that "contemporary life, by blurring and merging public and private spheres . . . destroys the qualities of intimacy rooted in family and friendship by vulgarly universalizing them. The Communist subculture . . . accepted and respected the fundamental distinction between public and private spheres." Thus Lyons suggests that the Party somehow showed respect for personal life in contradistinction to the vulgarizing trends of the contemporary world. It "allowed for primary group intimacy and personal discretion" in a way that mainstream culture did not.

On the other hand, there is a good deal of evidence that the CP eschewed the personal because its exploration or discussion was deemed unimportant and "bourgeois." An ex-Party member, interviewed by author Vivian Gornick, said that her Party comrades held that personal feelings should be "suppressed and despised." They "were harsh, most harsh with me, telling me that this was all *personal* and, therefore, trivial. That I should be more serious, more dedicated, a better Communist after all than that, to be so concerned with something as frivolous as my *feelings*." Whatever the reason, private life and personal feelings were not subjects of conversation. This taboo prevented one from raising personal issues so as not to detract from the urgency of the moment, potentially get oneself in trouble, contaminate the public sphere with the private, or reveal oneself to be undedicated and frivolous.

We may never know exactly what prevented Ethel and Julie from speaking about anything personal to their YCL friends, who were increasingly their only friends. But they followed the Party injunction perfectly and thus never discussed their feelings, problems, fears, or anxieties. This probably was not difficult for Ethel. In many ways the prohibition on personal revelation may have been a relief to her. Unaccustomed to speaking about herself, Ethel may have felt at ease in an environment where there was no expectation of sharing feelings and the intimate details of one's life. Certainly there is no evidence that Ethel balked at this norm, at least at this point in her life.

When they were not with his YCL friends, at a meeting or rally, Ethel and Julie spent most of their time in Ethel's bedroom, sequestered from the rest of the family. The Greenglasses did not particularly like Ethel's boyfriend. While they were impressed by the fact that he attended college and his family lived in the modern Lavanburg Homes, they were not impressed by his political interests. They were particularly concerned over how much time Julie spent talking to David. At fifteen, their youngest child was highly impressionable and looked up to Ethel's boyfriend with a great deal of respect. Julie encouraged Dave's interest in science by giving him books and a chemistry set, and talked with him frequently about politics, urging him to join the YCL. When Barney's oldest son, Sammy, came to visit, the Greenglasses would regale him with tales of how Julius was influencing Dave, and asked him to speak to Ethel about it.

It was not difficult for Sam to become annoyed with Ethel. He had always resented her and did little to hide his feelings. Perhaps it was sibling rivalry or jealousy at the fact that the little attention his father was capable of giving his children was often focused more on Ethel, the only girl. Little is known of Sam's history, what happened to his own mother, and under what circumstances his father married Tessie. He may have resented his father's new family altogether and chose to rivet his hostility on the first child born of his father's new union. Without more evidence, it is impossible to do more than guess at the origins of Sam's bitterness toward his sister, but the fact that it existed is clear.

In 1950, Sam Greenglass boasted to the FBI that he had always been an ardent anti-Communist and had had "many violent discussions with Julius and Ethel concerning Communism." In fact, during the nineteen-thirties he was so concerned about their influence over his youngest brother, Dave, that he seriously "offered to pay their transportation to Russia if they would agree to stay there." Much to his consternation, they told him they preferred to stay in the United States.

The Rosenbergs, on the other hand, were quite welcoming to Julie's new girlfriend. His mother liked Ethel and after getting to know her, told her that she [Ethel] and Julie were "as alike as two drops of water." Harry's initial reaction to his son's choice, however, is not well remembered. Father and son had become somewhat distant since Julie had become so absorbed in the YCL. His father did not understand his son's level of involvement, any more than he had comprehended Julie's religious fervor. But this was Communism, something he had always opposed, and it was interfering with his son's education, something his religious involvement had never done. Even with his father's remonstrances, however, the Rosenbergs' household was a more welcoming one than the Greenglasses'. But the Rosenbergs did not have a secluded room where Julie and Ethel could be alone without parental interference, and this made them favor 64 Sheriff Street.

The attitudes toward premarital sex among the YCL crowd to which Ethel and Julie now belonged were not sharply defined, nor are they easily characterized retrospectively. On the one hand, there was a strand of thought inherited from the early days of the Bolshevik revolution that held marriage to be simply a formal convention carrying none of the moral, religious, and emotional weight heaped upon it in capitalist countries. Although the CPUSA encouraged marriage, particularly during the Popular Front era, it consistently disdained the prevailing bourgeois conception of romantic love as an almost magical experience, separate from political life and activity. The Party regarded sex as healthy and natural and dismissed the idea that anything was "sinful" about its enjoyment. It argued for the availability and use of birth control, demanding, in 1934, *"free and legal information* for all working and farm men and women everywhere—and not only for the rich." On the other hand, the Party traditionally emphasized that its adherents live like "ordinary workers" and thus take on the moral standards then prevailing within the working class. This injunction became more broadly applied during the Popular Front, when the attempt to ally with a vast array of mainstream groups and organizations discouraged any emphasis on "social" issues such as birth control information.

The Party was consistent, however, in its plea for equality, respect, and commitment between men and women in marital and sexual relations. Even at the height of its Popular Front encouragement of marriage and family life, Earl Browder wrote that "Communist support for the family does not mean that we agree with the unequal status of women in the family, which characterizes capitalist society." Although this position could be readily translated into inaction regarding women's rights until the coming of socialism, it did cast gender inequality within the family as something negative and as a function of the hated capitalist system.

Sexual mores among Ethel and Julie's circle of friends were also shaped by education and religion. Since all the men, and a few of the women, were not only YCL members but college students as well, their attitudes toward personal and social issues tended to be more liberal than those of the noncollege educated. Sexual freedom was not celebrated in the thirties as it had been in the twenties, but, as a result of the progress made during the previous decade, sex was generally viewed as both a normal biological and emotional need. In a national survey of 1,400 college students in 1937, one-half of the men and one-quarter of the women in their junior and senior years had engaged in premarital intercourse, "while two-thirds of all the young women avowed themselves willing to do so for true love."

Conversely, the Jewish culture in which all of Ethel and Julie's friends and acquaintances grew up maintained a clear moral sanction against premarital sex, especially—as in all cultures—for the females. Yet this injunction did not carry the same weight and consequences as it did among Christians. Jews have never had anything resembling a cult of the Virgin or a Madonna syndrome, whereby a "good" woman is believed to lack any sexual drives or needs. Judaism does not separate females into good women and bad women, virgins and whores, as does Christianity. Rather, women's intrinsic sexual nature has always been recognized and considered at least equal to men's. In fact, the *Shulhan Arukh*, the authoritative sixteenth-century Code of Jewish Law, holds that one of the duties of a husband is to fulfill his wife's sexual needs. Within marriage, sex is considered necessary for both procreation and pleasure, and celibacy has always been condemned.

This attitude made premarital sex less psychologically burdensome for Jewish women in the thirties. If they engaged in premarital sex, they did not immediately have to think of themselves as whores, fallen women, or as unduly preoccupied with sex, as may have some of their non-Jewish counterparts living a few blocks away. If sex for pleasure was a normal part of marriage, and if a woman had found someone she truly loved and planned to marry, it was not difficult to rationalize away the moral prohibitions against premarital sexual relations.

As a married woman, Ethel was quite open about her own sexual needs and desires and clearly unembarrassed about how much she enjoyed sex, in fact, less embarrassed than her husband. While this does not tell us about her premarital relations, it does add some support to the assumptions of her friends from the late nineteen-thirties, namely, that Ethel and Julie had become lovers long before they married.

The year 1937 marked the beginning of the happiest period of Ethel Greenglass's life. She was in love with a man for the first time, and involved in a web of political activity that gave meaning and purpose to her existence. Julie was her closest friend and lover, as well as the comrade with whom she worked to fight injustice and bring about change in a world precariously poised for war. This was a life far removed from the emotional and intellectual emptiness of 64 Sheriff Street. It was also a life that reflected what historian Paul Lyons has termed the "honeymoon effect":

> . . . [the] *flush of radicalism, the emotional high of purposeful activity, the sense of accomplishment and sacrifice for the good of humanity, the work with fine and noble comrades, the love affairs with those sharing a common vision, the expectation that the future was indeed theirs, created a honeymoon effect for most young Communists.*

Ethel had not only fallen in love with a man but enormously deepened her commitment to a movement. Before she had met Julie, she agreed with the CP's line and valued political involvement, but these were decidedly less salient for her than the commitment to study voice and sacrifice everything necessary in order to realize her ambition to perform professionally. Knowing Julie gradually altered these priorities.

First, his admiration and love for her as she was must have satisfied some of the needs she had tried to fulfill through acting and singing. Julie provided her with the self-esteem that audiences had only ephemerally offered. Second, because Julie occupied so much of her time, she had to dispense with the rigid schedule of practicing singing and piano. They were together most evenings, and this had been a time reserved for practice. Lastly, the things he cared about *did* seem more important than her own personal ambition. Somehow her interest in singing seemed petty, perhaps even bourgeois, in the face of what appeared to be the coming conflict between fascism and socialism in the western world. Although Julie loved her voice and encouraged her to sing, her desire to become a singer seemed trivial compared to the concerns driving Julie and consuming his imagination.

Thus Ethel increasingly sang only in the service of a political cause, as when Julie taught her the words to "Tango de las Rosas" and "Ay-ay-ay." Together they went to Times Square with some of his friends and she sang these songs while the others held aloft the Spanish Republican flag and asked passersby to contribute to the Loyalist cause. On such an occasion, everything in Ethel's life came together—being with Julie, singing in public, engaging in work that benefited humanity, participating in politics with like-minded people. Ethel sang to help the oppressed and by doing so cemented her relationship to Julie.

In view of how close they had become, it is not surprising that Ethel and Julie began to talk about marriage. Harry Rosenberg, however, objected. His wife told an interviewer in 1953:

> They wanted to be married before. Ethel said, 'I like him, I want to marry, I will work all my life.' My husband, who never would let a wife work, said, 'And how can you? No, there will be babies, you cannot work. You must wait. Wait until Julie is through school.' They waited.

Harry's objection was by no means idiosyncratic. Jewish wives simply did not work on the Lower East Side. The very fact that Ethel was willing to challenge this proscription, to "work all her life," probably indicates her strong desire to marry, her willingness to break with the tradition in which she was raised and witnessed her own mother's despair, and/or her acceptance of and perhaps enjoyment in working outside the home. The fact that Ethel and Julie acquiesced to Harry's wishes undoubtedly reflects how much both of them still respected parental authority and Jewish custom, despite their more recently acquired radical political beliefs.

They postponed marriage until Julie graduated from City College, a wait that was prolonged by the fact that he had to stay in school an extra semester in order to pass a Spanish course that he had previously failed. Although he had never possessed any real interest or outstanding talent in engineering, nor taken his courses as seriously as studying Marx or engaging in political activity, Julius Rosenberg finally graduated from the City College of New York with a Bachelor of Science degree in electrical engineering in February 1939. He had only to find a job so that he could marry Ethel and support her as his father and society demanded.

Getting work as a graduate of CCNY's engineering school at this time was extremely difficult. As classmate Morton Sobell recalls:

> Going to school in the Thirties was strictly an act of faith or a manifestation of love of learning for its own sake. We were all aware that City College engineering graduates were not hired by the large corporations. For one thing, we were considered too radical; for another, most of the students were Jewish (to many people this was redundant).

Job applications required one to list the institution from which one had graduated, as well as one's religious faith. Sobell recalls making "the rounds of the employment agencies where I was told, without apology, that no Jews were wanted." Employment prospects seemed so gloomy that Julie and Morty would sit in the engineering labs, eating their homemade lunches and pondering emigration to the Soviet Union where engineers were desperately needed. Although neither of them seems to have seriously contemplated moving to the USSR, they, along with most of their classmates, despaired of ever finding work in the field in which they were trained.

While Julie looked for full-time work, he was employed part-time as an assistant by Paul Williams in his small business on West 17th Street. This job apparently did not provide enough money for Julie to support himself, let alone Ethel. Williams, who had recently returned from the war front in Spain as part of the Abraham Lincoln Brigade, worked as an aeronautical engineer and encouraged Julie to enter this field. Julie did enroll in a course that Williams taught for the Federation of Architects, Engineers, Chemists and Technicians on aeronautical drafting and details. The course was intense, requiring four hundred hours of classroom time spread over April, May, and June. Between working and studying for Paul Williams and his political work, Julie was far busier after graduation than he had been before.

Perhaps because Julie's schedule now made it more difficult for him and Ethel to see each other, they were less willing to wait to marry. Whatever the exact reason, when June arrived Ethel and Julie decided to get married.

The marriage itself did not require much planning or preparation. Most people attached to the Young Communist League eschewed big or formal weddings. A large, ostentatious ceremony and reception were considered bourgeois. According to one Yiddish "memorist," the only two groups on the Lower East Side who "preferred 'private weddings' without a big fuss" were the "aristocrats and radicals." In keeping with the taboo on private life, a newly married couple in the YCL "would come and announce they had gotten married and no one made much of a fuss over it." Typically, the betrothed couple would gather one or, at the most, two dozen family members and perhaps a few very close friends at a rabbi's house or synagogue. The ceremony would be brief, and perhaps a little wine would be drunk afterward. There was usually no party or celebration.

Ethel and Julie followed the prescribed pattern. On Sunday, 18 June 1939, they went to a Rabbi Zin's in the company of some of their family. The event was either so brief or so unimpressive that neither Julie's brother or sister were able to remember a single thing about it when questioned in 1985. Nonetheless, Ethel and Julie were intensely happy.

Directly after their wedding, Julie officially moved into the Greenglass household. Instead of secretly spending their time in Ethel's bedroom, they now could live openly as husband and wife. But their tolerance of the emotional and perhaps even the physical environment of 64 Sheriff Street was short-lived, for they soon moved into the Rosenbergs' flat at Lavanburg Homes. Here for the first time in her twenty-three years, Ethel lived with steam heat, a gas stove, and a private bathroom. She and Julie were completely happy and quite demonstrative in their love. "Always they were touching each other," Julie's mother, Sophie, recalled. If they were apart during the day, Julie's sister remembers, "they couldn't wait to get into the bedroom, that's how much in love they were."

In July, Julie's sister, Ethel, and her husband Oscar rented a cottage for the summer and invited Julie and Ethel to spend some time there for their honeymoon. When the newlyweds arrived in Spring Glen, it apparently was the first time they had traveled outside New York City together. Since Ethel and Oscar had five other family members visit the two-bedroom cottage at various times during Ethel and Julie's stay, the newly married couple was rarely alone. Nonetheless their "honeymoon" seemed very romantic to these products of the urban ghetto. They wandered arm-in-arm through the countryside, admiring the trees, watching the sun set or the moon rise in the sky. They would often sit together in the still air of the early evening as Ethel sang in her clear, sweet voice. The future must have seemed limitless in terms of the possibilities and happiness it promised. In pictures from this holiday, Ethel appears tanned and content. She seems to have some inner peace, a certain serenity, as she poses in her shorts, oxford shoes, and white socks. The memory of this idyllic retreat lasted for Ethel and Julie throughout their lives and they often gazed at the photographs Julie's sister gave them from the trip. Recalling Spring Glen helped to sustain them later when they had little else but memories of happier times.

Ethel Rosenberg

1939–1950

8

THE WALL
THAT SHIELDS

By the summer of 1939, the American Communist party had reached the acme of its power. "Few liberal organizations were without a significant Communist presence. Politicians in states all over the country vied for Communist support, albeit quietly. Hundreds of prominent intellectuals, performers, and artists applauded the Soviet Union's every action. Well-known Communists held leading posts in the trade union movement." When Earl Browder was arrested for vagrancy in Terre Haute, Indiana, while he was on a speaking tour, "the nation's press jumped to his defense with an unprecedented outpouring of concern for the Communist party's right to campaign without hindrance." In January, the Party announced that it had reached a membership of 100,000, but even this unprecedentedly large figure underplayed the CP's influence on American political life. "There were never more than 100,000 American Communists at any one time, yet labor unions, youth groups, peace organizations, civil rights bodies, and a host of miscellaneous clubs, gatherings, and assemblies faithfully followed the Party's direction." Because of the number of Party sympathizers in these organizations and because of the CP members' commitment, energy, and organizing skills, Communists typically dominated the liberal groups in which they participated. Communist party membership had never

114   before carried with it greater acceptance, respectability, and influence.

It was this Party—severed completely from its sectarian roots and revolutionary dogmatism—with which Ethel and Julie were familiar and to which they committed their lives in 1939. As the historian Harvey Klehr observed:

> These younger Communists knew little about the Party's past. Their formative political experiences were the Depression and the rise of fascism. . . . The spectre of revolution that had animated the first generation of Communists was less vivid among this one. They still desired a socialist society, but its urgency was no longer the political issue. Fighting fascism and struggling for reforms took precedence.

A year earlier the CP had altered its political platform and basis for organizing from the "Popular Front" to the "Democratic Front." This semantic transformation signaled the Party's intention both to ally itself with workers, farmers, and the middle class—as it had under the Popular Front—and to form coalitions with "important sections of the upper-middle class and certain liberal sections of the bourgeoisie," primarily through the institution of the Democratic Party.

The quintessential goal of the Democratic Front was fighting fascism. Party leader Browder described this goal quite simply: "With fascism wiped off the face of the earth, with the glorious achievements of the Soviet Union as an example, the rest of the world will find the transformation to socialism rather rapid and painless."

In the United States the Communists vociferously argued for an end to the American embargo on arms to the anti-fascists in Spain; they strove for the repeal of the Neutrality Act that limited American support of anti-fascists abroad; many of them fought and died battling Franco's forces in Spain; they supported a boycott of all Nazi goods; and they led the American League for Peace and Democracy, which was formed specifically to combat fascism. Denunciations of fascism were central in virtually everything CP leaders wrote and spoke.

Thus when reports surfaced in the American press that the Soviet Union and Nazi Germany were about to sign a nonaggression pact,

Party leaders dismissed them as mere propaganda. Earl Browder flatly rejected the suggestion by stating, "There is as much chance of Russo-German agreement as of Earl Browder being elected President of the Chamber of Commerce," and the Communist *Freiheit* denounced the socialist *Jewish Daily Forward* for "chewing the dirty lie of an 'agreement' with Hitler when the facts have always shown that this is a lie."

Nonetheless, on 23 August 1939, the Soviets and the Nazis signed a pact promising mutual nonaggression, agreement over the invasion of sovereign Poland, and division of eastern Europe into German and Russian spheres of influence. The pact heralded the Soviet Union's abrupt cessation of its struggle against fascism and its worldwide leadership of the Popular and Democratic Fronts. No longer was Nazism a barbaric force threatening peace, democracy, and perhaps civilization itself, but a "matter of taste" that one "may respect or hate . . . just as any other system of political views."

This shocking alteration in Soviet ideology reflected both the Soviets' real fear of a Nazi invasion and its leaders' territorial ambitions to dominate large parts of eastern Europe and the Baltic states. Although such political maneuvering was and is by no means unique, the fact that semiautonomous Communist parties throughout the world now had to change their political analyses and activities drastically to keep in line with the Soviet shift, comprises an unusual chapter in world history.

For the CPUSA, fascism suddenly was not the major threat to world peace, nor Nazism the unmitigated evil confronting humanity. Within a few weeks of the Nazi-Soviet accord, Party leaders were explaining why the pact was good for world peace. Within two months, they had completely reversed their positions on both international and domestic issues. England and France, which had stood as bastions of democracy and freedom during the Popular and Democratic Fronts, were now depicted as being as dictatorial, imperialist, and hostile to the proletariat as Germany was previously. William Foster, second only to Browder in the CP's hierarchy, went further: "The British empire is the very cornerstone of the world capitalist system, the main enemy of everything progressive, and its serious weakening or overthrow by Hitler, or by the world revolutionary forces, would shake the very foundations of the entire capitalist system." Franklin Roosevelt, whom the CP had championed and venerated since 1936, was now called a "warmonger" who was giving America "the same direction which Hitler gave for

Germany in 1933." After ardently campaigning for the repeal of the Neutrality Act so that the United States could come to the aid of countries threatened by fascism, the CP suddenly switched its position and argued for strict neutrality in the face of France and Britain's September 1939 declaration of war against Nazi Germany. The Party portrayed the war as one "between rival imperialisms for world domination" in which "all the belligerent countries are equally guilty. . . ." Accordingly, the Party dropped its support of the boycott of Nazi goods, contrived tortured justifications for the Soviet invasions of Poland and Finland, and dissolved the anti-fascist American League for Peace and Democracy.

The Party's drastic transformation and obvious submission to Moscow was met with disappointment, disgust, and outrage by people outside its membership. Progressive intellectuals, writers, labor leaders, politicians, and professionals who had been supportive of the Party broke with it, often becoming thoroughly anti-Communist in outlook. Much of the liberal and socialist Jewish community was incensed and repulsed. Jewish Communists were taunted on the streets and in their workplaces with "Heil Hitler" salutes and shouts of "Communazi." Fist fights broke out in the garment center and on the Lower East Side between Party loyalists and their opponents. The Yiddish *Morning Journal* called for the "annihilation of Jewish Communism," and the CP's *Freiheit* was regularly torn to shreds at newsstands. Dozens of liberal organizations and unions adopted "Communazi" resolutions, prohibiting both Party members and participants in fascist organizations from joining. The House Committee on Un-American Activities stepped up its harassment of Party members and CP front organizations. Consequently, Party leaders increasingly found themselves indicted for such past transgressions as using false passports or registering to vote under false names. In some states, people who carried around petitions to qualify the Party on local ballots were harassed, beaten up by angry mobs, and arrested. Those who signed qualifying petitions were threatened with prosecution, loss of jobs, and public exposure.

In the wake of this shocking series of events, many CP and YCL rank-and-filers accepted the new Party line and remained faithful to its leaders. On 11 September, at the first mass rally following the signing of the nonaggression pact, the Party was able to gather thousands of its followers into Madison Square Garden. The audience

cheered its leaders' denunciations of the war that had been declared
a week earlier between Britain and France, and Germany. As a
reporter for *The Nation* magazine observed about the rally, the
"thing that stood out in the meeting was the almost desperate hud-
dling together of people confronted by a monumental world crisis,
taking refuge in a reaffirmation of their own solidarity."

What many in the CP believed in their hearts to be the final
conflict between fascism and socialism had begun. The leaders to
whom they had looked for guidance and analysis were not going
to be deserted in the midst of what seemed to be world chaos. Party
adherents assumed that mainstream media were biased in favor of
the ruling class and therefore were automatically anti-Soviet and
anti-Communist. Truth only emanated from the Party press. If Stalin's purpose in allying with Hitler seemed wrong or confusing, it
was because the media—controlled by big business—wished to
portray it as such. The "Bolshevik Code," as historian Paul Lyons
terms it, requires such belief: "there are times when the revolutionary cadre has to simply maintain discipline and have faith that
information will eventually be revealed to clarify seemingly compromising situations."

Social reasons also caused many Party members to accept the
Nazi-Soviet Pact. Communists "tended to live in the same neighborhoods, they spent most of their social life with other Communists,
and their children played together. Breaking with the party over the
pact would have meant accepting a status as a social pariah, and
few were prepared for that step."

———————

Ethel and Julie certainly conformed to this description and supported
the Pact. After their "honeymoon," they had moved in with Julie's
good friends and fellow YCL members Marcus and Stella Pogarsky.
Julie had known Mark since high school. They had attended CCNY
together and now both were working for Paul Williams. The Rosenbergs were as close to the Pogarskys as they were to any couple,
so when Mark had suggested they share a four-room apartment he
had rented in the Williamsburg section of Brooklyn, Ethel and Julie
agreed.

In this new living situation, politics were discussed constantly.
The two couples prepared and ate their dinners together, and spent
their evenings at meetings, fundraisers, or other CP related activities.

Ethel continued to sing, but the songs were more likely to be "Songs for Democracy" penned by International Brigadistas in Barcelona than operatic arias by Puccini.

Over the preceding two years both Julie and Ethel had deepened their involvement in politics. While he was still attending City College, Julie had organized the Steinmetz Society. The society was affiliated with the campus YCL and was intended for engineering students exclusively. The society's name honored Charles Steinmetz, a German-born electrical engineer who had been employed by the General Electric Company during the first part of the century. He was an outspoken socialist whose political views were tolerated because he revolutionized electrical engineering through his discovery of the law of hysteresis, which made it possible to reduce the loss of efficiency in electrical apparatus and thus placed General Electric far ahead of its competitors.

Some twenty-five to thirty engineering students—about half the total enrollment—became members of the society, which met in a small hall a few blocks from the campus. Among the men who joined were Julie's friends Mark Pogarsky, Nat Sussman, and Morton Sobell, but also such acquaintances as Max Elitcher, Bill Danziger, Joel Barr, William Mutterperl, and Jack Shapiro. In addition to discussing what was taking place in the engineering school and at CCNY in general, the group talked about larger political issues and global events, particularly the rise of German fascism and the progress of the Spanish Civil War. For most of these discussions, Julie functioned as the group's leader.

Spurred on by his activity in the Steinmetz Society and the campus YCL, Julie started to attend meetings on campus of the Federation of Architects, Engineers, Chemists, and Technicians (FAECT), a Party-controlled union for white-collar workers and professionals. Formed in the early nineteen-thirties, FAECT found most of its membership among civil service workers and in the Works Progress Administration (WPA). By 1937, FAECT had been chartered into the CIO and was attempting to increase its membership in private industry. At the same time, FAECT began to establish affiliated chapters in technical and professional schools on college campuses. The union leadership believed this would help combat the traditional political conservatism of technical students, teach them the meaning and importance of unions, and make them more likely to join FAECT and become active union members once they moved into the labor market.

Julius Rosenberg was one of the engineering students FAECT
successfully recruited at CCNY in the fall of 1938. Because he had
been working part-time since the summer for Paul Williams, Julie
joined the union as an employed member. Although his participation in FAECT was minimal during this, his last semester in college, after graduation in February 1939, Julie contributed countless
hours to writing and producing FAECT leaflets, helping out at the
union's headquarters, and going to college campuses to enlist support among technical students for unions in general and FAECT in
particular. A member of FAECT remembers Julie, and later, Ethel,
from this period:

> I first knew Julius when he was coming out of school, on
> the verge of graduating. At the time, the field of engineers,
> technicians, etc., was mostly unorganized, but FAECT had
> begun to establish some rates and was getting some con-
> tracts. Many of the young men in school had no idea of
> what they would face when they emerged from school.
>
> He was very enthusiastic about the prospects [for FAECT],
> and undertook to help us organize other chapters with a
> real feel for it. He was a very pleasant personality, I re-
> member, very conscientious. I saw him occasionally, not
> often, and saw that he was making progress, and enlisting
> college youth in the Federation who he felt certain would
> put up a better fight for good conditions after they graduated
> than they would if left to learn about economics as they
> were after they went out armed with diplomas.
>
> Ethel used to come and help us—no, I didn't say help
> him, but us. She did it because she herself was interested,
> not just because he was. She typed for us at the office and
> took work home to type. She was devoted, conscientious.
> They were two wonderful people. Whatever we asked of
> either of them, they did—there never was any hesitancy.
> They had the feeling that they were part of the working
> staff.

During the same period, Ethel also deepened her political involvement, but in a way distinctly her own and quite autonomous from
Julie. In 1937 she had begun attending the Friday night lectures of
a new dramatic group that had recently formed on the Lower East
Side. Playwright Art Smith had been deeply moved by a tenement

fire at 137 Suffolk Street which occurred on 4 March of that year. A poor Jewish peddler, his wife, and another woman were killed when a fire raced through their substandard apartment and the roof collapsed over them. Smith wrote a play based on this tragedy, *Kingdom of 137*, and gathered a group of amateur actors to perform it. The only location the group could find in which to rehearse was the basement of the Lavanburg Homes, where the Rosenberg family lived. The ensemble called itself the Lavanburg Dramatic Group, and its members decided to remain together indefinitely to stage works by Smith and other plays of social significance that focused on Lower East Side life.

In addition to its regular stage work, the Group instituted a Friday night lecture series in which actors, directors, playwrights, and theater critics came to speak about the relationship of acting and politics. The most frequent and popular guests were members of the renowned Group Theatre, which was generally considered the foremost exponent of social realism and politically conscious theater in America. It had achieved wide acclaim for its 1935 Broadway production of *Waiting For Lefty*, which was undoubtedly the most popular radical play of its day. The Group Theatre had within it a very influential Communist cell that organized classes in acting and directing for workers' groups and was able to enlist some of its non-Communist members, such as director Lee Strasberg, to give practical demonstrations in these classes. The lecture series at Lavanburg was part of this program.

Ethel quickly became an avid patron of the Friday night presentations. Julie reserved these evenings for CCNY's YCL meetings, so Ethel was free to indulge her still lingering passion for theater before Julie called for her after his meetings. The Group Theatre's political perspective appealed to Ethel and the other young people who had come of age during the Depression, as did its equal commitment to quality acting and directing. In addition, its success on Broadway differentiated it from all other socially conscious theater groups. The list of guest speakers who appeared in the series was truly impressive. It included Group Theatre members such as Clifford Odets and Elia Kazan, as well as such other luminaries as Frances Farmer, Harold Clurman, Louise Reiner, Jerome Weidman, and Willard Van Dyke. On occasion Kazan also directed the young actors who by day, according to *The New York Post*, were "stenographers, shipping clerks, or unemployed inmates of candy stores and pool rooms."

The Friday night lectures temporarily rekindled Ethel's interest in acting. She began attending the Lavanburg Dramatic Group's rehearsals, so infatuated was she by this newly found melding of her old and new interests. For unknown reasons, however, she never joined the ensemble, although her desire to perform was stimulated enough that she again appeared in *The Valiant* and one or two other one-act plays at the Young Men's Hebrew Association Playhouse at Broadway and South Ninth Street. If she was willing to act in these rather obscure productions, it seems likely that she might have hoped to perform with the Lavanburg Dramatic Group. But, it is also possible that she was simply too shy or intimidated to make her interest known.

In 1938 the Lavanburg Dramatic Group changed its name to the East Side Dramatic Group and soon afterwards moved from its housing project basement to the 400-seat theater of the Henry Street Settlement Playhouse on Grand Street. These changes reflected the fame and prestige the Group was acquiring. Ethel followed it to its new location and so was introduced to the arts program attached to Henry Street Settlement House, a much larger, more affluent, and better-staffed settlement house than Clark House. Ethel continued to attend the Group's lecture series and rehearsals, and also enrolled in dramatic courses and modern dance classes given at the Henry Street Settlement House.

During this time, she became particularly interested in the new "Living Newspaper" style of play that had emerged in the Soviet Union, become popular among radicals in Europe, and finally found its way to the United States during the nineteen-thirties. Championed by the Federal Theatre Project of the WPA, "Living Newspaper" was "a blend of radio-play methods and movie newsreel, which sought to turn current events into the stuff of drama and had the advantage of using masses of relatively mediocre actors." Enacting the most contemporary themes, controversies, and events from a radical perspective, the "Living Newspaper" form of theater provided an ideal way of synthesizing acting and political agitation for Ethel, although there is no evidence that she ever appeared in any performances of this new kind of theater outside her drama classes.

After her marriage to Julie, Ethel further deepened her political commitment by joining the Ladies Auxiliary of FAECT. The CP vigorously encouraged married womens' involvement in the auxiliaries of their husbands' unions. According to author Elsa Dixler,

"Party theorists who discussed the labor movement frequently mentioned the value of women's auxiliaries in strengthening unions. . . . When women's auxiliaries supported men's unions, they buttressed the Communist contention that men and women had identical interests. . . . This message was spelled out in a poem, 'Lines to An Auxiliary,' " printed in the *Sunday Worker Magazine*:

> *I dreamed a dream last night, 'twas wondrous strange!*
> *I saw myself as Woman stretched prone on rocky earth,*
> *And yet the Earth, a pressing globe, lay heavy on my breast;*
> *I cried, 'Why must I be bound and you go free?' and then*
> *I looked and saw his foot caught under that same weight.*
> *'You suffer too and are not free,' I said, 'Let's use*
> *Our weights combined and from this pressure loose ourselves.'*

Although Party rhetoric hammered away at the theme of women's and men's shared interests, and the necessity for both sexes to work "shoulder to shoulder" against capitalism or fascism, women definitely were second-class citizens in the American Communist party. By the time of the signing of the Nazi-Soviet Pact, thirty to forty percent of the members were women, yet very few held leadership positions or wrote for the Party press. Since workers, and particularly workers in "basic industry" such as steel, mining, and manufacturing, were the true revolutionary agents in the Party's lexicon, women—the majority of whom did not work outside the home—were usually excluded from playing much more than a supportive or "auxiliary" role.

In the Party circles in which the Rosenbergs traveled, women were subordinate not only because of their lesser involvement in the labor force, but also due to the men's intellectual pretensions. Generally, both the women and men shared the expectation that women did not take part in theoretical debate, discussions of Marxist texts, or denouncements of the Trotskyites' deviation from the correct line. The Communist party thus simply mirrored the larger society and the Jewish culture from which most of its New York college-educated members came. Women could be intelligent, but they typically could not be intellectuals. Since the Talmudic scholar was always a man, by extension so was the Marxist. As Rebecca Kohut points out, "Jewish women were expected to stay at home. . . . To have opinions and to voice them was not regarded as good form even in the home." The Rosenbergs and their friends seem to have endorsed a version of this attitude, even to the point of believing, as Julius and Mark Pogarsky asserted, that "all the best radicals come out of the Yeshiva."

There is little question that Ethel played a supporting role to Julie's, that they both considered him to be the true political thinker and activist, and that Ethel accepted this as part of the natural order of things. Yet it was common for her to attend a meeting every night, and for a rank-and-file woman, "this was rather unusual."

It is also clear that Ethel was emerging as an independent thinker who was not afraid to hold to her own opinions and differ with her husband on occasion. Julie continued to follow the Party's leadership without question. His faith in authority figures was unshakable; his adherence to the Party line unquestioned. "He accepted the classical idea of democratic centralism," probably because it fit both certain conscious, political requirements and his lifelong, psychological need to believe in an external authority to which he could actively dedicate his life. Ethel, however, increasingly asserted herself politically, occasionally taking positions different from Julie's. Harry Steingart, secretary-treasurer of FAECT and one of Julie and Ethel's closest friends from this period, recalls Ethel from the meetings they attended together: "Ethel accepted it [the Party's leadership] more in order to minimize any family quarrels. I think she was more of an independent thinker [than Julie]. She didn't have to wait until the *Daily Worker* came out with an opinion." When she disagreed with her husband, she did so "cautiously" so as "not to hurt his feelings. . . . She would never personally attack Julius by saying 'you're not thinking' or 'you're not being rational' or 'you don't know enough about the subject.' She would persuade him by giving him good reasons and convincing him."

Ethel's independence of mind, however, did not challenge any of the Party's fundamental beliefs or stances. Accordingly, when Stalin signed the nonaggression pact with Adolf Hitler, both Julie and Ethel "heartily supported it," for basically "their positions were the Party's positions." They were not about to criticize or attack the institution that structured their thinking about the world, gave them sustenance, provided role models, and formed the nucleus of their social lives. For them the CP press and its leaders had invariably provided the truth about current events—about Spain, discrimination against Negroes, the exploitation of workers. Identification with the Communist party gave Julie his identity, his beliefs, his social, and, for the present, his professional milieu through his work for Paul Williams and FAECT. In addition to providing Ethel with many of these things, "the CP," according to her therapist from later in her life, "offered her a window to the world . . . where she could begin to see something different than the Jewish ghetto where she grew up, where girls were not educated and boys were."

The Party provided a way to have an internationalist perspective, a knowledge and analysis seemingly superior to most people's, a mission in life to transform the entire world. Thus many Party adherents could think of themselves as thoroughly cosmopolitan and sophisticated while they continued to live in their immigrant ghettos and share their perspective with other people exactly like themselves. For someone who would never leave the Lower East Side, the CP offered a way of being worldly without ever venturing out into the world.

Along with an estimated 75,000 other Americans who joined the Communist party in 1938 and 1939, Julius Rosenberg proved his faith by becoming an official member on 12 December 1939. We know this because his membership card was eventually confiscated by the FBI, and at least one of his friends admitted to that agency that he was in Julius's CP branch. No such definitive material exists regarding Ethel. Although she would never be as politically active as her husband, nor as wholly consumed with or committed to the Party, in the late thirties and early forties her activities and beliefs could not be differentiated from those of a member.

Altering one's status from YCL membership to that in the Communist Party was an easy affair. One signed a Party card and paid an initiation fee of fifty cents. Assignment to a branch then followed. There were both neighborhood and industrial branches, each composed of about fifteen to fifty people. Meetings took place every other week and usually were held in members' homes or at Party headquarters. On the Lower East Side (which constituted a CP "section") there were some thirty branches.

According to Carl Marzani, who was the Lower East Side section organizer from 1939 to 1941, rank-and-file members spent four-fifths of their time following Party directives and one-fifth of their time on their own. Unaltering staples of a member's "four-fifths" time commitment were to attend branch meetings, to sell the *Daily Worker*, and to contribute dues of a week's wages a year to the Party. It could also consist in recruiting other members, campaigning for Party-endorsed candidates, organizing in the neighborhood or workplace around issues decided upon by the national leadership, joining CP mass organizations or nonaffiliated organizations and attempting to win members' acceptance of the Party's line on particular issues, running off leaflets, and attending CP rallies, demonstrations, and meetings. The "one-fifth" involved responding to ad hoc situations. If there was a tenant eviction, an understaffed picket line or a comrade who was ill, rank-and-file Communists were expected to respond to the situation quickly and without appealing to their superiors for direction.

Julius Rosenberg became a model rank-and-file member. He became chairman of his CP unit, branch 16-B of the Party's industrial division. The branch had nine members: Sol Tannenbaum, Al Sarant, Nat and Gertrude Sussman, Joel Barr, Morris and Shirley Savitsky, and Marty Hamburger. Despite the fact that the group often met at the Rosenbergs' home, Ethel never officially joined, although she occasionally sat in on meetings. According to one of its members, the branch functioned largely as a "Marxist discussion group . . . , a quiet group which took no part in mass activity which would indicate CP membership inasmuch [sic] as the group largely consisted of federal civil service employees." In addition to this, both Julie and Ethel sold the *Daily Worker*, continued to work for FAECT, and espoused the CP's perspective.

The Party had become the world for the Rosenbergs but, in fact, the world had a much dimmer view of the CP than either of them were ever able to fathom. Even their intimate environment had its watchdogs, its informers. We know this because a Miss S. Liggetts, a fellow tenant of the apartment house in which the Rosenbergs lived, reported to the FBI that Ethel Rosenberg and Stella Pogarsky signed Communist party nominating petitions on 13 August 1939. Although the FBI took no action in response to receiving this information, it established a file on Ethel ten years before she and her husband were arrested for allegedly stealing the secret of the atom bomb. Ethel and Julie's faith in the Communist party blinded them to many of the realities in the world around them. As Irving Howe has pointed out: "It is hard for those who have never gone through an ideological movement, especially the Stalinist variety, to imagine how self-contained its life can be. Ideology and organization fuse to create a wall that shields those within the inner precincts from doubt. . . ."

9

SETTLING DOWN

Their lives may have been thoroughly dedicated to the Communist party, but the fact that Julie was still unable to find full-time employment plagued the Rosenbergs just as it would any newly married couple. While he continued to work for Paul Williams on a part-time basis, he found a job for a month as a tool designer for E.B. Bliss and Company in Brooklyn. He enrolled in courses attempting to learn skills he thought might improve his chances in the job market. After completing the class with Williams on aeronautical drafting, he studied airplane structure, aerodynamics, and aviation motor design at the Guggenheim School of Aeronautics. He also took a course on tool design at the Polytechnic Institute of Brooklyn.

When Julie learned that the federal government was hiring junior engineers at a salary of $2,000 a year ("a fantastic salary for any of us," recalled Morton Sobell), he took the civil service examination to place himself on the eligibility list. A number of his acquaintances from engineering school had already been hired by the government. Sobell, Max Elitcher, and Bill Danziger were working for the Navy Bureau of Ordnance in Washington, D.C. The federal government was far less discriminatory against Jews and graduates of CCNY than was private industry. It did not automatically disqualify a job applicant simply because he had been a stu-

dent radical and graduate of left-leaning City College, as did many
New York City employers.

It had been over a year since Julie had graduated and he was still doing little more than odd jobs when Ethel decided that she, too, would take a federal civil service exam. The $700 a year she continued to earn from the Bell Textile Company was simply not enough to support both herself and Julie, particularly since they had to pay both their routine living expenses and the tuition required for the classes Julie attended. The federal government was advertising for clerks at a salary twice what she was presently earning, so she took the exam.

When Ethel applied to be a federal worker, she used her maiden name and 64 Sheriff Street as her home address. Most likely she did this because during the Depression "[m]any employers, including the Civil Service, fired married women, on the fallacious assumption that their husbands would be able to support them." The Democratic party's policy actively discouraged married women from holding jobs, and the American people seemed to agree, as reflected in Gallup polls of the time. The CP, however, opposed this view, arguing that all women had the right to work.

While Julie continued unsuccessfully to look for a job, Ethel was notified at the beginning of May 1940 that she had been appointed a temporary clerk with the Census Bureau in the United States Department of Commerce at the astronomical yearly salary of $1,440. This sum amounted to more than she or Julie had ever earned and probably rivaled the income of each of their fathers. Although moving out of New York, leaving their families, friends, and the Party circles they had been part of for years must have seemed traumatic, the opportunity was undoubtedly too good to forgo. After fourteen months of looking for work, perhaps a new city beckoned to Julie with untold opportunities for employment. And it was not as though Washington, D.C. was as foreign as it might have been for two people who had never lived more than a few miles of their birthplace. Julie had friends and colleagues from school there, and the Party maintained a sizable membership in the District, although far smaller and more clandestine than in New York.

Ethel unselfconsciously told people of her newfound luck. To her, as to so many in and near the Party, there was nothing incongruous in working for the American government and identifying oneself as a Communist. The Party as she knew it maintained that

128   Communism was twentieth-century Americanism. The Nazi-Soviet Pact may have effectively ended Popular Front policies, but it did not erase the ideas and perspectives with which recruits from the mid-nineteen-thirties had been inculcated. Ethel and Julie registered as Democrats for the 1940 presidential election and continued to adhere to the democratic and American themes Party leaders had put forth in February 1940: "Keep America Out of the Imperialist War!"; "Higher Wages, Shorter Hours—An American Standard of Living for All!"; "Put America Back to Work; Curb the Monopolies; Jobs, Security for All!"

Since she lived in an atmosphere where the Communist party was seemingly accepted, and at worst tolerated as a necessary evil, Ethel apparently was indiscriminate about who she told of her impending government employment. Thus on 25 May the FBI received a phone call from a woman "who stated she was a distant relative of one Ethel Rosenberg." The unidentified relative reported that "Miss Rosenberg is extremely Communistic and has recently received an appointment to go to Washington, D.C., as an employee of the Census Bureau." Therefore, by the time the Rosenbergs set out for Washington, there were already two entries in Ethel's FBI file.

In the first or second week of June 1940, Ethel and Julie arrived in the nation's capital. Julie's best friend from high school, Milty Manes, had lived there since 1937, and it was to him that the Rosenbergs turned for help in their new environment. Manes lived in a rooming house at 1935 Baltimore Street in the northwest section of the city, and he was able to secure a second-floor room for his friends in the same house. For the next three months, Julie and Ethel lived in their one room, with the bathroom down the hall. Ethel went off each day to her clerical job at the Census Bureau. Julie spent most of his time in Washington looking for work, taking government eligibility tests, and visiting with Milty and his roommate, Sidney Magnes. The three men became very close over the summer months as they discussed the progress of the European war, the pros and cons of New Deal legislation, and prospects for political change in the United States and abroad. Although Milty had never been attracted to the CP or its ideology, Julie considered him "a brilliant thinker," and tremendously enjoyed his company.

Ethel also contacted an old friend from New York. Morris Fleissig now lived in Greenbelt, Maryland, a government housing project seven miles from Washington. He had married, and upon hearing from Ethel, invited her and Julie to visit him and his wife. During their second weekend in Washington, the Rosenbergs visited the Fleissigs and went swimming at a pool in what the Roosevelt administration dubbed the "model American town of the future." Morris invited his good friend, Barney Weinstein, along. Since Barney had grown up in the Lavanburg Homes, Ethel and Julie began to feel as though they were again part of a community that had its roots on the Lower East Side. Although Washington did not have a large or residentially concentrated Jewish population, and although its Communist party did not operate openly, the Rosenbergs quickly found like-minded people with whom they could overcome the loneliness of living in a new city.

The hot, humid months of July and August passed slowly. Julie visited friends and tried to make connections that would help him secure a job. For a year and a half he had been unsuccessfully looking for employment. He was now supported exclusively by his wife—an unheard of situation for a young, healthy, Jewish-American man in 1940. There is no record of how Julie felt about this or of how Ethel responded. It is unimaginable, however, that his failure at being a breadwinner could have left them both unaffected. Yes, he was a Jew, a radical, a graduate of City College. But almost all of his Jewish and/or radical classmates had found work—many in the government, and many at starting salaries higher than those their fathers were earning at present. The Party offered explanations for unemployment, for discrimination in the labor market, but it did not address the psychological and emotional reactions real human beings experienced about their own inability to find work. The Rosenbergs may have been better equipped than some to analyze the forces operating against Julie's finding a job, but they probably had as much difficulty as anyone trying to make sense of why he— and not others—was at such an impasse.

Thus when the federal government finally notified Julie in late August that he had been appointed a junior engineer for the Army Signal Corps, he must have been elated. He was to begin training for the job at Fort Monmouth, New Jersey, right after Labor Day. With so little forewarning, he planned to leave immediately for New York and return to his parents' apartment. Ethel had to give a month's notice to the Census Bureau, so it was planned that she would quit as of 1 October and follow Julie home.

The position of junior engineer with the Signal Corps translated into inspecting electronic equipment manufactured by private industry for the United States armed forces. The Roosevelt administration had begun to expand America's defense industry, "urging the United States to take on the responsibility of serving as the arsenal of democracy." Industrial production of military materials had been increasing steadily throughout the year as private industry converted to war production. Consequently, the government had a greater need for supervision and inspection of the industrial output for which it was contracting. The Signal Corps was the agency through which a vast number of new inspectors was recruited.

At Fort Monmouth, Julie and the forty to fifty other recently hired junior engineers were trained in the technical information required to perform inspections. The position did not demand vast amounts of knowledge in engineering, which was probably fortunate given Julie's general lack of interest in the field. The job, however, did require long periods of travel and a certain amount of overtime. Inspectors were stationed at various industrial plants as far away as Ohio and Florida and for as long as a year at a time. A forty-eight-hour work week was typical, but the salary and benefits were impressive. While private companies were generally offering $20 a week to engineers with Bachelor of Science degrees, the Signal Corps paid $40 a week with a $5 per diem during the periods inspectors were stationed at industrial sites. FAECT was also relatively strong in the Signal Corps and a number of men from CCNY were among its employees. Thus, aside from the prospect of having to be frequently away from home and apart from Ethel, Julie probably was quite excited by his new job and considered himself lucky finally to have found employment so well suited to his needs.

After he finished his training at Fort Monmouth at the beginning of November, Julie began to work out of the inspectors' headquarters in Brooklyn and resumed his activities with FAECT and the Party. At last he was truly a part of the work force. For so long he had been involved with the Communist party and had subscribed to a Marxist perspective, yet he had never been able to engage in the most critical work demanded of any Communist—to organize at the means of production. As an inspector for the United States government, he clearly did not even remotely approximate an industrial worker—the privileged actor and venerated hero of Marxist-Leninism—but he was now in a situation where he could convert other workers to Communism. Unlike his activism at CCNY, or his work recruiting students for FAECT, Julie's first full-time job

would allow him to achieve a certain status within the Party reserved
exclusively for workplace activists.

As a stalwart follower of the Party's perspective, Julie believed that workers, the proletariat, the masses in general, could be won over to Communism by successful argument. Through the correct analysis and revelation of the truth, heretofore concealed and mystified by the ruling class and its agents, an organizer could instill in workers revolutionary class consciousness. Julie set himself to this task. He spoke of the Party frequently and openly. "He was not always cautious. . . . I think he sold the *Daily Worker* or at least introduced it to some of his fellow workers." He "shot off his mouth." A staff member of FAECT recalls that Julie "was very, very outspoken, very active, very eager. He was always more eager than most people in doing what he thought was the correct thing. . . . There were those who thought it was not discreet to tell the world wherever you were what you thought. There was a limit to this regarding your bosses, regarding the ownership of whoever you were working for."

Julie did not know discretion. He had never concealed his beliefs, and employment by the United States government did not seem to change his behavior. Having grown up in an environment where Communism was tolerated; having attended a college in which membership in the Young Communist League conferred status and respect; having had little real work experience, and having spent his adult life in a social world that revolved around the CP, Julie seemed to assume that everyone he encountered would at least countenance his views.

Thus, when he was called in for a Signal Corps loyalty hearing on 20 January 1941, he was utterly surprised. The government had checked into his background and discovered the material the FBI had on Ethel and some of their friends. His new career in the Signal Corps suddenly appeared to be in jeopardy. A hearing officer confronted him, stating that he was in possession of information showing that the Pogarskys, with whom the Rosenbergs had lived, were active Communists and that Ethel had signed a CP nominating petition in 1939. Julie defiantly retorted that "[e]ven if [Ethel] did sign a petition, I don't see how that would affect me. After all, she is a different person and has rights." He then took the offensive. His strategy was to lie: "I am quite sure she [Ethel] is no Communist. We never discuss politics or government very much, but I believe that her views are similar to mine [sic] own." And what, he was asked, were his own views? His description of his life in college was intended to explain them:

> I never took part in any student demonstrations. I remember signing a petition once relating to aid to Spain, but I don't remember who sponsored the petition. . . . So far as I know, none of my friends at college were interested in the Communist Party. . . . At no time in my life have I ever had anything to do with distribution of Communist literature.

Although he was able to avoid swearing under oath that he was not a member of the Communist party, he was called back for a second hearing on 8 March. At this time he lied under oath:

> I asked my wife about her signing a Communist Party petition. Her memory on the matter is not entirely clear, but she told me that a man who she did not know, came to the door one day. He said he lived in the neighborhood and gave her a long rigamarole, all to the effect as to whether she wanted all sides of a question represented. She said that she guessed she did. He said, then sign this. She asked what it was and he said it would put the Communist Party on the ballot. She asked, 'Will this make me a Communist if I sign?' He said, 'No', so she signed. I guess it was carelessness on her part, or maybe she just lacked sales resistance. However, I know that she is no Communist.

The hearing officer was persuaded and the matter was dropped, for the time being.

Thereafter, Julie became somewhat more discreet, and dedicated himself to preventing the harassment of fellow comrades by the United States government. With this purpose in mind, he became chairman of the federal civil service committee of FAECT. In this capacity, he attempted to secure higher wage rates for overtime, tried to initiate on-the-job training to allow employees to be professionally upgraded, and obtained allowances for carfare for travel between worksites. But the work that drew his most passionate involvement was always the attempt to reinstate employees who were fired for political reasons.

It is not known how Ethel responded to Julie's loyalty investi-

gation. At the beginning of October she had moved back to New
York and into Sophie and Harry's apartment to take up residence
with her husband again. As was expected of a woman in her position, she did not look for work since her husband was able to
support her. To have his job so quickly threatened may have been
quite unnerving. She had forfeited a well-paid job in Washington,
while the chances of Julie finding another position must have appeared virtually impossible, given the difficulty he had had in securing his present job. Ethel had never cared about money and she
never overcame her revulsion at her parents' concern with it. Yet
she was doggedly practical. People had to work regardless of their
ideals. She had maintained this view for herself throughout her
infatuation with the stage, and she undoubtedly maintained it now.
The Signal Corps job was a good one. Julie recently had been
suffering from boils, and his employer did not assign him work
outside of New York City in consideration of his need to care for
this problem. Thus at his March hearing, Julie reported:

> I . . . talked it over with my wife and . . . I feel under
> obligation to the Department. It takes two solid months of
> training for a Radio Inspector to do any work at all. Besides,
> they have been very good there to me. My health has been
> a little bad lately . . . I have had to take special injections
> every day and they have kept me on work in the city and
> they have not sent me away on any work.

If we are to believe this statement (and since it does not bear on
Communism it is more likely to be true), Ethel's practicality and
Julie's ever-present concern about his health probably helped mo-
tivate his somewhat more conciliatory tone at this hearing.

Once Julie's job was no longer threatened, Ethel had to construct a new life for herself as a married woman who did not work
outside the home. She had never enjoyed idleness; she needed to
feel she was fulfilling a purpose, achieving a goal. Now, for the
first time in her adult life, she did not have to worry about economic
survival. Julie was not making a fortune but, given both of their
expectations and standards of living, they had more than they needed
to live comfortably.

After Julie received his first paycheck, Ethel began looking for
a place for them to live. Sharing an apartment with Sophie and
Harry might have been acceptable as a temporary situation, but

clearly was not something Julie and Ethel wanted to continue indefinitely. Therefore when Ethel saw a room-to-let notice posted in a grocery store across from Tompkins Square, she quickly inquired about it. At 103 Avenue A, three doors down from the corner of Seventh Street, stood a six-story, gray stone tenement with twenty one-room apartments. A widow took Ethel upstairs to a corner room that seemed to meet Ethel's minimal requirements. Although it had a bathroom down the hall, it was "furnished" with the barest of necessities and it did have steam heat and electric lights, and the price was right. A short time later, Ethel took Julie to see it, and they rented it immediately. At the beginning of the new year, the Rosenbergs moved into their new home and set up housekeeping.

Although she was now a twenty-five-year-old married woman, Ethel maintained her new living quarters just as she had her bedroom at 64 Sheriff Street. There was no color in the room, no pictures on the wall, nothing to personalize the surroundings, except for mess and clutter. Ethel almost never dusted, swept, or washed anything in the room. She was a *shlimazolnite*, a sloppy housekeeper, just as her mother was. The widow who owned the tenement house described Ethel as "the poorest housekeeper [I] ever knew and the Rosenberg apartment was a complete mess. . . ." Both Julie and Ethel accepted the cultural prescription that the home was solely Ethel's responsibility. Although the home in which Julie was raised had always been kept neat, orderly, and clean, he did not seem to mind Ethel's neglectfulness and accepted it with a certain amount of humor. A friend of the Rosenbergs recalls meeting Julie at a store, "thumbing through birthday cards, looking for one for Ethel. One was an elaborate tribute to a man's helpmate, and in rhyme told how he always came home to find an ordered, immaculate house. He showed it to me, laughed and said, 'Well, I can't in all honesty send that one.' "

This tolerance undoubtedly emanated from Julie's steadfast and unambivalent love for Ethel that endured throughout their marriage. A friend remembers: "He was very much in love with Ethel. He would evince it in his attitudes; he would always talk about her. We would have meetings, there would be other women around, and Julius had no eyes for any other woman or show any apparent interest in any other woman. When they were in the same room they would always look to one another."

Another reports that: "All was harmony. In everything they were together, there was no conflict. In the early days they were that way about the union, both of them doing work. Julie and Ethel were so truly united that when they were together each seemed to come alive with an added vitality."

By all accounts, Julie was a "sensitive" man. "Actually, I never knew anyone so sensitive to people. I can say with utter lack of exaggeration that his love for people was overwhelming." He was as comfortable talking with women as with men and cared deeply about friends' problems. "He was always worrying about some friend who was broke or out of a job, and would ask if something couldn't be done for him. He always would give something, and often get others to, if there were children involved." It was not uncommon for him to become physically ill upon learning of a personal tragedy or of some major social injustice. His reaction to a black prisoner's unjust execution is fairly typical of his response: "He became sick to his stomach, found it difficult to swallow and his eyes filled with tears." His feelings could also easily be hurt in arguments or political debate. Ethel recognized his sensitivity and approached any difference of opinion with extreme delicacy. Harry Steingart was impressed by this and as a result judged Ethel to be "a good wife" for her empathic understanding of her husband.

In his relationship to Ethel, Julie never showed anger. When he was unhappy with her or with something she had done, he sulked, perhaps making her feel guilty for whatever "crime" she had committed. He was also unselfconsciously demonstrative with her, freely placing his arm around her, holding her hand, or kissing her in public. They both called each other "darling," "sweetheart," and "honey," but also "bunny" and Julie sometimes called Ethel his "sweet *vibella*."

The security of knowing she had Julie's unceasing love and acceptance allowed Ethel to express more readily the warmth and concern she had for other people. Those who knew her at the time remember this well: "She was a warm human being. She was concerned, not only in the abstract, she was also concerned about me—how I felt, how we were getting along, what your problems are and so on." "Ethel radiated a warmth one didn't find in many people." She was "very solicitous, always making sure I had my rubbers on when it was snowing, put a hat on, button up your coat, that sort of thing." Ethel "was amazingly soft and warm. . . . so thoughtful, very solicitous." "She was quite a dame, alert, aware, very warm and interested in others. If she said, 'You look pale, I'll bet you're not getting enough rest; why don't you?' you felt she meant it." Ethel and Julie's concern for their friends frequently turned their one-room apartment into an open house. A friend of theirs from FAECT remembers:

> They didn't have any money, but they were happy as anything. Without a dime, they made marriage look like something wonderful. And there was always open house there on Saturday night, always people around, sometimes sleeping on the floor. Julie'd give the shirt off his back, and he'd never say 'no' to someone in from out of town, or broke, who wanted a place to stay.
>
> I never saw liquor in their house. Ethel would sing, and we'd talk and maybe she'd get coffee from the landlady. They were young and carefree then.

By the summer of 1941, Ethel and Julie had saved enough money to take their first real vacation. They both had an appreciation for nature that bordered on awe, given their extremely limited exposure to it, so they decided they would like to visit a farm, something that seemed exotic to these lifelong city dwellers. Julie called the Farmers Consumers Cooperative to locate a farm that accepted visitors for the summer and was referred to Waldo McNutt who worked for the Cooperative. In keeping with the Rosenbergs' CP-delimited social world, McNutt apparently had been a member of the YCL and a former chairman of the Party-dominated American Youth Congress. He invited the Rosenbergs to his farm in Haddam, Connecticut on the Connecticut River. Since neither Ethel nor Julie knew how to drive a car, McNutt volunteered to pick them up in Astoria and drive them to his farm. What followed was a three-week vacation in which the Rosenbergs experienced an entirely new manner of living and the beginnings of a new friendship with Waldo McNutt and his wife.

Once back in New York, Ethel sought volunteer work through which she could make a contribution politically. She made it known to the local Party section that she was willing to volunteer her services because she had a fair amount of time on her hands. Since she had moved out of 64 Sheriff Street shortly after her marriage, she had spent less and less time on music and her pursuit of a career as a singer. She had been unable to transport her piano to the Rosenbergs', the apartment she had shared with the Pogarskys, the rooming house in Washington, or their present one-room apartment. All were too cramped, and her involvement in politics had taken the energy and time she needed to practice. Lessons with Madame had taken money that she and Julie had desperately needed during his long period of underemployment, and they seemed increasingly irrelevant given the imminent threat to world peace the Communist party had been predicting. So she had quit. Marriage and the Party finally extinguished the ambition Ethel had clung to since she was a girl.

―――――

When Hitler invaded the Soviet Union on 22 June 1941 in defiance of his nonaggression pact with that country's government, the Communist party began to argue vociferously for America's intervention into the war that now threatened the Communist homeland. Just as quickly as it had altered its position at the time of the signing of the Nazi-Soviet Pact, the CPUSA now reversed its policy against military intervention, war preparations, and support of the "imperialist" war that raged in Europe. As soon as they learned of Hitler's deception, "the Communists responded as if German bombs were landing on their own homes. . . . In a remarkably short period of time the Communists pulled together a network of new pro-war front organizations, which in the course of the war would attract considerable public support." These new organizations acted to arouse support for both America's military intervention against the Axis powers and material aid to the Red Army, and also raised funds for food, clothing, and medical supplies for the people of the Soviet Union.

One such organization, formed in September, was the East Side Conference to Defend America and Crush Hitler. The Party section leader, Carl Marzani, was chosen to be the Conference's executive secretary. Shortly after he established the Conference headquarters on the second floor of a building at 137 Avenue B, directly across from Tompkins Square, a woman came into his office offering to be his secretary. Her name was Ethel Rosenberg. Marzani recalls, "I assume the Party sent her. I'm sure she was assigned. I took it for granted. You never ask if someone's in the CP." Ethel immediately assumed her duties as full-time, volunteer secretary to this newly created Communist "mass" or "front" organization.

Marzani was in charge of shaping the Conference's direction

and planning its day-to-day operations, but to attain wider recognition and legitimacy, the group's official chairman was New York City Councilman Meyer Goldberg, and its vice-chairs were a rabbi and a Polish Catholic priest. Its board of directors included Alan Hall of the Henry Street Settlement and Harry Schlacht, editor of the *East Side News*. Despite the rather strident sound of its name, the East Side Conference to Defend America and Crush Hitler had the appearance of a local Popular Front organization.

Ethel began to work at the Conference in early September. In addition to her regular office duties, she had to help organize an East Side parade that Marzani was planning for 24 September. This parade was intended to demonstrate how all Lower East Side residents were united behind President Roosevelt's defense preparations and "against the Hitlerite menace." The *Daily Worker* of 16 September 1941 proclaimed:

> *Chinese, Poles, Jews, Russians, Ukrainians, Italians, Spanish, Czechs and Slovaks, dressed in national costumes, will parade through [the] East Side on Wednesday, Sept. 24, in support of President Roosevelt's anti-Nazi program.*
>
> *The unity of all nationalities of the crowded downtown neighborhood will give the answer to Lindbergh's fascist lies and will rally the peoples of the East Side against the fascists at home and abroad, Carl Marzani, executive secretary of the East Side Conference to Defend America and Crush Hitler announced yesterday.*

The Conference was supposedly composed of some 296 organizations, groups, societies and clubs, and Ethel had to help contact each of them about their participation in the parade. She also had to try to secure press coverage, and field questions from callers and visitors to the Conference's office, which was open to the public for four hours each day. Suddenly she was in the middle of the Party's work, believing perhaps, as did so many other CP adherents at the time, that each day's work represented "a shovelful of earth over the grave which Hitler and his crowd dug for themselves" when they invaded the Soviet Union.

When the "Parade of Nationalities" actually occurred on the 24th, the Party deemed it an unqualified success. According to Party estimates, 100,000 East Siders turned out to watch 7,000 people, many of whom dressed in costumes as they paraded from Tompkins

Square to the intersection of Madison and Grand streets for a rally.
The *Daily Worker* reported that "100,000 East Siders cheered.
. . . as the crowded downtown community gave its ringing answer
to Hitler and his appeaser pals."

Once the parade was over, Ethel's work settled into a more
normal routine. She acted as Marzani's personal secretary, taking
dictation, typing his letters, and screening his phone calls. She cared
about his welfare; "she mothered me to death," he recalls. If there
was extra work, Marzani only had to mention it and Ethel would
arrange for it to be done. She was extremely attentive to detail,
obsessively concerned about punctuality and order, despite her
tolerance of clutter and dirt. This made Ethel an excellent secretary.
Marzani remembers her as "very cheerful, very competent, a very
hard-working person. She seemed to me to have no ambitions, was
content to do her typing and phoning and taking dictation, very
happy to do whatever had to be done, not talking much." Of course,
Marzani adds, he was a "male chauvinist" at the time, and took
for granted that she would take care of him. "After all," he asks
sardonically, "what are women for?"

Ethel certainly did not question her role at the Conference office.
The cheerfulness Marzani recalls is similar to reports of Ethel from
her days at National New York Packing and Shipping and of her
readiness to do "whatever had to be done" as when she worked
for FAECT. Ethel did not seem to dislike clerical work as such, and
seems to have found it fulfilling when it was in the service of a
larger cause, such as building a union or working for the defense
of the Soviet Union. After marrying Julie, it was through clerical
work more than any other activity that Ethel contributed to the
Communist party. There are no reports of her singing at any fund-
raiser or CP sponsored event after 1939. Her former manner of
combining politics and art ceased to matter as she abandoned her
vocal ambitions and gave her life so completely to the Party. Carl
Marzani confirmed this:

> When I tell you that I had no idea that she ever had studied
> voice or dramatics, or done any singing whatsoever, you
> can get an idea of the sort of person she was. It would have
> been natural for many persons to mention it, as we had
> affairs where she might have sung. But nothing ever was
> said about it. And while I didn't know her husband well—
> I met him once or twice—he never mentioned it.

Marzani's ignorance of Ethel's past accomplishments was echoed by all those she met in the late thirties and early forties. One of her closest friends from this period learned of these achievements only after reading Ethel's testimony from her trial in the early nineteen-fifties. Another friend remembers:

> Ethel was always worrying about others, asking how they felt, mothering them. Sometimes she visited our home and listened to our records, but she almost never talked about her own life—it was too average to be 'interesting.' She thought mine romantic because I was born in Europe—she said she just had an ordinary American childhood.

Ethel's reticence far exceeded the prevailing prohibition against speaking about one's personal life in Party circles. She simply never told people of her membership in the Schola Cantorum, her amateur night successes, her stardom on the stages of Seward Park High and Clark House. Perhaps she assumed that her political friends and acquaintances would be uninterested in such silly, apolitical endeavors. Perhaps her early family life had conditioned her to assume that no one could find her achievements praiseworthy. Maybe she actually had come to denigrate these accomplishments in her own mind. Did she now see them as nothing more than puerile diversions?

Although she had thoroughly discarded her ambition to be a stage performer, her love of singing continued. This certainly was no adolescent infatuation. She sang whenever and wherever she could. Sylvia Steingart remembers attending Sunday brunches at friends' houses with the Rosenbergs and hearing Ethel sing in her "beautiful coloratura soprano." Another friend from FAECT remembers social gatherings where Ethel "loved to sing and some of the guests would join in. She sang a Russian song and an Italian song, folk music and a few operatic airs." To one woman, a grandmother who occasionally volunteered at the Conference's office, Ethel confided her past desire to be a professional singer. This woman had been trained as a singer. Ethel sometimes would drop by her rooms after work and the two would sing duets or hunt for sheet music at the secondhand stores on Fourth Avenue. The older woman remembered:

> I am sure she felt no regret that she had not gone on with a career in voice. And always she made such a fuss over

*me. 'Now if I had had a big voice like yours I would have
wanted audiences,' she'd laugh. 'But mine is small'. . . . I
never even knew she acted; that was so far in the past.
Singing was simply a joy to her.*

As late summer turned to fall and the United States had still not
entered the war, the Conference continued its drive to influence
public opinion and provide material aid to the Allies. Ethel often
was forced to work overtime or to bring typing home with her at
the end of the day. Despite her long hours, she seems genuinely to
have thrived doing what she believed was such purposeful work,
and she also liked her boss enormously. Carl Marzani was the
consummate Communist intellectual; educated at Oxford, a teacher
at New York University, he was probably the most well-read, erudite
man Ethel had ever encountered. He was also ebullient, egoistic,
and charming. If his dedication to a socialist transformation today
is any indicator of what he was like in the past, he must have inspired
all those with whom he came in contact.

In October, the Conference announced plans to hold a mass
rally as part of the Eleanor Roosevelt-sponsored "American All Week."
On 27 October, 1,000 East Siders listened to various civic leaders
call for America's entry into the war against Hitler. They also voted,
at the suggestion of their chairman, Meyer Goldberg, to change the
group's name from the East Side Conference to Defend America
and Crush Hitler to the East Side Defense Congress, a less strident
and sectarian-sounding name. They also voted to enroll themselves
as air wardens, buy defense bonds, and raise $50,000 for aid to
the nations fighting Hitler.

Coordinating these activities fell to Carl Marzani, and second-
arily to Ethel. Her workload also increased in November when the
again renamed East Side Defense *Council* decided to begin a drive
to register blood donors for the Red Cross in preparation for the war
that most people in the Party believed (and hoped) was imminent.
By the end of the month, "Ethel was working night and day at the
Defense Council."

Ethel's absence from home probably would have been difficult
for Julie had he found himself alone in their one-room apartment
much of the time, but this was not the case. On 14 October he had
been transferred from Brooklyn to the Signal Corps headquarters in
Philadelphia. From there, he was assigned to an RCA plant in Camden, New Jersey. As it was too far for him to commute daily from
Manhattan to Camden, particularly since he often worked overtime,

he and three other inspectors assigned to the RCA plant rented an apartment in Philadelphia, directly across the Delaware River from Camden. Julie spent the weeknights there and returned home on Friday night.

This new living arrangement marked a turning point in Ethel and Julie's relationship. Never again would they have the opportunity to spend as much time together as they had since they met in December 1936. Since then they had passed most of their evenings together, alone, in meetings, or with friends. Their social world had been a tight one, drawn from the close circle of Party members and followers who usually lived close by. As Julie began to travel and actually live away from home, the Rosenbergs' Saturday night open houses became fewer, and the intensity of their social networks began to diminish.

When the United States finally entered the war at the beginning of December, Julie had been living in Philadelphia for a month and a half, and Ethel had just finished the Council's blood donor drive, which was being hailed in many local newspapers as the first of its kind in the country. Communists everywhere were relieved and elated by the country's declaration of war. At last their desire to fight directly against fascism and in defense of the Soviet Union seemed far closer to reality. The *Daily Worker* printed a new slogan under its masthead, "National Unity for Victory over Nazi Enslavement," and the paper soon began arguing for a "Second Front" in Western Europe to divert Hitler's energies away from the USSR.

Once America entered the war, the East Side Defense Council affiliated with the Civilian Defense Volunteers Organization. The Council's work was to proceed as it had, but now it would be an official branch of United States civil defense operations. A week after this decision, however, Carl Marzani was drafted. In February 1942 he departed for Washington, leaving the Council without its main link to the Party and its intellectual and organizational leadership. The Council therefore acted throughout the war years as a rather unexceptional member of the civil defense organization, its connection to the CP rendered unnecessary by America's entry into the war.

Before he left for Washington, Marzani gave Ethel a copy of the recently published best seller, *Mission to Moscow* by Joseph E. Davies. This book, which the *New York Times* acclaimed as "the one book above all to read on Russia," praised the Soviet experiment under Stalin's rule, while assuring Americans that Communism in its Marxist-Leninist form was disappearing from Russia and consequently posed no threat to the United States. One reason for the book's popularity and influence was that its author was not a left-wing intellectual or radical journalist, but had been the American ambassador to the Soviet Union from 1936 to 1938.

Mission to Moscow captured what a great many Americans wanted to hear at the time about the USSR. In early December, the Red Army had launched a major counteroffensive against Hitler's troops and gave the Germans their first military defeat within twenty-five miles of Moscow. This victory demonstrated to Americans for the first time that the Nazis were not invincible and that the Soviets were brave, heroic, and trustworthy allies. The American Communist party shared in some of this newfound good will toward the Soviet Union. Since the Party now had resumed its support of the Roosevelt administration that it had surrendered during the months of the Nazi-Soviet Pact, the CPUSA regained some of the acceptance it had gained during the Popular Front. Although it would never again enjoy the tolerance and respect it had in liberal circles in the mid-to-late thirties, the Party experienced a renewed vitality as it fought indefatigably to defend the Soviet Union and the United States and wipe fascism off the face of the earth.

For the Rosenbergs, America's entry into the war signaled not only positive political movement—given that the United States and the Soviet Union would now be allies—but a certain amount of personal security. Armaments production would necessarily escalate; therefore for the remainder of the war, a steady demand for Signal Corps inspection of private industry would keep Julie steadily employed. On 1 January 1942 Julie was promoted from junior engineer to assistant engineer, and his salary was increased from $2,000 per year to $2,600. At last it seemed as though the Rosenbergs were proceeding on the same trajectory as Julie's classmates from college. Their future looked promising. After receiving a relatively large check for his latest per diem expenses, Julie bought Ethel an $80 fur coat. They began looking for a real apartment, one with its own bathroom and kitchen.

At the beginning of spring, Ethel and Julie found an apartment they could afford at Knickerbocker Village, a housing project on the Lower East Side. Built in 1934 by the Metropolitan Life Insurance Company, Knickerbocker Village occupied an entire block bordered by Monroe, Market, Cherry, and Catherine streets. Its two thirteen-story brick buildings contained about 1,600 apartments. It boasted its own nursery school and playground for children, elevators, laundry facilities, steam heat, and electricity throughout. The Rosenbergs secured a two-year lease for GE–11, a one-bedroom apartment on the eleventh floor facing the courtyard. Their rent was $45.75 per month, including electricity.

On 15 April they moved into their new home. According to one friend, it was "a big event for them to get an apartment of their own, and they were walking on the clouds. This was the most modern apartment in which either had ever lived. A technological revolution stood between Knickerbocker Village and 64 Sheriff Street, although the two were separated by no more than a mile. Ethel now could cook on a gas stove, keep every room heated in the winter, and use her own bathroom whenever she desired.

The Rosenbergs were also very fortunate since their move into Knickerbocker Village coincided with Harry and Sylvia Steingart's move to California. When he realized that Julie and Ethel owned almost no furniture, Harry suggested to Julie that "I would let you use my furniture and I would save the storage money and you would have the use of the furniture." The Rosenbergs readily agreed. Harry and Sylvia gave the Rosenbergs not only their furniture, but their dishes, linens, and books. Ethel and Julie were able to fill their kitchen shelves with the Steingarts' dishes, furnish their living room with the Steingarts' tables and chairs, and their bedroom with a single chest of drawers and a bed. There were, however, no rugs on the linoleum floors, curtains on the windows, nor pictures on the walls. And, probably within months of their arrival, the apartment was covered with the dust and grime resulting from Ethel's remarkable "housekeeping."

Their new neighbors in the housing project were similar in many ways to Ethel and Julie. Most of them were young couples who had grown up on the Lower East Side. Many of them did not yet have children or had youngsters who were only of preschool age. A remarkable number of Party members and followers lived at Knickerbocker Village, and they formed the backbone of the tenants' association. Because of Ethel's full-time work at the Defense Council and Julie's presence only on weekends, however, the Rosenbergs did not seem to have much of an opportunity to integrate themselves into the social circles of Knickerbocker Village. Yet they gradually did form good friendships with Ruby and Isidore Goldstein, and with Harry Lande and his wife. A few months after the Rosenbergs moved in, they were also able to tell some friends of an apartment on the twelfth floor that was becoming available.

When Mike and Ann Sidorovich moved upstairs from the Rosenbergs, they quickly became Julie and Ethel's closest friends. Julie and Mike had attended Seward Park High together and later worked for Paul Williams at the same time. Mike was active in FAECT and had been a member of the Abraham Lincoln Brigade that fought in the Spanish Civil War. Clearly, the Sidorovichs and the Rosenbergs had a great deal in common, and for the next year they spent much of their free time together.

After settling into their modern apartment, Ethel and Julie took a step that would radically transform their lives forever. At the age of twenty-six, and after three years of marriage, Ethel was pregnant for the first time. Throughout the summer and fall Ethel continued to work as a full-time volunteer at the East Side Defense Council. Although she was able to maintain her full schedule until shortly before her delivery date, she often experienced acute back pain while standing. The added weight from her pregnancy apparently strained her back, which was frequently a source of pain even under normal conditions. Outside of work and meetings, Ethel spent much of her pregnancy lying down so as to relieve the pressure on her back. She may often have been alone, since Julie was still spending one or two weeks at a time on inspections in New Jersey or Pennsylvania. When he was home, however, he pampered his pregnant wife and treated her with love and renewed respect. He relished the idea of becoming a father, and doted on the woman who was carrying their child.

Thus as Ethel looked forward to the birth of her baby in March 1943, she was extremely optimistic. Not only did she anticipate that the "war was going to end fascism for good and all," but she expected to find untold happiness and fulfillment in becoming a mother. Unfortunately, her expectations were unfounded.

10

THE PERFECT MOTHER

Michael Allen Rosenberg was born on 10 March 1943. He was delivered at Physicians Hospital in Jackson Heights, Queens, probably because Ethel's doctor, Max Hart, had his practice in nearby Rego Park. We have no record of who accompanied Ethel to the hospital or of how she experienced childbirth. We do know, however, that Julie was not present; he was on assignment for the Signal Corps at Orlando Field, Florida. His absence at Michael's birth presaged the isolation Ethel would experience in the next few years while raising her son.

A month before his son's birth, Julie had again been promoted. He was now an associate engineer with the Army Signal Corps and commanded a salary of $3,200 per year. His new job consisted in supervising the work of forty-six other inspectors, aiding in the review of contracts, assisting in the establishment of inspection procedures, giving classes and training inspectors, administering technical and design checks, periodically meeting with the heads of the defense contractor's departments, and aiding in the handling of personnel problems. These new responsibilities made it more difficult for him to miss work or refuse a placement away from New York. Thus he was forced to accept an assignment that caused him to be 1,100 miles from his wife at the birth of their first child.

On Thursday, 18 March, according to Jewish custom and law, Michael was circumcised. Because this was a work day, many of the people Julie and Ethel might have wanted to be present for the ceremony were unable to attend. Ethel's father, Barney, was there, however, and he was given the auspicious role of *sandek*, the man who holds the child during the circumcision. Julie's brother, Dave, who was now a practicing pharmacist, and his wife Ruth, a nurse, were also present. They became Michael's godparents, implicitly assuming the roles of Michael's protectors and guardians should anything happen to his parents. Also in attendance was another Ruth, David Greenglass's new wife. Although married only the previous November, this Ruth was well acquainted with both Ethel and Julie. The former Ruth Printz had been Dave's girlfriend for years. Her family lived on Rivington Street and she had attended Seward Park High, from which she had graduated only the previous June. The daughter of Galician Jews, Ruth had grown up in poverty similar to that of the Greenglass family, and now at the age of eighteen was an impressionable young woman, very much taken with her in-laws and their relatively affluent life-style in Knickerbocker Village.

During the first month of Michael's life, while Ethel adjusted to motherhood and recovered from childbirth, the Rosenbergs employed a young black woman to do the housework and to help Ethel with the baby. Bertha Britain had worked for three of Ethel's first cousins and was recommended to her by them. She was enormously helpful since Michael was a cranky, somewhat sickly baby who demanded all Ethel's attention, leaving her little energy to shop, cook, or care for the apartment.

Although this first month undoubtedly was a difficult one for a young couple suddenly confronted with a newborn baby who was hard to soothe and woke frequently during the night, the Rosenbergs remained delighted with their first child. In April they gave a party in honor of his arrival at their apartment. In addition to many of their friends, they invited their families. Although neither Ethel nor Julie had been very close to their parents or siblings since their marriage, Michael's birth signaled a reawakening of familial involvement. Both sets of grandparents were eager to see their newest grandson, and being parents now gave Julie and Ethel a new basis on which to relate to their brothers and sisters, many of whom already had had their first child. The party, however, was a bittersweet experience for the Rosenbergs.

Ann and Michael Sidorovich, who had become Ethel and Julie's closest friends and neighbors, were shortly to move to Westchester County. Ann had been someone on whom Ethel had relied during her pregnancy and in the past month. Since traveling beyond the confines of the immediate neighborhood was now arduous for Ethel, her ability simply to take the elevator one floor up to see Ann for companionship and assistance had been a godsend. The party honoring Michael's birth was one of the last times the Rosenbergs would see the Sidoroviches as neighbors, and their imminent departure most likely saddened the occasion, particularly for Ethel.

Of a more conflictual nature for the Rosenbergs, however, was the appearance of Mark and Stella Pogarsky. Since Ethel and Julie's move to Washington three years earlier, the two couples had grown apart. Julie and Mark had had a rather serious disagreement, the cause of which remains unclear. Tension must have permeated their meeting, for this party would be the last time the two couples intentionally saw one another.

Worse yet, over the course of the day Julie and Ethel managed to get involved in a political argument with Ethel's brother, Sammy. Since offering to pay their way to the Soviet Union in the late thirties because of what he believed was their harmful influence over his younger brother Dave, Sam Greenglass had remained distant and cold toward his sister and her husband. Unlike most of the Greenglasses and Rosenbergs, who were fairly apolitical, Sam prided himself on his anti-Communism and seems to have taunted Ethel and Julie about their political views. According to Julie's sister Ethel, the Rosenbergs refrained from discussing politics with their families; yet it seems likely that if Sam pushed them, neither Julie nor Ethel would hesitate to defend the CP's viewpoint. It is unclear who sparked the argument or what it was about, but after it was over Sammy decided never to see his sister and her husband again. He remained true to his promise. The next time he would see Ethel, she would be behind bars, and then he went only to aid the FBI in its attempt to make her confess.

Many people at the party probably were also somewhat saddened by the absence of Ethel's other brothers. Bernie Greenglass had joined the army the previous year and was serving on the African front. Ethel's youngest brother, Dave, had just been sent to Aberdeen, Maryland, for basic training, and it was unclear if and when he would go into battle. Pictures of Ethel's brothers in military uniform began to adorn the bedroom dresser.

As she closed the door after saying goodnight to her last guests,
Ethel most likely turned her attention to the object of the day's celebration. She was probably not then aware that her attention would remain riveted there until forced away against her will.

———

Virtually from the day of Michael's birth, Ethel felt overwhelmed by the demands of motherhood. She wanted desperately to be a good mother, a perfect mother, to do all the things that her own mother had seemed unwilling or unable to do. Yet Michael confounded her. He cried and she could not soothe him. He would not go to sleep when she wanted him to, and then he would awaken repeatedly during the night. He was continually ill, and she was helpless to protect him from an onslaught of infections. In her own words, it "wasn't the usual thing of where a baby gets sick occasionally. It was practically every week in and week out." His will seemed intractably set against her own. Michael's Aunt Ethel recalls that he cried "twenty-four hours a day. . . . He was a very nervous child; he would cry and scream; I couldn't stand it."

Julie was away most of the time. His Signal Corps responsibilities frequently kept him in Philadelphia or New Jersey overnight. He continued to be absent for entire weeks, returning home only for weekends. Even when he was home, however, neither he nor Ethel expected him to care for Mike. A baby was a mother's responsibility, particularly when it was in distress, as Michael was frequently. Thus Ethel's days and nights were often spent alone with Michael as she tried desperately to comfort this baby who seemed prey to perpetual discomfort.

The companionship she had found with Ann Sidorovich was lost by the end of April when the Sidorovichs moved to Chappaqua, New York. Although there were literally dozens of young mothers in Knickerbocker Village with babies and toddlers, Ethel found it difficult to associate with them. Typically, they sat together in the housing project's inner courtyard with their children, or walked in twos or threes on the nearby streets with their children in baby carriages and strollers. When Ethel attempted to join them, Mike often cried ceaselessly while the other babies slept, lay contentedly in their carriages, or crawled on the grass. Ethel could never relax and it was virtually impossible to carry on a conversation with another mother since Michael was so frequently in distress and demanded her attention. Ethel's old friend Betty Birnbaum relates an illustrative incident. After not seeing each other for two or three years, Betty ran into Ethel as she was pushing Mike's baby carriage on Delancey Street:

> *Michael was sleeping on his belly, and I got very excited. 'Ethel, I want to see the baby,' and I said, 'turn him over, turn him over.' She said, 'I can't do that; it'll wake him up.' 'Turn him over; I have to see his face!' So very reluctantly, and only because she was soft and gentle did she do this to please me. I didn't know what I was asking. . . . She turned him over and Michael howled, outraged. . . . I could see she was upset. She looked harried. She put him back on his tummy, but I had got a look at him. What I remember is that she seemed quite harried then.*

Ethel's acquaintances and friends from political work were of little help at this time. The war in Europe raged; the CP continually demanded a second front. Those who worked with the East Side Defense Council, FAECT, and the Communist party were preoccupied with supporting the war effort and contending with its domestic ramifications. Since many of those she knew in the Party were explicitly opposed to having children because of the restrictions it imposed on people's political activities, it is not surprising that she quickly lost contact with many of her former political associates. Ethel's experience was similar to that of a woman whom historian Robert Shaffer describes: "A woman took a leave of absence in her ninth month of pregnancy from the Young Communist League unit in which she had been active for four years. Few of her colleagues visited her while she was away from her branch, and she wrote dejectedly [to the *Party Organizer*]: 'It makes me feel that all the work and energy I put into the movement did not mean anything to anyone.' "

In the absence of friends or neighbors with whom she felt comfortable in her new role as mother, Ethel found herself spending increasing amounts of time with her family. Now that she had had a child and no longer worked outside the home, her life was both more similar to theirs and more acceptable to them. For the first time in years, she had things to talk about with her mother and often relied on her to baby-sit on the rare occasions when she went out without Michael. More important, however, were the two new additions to the Greenglass family. Gladys, or "Gladdy" as she was affectionately referred to, had married Ethel's brother Bernie, and was someone with whom Ethel genuinely enjoyed spending time. Ruthie, Dave's eighteen-year-old wife, was pleasant and had developed a close relationship with Tessie. Since she was nine years younger than Ethel, she looked up to her sister-in-law who seemed so much more worldly and experienced than herself. Ruth also admired Ethel because of her political views.

Ethel seems to have warmed to the role in which her sister-in-law placed her. She counseled Ruth on political matters and organized outings for Ruth, Gladys, and herself to attend some of the larger CP functions that were staged in Madison Square Garden and elsewhere. Outside of Julie, it was now with family members that Ethel maintained an increasingly tenuous link to the world of organized Communism.

As contact with her family increased, Ethel, Julie, and Mike began attending Friday night *shabbes* dinners at 64 Sheriff Street. Now that all their children had left home, Tessie and Barney leased the upstairs flat to Tessie's unmarried sister and converted what originally had been Sammy's bedroom into a dining room. Here the Greenglass family would gather, frequently along with Tessie's sister and brothers, Abe and Issy, and members of their families. Even if Ethel had not seen Ruth, Gladys, or her parents during the week, Friday nights became an institutionalized means of maintaining ties, keeping up on each others' lives, and hearing news of Bernie and Dave.

All of this new familial closeness did not mean, however, that Tessie and Ethel had finally repaired their relationship. Tessie remained critical of Ethel—of the way she was raising Michael, her ideas of how the war should be conducted, her attitudes toward Negroes, and on and on. Ethel was an American whose radical views set her apart from her immigrant mother who remained rooted in her *shtetl* upbringing. Nonetheless, in 1943, Ethel's life more closely resembled her mother's than ever before.

For Ethel, however, pleasing her mother came at a high cost. Some part of her probably responded to Tessie's greater acceptance of her. For all her rebelliousness, Ethel in many ways longed for her mother's approval and love. Yet this small degree of maternal approbation may have paled in comparison with the enormous difficulty Ethel was experiencing in her new role as full-time housewife and mother. Caring for Michael continued to be a perpetual struggle. Just as it was so hard for Ethel to calm Michael when he was an infant, as he became more mobile and began to talk, she found it almost impossible to control or discipline him. She believed that discipline, in virtually any form, was cruel. She not only held herself accountable to this standard, but believed in its universal applicability. Author Virginia Gardner writes of an interview she conducted with a neighbor of Ethel's at Knickerbocker Village: "Ethel couldn't stand to hear a child cry, any child. . . . [Upon calling on this neighbor] Ethel found she'd punished her eldest, then about 5, for using some bad language he'd picked up from older boys. He was crying, and Ethel 'took me to task—she was that way, couldn't bear to see a child punished, or suffer in any way.' "

This belief in the evil of punishment, coupled with an inability to tolerate a child's tears, took an enormous toll on her. She became captive to her own son's bad moods, fits of temper and disobedience. Virtually bereft of punishment as a tool with which to train Michael, Ethel was molding him into a child who was simultaneously unmanageable and extremely dependent on his mother for the satisfaction of his needs. Ethel's sister-in-law remembers the situation well: "He was such a disturbing child. . . . I would grab him away from her [Ethel] and say 'you're gonna sit down and eat or you're gonna lie down for a while. . . . I couldn't take it; that woman was wearing herself down. Every little beck and call, she'd run to his side. That's how Ethel was. . . . Never punished him in any way. I punished my kids. . . . But Ethel was different."

It seems that the more her son's behavior troubled her, the more Ethel turned to child-rearing literature to find answers, techniques, and counsel. She subscribed to the most popular source of advice at the time, *Parents' Magazine*. With a circulation of 1 million, *Parents'*, according to sociologist Terry Strathman, "was ubiquitous, and during these years its publishers sought to reshape every aspect of home life to conform to 'the child's best interest.' " In the nineteen-forties this reshaping was based on a new permissive attitude to the rearing of children. Responding to strict, behaviorist methods of raising children that had prevailed in the twenties and thirties, *Parents'* increasingly advocated that children should decide for themselves when to sleep, eat, and play rather than adhere to the schedules and routines of parents. Punishment of any kind was looked upon as a "last resort," a sign of "failure on the part of the parent to prevent the development of a situation to the point where punishment is inevitable." Through "imposing *any* kind of punishment upon the child," Strathman notes, "the parent's behavior was seen as more suspect (and perhaps more irrational) than the child's."

Dr. Arnold Gesell was the researcher and author generally credited with introducing the idea of permissive child rearing, and whose work and insights Dr. Benjamin Spock was to draw upon and popularize in the late nineteen-forties. According to Morton Sobell, it was Gesell's book, *Infant and Child in the Culture of Today* (with co-author Frances L. Ilg) that was most often followed by parents in Sobell's group of friends. Gesell not only influenced mothers directly through his books, but as one of the most prominent advisory editors of *Parents' Magazine*, he had a sizable impact on that periodical's substantive direction.

Parents' Magazine and *Infant and Child in the Culture of Today* suggested that there were right and wrong methods to raise a child, and that these methods were arrived at through scientific study and observation. As the founder of the Yale Clinic of Child Development, Gesell derived behavioral summaries of a child through every stage of its development. According to him, "The summaries then become standards of reference for estimating the maturity of the observed behavior in children. . . . An approximate estimate is arrived at by the simple method of best fit."

This seemingly scientific exactitude probably had a certain appeal for Ethel. Like most new mothers searching for help in understanding their children, Ethel must have felt some degree of support from these authors who were regarded as "experts" in raising children. Yet it seems as though she responded to what she read with a zeal and reverence bordering on the extreme. She thoroughly believed what she read without hesitation.

In fact, Ethel already was used to this manner of thinking, for it was not unlike that presented by the Communist party. The world was understandable through laws arrived at through scientific methodology and interpreted by experts—Lenin, Stalin, and to a lesser degree, Browder and Foster. Complicated world events could be comprehended only through the application of scientific socialism, although only the CP "expert" was typically able to make such application. Ethel generally believed what she read in the Party press and seems to have believed what she read in *Parents' Magazine*. She had faith in the superiority and objectivity of "science," and both the Party press and the child-rearing literature she consumed claimed exclusive rights to scientific understanding in their respective fields.

Reverence for the scientific expert can, of course, diminish one's ability to act and think autonomously. If the experts have a monopoly on the truth, lay people can only be dependent followers and foot soldiers. Some have suggested that this was Ethel's relationship to the Communist party. What seems to be true is that this also was her relationship to the child-rearing expert.

According to Elizabeth Phillips, one of her psychotherapists from the late nineteen-forties, Ethel was extremely "dependent" and "naive" in her attitude toward expert advice. She believed if she did "all the right things" she could be a "supermom," but in reality "was so naive, and that's how I perceived her, as completely naive, a person whose heart was in the right place but didn't know how to get from one to two. . . ." Ethel took the tenets of permissive child rearing to be unquestionable, scientific truths. If punishing a child was deemed "a failure on the part of the parent," Ethel undoubtedly vowed to banish punishment of any kind from her relationship to Michael. "It was kind of the misrepresentation of Spock," Phillips notes.

In addition to permissiveness, another strain in the child-rearing literature of the time to which Ethel would have been particularly sensitive was the theme of democracy as an ideal for the American family. In response to the spread of fascism throughout the western world, the virtues of a democratic, nonhierarchical family were set against the horrors that could result from authoritarian homes believed to produce goose-stepping Nazis. The war transformed "child raising from a problem in hygiene or psychology to a political struggle; *our* system had to be defended against *theirs*." The idea that child rearing was more than a diversion from political work but rather a fundamental, yet personal means of combating fascism must have appealed to Ethel due to her hatred of fascism, and because of the implicit political importance it conferred on her new role as full-time mother. Thus the political implication of child rearing, such as that referred to in the following example from the introduction to Gesell and Ilg's *Infant and Child in the Culture of Today*, may have influenced Ethel's beliefs about her relationship to her son.

> The spirit and organization of the family . . . reflect the historic culture. A totalitarian 'Kultur' subordinates the family completely to the state, fosters autocratic parent-child relationships, favors despotic discipline, and relaxes the tradition of monogamy. It is not concerned with the individual as a person. A democratic culture, on the contrary, affirms the dignity of the individual person. It exalts the

status of the family as a social group, favors reciprocity in parent-child relationships, and encourages humane discipline of the child through guidance and understanding.

Ethel adhered to the ideals of "humane discipline" and "parent-child reciprocity" not merely by forgoing punishment of virtually any kind, but by trying to equalize the relationship between herself and Michael as much as possible. Rather than being an autocratic parent, Ethel attempted to be a kind, accessible "baby-sitter" according to Elizabeth Phillips. "She tried to get on a 'baby-sitter level' with him. . . . She wanted to make life good for him in the way a baby-sitter wants to make the evening good. . . ."

A neighbor at Knickerbocker Village describes an incident which at the time was inexplicable, but in some part may be understood in light of Ethel's wish to diminish the "undemocratic" gulf that separated her from her son.

One day—the boys [her son and Michael] were two, three years old—she [Ethel] asked to bring Michael to play with Steve because he liked Steve. . . . So she had never asked me before. As I said, she never talked to anybody and I was very surprised, but you know, I was friendly. So I said, "Come up," and she came up to my house and she sat down on the floor and played with the children. She did not say three words to me. . . . I was just astounded. . . . You would think she'd sit and talk and watch them. . . . Whatever toys my son brought out—the blocks—she'd help them build. She was there maybe two hours, and I'm sitting there, and I finally I just took a book and read it. . . . So she was a very peculiar girl.

To others she may have seemed "peculiar," but Ethel honestly believed she was "doing all the right things," following the experts' advice in an attempt to be a "supermom."

Certainly Ethel's rather extreme interpretation of the permissive child-rearing literature cannot be the only reason that she consistently refused to punish Michael and had such difficulty in managing her son. Another possible motive may lie in her conscious desire to make Michael's childhood better than what her own had been, to correct or compensate for what she considered her mother's many grievous errors in raising her. Ethel was quite explicit about this.

She "felt she was raised in a strict way, [and] did not want to be a stern disciplinarian. She wanted her children to be raised differently than she had been raised." In many ways, Ethel continued to see her mother as a "witch" who had flagrantly favored her brothers, restricted her involvement in anything outside the family, and denigrated her accomplishments. Just as she had rebelled against her mother's way of life as an adolescent and young adult, she now rebelled against her mother's way of taking care of her. If her mother had been strict, she would be permissive; if her mother had neglected her, she would devote herself to Michael; if her mother had discouraged her creativity, she would see to it that her son's flourished, and so on. In short, she wanted to be the perfect mother; "she had enormously high standards" by which she judged her success as a parent.

A neighbor from Knickerbocker Village recalls, "Never did I see such patience as Ethel had. . . . When my boy would return from their [the Rosenbergs'] house he'd expect me to drop everything, even if I was in the midst of making a cake or sewing, and 'play with us like Ethel does.' "

While Ethel's wish to be a perfect mother is understandable, particularly in light of how she viewed her own unhappy childhood, her idea of what a perfect mother was seems unrealistic. For her, a perfect mother never frustrated her child because she could gratify his every need. Setting limits, disciplining and punishing—the acts that cause children to cry—were tantamount to being a bad mother. Perhaps in her drive to undo and compensate for her mother's inadequacies, she was unwilling or unable to understand that all of a child's needs cannot be gratified, that children often want limits and need to know that a parent is capable of setting them. Some of this is revealed in Michael's own recollections of his childhood:

> I had a tremendous sense of being the center of the universe. Of course most infants have this outlook and gradually and tenderly they are disabused of it by experience. . . . I was catching on very, very slowly—too slowly. . . . She [Ethel] generally dealt with me by giving me what I wanted. If I fussed over meals, she rarely made me leave the table; instead, she tried to make a game out of eating. I was a wild lion and she a lion tamer who danced around me and

fed me scraps of meat as I 'performed.' That was her way
of having me eat and keeping me happy. . . . As I demanded
more of her time, pushed further against her nonexistent
limits, I became a very tense child.

Michael, however, was not the only one who was becoming increasingly tense. Despite the unerring patience and self-denial she evinced with her son, Ethel became ever more upset and angry. Often at the end of a long and arduous period of attempting unsuccessfully to be the perfect mother to her demanding, precocious son, she would spank Michael or lash out in anger at anyone who was around, typically Julie or a member of the Greenglass family. Afterward she would feel enormously guilty and remorseful.

Given Ethel's rigid standards about the harmfulness of punishment and the endless days and weeks she spent being "democratic," patient and unceasingly understanding with her child, her sudden, angry outbursts must have made her feel wretched about herself and her ability to be the perfect mother. Although these instances seem to have been rather rare, given that only Julie, Ethel's psychiatrist, and Michael make any reference to them, they do perhaps reveal what was another reason for Ethel's inability to control Michael and her normal refusal to mete out punishment.

Ethel may have felt so negatively about disciplining children—to the point of reprimanding a neighbor for scolding her own son—because she felt guilty for secretly having the very strong urge to do so herself. "The lady doth protest too much, methinks." Certainly in ascribing such unconscious motivation to a person who is unable to speak for herself, we are on shaky ground. Nonetheless, Julie referred repeatedly to her seething anger; her psychiatrist acknowledges her "pent-up anger" and states that she was "caught-up in her anger," and Michael distinctly remembers being repeatedly spanked for disobedience. Although most people do not like to see a child punished or cry, Ethel's extreme reaction, her typical refusal to discipline Michael and her oversolicitousness toward him whenever he was in any kind of discomfort or distress reasonably raises the question of what motivated this kind of reaction. It may be that she was only following what the advice literature urged or was seeking to reverse what her mother had done to her. It also seems possible that she was afraid of or guilty about her anger toward her son. Since there are no earlier references to Ethel's fits of temper, it may be that the birth of her first child reawakened a long-silenced anger that may have had its origins in Ethel's feelings toward her own family.

Did Michael's childhood frustrations and tantrums unconsciously reevoke or even consciously remind Ethel of the enormous frustration and rage she had experienced in relation to her mother and brothers? If this is true, once reawakened it may have been difficult for Ethel to repress or forget. Alternatively, it is possible that despite her resolve to make Michael's childhood wholly unlike her own, she occasionally expressed the same sort of hostility that had been directed toward her by her own mother and brothers. Some would call this an unconscious "identification with the aggressor," and the psychological literature is replete with examples of such identifications. Despite a parent's intentions, she or he may act in ways that can only be understood in light of her or his own childhood. Child psychologist Selma Fraiberg describes this phenomenon nicely: "In every nursery there are ghosts. They are the visitors from the unremembered past of the parents. . . . Even among families where the love bonds are stable and strong, the intruders from the parental past may break through the magic circle in an unguarded moment, and a parent and his child may find themselves reenacting a moment or a scene from another time with another set of characters." To say this is what may have occurred for Ethel is indeed speculative, yet it gives us one more possible level on which to understand the genesis of the problem that was swiftly coming to dominate Ethel's life.

As 1944 progressed, Ethel moved further into the private world of mothering and family life. Her connections to political work diminished as Julie continued to be away from home, leaving her alone to care for Michael, and curtailing the visits of political friends and associates whom he had brought into their apartment.

As though heralding the end of an era, the CP branch in which Julie had been active was ending. According to Nat Sussman, who had been in the branch, "the Industrial Division headquarters of the Party issued transfer cards to neighborhood units," thus sending members into new and different CP groups. In February, Branch 16B held a farewell party for itself at a restaurant in the city, and Ethel provided the entertainment by singing. It is doubtful, however, that either Julie or Ethel had been very involved with the branch in the past eleven months. The group typically met on a week-night, and this was precisely when Julie was most often on assignment outside New York City. It is unlikely that Ethel attended meetings without her husband before Michael's birth, and it seems improbable that she would do so after he was born. Nevertheless, the branch's close may have had a certain poignancy for Ethel, given her present isolation from organized political work. This is not to say that she suddenly lost interest in the Party or its activities. She continued to read and follow the *Daily Worker* and still tried to attend Madison Square Garden rallies. These were slender threads, however, when compared to the texture of her active political involvement prior to Michael's birth.

In the spring of 1944, Julie took vacation time off from the Signal Corps to accompany Ethel and Michael on a visit to Mike and Ann Sidorovich's home in Chappaqua, New York. Ethel had still not found anyone with whom she could talk as freely as she had with Ann, so this was probably a much anticipated event. She had taken Michael to Chappaqua for a brief stay during the previous summer to escape Manhattan's heat and humidity and to find the companionship she lacked at home. This time, having Julie with whom to enjoy the semirural environment and the Sidorovichs' company, must have made it a happy retreat for Ethel, although we do not know how well Michael adapted to the new environment.

Shortly after the Rosenbergs returned home, Julie was sent to Washington, D.C., to receive training at the Bureau of Standards for the newest inspection assignment he had received. He had been stationed at last in Manhattan, at Emerson Radio and Phonograph Company, but he was not fully able to supervise inspection on some of the equipment the company manufactured. Apparently, the Bureau of Standards offered the necessary training on this equipment, so Julie spent the latter half of June once again separated from Ethel and Michael.

When he returned at the beginning of July, he found Ethel more exhausted than ever in her increasingly futile attempts to control Michael. Their son was now walking and talking, and his new abilities gave him newly discovered means to resist his mother. He refused to eat what was prepared for him; he never wanted to go to sleep; he defiantly did what his parents asked him not to. Simultaneously, he constantly demanded his mother's attention, breaking into outraged cries if she failed to gratify his wishes. The apartment was in complete disarray. Ethel adamantly believed that

160 "children were more important than the house," so that Michael's toys, projects, and possessions virtually covered the floors. Neighbor Ruby Goldstein was appalled when she looked into the Rosenbergs' apartment since they "took no care of their home . . . [it] was very upset and untidy." To add to the household confusion, Ethel had decided that Michael needed his own room, something the middle-class child-rearing literature assumed was prerequisite for normal child development. Typically, Julie followed Ethel's lead on any matter related to their son, so he and Ethel dutifully dispersed their belongings throughout the house and began to sleep on the studio couch in the living room, while Michael took possession of the bedroom. Apartment GE-11 became visual evidence of how much Michael had become the "center of the universe" for Ethel, how she now "was literally a mother 24 hours out of 24."

In the midst of the continual tension in Ethel's relationship to her son, exacerbated by the summer heat, a stuffy apartment and Michael's increased mobility, Julie's sister, Ethel, called, asking the Rosenbergs to share a bungalow with her family for the remainder of the summer. Although they had never indulged in such a luxury before, Ethel and Julie agreed that this was something their small family desperately needed. A few months in the country where they could breathe fresh air, Mike could run freely, and Ethel could have her sister-in-law's companionship seemed to outweigh the financial costs. Of course, Julie could only come out for the weekends and would have to live by himself during the week, but both he and Ethel had grown accustomed to being apart.

Ethel and her husband, Oscar Goldberg, had rented a pleasant two-story, green-shingled house on Baker Lane in Budd Lake, New Jersey. Located in the north-central part of the state, it was roughly forty-five miles from the city. Oscar, who was fourteen years older than his wife and an immigrant from Poland, was a successful grocer in Maspeth, Queens. The two couples got along well, although the Goldbergs had a much higher standard of living than the Rosenbergs and were not at all interested in politics. Julie always had considered Ethel his favorite sibling. Closest in age, she had a lively sense of humor, was extremely outgoing, and could be quite forceful about subjects that mattered to her. In contrast to both their other brother and sister, Dave and Lena, who were rather introverted and low key, Ethel and Julie seemed more like kindred spirits in their exuberance, humor, and ability to hold forth.

In many ways Ethel's husband, Oscar, was removed from the

Rosenbergs in age, background, and disposition, but he admired
Julie for his college education and his knowledge of world events.
As a Jew whose entire family was to perish at the hands of the Nazis
and their collaborators by the end of the war, Oscar was preoccupied with the events in Eastern Europe. This, of course, was a
subject Julie read about daily, so the two men often passed hours
absorbed in conversation.

The vacation started off badly, however. When they arrived the
cesspool was overflowing and the refrigerator did not work. They
were paying $375 for two months' rent, yet they were subjected to
foul odors and were forced to go shopping every day for food. Ethel
Rosenberg's back, which occasionally gave her trouble, now seemed
to have gone into some kind of spasm or strain, and she was in
constant pain, although she "suffered in quiet." Worst of all, Mike
did not adjust well either to his new environment or the company
of his aunt's children. He cried "24 hours a day." What Ethel
Goldberg could not understand was why Ethel allowed Michael to
do anything he wanted: "He would throw things around, drive me
crazy; I couldn't take it. Not a word from her and Julie was the
same way. . . . I went to Budd Lake and had a miserable time there
because of Michael's behavior."

Household tension and commotion grew during the weekends.
Not only were Julie and Oscar then present, but both the Goldbergs
and the Rosenbergs invited members of their respective families to
visit. Sophie and Harry Rosenberg accepted an invitation, and it
was depressing to see how Harry's health had deteriorated over the
past few years. He had had a serious kidney ailment since 1941,
and now, removed from the familiar environs of the Lower East
Side, amidst the sunshine and greenery of Budd Lake, he looked
old and weak. Tessie and Barney also came for a weekend. Both
of them also seemed older in the outdoors. Tessie had begun to
walk with a noticeable stoop, and Barney had become obviously
senile. Ethel was extremely patient with her enfeebled father, whereas
Tessie was usually exasperated and angry over her husband's often
stupid behavior and his inability to remember things. Ethel quietly
came to his rescue, as the following incident demonstrates: "He
came to Budd Lake once, and he came out with his bathing suit
with his penis sticking out. Ethel went up to him and gently told
him. . . . Ethel loved her father. She was a good daughter."

At last, with the arrival of the Labor Day weekend, the Rosenbergs and the Goldbergs packed their possessions and returned to

New York City. Ethel Goldberg was relieved to be rid of Michael, his crying, his constant need for attention, and his insistence on getting his own way. Ethel Rosenberg came away convinced that something was terribly wrong with her as a mother and with Michael as a child. The articles and books she had read on child rearing simply were not enough; she needed more formal instruction. She looked for classes that might be helpful and enrolled in one at the New School for Social Research on "The Child—From Birth to Six Years." The class met once a week for two hours and was taught by Eleanor Reich and Edith Buxbaum.

At the beginning of October, Ethel sat in a classroom for the first time in thirteen years. Just as she had loved school and found it a means of escape from an unhappy home life, she relished the course at the New School which gave her new tools for understanding her present difficulties at home. Just as she had respected her teachers at Seward Park High as unquestioned authorities, she now listened to her instructors and accepted their perspective on child rearing.

Although there is no extant syllabus from the course, it is possible to get a good idea of the general orientation of the class by looking at Edith Buxbaum's book, *Your Child Makes Sense* (1949). According to Buxbaum, this book "originated in a series of lectures and seminars on child development, which I gave to groups of parents and teachers in different schools, including most recently some from the New School of Social Research in New York."

Edith Buxbaum had studied psychoanalysis at "the Vienna Institute of Psychoanalysis, in the group over which Freud personally presided for a long time; Anna Freud conducted the seminar on the analysis of children and adolescents in which I participated." The purpose of *Your Child Makes Sense*, which makes it possible to imagine the course on which it was based, was to introduce a psychoanalytic perspective on child development into the average American family. By so doing, Buxbaum attempts to show that childhood conflict—between the child and its environment, and within the child itself—is a normal result of unconsciously based and universal instinctual urges. Although many of Buxbaum's ideas have now become unquestioned assumptions in our thinking about child development, her emphasis on guidance rather than control, and her belief that "children know best," mark her work as one of the most permissive child-rearing tracts. There is little question as to who in the family is prone to mistakes and must sacrifice and compromise in order for proper child development: the mother.

> *Although we tend to think, 'mother knows best what's good for the child'—actually, the healthy baby knows even better. . . . Children have their own needs. From the first day on they let their mothers know what those needs are. As they get older their desires become more complex and more difficult to fulfill. However, when the mother is willing to learn from the child and to follow his lead in his training and education, they may all live happily ever after. . . .*
>
> *If we want our children to be physically healthy, happy in their relations with people, able to function at the highest level of their abilities and able to control their instincts adequately through their conscience we must provide the opportunity for them to do so. We can assist their development by the use of guidance rather than by the use of control which means superimposing our ideas upon them with the help of punishment. Children who grow up establishing a sound control of their emotions are likely to become the kind of adults who may be able to build the true democracy which we all wish to achieve: a democracy governed by intelligence and free of the errors brought on by irrational fears.*

Here were the themes that *Parents' Magazine* had presented in somewhat diluted form: the importance of a mother's subservience to her child's needs, childhood determinism, the injustice of punishment, emphasis on the rearing of *democratic* children through not "superimposing our ideas upon them." Buxbaum, however, did not rest her case on some isolated studies at the Yale Clinic of Child Development (as did Arnold Gesell), or on idiosyncratic observations of children through a pediatric or psychology practice, but rather on the weight of the fifty-year-old tradition of psychoanalysis. While a Freudian perspective had been creeping into standard child-rearing advice for some years, once fascism began to force analytically trained clinicians and educators to flee Europe for the United States, psychoanalysis established a strong foothold in the American ideology of how to bring up children.

The effect on mothers of Buxbaum's psychoanalytic proselytizing was often detrimental. As author Daniel Beekman points out, "Unfortunately, misinterpreting these theories, the tendency was all too often to avoid frustrating the child at whatever cost in frustration to the parent. . . . Instead of simplifying the relationship between mother and child, this vision of the child's emotional fragility encouraged the mother to be more anxious rather than less."

Whether or not Beekman's assessment has universal applicability is uncertain, but it may correctly describe Ethel's experience of Edith Buxbaum's class. By November, Ethel had reached the nadir of her relationship with Michael. At twenty months he was worse than ever—defiant, demanding, constantly crying, sick, unmanageable. Ethel's back was killing her; she began to suffer from terrible headaches and often felt dizzy. It seemed as though she could not go on like this. In 1951, during her trial testimony, she described this period in the following terms:

> A. *Well, it so happens that I have had a spinal curvature since I was about 13 and every once in a while that has given me some trouble, and at that time [fall 1944] it began to kick up again, and occasionally I have to get into bed and nurse a severe backache. Through the bargain, I developed a case of low blood pressure, and that used to give me dizzy spells, sometimes to the point where I almost fainted. I also had very severe headaches, and it finally got so bad that I went to visit my doctor. . . .*
>
> Q. *Now, during that period how old was your first born baby? . . .*
>
> The Witness: *It was right after he was a year and a half old. From a year and a half to the time he was two.*
>
> Q. *And what was the condition of your child's health? . . .*
>
> A. *The condition of my child was very poor. I had had a very difficult time ever since his birth, I mean, with him. . . . By the time he was a year and a half old, that winter was extremely severe, the winter between the time he was a year and a half to two.*

Since the attorney then led her testimony in a different direction, we never learn how Ethel would have linked her physical symptoms to Michael's experience between the time he was one-and-a-half and two years of age. Nonetheless, that they were linked for her is evident from the fact that this line of questioning was conducted by Ethel's lawyer, indicating that she had previously described the circumstances of fall 1944 to him. He undoubtedly connected Ethel's and Michael's conditions through his questions because this is how he had learned of them.

Ethel's symptoms—her backache, headaches, and dizzy spells— caused her to take to her bed, not just occasionally, but for most of the time from November 1944 through March 1945. During this period she was unable to do any housework and found it difficult to take care of Michael for any length of time.

Directly after she returned home from Budd Lake, Ethel had called Bertha Britain who had helped her out for the month after Michael's birth. She wanted someone to come in and clean the house while her back was bothering her. Bertha was moving to Boston and recommended an older woman, Evelyn Cox, whom Ethel immediately hired at 75 cents an hour. As the months progressed and Ethel developed her headaches and dizziness, Mrs. Cox began working Mondays, Wednesdays, and Fridays from ten in the morning until four in the afternoon. She cleaned, washed, mended clothes, and cared for Michael. Since Julie was now working in Manhattan, he usually left for work about 8:30 A.M. and returned home by 5:30 P.M. Thus he often was able to supervise Michael when Mrs. Cox was not present.

Ethel's physical problems had the effect of separating her from her son. Her poor health was a legitimate reason from her, Julie's, her family's, and probably even Edith Buxbaum's point of view to cease caring for Michael on a full-time basis. Therefore her illness sounds not wholly unlike that of women in the late nineteenth and early twentieth centuries who developed "hysterical" physical symptoms as a means of opting out of restrictive lives and responsibilities.

This is not to say that Ethel, or nineteenth-century "hysterics," consciously feigned their maladies to deceive those around them. As all informed studies of hysteria and psychosomatic illness indicate, the origin of physical problems remains mysterious to their subject and bears little or no psychological meaning of which the subject is consciously aware. In the nineteenth century, middle-class women developed curious symptoms such as headaches, dizziness, weakness, numbness when there were no other acceptable means of protesting their situations and when their socialization prevented them from having the ability to conceptualize the source of their discontent. Although Ethel certainly was no nineteenth-century Victorian, by the fall of 1944 she seems to have become overwhelmed by her responsibilities as a mother and to have lacked the emotional or intellectual resources to see beyond her circumstances. Within a very short period of time, her life had been transformed from one deeply involved in the world of politics, service, and networks of friends and acquaintances, to one focused entirely on a small, troublesome child. She had made this "choice," but it was one selected from a field that—for Ethel—probably contained no alternative options. She had been raised in a culture that held women's ultimate identity to be that of mother; child-rearing experts confirmed this view and asserted an unquestioned cause-and-effect relationship between a woman's mothering abilities and the emotional health of her offspring. Even the Communist party did nothing to challenge such ideas. Although the Party denounced women's subservient roles, as historian James Weinstein points out, this sentiment conflicted with the more fundamental Communist "emphasis on party members living like 'ordinary workers'. . . ." Ethel had taken all these societal prescriptions a step further through her desire to be a "perfect mother." Yet the more she strove for perfection—through almost never disciplining or frustrating her child and directing all her creative energies toward him—the more Michael's behavior and her own angry outbursts reflected back to her, her own imperfections.

11

HARD TIMES

During Ethel's illness, Julie seems to have been only too willing to assume some of Ethel's duties and to pay for Mrs. Cox's services. His salary was higher than ever, $3,600 a year, so he could afford the relative luxury of employing a maid. In fact, the Rosenbergs had been doing so well financially that Julie became an investor in a development scheme hatched by some acquaintances in November 1944. Russell McNutt, Waldo's brother, and his brother-in-law Sigmund Diamond were purchasing a stretch of property along the Taconic State Parkway, intending to clear the land and build a community of homes. Julie invested between $1,000 and $1,500 in the Yorktown Development.

Julie's employment appeared utterly secure so he probably made his investment without worry. Although there continued to be dismissals in the Signal Corps based on alleged Communist affiliation, Julie had no reason to believe he was at risk since the successful resolution of his loyalty hearing nearly four years earlier. Consequently, it came as a complete surprise to him when, at the beginning of 1945, he was again the object of a loyalty investigation.

Since 1941 he had disguised his pro-Communist sympathies on the job. His first investigation had taught him a powerful lesson in discretion; there is no evidence that he broadcast the virtues of the

CP as he had prior to his loyalty hearing. What then had sparked the Signal Corps' renewed interest in his political beliefs?

Julie turned in desperation to the Intelligence Officer of the Newark Signal Corps in an attempt to discover the reason for the investigation. Captain John Henderson responded sympathetically. He showed Julie a copy of a summary prepared on him by security investigators. This referred to Julie's membership in the Communist party, his transfer from one unit to another within the CP, and his membership in FAECT, a union suspected of Communist affiliation. Julie was indignant. Here were the same allegations of CP membership without substantive proof that he had faced in 1941. Now, however, the Army also was trying to dismiss him on the basis of his membership in a legal labor union, chartered under the CIO.

Julie intended to fight this blatantly antilabor charge. He would deny Communist sympathies, just as he had in 1941, and demonstrate that he could not be dismissed for simply belonging to a union. He would enlist his FAECT brothers; Victor Rabinowitz, the union's attorney; perhaps even his congressman, Samuel Dickstein. Without proof of CP membership, the whole investigation could be shown to be an unwarranted attack on his legal right to belong to a labor union. He actively began to gather support for a delegation of FAECT members to protest what appeared to be a totally unfair inquiry.

What Julius Rosenberg did not know as he worked to challenge the findings against him was that the Signal Corps had not initiated an investigation into his background on the basis of the same circumstantial evidence that it possessed in 1941, or because of his union membership. Rather, it proceeded at the instigation of the FBI. That agency had forwarded to U.S. Army Intelligence a photostatic copy of a CP membership card showing that a Julius Rosenberg had enlisted in the Party on 12 December 1939. Army Intelligence believed that this was insufficient evidence to prove that the Julius Rosenberg indicated on the card was synonymous with their Signal Corps employee. The FBI persisted, however, and in the fall of 1944 sent Army Intelligence yet another photostat. This one was a copy of a card showing a Julius Rosenberg's transfer to the Communist party's East Side Party Club. The Army was now convinced because their employee's address appeared on the card.

On the basis of this new, concrete evidence, the Army ordered a loyalty investigation. The summary of this investigation, which Julie was shown, made no mention of the photostats the Army had in its possession. As a result, Julie genuinely believed that the only real evidence the Signal Corps had against him was his open membership in FAECT. He thus felt free to proclaim in a letter to Captain Henderson, which Ethel undoubtedly typed:

> *I am not now, and never have been a communist member.*
> *I know nothing about communist branches, divisions, clubs*
> *or transfers. I never heard either of the Division or the Club*
> *referred to. I had nothing to do with the so-called transfer.*
> *Either the charge is based on a case of mistaken identity or*
> *a complete falsehood. In any event, it certainly has not the*
> *slightest basis in fact.*

He had boldly lied in 1941 and that had succeeded in saving his job. Apparently he believed the same tactic would work in 1945. He seemed thoroughly oblivious, however, to the enormous network of informers that had infiltrated the Communist party and the FBI's unceasing interest in ferreting out CP members and sympathizers from any kind of government employment. As historian Maurice Isserman points out, World War II depleted the Party of many of its most experienced members through enlistment and induction into the armed forces. One "consequence of the CP's wartime shortage of experienced cadres was the ease with which government informers now found it possible to move up in the party hierarchy. . . . In May 1942, CP waterfront leader Al Lannon wrote: 'We must follow a bold policy of promotion of comrades from the ranks even without any previous experience, who show possibilities for development.' " The fact that these "comrades" were often government informers is shown by the large number of informants who surfaced in the late nineteen-forties and early nineteen-fifties to testify against former and current CP members that they had known or befriended. According to Ronald Radosh and Joyce Milton, it was "almost certainly" an informer within the Party who alerted the FBI to Julius Rosenberg's membership in Branch 16B.

Julie knew none of this. He possessed a profound, albeit naive, faith in people. He also believed the Popular Front ideology that the American legal system under the Roosevelt administration was ultimately a fair one. Thus when he was notified on 9 February 1945 that he had been placed on "indefinite suspension" from the Signal Corps, he was simultaneously outraged and convinced he would inevitably win reinstatement.

As the chairman of FAECT's Federal Civil Service Committee, Julie had repeatedly and unstintingly fought for the reinstatements of union brothers who had been dismissed by the federal government. Now that the case was his own, we can only imagine the energy and emotional resources he summoned to defend himself. He organized a delegation of FAECT men that formally protested to the Army Signal Corps. He fired off letters to the union's attorney and Captain Henderson. He lodged a formal appeal. All, however, was in vain. On 26 March his employment with the Signal Corps was officially terminated.

Unable to accept what he believed to be a completely unjust and illegal firing, and afraid that the grounds on which he was terminated would permanently hinder his future job possibilities, Julie decided to seek the assistance of his congressman. After unsuccessful attempts to reach him at his New York home and office, in April, Julie took the train to Washington to see Samuel Dickstein in person. Again, he was stymied. Congressman Dickstein was not in his office and was thought by his staff to be in New York. Julie then called an old friend from CCNY, Max Elitcher, who drove him to a federal workers' union hall. Here he discovered where to find some union officials who could help him appeal his case and who could perhaps accompany him to a meeting with Dickstein. Julie dutifully took a trolley to the offices of these officials, but found out that they too were not at work. Disappointed, he took the train back to New York the evening of the day he had arrived.

This journey of missed opportunities provides some insight into how Julius Rosenberg thought about and reacted to the American legal system. First, he seems to have had a fundamental faith in the fairness of the United States government. Rather than harboring a cynical view of how the "system" or "big government" worked, he believed that an injustice—his dismissal—could be rectified if his elected representative could hear his logical explanation of what was unfair about his firing. From Julie's viewpoint there seemed to be nothing systemically unjust; rather, some individuals within the government had acted unfairly, and their error needed to be rectified. Ultimately, if the facts were known, if the injustice was revealed in broad daylight, Julie believed he would be reinstated in the Signal Corps.

Second, his Washington trip demonstrates his decided naiveté about how to act effectively in the world. He traveled to Washington on a Saturday, without previously making an appointment with

either his congressman or the union officials with whom he wished
to speak. He assumed he could call Samuel Dickstein from the train station and, upon summarizing his case on the phone, be asked to come over and confer with the congressman. Similarly, he had not previously contacted the union officials he wished to see. After learning their address while in Washington, he did not call them to see if he could meet with them, but traveled by public transportation to their office only to discover that they were out. His trip to the nation's capital was a failure. He went home, defeated by the seeming inaccessibility of the system in which he had placed his faith.

To what did Julie owe both this trust and naiveté? Clearly, he believed the Popular Front ideology of patriotism and faith in American democracy. In fact, by April 1945 the CPUSA had been transformed into the "Communist Political Association." Eleven months earlier, Earl Browder had orchestrated this metamorphosis, which made the Party into an association much like "all other democratic and progressive groupings which operated through the two party system. . . ." The feasibility of socialism was eschewed, and a new constitution banned any group from the CPA that "conspires or acts to subvert, undermine, weaken or overthrow any or all institutions of American democracy." More than ever, the Communists stated their adherence to the "traditions of Washington, Jefferson, Paine, Jackson and Lincoln." This renewed fervor for democracy, patriotism, and the celebration of the American heritage probably helped to ignite Julie's fantasies of a successful meeting in Washington with Samuel Dickstein. But, because so much of his understanding of the world was from reading, listening to speeches, and conversations with like-minded friends, many of his ideas were untempered by any lived experience. His unabashed idealism, his wholehearted faith in those he imbued with authority, ill-prepared him for a world that often bore little relation to what the *Daily Worker* portrayed. Just as he had been astonished at fifteen by the indifference of the rabbis he respected toward the plight of political prisoners, he was unprepared at twenty-six for the difficulties he encountered as he attempted to rectify the injustice he felt had been done to him.

After his defeat in Washington, Julie, according to a friend from FAECT, "tried for a year to drum up activity on his appeal." Unfortunately, his friend adds, "It was pretty clear the days were over when we could win reinstatements. So not much of a fight was put up on it."

Julie knew that a dismissal from government employment for being a Communist could haunt a man for life, ruin his career chances and exclude him from better-paying jobs. Thus it was probably a great relief to him when he was quickly hired by Emerson Radio and Phonograph Corporation to do research on new projects the company was designing for the Army and Navy. Emerson had been one of his assignments as a Signal Corps inspector, and he undoubtedly made such a positive impression through his ability or personality, that the circumstances under which he was forced to leave his former job did not matter.

Julie began work on 26 February 1945 at $70 a week, a salary comparable to what he had been earning in the Signal Corps. He soon received a raise to $77 a week, but since he was typically requested to work overtime, he averaged $100 a week. This was more money than Julie or Ethel had ever seen, but it came at a rather high cost. Julie now frequently worked until midnight and was often exhausted when he was at home. Yet he could purchase things for the family that only a few years before had seemed extravagant. He bought Ethel a $30 watch for her birthday and a $21 console table from Macy's, the only store-bought furniture the Rosenbergs acquired for their apartment. The Rosenbergs also purchased a used upright piano for $25 from another resident at Knickerbocker Village, who had advertised it through the tenants' paper, *The Knickerbocker Village News*. Now Ethel could play and sing once again in her home, which she had not done since she moved out of 64 Sheriff Street six years earlier.

Julie was doing so well financially that he and Ethel were able to rent their own bungalow for the summer in Lakewood, New Jersey. Despite the previous year's difficulties at Budd Lake, the attractions of spending the summer outside New York City were so great that Ethel and Julie were determined to repeat the experience. Ethel had not been bedridden since March, but she was still prone to frequent headaches, backaches, and often slept poorly. It was hoped that a summer in the country would have a curative effect.

When the Rosenbergs reached Lakewood, however, they found the bungalow they had rented to be too dirty to unpack their belongings. Having never rented a vacation home before, perhaps they did not know what to look for or how to arrange for what they wanted. The thought of staying in such a run-down, filthy environment seemed untenable. They turned to the only people they knew in the vicinity, Sonia and Ben Bach who lived about twenty miles away near Toms River. The Rosenbergs had been introduced to the Bachs years before by the Bachs' cousin Sylvia Steingart. Sonia and Ben were Jewish radicals, in or close to the Communist party, and, most importantly, they had a cottage on their property that they offered to the Rosenbergs as a place to stay until they could sort out what to do about the bungalow in Lakewood. This kind invitation was extended so that Ethel and Michael stayed for several weeks, while Julie visited on at least two weekends. Ethel and Michael eventually moved into a nearby rooming house that accommodated some thirty people. They continued to see Sonia and Ben on a regular basis, however, and strengthened a friendship that would serve them in an important way in the future.

———

The most important event of the summer came on 6 August 1945 when the United States announced that it had dropped the first atom bomb on Hiroshima, Japan, and obliterated that city. A second bomb was dropped on Nagasaki on 9 August. The world watched in disbelief, horror, and for some, relief. The United States had developed a weapon more powerful and more destructive than any previously imaginable. It had altered conventional warfare forever and demonstrated with shocking swiftness and force its newfound hegemony over other nations. It became known within days where and how the atom bomb had been developed. On a barren mesa, thirty miles from Santa Fe, New Mexico, stood "Site Y," a former boys' school where some of the best scientists in the world had labored in complete secrecy for two years to construct the most terrifying weapon then known to humanity. Here, at what was better known as Los Alamos, J. Robert Oppenheimer had led a group of some 6,000 people in the development of the atom bomb.

The dropping of the atom bombs effectively ended the Second World War and ushered in an enormous transformation in the way Americans lived, worked, and thought about the world. Upon returning home from overseas and after discharge from the armed forces, American servicemen married at a spectacular rate, moved to newly built suburbs, started raising families, and focused on the best means of getting ahead in the rapidly expanding American economy. Postwar prosperity allowed these newly created families to experience a vastly improved standard of living. For a generation that had come of age in the Depression, the second half of the nineteen-forties heralded a period of relative affluence that was unimaginable before the war. Of course, such affluence was not uniform; individuals and groups of people continued to be locked out of the postwar boom. Nonetheless, this newly gained prosperity was so widespread that suburban home ownership, at least one car in every garage, and access to the products of the greatly expanded postwar consumer industries moved within reach of most white Americans.

This new emphasis on family, career, and consumption affected members or followers of the Communist party as much as it did other Americans. Many CP adherents already had begun to question their allegiance to the Party during the war itself. As historian Maurice Isserman suggests, "For some, service in the armed forces had a dramatic impact on the way they looked at the world, lifting them out of parochial party circles, throwing them into direct, intimate contact with the 'masses' whom they had so often discussed in abstract or romantic terms." When the tenets of Marxist-Leninism were confronted by reality, they were often found to be sorely lacking. The "masses" were often thoroughly uninterested in Communist analyses. Without Party structures and networks to offer support and meaning, CP followers in the military often became critical of what they had formerly believed or simply found it irrelevant in their new environments. Thus, upon returning to civilian life, many let their memberships lapse and ceased to move in Party circles.

For others, however, postwar prosperity simply did not square with the Communist party, which so many people had joined either in hopes of altering the economic system that had engendered the Depression, or out of a desire to combat fascism. With what seemed to many as the permanent eradication of fascism as a global threat and the ascendance of economic well being, the reasons for maintaining ties to the Party were erased.

In fact, after the war the CP exacerbated its seeming irrelevance by taking a distinctly more orthodox Marxist-Leninist line, denying the possibility of a rising standard of living (despite continual evidence to the contrary), and anticipating an impending economic depression. Such grim predictions were not welcomed by a population increasingly enthralled with its new consumer goods, tract homes, and the purported joys of marital bliss.

Steve Nelson, who was a member of the Party's national board after the war, recalls that

> *despite our recognition of these changing cultural patterns, we were limited in what we could offer, for we were still trying to present a socialist vision based on the model of the Soviet Union. . . . The Party, which had historically been rooted in a heavily immigrant working-class culture characterized by economic insecurity and political alienation, was unable to adjust to these changes. We could not evaluate the changing composition of the work force and its new patterns of community life and consumption.*

The ethnic, working-class enclaves that had served as CP strongholds throughout its history were now declining as older members died and younger ones moved away. Thus, despite its ability to recruit new members directly after the war, the Party's backbone was weakening. Between mid-1944 and the beginning of 1946, 50,000 members had left the CPUSA.

Ethel and Julius Rosenberg were not to be part of this larger social trend. Although they had some middle-class aspirations, as evidenced by their summers in the country and their desire to provide every creative opportunity for their son, their inclusion in the postwar boom was forever stymied when Julie learned that he was to be laid off from Emerson Radio and Phonograph. Probably due to demobilization, the research that the company had been conducting for the Army and Navy was curtailed. Since this was the work for which Julie had been hired, his discharge probably had more to do with the war's end than with anything regarding his performance on the job.

Julie's prospects were not promising. Unlike most of his fellow graduates from the CCNY School of Engineering who had experienced employment difficulties because of their political affiliations, Julie had no real engineering ability on which to fall back. When someone such as Joel Barr was dismissed from the Signal Corps for signing a Communist nominating petition in 1942, he was able to find work at the Western Electric Company because of his outstanding engineering capabilities. Julie did not have such opportunities. He began to look for work, filling out job applications and giving as character references people whom he deemed respectable, such as Ethel's physician, Dr. Hart. He was not beyond exaggerating his abilities, as when he claimed that he could speak, read, and write Spanish, and could read French. He turned to friends and associates he had known through FAECT for help in finding him employment. Yet, there seemed little these friends could do. Here was a twenty-seven-year-old man who was not particularly skilled at engineering—his chosen field—and whose major employment experience was in the Army Signal Corps from which he had been fired for being a Communist. In what increasingly became a desperate search for work, Julie gave the impression (in the words of a friend from FAECT whom he used as a character reference) that "wherever he went there was a cloud over him, a shadow over him . . . he could not get employment."

With little hope of finding work, Julie's worst fears of what his Signal Corps dismissal would inflict were realized. Virtually all the engineering graduates he knew from CCNY were embarking on successful careers. Morton Sobell worked for General Electric; Joel Barr had just resigned from Western Electric to work toward his master's degree in engineering at Columbia University; William Mutterperl had worked at the National Advisory Committee for Aeronautics since 1940 and was advancing rapidly; Max Elitcher continued his employment at the Navy's Bureau of Ordinance in Washington, and so on. Many friends were buying houses; neighbors at Knickerbocker Village were moving to the suburbs. His own brother was a successful pharmacist, and he could not even find a job.

There seemed to be only one alternative left—to start his own business. This required no job application, references, or questions about membership in the Communist party. Small business ownership had a long and respected history in the Jewish community; it was, in fact, something to which a great proportion of working-class Jews, including Julie's father, aspired. All that was needed was capital—and therefore partners.

The Greenglass brothers—Bernie and Dave—were the natural candidates to join Julie in business. They had virtually no plans for what they would do after the war and seemingly little ambition. After being discharged from the Army, Bernie had borrowed $5,000 from his uncles to invest in a firm called Radar Fabrics. Since this venture never got off the ground, Bernie had the money to invest elsewhere. Julie persuaded him to capitalize a small shop that would buy and sell surplus hardware such as screws, nuts, bolts, and wrenches. Julie would be responsible for attracting business through the many engineering contacts he had developed over the years from CCNY, FAECT, and the many places he had worked as a Signal Corps inspector.

Julie probably also wanted Dave as a partner, in part because he was very familiar with machinery and had been working as a machinist for the Army. He probably also sought him out since he had always taken a paternal role toward Dave, guiding and giving counsel to his impressionable and somewhat passive younger brother-in-law.

When Dave was a teenager, Julie had introduced him to the Young Communist League, which he joined and with which he became quite infatuated. He, in turn, enlisted Ruth in the organization. Neither Dave nor Ruth evidenced much understanding of Marxism, the Party's strategy, or current events, but they both possessed an adolescent zeal born of naiveté, inexperience, and an idealized and romantic vision of life as revolutionaries.

When Dave was inducted into the Army shortly after he and Ruth were married, he sorely missed the political discussions he had had with Julie and Ethel, and asked Ruth to send him the Rosenbergs' opinions on political matters. "Please don't delay in sending me the Browder speech," Dave implored his wife in a typical letter. "Find out from Ethel what she and Julie think about it."

In August 1944, Dave had been transferred to Los Alamos, New Mexico, to work on some unspecified "top secret" project. When he wrote to Ruth about it, he was nervous about disclosing any information, since it was "a classified top secrecy project and as such I can't say anything." He did however state, "Not a word to anybody about anything except maybe Julie." Julie probably was the most informed and worldly person Dave knew. He alone among Dave's family and friends could be expected to grasp the seriousness of Dave's assignment and offer suggestions regarding Dave's passion at Los Alamos—recruiting fellow GIs into the Communist party. As Dave informed Ruth, "I'll raise the red flag yet so don't worry about the future."

When Julie invested in the Yorktown Development later in the year, he asked Dave and Ruth to participate in the venture, anticipating that once the homes were built, they would occupy them and be neighbors. When Ruth wrote Dave of Julie's proposal, he happily replied: "I most certainly will be glad to be part of the community project that Julius and his friends have in mind. Count me in. . . ."

In September 1945, Dave came back to New York on furlough. He revealed that he had been working on the atomic bomb that had been dropped on Japan the previous month. Since the bomb had led to Japan's surrender, it seemed certain Dave would be discharged shortly, so the family venture was discussed and the necessary plans were made to set up the business. David was probably honored that Julie had included him in his plans and relieved that work would be waiting for him after he left the Army.

Julie had attracted another partner, his neighbor Izzy Goldstein, to enter the business as well. Each of the four—Julie, Bernie, Izzy, and Dave—would invest $1,000. The three relatives would assume Bernie's $5,000 debt among themselves, and they would use Barney Greenglass's old shop at 64 Sheriff Street to work. This would help them save on rent, and it would provide their small business with a storefront.

In December, after Julie was officially laid off from Emerson, United Purchasers and Distributors was opened. It must have been a complete failure, however, since the partners dissolved it only a few months later. They quickly regrouped and formed a new business, G and R Engineering Company. Named after Greenglass, Goldstein, and Rosenberg, G and R was a machine shop. Most of Bernie's $5,000 was used at this time to purchase machinery from the War Assets Administration, and since Dave Greenglass had been discharged from the Army at the end of February, he became the shop's principal machinist. The newly reformed company rented a shop at 200 East Second Street on the Lower East Side, and Julie, as president, began to hunt for jobs G and R could execute.

His quest, however, would never be successful. Although he was able to secure some work for the company, it was almost never enough to return a profit and pay the partners anything more than the most minimal salaries. Julie would never again see the kind of money that he had made in the Signal Corps or during his brief employment at Emerson Radio and Phonograph. From 1946 on, the Rosenbergs' standard of living declined, and their simplest desires for certain aspects of a middle-class life-style were permanently thwarted.

———

As many of their contemporaries drifted away from the Communist movement, Julie and Ethel cleaved to it. Their life in the postwar period did not focus on a new tract home, upward mobility, and the joys of suburban consumerism. Rather, they remained mired in the urban working class. The grim predictions of impending economic depression that were provided regularly by the *Daily Worker* may have seemed more realistic to them than to their better-heeled contemporaries. They remained residents of the Lower East Side both in actuality and in spirit. Julie did not have the experience of service in the armed forces to afford him a different perspective on life. His closest approximation to basic training had been his two-month training period at Fort Monmouth, New Jersey, where his closest friends had been fellow FAECT and CP members. Ethel did not have PTA meetings, play groups or the upkeep of a new home to focus her interests. She continued to live within the same three-mile radius that had constituted the geographic boundaries of her entire life. Relatively isolated within their ghetto, intent on the struggle to survive, and no longer as active as they had been politically, the Rosenbergs had little current experience by which to judge the increasingly extreme and dogmatic analyses of the *Daily Worker*, which they, of course, continued to read regularly.

Having deposed Earl Browder, who had led the Party during its most reformist, patriotic Popular Front years in the mid-thirties and early forties, the CP now had William Z. Foster as its leader. As the elder statesman of the Communist movement, Foster was thoroughly orthodox and deterministic in his outlook. Foster perceived Leninism as being as accurate in postwar America as it had been in 1915 Russia. His frame of reference was not the founding fathers or the American heritage of which Browder was so fond of speaking, but an impoverished working class following the glorious path of the Soviet Union. Once Foster firmly controlled the Party leadership, there was no more talk about shaking hands with J.P. Morgan to further American-Soviet friendship, as Browder had suggested at the end of 1943. Friendship and cooperation were not words in Foster's vocabulary, but the following from an article written in July 1946 were: "The axe must be applied to the root of the evil, the power of finance capital, the breeder of economic chaos, fascism and war, must be systematically weakened and eventually broken."

Words such as these may have given Julie solace in his gloomy economic situation, but there seems to be evidence that Ethel was less affected by their precarious finances than was her husband. She was used to poverty, unconcerned about her physical surroundings, and lacked material desires. What she did care about was how Julie's floundering career was affecting him. An old friend from FAECT recalls her imploring him to help find Julie some work for his business: "It happened that in 1946 or '47, I was in a job where I was in a position to throw some work his way. My family and I were living out of the city at the time and Julie came out to call on me to plead with me to try to get him some business. I decided I'd try to get him something, though it wouldn't be much—but that I wouldn't risk my job by recommending a place until I saw what they could turn out." Thus he visited G and R Engineering and met Dave Greenglass, whom Julie had described as "a smart technical man," for the first time.

> *I'm not saying there's anything criminal about being fat. I'm not saying there's anything criminal about being dirty. Or that if a man doesn't look you straight in the eye and give you a firm handshake that I know he's a crook.*
>
> *I'm not claiming to have been prophetic. But here I was, a good friend of Julie's. Greenglass probably knew I was anxious to do something to give them some business. He could at least have wiped the dirt off his hands and come up and given me a decent handshake. He was sulking . . . and Julie tried to pass it off with a 'don't mind him, he's like that sometimes.'*
>
> *We left the shop and I told Julie, 'I'm sorry, but I can't see a smart man there.' I felt like a heel but I didn't recommend his shop. It would have meant at most a $500 order, at that time. But I couldn't see competent work coming from a slovenly, shifty-eyed machinist like that one.*
>
> *I went out to dinner with Julie. I found he didn't have any money at all. I had to take his check, I remember.*

Some time later he met Ethel at a mutual friend's house. She pleaded with him to "do what you can to help Julie in the business."

People's memories of Ethel and Julie from this period confirm that they were not doing well. Another friend from FAECT who, as a bachelor would stay with the Rosenbergs when they lived in their furnished room on Avenue A, recalls visiting them after the war with his wife: "The few times we did see him at Knickerbocker Village, he would come in late from the shop, flop down in a chair, seem dead beat. Guess he was having a struggle there then and putting in long hours and feeling it. . . . Both of them seemed tired.

She was up with Michael a lot at night. He was taking very little money from the business at that time."

A Mrs. Berger, one of the Rosenbergs' neighbors at Knickerbocker Village, recalls that she felt sorry for Ethel because she was always so poorly dressed. Despite the fact that most of the tenants in the housing development had little money, Ethel "appeared to have less than the majority of them." The Rosenbergs were forced to start asking for credit from the Village Grocery and Dairy across the street from their apartment, since they often did not have the cash to pay for food. Mrs. Berger and another neighbor report that Ethel occasionally borrowed small food items that she never returned and for which she never reimbursed them.

The Rosenbergs' difficulties were exacerbated in the summer of 1946 when Julie's father had to be hospitalized. Although the two had not been particularly close for many years, Julie continued to respect his father despite Harry's displeasure at his son's involvement in the Communist party and his seeming inability to secure employment. Harry had been in ill health for the past five or six years, yet his family found it difficult to contend with his hospitalization. Sophie, Lena, and Ethel Goldberg were constantly overcome with tears, fits of crying, and unabashed grief that prevented them from doing little more than sobbing at Harry's bedside. Dave Rosenberg could do little to comfort his mother and sisters, nor did he seem to have the ability to give solace to his father or the time to visit frequently. The emotional leadership of the Rosenberg family thus fell to its youngest member who, according to his mother, "just moved over to the hospital and stayed night and day that last week; he had a good wife—she said, 'Go, that is where you must be.' " Harry Rosenberg died on 1 August 1946.

Although the Rosenbergs spent August mourning Harry's death, the month also brought with it another startling event: Ethel became pregnant once again. There is no information to indicate whether this pregnancy was planned or accidental, whether it was greeted with joy or resignation. Friends knew that Ethel wanted children, but after her experience with her first born and the family's current financial situation, it cannot be assumed that she wanted another child and at this point in time. Cultural prescription on every level, however, mandated at least two children per family, and child-rearing literature bemoaned the fate of the "only child." Michael was already three-and-a-half, and would be over four when his new brother or sister arrived—a space between children that was more than ample in these baby-boom years in which a mere two years between siblings was increasingly the norm. Further, if Ethel had wanted another child, it is unlikely that she would have let economic difficulties stand in her way. The year 1947 may not have been the best one for the Rosenbergs to support a new child, but it was unclear when, or even if, there would be a better time.

Whatever the initial circumstances surrounding this pregnancy, Ethel entered into it with her newly developed determination to do everything "right," that is, according to expert opinion. She was particularly concerned with Michael's reaction to her pregnancy and his ability to cope with a younger sibling. Having been the "center of the universe," Michael might find the arrival of a new baby a narcissistic blow from which it would be difficult to recover. Thus Ethel made every effort to prepare him well in advance of her delivery date for what to expect. Shortly before she went into the hospital, for example, she went to the expense of actually recording her voice so that Michael would not feel abandoned while she was away. Long before tape recorders were widely available consumer items, one of the only means of making a recording was to go to a recording studio. In her ninth month, Ethel took the subway to Times Square to visit Sanders Recordings on Sixth Avenue. Although she dressed so shabbily her neighbors pitied her and was often unable to find the cash to pay for groceries, Ethel chose to buy a Sanders recording disk imprinted with her message to her four-year-old son. The record was probably far more expensive than two weeks of groceries or a new dress, but it perfectly exemplifies Ethel Rosenberg's priorities.

12

"SHE WASN'T PART OF US"

When Ethel left for Beth Israel Hospital in the middle of May 1947 to bear her second child, she and Michael had never been apart for more than a few hours. He had grown from a crying, demanding, often inconsolable toddler into a hyperactive, extremely tense, and precocious child. A friend from FAECT remembers him as a "bright, fragile child, who, though too young to read, had memorized and recited captions below pictures in [an] entire book, ten or fifteen pages." Ruby Goldstein, the Rosenbergs' neighbor whose husband was a partner in G and R Engineering, remembers that Ethel would never leave her apartment without Michael:

> Ethel would stop and talk with the women in the building and after a few moments, Michael would insist on continuing to walk up the block or along the street, or Michael would insist on lighting a fire or doing some other mischief which would attract his mother's attention, and Ethel would leave the group after a short time. . . . The women in the neighborhood were annoyed with Ethel because they noted that whatever Michael wanted to do Ethel would permit him. . . . Michael would gather wood and paper that he found on the street and would insist on lighting a fire, and

though the mothers stated that he should not do so because it might blow and cause a larger fire, Ethel would permit Michael to light a fire.

Mother and son were quickly becoming pariahs in the domestic circles of Knickerbocker Village. Parents would not allow their children to play with Michael because if they did see him, they returned home unmanageable, whining "that Michael was allowed to do anything that he cared to." When interviewed by the FBI in 1950 and 1951, neighbors were unanimous in their assessment that Michael "could do anything he pleased" and that "Ethel exercised no control or discipline over him." Anna Lauffer, who lived next door to the Rosenbergs, complained that the family was very noisy because Michael "would play the phonograph as late as midnight and as early as five A.M." She discussed the problem with Ethel on "several occasions with no success, and as a result . . . tried to have as little to do with them as possible."

As an acutely sensitive, empathic woman, Ethel no doubt sensed the contempt and ridicule of the other mothers for her handling of Michael. She reacted as she had in the past: she feigned indifference. As a child she had pretended to be untouched and unhurt by what she perceived as her family's malice; as an adolescent who never dated, she impressed her girlfriends with how aloof she remained from boys and any discussions about them. Now, as a mother in a housing complex with literally hundreds of other mothers, she acted as though she was thoroughly disinterested in them or their companionship. The warm, immensely caring and thoughtful woman of the nineteen-thirties and early nineteen-forties, was increasingly known in her immediate neighborhood as cold and unfriendly. "It was not easy to be friendly with her . . . [Ethel did] not evidence any desire to become friendly with her neighbors." Ethel "wasn't a person who was part of the pack. She wasn't part of us. She was aloof from us. She was a loner; she never bothered with anyone; she was superior to us. . . . She acted as if she wouldn't deign to talk to us." Ethel was "nice but withdrawn from people around. . . . She was not outgoing; she did not reach out to people. . . . You couldn't get through a barrier there."

Yet, as her subsequent disclosures in therapy reflect, at this time Ethel was overwhelmed by anxiety for her son, herself, and their relationship. She probably was enormously hurt when her next-door neighbor, Anna Lauffer, virtually stopped talking with the Rosenbergs, and when such neighbors as Ruby Goldstein refused to let their children play with Michael. But, from Ethel's perspective, there may not have been any choice. She probably could not force Michael to turn down his phonograph so the Lauffers could sleep, just as she so frequently could not make him go to bed, or eat, or do any of the things she requested. If mothers did not want their children to play with Mike because of how unmanageable they were when they returned home, what was she to do? Her response was to disavow her need for acceptance among the Knickerbocker Village mothers and to become immersed in the permissive child-rearing literature of the day, which had explicit advice for her: "Steel yourself to family and friends who may argue that you are ruining your baby . . . develop a powerful indifference to their comments."

This then is the maternal environment into which Robert Harry Rosenberg was born on 14 May 1947. From the start, however, this wide-eyed, curly-haired boy was the opposite of his older brother. Robert, or Robby as he was affectionately called, "was a contented child." Undemanding, easily pacified, he came to be thought of by his parents as their normal child, in contrast to his older brother who Julie characterized in 1951 as being "very emotionally disturbed for quite a number of years."

This parental attitude obviously was perceived by Michael who became quite jealous of his younger brother. He simply could not tolerate the fuss being made over Robby and often threw tantrums when his mother was absorbed with his younger brother. Ethel tried new tactics to appease Michael. One such attempt was over the issue of putting her two children to sleep. So that Michael would not throw a tantrum as she nursed Robby and prepared him for bed, she gave him the run of the living room and the promise of staying up later. Helen Sobell, the wife of Julie's old college friend, was surprised that Ethel followed this procedure even when she was entertaining guests:

> One of the three times that I was over at the Rosenbergs' apartment . . . there was some question of Michael being jealous of Robby, and their putting Robby to sleep first and permitting Michael to stay up for a while longer. I remember they actually let Michael have the living room for awhile and we, the adults, went into the kitchen so that Michael could settle down separately from Robby before he went to sleep. . . . She had quite definite ideas in terms

of what methods were good or productive [regarding child rearing]. . . . She had done a lot of studying and a lot of thinking on the question of raising children.

Robby and Michael accompanied Ethel on almost every occasion— to the grocery store, her parents', or the rare visit to friends. Since the war's end and since Julie had renewed a number of acquaintances and friendships through his search for business for G and R Engineering, the Rosenbergs did have more people to their apartment than in the past. Yet Ethel's life remained focused almost entirely on her children, and even when the Rosenbergs did socialize with other couples, the conversation often centered on children and child rearing. Ethel's interest, according to occasional guest Morton Sobell, "was more than normal preoccupation, a deeper concern than other people manifested about whether she was bringing them up right."

The one person to whom Ethel seems to have confided her fears and anxieties about her ability as a mother was Vivian Glassman. One of the Rosenbergs' few friends still active in the Party, Vivian was a professional social worker. She had a bachelor's degree from Hunter College and had gone to graduate school at CCNY. Julie had known her from his Signal Corps training at Fort Monmouth. She had worked there and in fact met her fiancé, Joel Barr, there. In 1945, she was canvassing for the American Labor Party at Knickerbocker Village and knocked at the door of apartment GE-11. Although she may have met Ethel before this time, this was the first opportunity that the two had to talk together at length.

What Vivian offered Ethel was not only a friendship in which political matters could be discussed, but a comradeship in which Ethel could speak about psychology with someone who was a trained social worker. Through her attempt to better understand her son and her relationship to him, Ethel had become increasingly intrigued by the field of psychology. The Communist party generally referred to individual psychology with disdain and contempt. As historian Paul Lyons explains: "Party culture always eschewed psychological explanation, seeing it as a bourgeois smokescreen obfuscating the realities of the material and objective world. As a result, Communists often seem to have a poorly developed sense of dynamics of individual behavior that is not at the level of the rational, the material,

or the political." Thus Ethel had never known people who typically
talked about psychological motivation, unconscious mental life, or child development in a serious way. In fact, such a focus was generally frowned upon. Vivian challenged the CP's stereotypes. Reputed by the FBI to be a Party leader, she nonetheless made her living as a social worker and was quite willing to talk with Ethel at length about Michael and Ethel's problems with him. She became a regular visitor to the Rosenbergs', usually by herself but occasionally with Joel Barr before they ended their engagement and he left for Europe in 1948. She had enormous patience with Mike and took care of him the few times Ethel and Julie went out in the evening.

Vivian urged Ethel to take Michael to the Jewish Board of Guardians, a nonprofit organization for whom she had once worked that offered family therapy, charging on the basis of what a client could pay. After years of trying desperately to be a perfect mother, of devoting herself single-mindedly to Michael's care, growth, and education, and of constantly feeling like a failure, Ethel acquiesced. In November 1948, she made an appointment with the Jewish Board of Guardians to see a family therapist.

Seeking therapy for a child could easily be seen as a defeat. It meant that a mother was not able to manage her child's problems adequately. It was an open acknowledgement that a child, and perhaps the mother, had serious emotional difficulties. This was 1948 and most Americans were not yet familiar with psychotherapy as a means of helping adults, let alone children. The idea that a five-and-a-half-year-old boy might need or benefit from therapy probably seemed absurd or unfathomable to all but a small number of intellectuals and members of the avant-garde.

Seeing Ethel Rosenberg in 1948 wearing her cheap, shapeless housedresses inside her dusty apartment filled with second-hand furniture, one would never take her for either an intellectual or a trendsetter. She seemed unusual to her neighbors only in so far as she was poorer than most, aloof, and unable to discipline her son. Yet she did have an ambition that was not readily discernible. She was driven to "do right" by her children in the same way that she had been driven to be an actress and singer in her youth. Class, social convention, and the opinions of others were not the sort of issues that would prevent her from realizing a goal she truly wanted to achieve. One could say that Ethel's life's problem was not that she lacked initiative and drive but that she desired so little.

If intelligent people she respected, whether they were friends such as Vivian Glassman or authors whose articles she read, believed that psychotherapy would help Michael and her relationship to him, then he would see a therapist. As a first-generation American, Ethel had grown up with contempt for her parents' old-fashioned, superstitious ways of approaching life's problems. As a present-day adherent of scientific socialism, she placed her faith in scientific progress as historically necessary and ultimately beneficial. The idea of placing a five-and-a-half-year-old in therapy may have seemed novel or strange, but then so had every real scientific advance in the twentieth century.

This may have been Ethel's thinking along one plane, but it is probably not the most salient reason she made an appointment at the Jewish Board of Guardians. In truth, she was distraught about her relationship with her son, so much so that she had begun to think of giving him up to foster care. For Ethel to have entertained such a thought reveals an astounding level of hopelessness and desperation for her son and for herself as a mother. She completely accepted that she alone was responsible for Michael. If she could not satisfy her own internal needs to be a "perfect mother"; if she could no longer cope with her son's demands, his tantrums, his stubbornness; if she could not resist lashing out at him in anger any longer, Ethel could not think of what action to take other than the unspeakable act of giving up her child. Vivian's recommendation of psychotherapy may have represented a defeat, but more importantly it probably gave Ethel a hope that otherwise she could not have imagined.

When Ethel arrived at the Jewish Board of Guardians, she was interviewed by a social worker while Michael was given a battery of psychological and intelligence tests. Although this first encounter with the world of clinical psychology was a novel experience, Ethel had some familiarity with psychological theory through her reading and her course at the New School. It was probably fortunate that she had been previously exposed to a psychoanalytic perspective on child development since this was the general orientation of the clinic. Open discussion of sexual and aggressive instincts in a child probably did not have the effect on her that it might have had on someone who was thoroughly unfamiliar with a Freudian approach.

Ethel declared on her application to the clinic that her family's sole source of income came from her husband's business, "which was not turning a profit." Determination of a fee was postponed, and Ethel and Michael were assigned to a young social worker, Elizabeth Phillips, who had just received her master's degree from Columbia University. In what was then routine fashion, appointments were arranged for Ethel to see Mrs. Phillips once a week, and for Michael to see her once a week.

Michael's first meeting with his new social worker indicated both his obstinacy and his precocity. Elizabeth Phillips recalls:

> I saw him for his first treatment session which I happen to remember because it was so unique. He was really an incredible little boy. He came in and said, 'Do you have any ink?' And I said, 'No, but I have paint.' And he said, 'Okay. Do you have any paper?' And I said, 'Yes.' So he took the piece of paper and he put a blob of paint in the middle of the paper, and he folded it and then opened it up and said, "Do you want me to tell you what I see in it?" He was going to do me another Rorschach which I thought was wonderful! Then we had a big fight. We fought for I can't tell you how many months. I went home every Friday afternoon with a headache because I had let him play with the [recorder] . . . and then I decided it was getting in the way of his doing anything in treatment. So I told him he couldn't use it any more. And so we had an argument every Friday afternoon over why he should be able to use the [recorder]. He was really hard to manage and he was very nervous, a very tense kid. He would just freeze up, space out. He just became enormously tense and not communicate.

Michael could not accept the word "no." Given that he had tested in the "genius level" on his IQ tests, he was a very logical and articulate five-year-old whose insistent arguments exhausted even a trained clinician.

Ethel, on the other hand, was "very easy to relate to and she was very dependent," remembers Elizabeth Phillips. She also recalls:

> She would come each week and recite the events of the week and the troubles she had had that week in coping. She wanted me to tell her what to do. . . . You know I was younger than she was. . . . I would say she tried to please

me, and I would say also that her transference to me was to a parent and not to a peer. It was not a sisterly kind of thing. She was looking for parental approval.

As the therapy unfolded, Mrs. Phillips learned how Ethel "set no boundaries [with her children]; those kids were the most boundaryless, fused with her. . . . It was hard to tell where they left off and she began. . . . She was left with those kids a lot. In those days there was not joint-parenting. Julius had a full-time job, and it was she and these kids. It was like three kids. . . . You know I never heard her talk about going to meetings. . . . I got the feeling she was home, just stuck at home, and that they didn't have baby-sitters a lot. . . . It would have been great if she had had a 'homemaker' which could have been provided. A 'homemaker' is somebody who comes in and takes care of the home *and* the children for periods of time so the mother can get some time off. I can't remember her talking about much that was autonomously hers."

Going to the Jewish Board of Guardians began to approach something that was autonomously hers. In Elizabeth Phillips, Ethel found an intelligent authority figure to trust with her problems and turn to for advice. But, apparently, it was not enough. Rather than satiating her needs, it stimulated her desire for greater self-understanding. Although Ethel could unburden herself in her therapy with Mrs. Phillips, the parameters of what she could discuss were relatively narrow: she was there to work on her relationship with Michael; material that did not bear on this was technically outside her therapy. Once-a-week sessions that chiefly centered on recitals of Michael's actions and Ethel's reactions to them did not begin to unearth the origins of Ethel's feelings toward her children, herself, and her family. What began as a desperate attempt to rescue her relationship to her son tapped a far greater yearning for self-knowledge.

To most people today such a yearning would seem understandable, perhaps even praiseworthy. Yet Ethel's desire to take part in a more intensive form of psychotherapy radically conflicted with what she had learned in the Communist party over the past twelve or thirteen years. Focusing on personal problems and emotional life was bourgeois and self-indulgent. Individual unhappiness found its origins in economic and political inequalities. Therefore solutions rested in political struggle, not in a privatized and depoliticized psychotherapy. Worse yet, what Ethel attached her yearnings to was orthodox psychoanalysis. This is what she had been exposed to in Edith Buxbaum's class and through the Jewish Board of Guardians, one of the chief training sites for the New York Psychoanalytic Institute. Ethel responded to this mode of thinking. It claimed to be "scientific," offering precise stages of development, categories of thinking, specialized vocabulary, and a systematic way of interpreting the world. It also was modern in that it was rational and antithetical to the religious and superstitious thinking of her *shtetl*-bound parents. It went far beyond the psychological platitudes that were offered in *Parents' Magazine*. And, most importantly, it spoke to an inner life that experienced pain, rage, and desire that were unmentionable in the circles of the Communist party.

In fact, the CP had an official line on psychoanalysis: "[M]aterialism cannot conceive and does not accept a concept of mind which blocks off any large segment from interaction with reality. Hence the strenuous objection to the concept of the Freudian unconscious, to the instinct theory. . . ." In 1936 the Soviet Communist Party had decided that all of Soviet psychology should emphasize conscious reason and concrete practice. The standard Soviet medical encyclopedia stated:

> It must be stated directly that the only true evaluation of psychoanalysis is to consider it as a fragment of bourgeois democracy. . . . It must be pointed out that as a method of treatment psychoanalysis is too complex. . . . Patients who are being analyzed for two years and more become too submerged in themselves, they are constantly stewing in their own juice and are torn away from reality. [Neuroses stem from the] mistaken thoughts of misguided people [that is, the] reflections of the material reality of press propaganda, of selfish class influences, of scientific reaction, or [the] unwarranted extensions of special or peculiar experiences. . . . For these reasons political insights and a solid class orientation are regarded as indispensable prerequisites to a realistic approach to life, to a sound social integration or to wholesome psychological development.

The American Communist party took its lead from the Soviets. According to historian Paul Lyons, the people who became involved with the CP in the nineteen-thirties were "a generation taught by the Party to mistrust depth psychology as subjectivist and to treat

Freud and psychoanalysis as a 'bourgeois' phenomenon." Furthermore, in the postwar period, as psychoanalysis was attaining greater popularity and as Americans were evidencing greater interest in personal and family life, the Party became even more aggressive in its campaign against psychoanalysis. At this time one found "in the pages of the *Daily Worker* as well as *Political Affairs* a wholesale onslaught against psychoanalysis and, indeed, against all schools of psychological thought except Pavlov's."

This then was the ideological environment in which Ethel had spent all her adult life, an environment in which psychoanalysis was denigrated, and virtually any exploration of psychological problems was taboo. As one Party member recalls, in the late nineteen-forties, he and his fiancé, who was also in the Party, "never discussed anything remotely connected to our emotional lives. We would have been mortified to reveal our sexual or emotional confusions to each other, we all pretended we didn't have any. All personal doubts or pains got submerged beneath Party language. If you stopped talking that language you felt guilty, confused, trivial."

As a loyal, although inactive follower of the Party, the internal pressure against entering analysis must have been enormous for Ethel. It is perhaps likely that such guilt might have prevented her from seriously considering treatment had it not been for the events of March 1949, the month that Barnet Greenglass died.

Ethel's father had fallen and broken his hip in February of the previous year. Since that time he had been in ill health and even greater diminished mental capacity. As he had aged, his submission to his wife had increased so that there simply was no question as to who made the decisions in the Greenglass marriage. Yet Barney, even as a demented and frail old man, offered his only daughter a genuine fondness and love unequaled by any other member of her family. There is no evidence that he provided Ethel with emotional support in her battles with her mother and brothers, but the knowledge that he cared for her, even in his inept way, undoubtedly gave Ethel some emotional sustenance. Even though Ethel was dismayed by her father's passivity, and probably resented his inability to defend her to her mother and brothers, his death affected her. In fact, her firm decision to find a psychoanalyst crystallized after Barnet died. Her one, albeit ineffectual, familial ally was gone. Her problems with Michael continued to overwhelm her, despite Mrs. Phillips' intervention. At last, Ethel broke with the Party's line on psychoanalysis.

The psychiatrist Ethel went to see was a short, stocky man, who was then forty-two years old. Although Saul Miller was a native New Yorker, he had something of the European about him since he had received his medical education in Vienna and Lausanne, Switzerland. After completing his psychiatric residency in 1946, he began training to be a psychoanalyst. As a candidate at the psychoanalytic institute he offered treatment at greatly reduced fees, which enabled Ethel to see him. He also had a reputation as someone who was sympathetic to the political left. His office was at 400 West End Avenue on the Upper West Side, and it was there that Ethel began to meet with him three times a week for psychotherapy. The expectation was that after a period of face-to-face therapy, Ethel would begin lying on the couch for a traditional analysis.

As she sat in Miller's darkened office with its heavy wood furniture and thick, drawn drapes, Ethel Rosenberg confessed her anxieties, anger, and deep sadness. Her pressing problem was her relationship with Michael. Unlike her appeal to Mrs. Phillips, however, to whom she turned for advice on how to be a better mother, here she simply poured forth her anxieties and guilt. "She couldn't control him. When she felt beaten down by him, she'd lash out at him; he rebelled, and she felt guilty about this." She also felt extremely guilty about her wish to place him in a foster home. "She blamed herself for not being a good mother; she believed she handled Michael nastily." She was not sleeping well and she could not control how much she was eating. Ethel gave the impression that she did not talk to other people about her problems, and her psychiatrist believes this was one of the reasons she wished to be in psychotherapy.

From the start, Ethel was a "good patient." She spoke freely, could recount her personal history in great detail, remembered her dreams, and never missed appointments. She seemed to be psychologically minded and was quick to point out that she believed her problems stemmed from her family of origin. She called her mother a "witch," felt that her brothers had "denigrated her," and although she liked her father the best, she thought of him as a "namby-pamby." "She spoke about her poverty [while growing up], about how her brothers were given better chances for education than she. Although she resented this she didn't speak about her resentment." It was clear to her psychiatrist that she was "caught up in her anger." Most of her dreams "reflected pent-up anger," yet she "suppressed her anger" in her therapy sessions. She spoke of how she could express resentment toward her mother and brothers and of her belief that her rancor found its source in the treatment she received from her family. Yet she wanted so much for Miller to like her, "to be on her side psychodynamically," that she checked her anger with him, presumably feeling that he would reject her if he saw how angry she truly was.

In the course of her therapy, she made "a very quick transference" to her analyst. "She felt safe with a man who was on her side," he believes. It was clear to him how much she was coming to care for, respect, and fantasize about him, yet she would never speak about these feelings in their sessions. As the therapy progressed, she became "attached" to him "in the same way she was attached to her husband." They were both "saviors"—intelligent, empathic men (not "namby-pambies") who actively valued and respected her, and took her side in her internal and external battles with her family. "She seemed more needy than most," he recalls. Her desire to have him accept and approve of her made her seem like "a grown child."

As with Mrs. Phillips, Ethel never spoke to Dr. Miller about politics or anything having to do with the Communist party. According to him, "she knew he knew she was in the CP," but never spoke of anything pertaining to that organization or its activities. Apparently for Ethel discussion of the social world and politics had no place in her therapy sessions, just as psychotherapy had to be excluded from her social life. Although "she had a lot of faith in psychiatry," and was growing increasingly enamored of a psychoanalytic perspective, she would never discuss either of her therapy situations with friends or acquaintances. A neighbor recalls that around this time Ethel was often seen rushing off somewhere, dressed better than usual:

> [These] times made more of an impression on me maybe because we wondered about her; why wasn't she like the rest of us? Why didn't she participate with the rest of us and make friends so that we could share responsibilities? If you'd meet and say, 'Oh, hi; you're so dressed [up], where are you going?' She would reply 'I have an appointment.' It was always something that you couldn't get through a barrier there.

With four therapy sessions for herself per week and an additional one for Michael, it is not surprising people remembered Ethel as always rushing somewhere. She never felt comfortable, however, admitting to her neighbors, many of whom were close to or in the Communist party, where she was going. Of course, this might also have been due to the fact that she was simply embarrassed telling mere acquaintances that she was being treated for emotional problems. Yet there is no evidence that she confided this news to any of her family or friends either. Given the Party's vehement opposition to psychoanalysis and her own reluctance ever to discuss personal issues, Ethel kept her two worlds, her two systems of thought, rigidly separate.

13

WITCH-HUNT

The U.S.-Soviet alliance that was responsible for Nazi Germany's defeat began to wear thin as soon as World War II had ended. The Soviet Union's aggression in Eastern Europe and its brutality toward individuals and groups in its newly occupied lands stirred the imaginations and emotions of Americans ready to believe the worst about Communism. Conservatives and others on the political right, who had been excluded from power since Roosevelt's first election in 1932, exploited these sentiments by repeatedly trying to connect Communism, spying for the Soviet Union, and the New Deal. In 1946 J. Edgar Hoover, director of the FBI, set the stage for this string of associations by claiming that "Red Fascism . . . had become a major force in unions, newspapers, magazines, book publishing, radio, movies, churches, schools, colleges, fraternal orders, and the government itself."

Just before the 1946 elections, the Republican Party distributed 683,000 copies of a thirty-eight-page pamphlet published by the U.S. Chamber of Commerce entitled, *Communist Infiltration in the United States: Its Nature and How to Combat It*. Clearly identifying the New Deal as laying the groundwork for Communist ideology, the pamphlet was expanded into a fifty-seven-page booklet published in January 1947 with the title *Communists Within the Gov-*

ernment: *The Facts and a Program*. It claimed, although never offered any evidence, that:

> *Evidence is clear and irrefutable in regard to three major points. First, Communists in our midst have a unique loyalty to the Soviet Union. They will use government positions in order to further the interests of a foreign power. In doing this, they will go as far as treason. Furthermore, their sympathizers and dupes have been led, sometimes unwittingly, to do the same.*
>
> *Second, Communists and their followers have achieved positions in our government where they can do immense harm to national welfare and security. . . .*
>
> *Thirdly, it is clear that our government has shown appalling laxity in meeting this problem. . . . [C]ases of espionage and treason were ignored, lest their disclosure 'prejudice our relations with the Soviet Union.'*

The newspapers in February 1947 carried the story that Louis Budenz—the *Daily Worker* editor who had become a professional witness against the Communist party in 1945—charged that a German, Gerhardt Eisler (who Budenz also claimed had secretly directed the Party's policies since 1941) had been an "atom spy." According to the papers, Budenz accused Eisler of passing secrets regarding the atomic bomb to the Soviets. Although the newspapers misinterpreted and exaggerated what Budenz actually said, and although no evidence was ever produced linking Eisler with espionage or the atomic bomb, this event further cemented the idea that Communism and spying were intrinsically related.

Democrats began to add their voices to the growing anti-Communist clamor, in part to try to prove that they were not responsible for the alleged Communist infiltration of the government and were not so tainted by New Deal liberalism as to tolerate the spread of "Red Fascism" within the United States. In March, Roosevelt's former ambassador to the Soviet Union, William C. Bullitt, informed the House Committee on Un-American Activities that the USSR would attack the United States as soon as she was able to match U.S. atomic power. Secretary of Labor Lewis Schwellenback proposed outlawing the Communist party, and the Attorney General asserted that there were "many Communists in America. They are everywhere—in factories, offices, butcher shops, on street corners, in private business—and each carries with him the germs of death for society." President Truman, who had hitherto considered the myriad of accusations regarding Communist spies as a "red herring," succumbed to mounting political pressures and in late March 1947 instituted a federal loyalty program that required extensive background investigations of all federal workers and dismissal of those found to be "disloyal." CP membership, even "sympathetic association" with the Party, were prima facie evidence of disloyalty, and hence mandated dismissal.

Contrary to its intended purpose, the President's Loyalty Order did not diffuse the issue of Communist infiltration into government, but rather acted to confirm the existence of a problem. The House Committee on Un-American Activities, commonly known as HUAC, stepped up its hearings into Communist influence and espionage, while J. Edgar Hoover announced in May 1947 that all 74,000 members of the CPUSA were "masters of deceit," ominously noting that America had 1 Communist for every 1,814 people, whereas in 1917 the Bolsheviks had only 1 for every 2,771.

It was not altogether surprising then when former Assistant Attorney General O. John Rogge charged on 7 November 1947 that the Department of Justice was planning a "dramatic round-up of dozens of Communist leaders and alleged fellow-travellers." This allegation tended to confirm the CP leaders' anticipation of impending American fascism, which had been a Party theme virtually since the close of World War II. Although this did not happen, the year 1948 did usher in the harshest repression of the Communist party in United States history and led to the demise of the Party as a force in American political life.

On 20 July 1948 twelve out of the thirteen members of the CPUSA's governing national board were indicted for violating the Smith Act, which made it a crime for anyone "to knowingly or willfully advocate, abet, advise or teach the duty, necessity, desirability or propriety of overthrowing or destroying any government in the United States by force or violence." Passed in 1940, the Act had only been invoked twice before: once against the Socialist Workers party and once against thirty-three Nazi sympathizers. In both cases, the CP had supported the government's action. Now, however, it undoubtedly regretted that stance.

Soon after the indictment of the Party leaders, American newspaper, magazine, and book publishers began a frenzied competition to report the latest revelations of former Party members-turned-professional informers. Among them were Elizabeth Bentley, Louis Budenz, and Whittaker Chambers. They, along with a host of lesser known personalities, regaled their audiences with tales of spy rings, espionage, and shockingly successful Communist infiltration of the federal government. When Chambers accused Alger Hiss, the quintessential New Dealer and former State Department employee, of espionage in August 1948, it seemed as though anyone with liberal credentials was open to charges of Communist sympathies and hence spying, conspiracy, or espionage on behalf of the Soviet Union. In a period of three short years, the Communist party had gone from being a barely tolerated domestic representative of America's wartime ally to the most vilified and menacing force known to the American people. To be a Communist, know a Communist, or to have had the slightest association with the American Communist party quickly became the secular equivalent of consorting with the devil. In this new religion of anti-Communism, redemption was possible only through the public act of informing, by renouncing one's previous political beliefs and naming names.

Reeling from the shock of learning how many of its members had been either FBI informants or traitors willing to inform against old friends and comrades, Party members responded swiftly by tightening security, regarding each other with heightened suspicion, and preparing for the complete political repression they believed would follow in the wake of the Smith Act indictments. Joseph Starobin, a CP member who attended CCNY four years earlier than Julius and who remained a rank-and-filer for most of his twenty-five years in the Party, recounts how the CP reacted at this time:

> *Those members who remained placed a greater premium than ever before on loyalty. . . . An inner cycle of self-justification developed which militated against any re-examination within the Party's ranks. Re-examination could easily be equated with doubt and weakness. For members of an ideologically bound community the greatest crime is disloyalty when that community appears in danger. . . .*
>
> *As the American Communists staggered, they turned inward. . . . Communists began to measure each other for deviations and heresies. Thus the strange paradox: in the name of defying the witch-hunt against them, the American Communists complemented it by engaging in a witch-hunt*

of their own. Beleaguered from without, they went through agony from within.

Thousands of members left the Party out of fear of being indicted, losing their jobs, their friends, or their families due to the militant anti-Communism sweeping the country. Thousands more were pushed out: they had questioned or disagreed with Stalin's expulsion of Yugoslavia from the association of Communist states; they showed evidence of being "white chauvinists," through their real or alleged insults to black members or black people in general; they objected to the Party's line on psychoanalysis, biology, or genetics. The Party fed on itself. Impotent to challenge effectively the unrelenting attacks made upon them from without, members seemed to turn their alarm and anger on each other, ever fearful that others' claims to being loyal Communists were insincere, false, or paid for by the FBI. In this atmosphere, individuals who had given the majority of their lives to the Party were expelled, apparently for no logical reason. As Vivian Gornick recounts:

> A Party member who visited her sister in Florida was accused of being a racist and was expelled; another served watermelon at a garden party and was expelled; a third did not invite a black Party member to sit down at his table in a restaurant and he was expelled. Those who called for reason were immediately suspect. And once the stigma of suspicion fell on you, you were lost; suspicion had become the mark of Cain.

There is no evidence that the Rosenbergs took part in this internal witch-hunt, other than through their reading of the Party press. It does seem, however, that they agreed with the Party's line and sided with it in its expulsion of members who were in disagreement, given the unceasing and uncritical devotion to the CP they demonstrated until their deaths. The Rosenbergs' distance from the day-to-day workings of the CP, and their general isolation from people who were active in the internal scrutiny of others' loyalty, allowed them to remain true to Party ideology without suffering the consequences of repudiating fellow comrades and losing friends. Being at a remove they did not witness first-hand the unbelievable cruelty that was meted out under the guise of preserving the sacrosanct "correct line." Most of their friends also remained loyal to the CP abstractly and continued to view themselves as Communists or at least friendly to Communism, but they had become too preoccupied with their careers and domestic lives to be active Party members, and were loath to rejoin the Party given the current repressive atmosphere. Morton Sobell, who had bought a house in Flushing, Long Island (something "I had said I never would do") and was working for Reeves Instrument Company in New York (with a salary of $7,000 a year), describes what had become rather typical for many of the Rosenbergs' friends:

> I wasn't reading the Worker regularly nor had I given any consideration to rejoining the Communist Party since our move to New York. Perhaps it was because my energies were fully absorbed by my job and family. I had also begun to feel a slight uneasiness about the affidavits Helen and I had so unconcernedly signed at Reeves. When Julius had been accused of membership in the Party, in 1945, the only consequence (serious enough for him) was the loss of his government job. But by 1947 the federal loyalty program had been instituted. The result of a federal employee's being accused of falsely signing a loyalty oath was not simply a lost job: it was a perjury charge, carrying a possible five year sentence.

Against this backdrop of mounting political repression, G and R Engineering was not succeeding. By the summer of 1947, Izzy Goldstein wanted to get out of the partnership. A fresh source of capital was needed to keep the company in operation. Julie located a local matzoh manufacturer and speculator in small businesses who was willing to invest in the company if it was reorganized. David Schein invested $15,000 in return for receiving twenty-five shares of common and preferred stock, the right to approve all expenditures, and an agreement that the company would expand its machine shop so it could perform larger and more complicated jobs. The Greenglasses and Julie agreed. They located a larger space to rent at 370 East Houston. Downstairs from an Orthodox synagogue, the shop formerly had been used as clubrooms for girls attending Downtown Talmud Torah, which had been Julie's religious school and was located only a few doors down the street. Although as a child and young adolescent Julie had spent innumerable hours in zealous study and prayer there, he would never again step through its doors, despite the fact that he would pass it literally hundreds of times during the next two and a half years.

Incorporated in October under the name Pitt Machine Products Co., Julie became president, Dave vice-president, Bernie secretary, and David Schein treasurer, although the latter had no role in day-to-day operations. With Schein's money, the partners were able to purchase a turret lathe and a kick press so the shop could perform more varied tasks. They hoped that this, the third of their ventures, would bring them the prosperity that so many in postwar America were experiencing. By the end of the year, Julie's annual income amounted to only $2,451, somewhat more than half of what he had earned in 1945 when he worked for the Signal Corps and Emerson Radio and Phonograph. In fact, by 1947 it was clear that Julie's career had been ruined by his dismissal from the Signal Corps for being a Communist. He had formed three different companies in two years and each had been unsuccessful. He was no more a businessman than he was an engineer. His one passion in life was politics, an unremunerative interest for a Marxist in the United States.

Business conditions and working relations deteriorated at Pitt throughout 1948. As the partners' renewed hopes were disappointed, they began to fight among themselves about why they were unable to turn a profit. Tension was particularly acute between Dave and Julie. As Dave's interest in the CP declined and his need to support a family and his desire to enjoy a more middle-class lifestyle increased, he directed his frustration over his financial plight at his brother-in-law. His admiration gradually was turning to resentment as Julie continued to treat him as a younger, less knowledgeable subordinate.

Dave was a full partner in the company and he wanted to be treated as such. He was no longer just Ethel's kid brother. He had spent almost three years in the Army, had worked on the atom bomb, was married, and since the fall of 1947 had a young son to support. Ruth also experienced growing bitterness toward Julie as the business continued to fare badly. When she married Dave, she had envied the Rosenbergs' political sophistication, their modern apartment, and their college-educated friends. She probably imagined that as she grew older, she too could live like the Rosenbergs. Yet, after four years of marriage and the birth of her first child, she was no longer as impressed by the Rosenbergs' political views and had become unabashedly envious of their life-style. Author John Wexley, who interviewed Ruth's neighbors and former friends on the Lower East Side, discovered that she

> envied Ethel's modern apartment with its steam heat and resented that her own child had to play in a filthy back alley while Ethel's children had a 'fancy' playground. Whereas she had to lug parcels up three flights of stairs Ethel could step into an elevator and just press a button. On the East Side, to describe someone's social standing in the most awesome terms it was enough to say the lucky one lived in a house which had an elevator.

Ruth believed David did "most of the hard work," and that Julie just "handed out orders instead of obtaining any." Since the Greenglasses' apartment on Rivington Street was only five blocks away from the machine shop, Ruth began dropping by frequently after her son's birth. With Stephen in his carriage, Ruth often took part in heated discussions and arguments over how the business was run and who was to blame for its lack of success.

Julie, conversely, believed that Dave was not working hard enough and kept irregular hours. In Julie's words:

> David decided to go to night school . . . and he had to leave the shop for three nights a week . . . at about 3 o'clock. And he was foreman of the shop and he had to supervise the employees and I am in the shop on a number of occasions and notice that there wasn't anybody there to supervise the employees and I got hold of Dave the next day and I says 'Look here, Dave, you are shirking on the job. You are not doing your work. The fellows aren't getting stuff out'. . . . and we had arguments about that, and finally David quit school because of that.

Ruth was furious on her husband's behalf. According to Julie she told him: "You are taking advantage of my husband. After all you have an education, he should have an education and he is contributing more than you are to the business anyway, because he produces the work and you just get it, and if he gave you four hours a day, that is enough for you. You should let him go to school." Julie did not yield. He took a superior attitude toward his wife's youngest brother, referred to him in conversation as a "boy," and yet was thoroughly dependent upon his skills as a machinist. The machine shop was Julie's last hope for supporting himself and his family, and Dave was crucial to the shop's success. If he did not take his responsibility seriously, or, worse yet, if he were able to secure a better job as a result of attending night school, Pitt would be without a foreman. Given the shop's poor financial situation, Julie may have thought it would be impossible to find a machinist as good as he believed Dave to be for what Pitt could pay. Thus Julie's hostility to Dave's educational ambitions may have been born out of fear as much as feelings of disdain for the "boy" who had looked up to him since he was fourteen and now demanded equality.

Ethel completely agreed with her husband. She had never differed with Julie over anything substantial, particularly if he expressed strong feelings over it. Even when she may not have thoroughly concurred, she would evince "patient indugence" toward what he did or said, intuitively sensing his need for her support. In Julie's uphill struggle to provide for his family and maintain some semblance of a career, Ethel probably would have been particularly supportive and especially reluctant to criticize his increasingly desperate attempts to secure a livelihood. Dave was her favorite brother but in a conflict with her husband, her allegiance to a Greenglass could never compare to the respect, loyalty, and love she felt for her husband. Julie continued throughout her life to be her "savior." Just as he alone had emotionally rescued her from her family, he continued to be the one person who loved her for who she was.

Ethel, like Julie, saw Dave as a little brother who could never truly stand in anything other than a subordinate position to her husband. Thus Ethel believed that Dave, and Bernie as well, were letting Julie down. According to Ruth, Ethel complained that her brothers "were not paying attention to the shop, that Julius was doing all the work, working hard, David and Bernie weren't keeping the proper hours, and they were wasting their time in talking where Julius was coming in there in the morning hours, that they were coming in at ten or ten-thirty, and he was sick a great deal of the time and he was tired of the whole business."

Quite predictably, social intercourse between the Rosenbergs

and the Greenglasses diminished as animosity rose. The only occasions on which the couples routinely saw each other were the
Friday night *shabbes* dinners at 64 Sheriff Street. It is quite possible
that these gatherings became filled with conflict due to the couples'
differences, and because Tessie openly sided with Dave and Ruth
against Ethel and Julie. It was Tessie's brothers who had loaned
Bernie the money that had been used to purchase the machines for
the shop. They were still owed $4,000, yet it was unlikely that they
would be repaid in the foreseeable future. More importantly, she
had *always* supported her sons in conflicts with her daughter.

The somewhat greater acceptance Tessie had expressed toward
Ethel since Michael's birth may have started to erode as early as
1948 when the Rosenbergs and Greenglasses started to quarrel openly
over their joint business venture. That her mother once more openly
favored her brother probably was a fresh reminder to Ethel of how
she could never truly win her mother's love and was forever rele-
gated to being the inferior member of the family. What may have
been new to Ethel was Tessie favoring Ruth. Simply by being Dave's
wife, Ruth had a certain status in her mother-in-law's eyes. Ruth
also conformed more closely to Tessie's standards. Since she only
seems to have parroted her husband's interest in politics, Ruth easily
shed her infatuation with the Communist party as her husband became more disaffected with politics after the war. Her consuming
preoccupation now was to get ahead, to make enough money to
climb into the middle class. Since this ambition was poignantly
familiar to Tessie, the two shared a basic orientation to the world
that Ethel continued to find repugnant. Thus a kinship was formed
between the two women, which some might characterize as founded
in aspirations for financial betterment, and others might say was
premised in greed. Whatever it is called, Ethel had grown up re-
belling against such an ethos and was unable to see it in a positive
light. According to her, "it was common knowledge that Ruthie
always nagged Davey about money." Ruth, because she was an
in-law, because she had won Tessie's acceptance, and/or because
she was, in fact, far more driven toward material gain than her
husband, increasingly drew Ethel's ire in the couples' arguments
about how Pitt was run.

What was now perpetual conflict and irritation exacerbated an
already tense life for the Rosenbergs. Money was a constant issue.
Although Ethel maintained that it did not matter, it probably was

difficult to be so glib when confronting the clerk at the Village Grocery and Dairy. The family's income for 1948 was a mere $2,035, $400 less than during the previous year, and half as much as what Julie had earned three years earlier. In 1945, however, the family had been smaller and prices had been lower.

By 1949 the Greenglasses' accusations had become more acrimonious. They accused Julie of being determined to "be King Tut or nothing." They believed he was at fault for not locating jobs for Pitt, and resented the air of superiority he assumed in relation to them. Julie, conversely, believed the company's failure was caused by Dave's poor workmanship and inability to supervise the staff. He repeatedly found himself arguing with Ruth, who was increasingly the representative of her more passive and less ambitious husband. In Julie's words:

> She said I was taking advantage of him; I was trying to make him a menial; I was trying to treat him like a worker and not a partner. As a matter of fact, we had so many arguments concerning his technical ability that at one point in the business I had to hire a foreman over him, and he told me in many words after that, 'How do you think I felt, Julie, when I had to work for my own worker?' I told him, 'Well, if you keep on producing rejects and losing money in the business and you don't know how to handle the men, we will never make a living.'

Arguments had become constant. Dave stated that "[t]here were quarrels of every type and every kind. I mean there was [sic] arguments over personality, there was arguments over money, there was arguments over the way the shop was run, there was arguments over the way the outside was run."

The overt hostility between Julie and Dave had become so intense that they almost came to blows. One day, in the midst of an explosive argument at a candy store near the shop, Bernie had to physically separate the brothers-in-law as their verbal sparring erupted into a near fist fight.

Certainly the cause of this heightened antagonism was the plummeting fortune of the machine shop. Business had become so poor that none of the partners was able to draw a salary. Each was forced to borrow money just to maintain himself and his family. Julie turned

to his friends for help. He borrowed $400 from Al Sarant, a former
member of Julie's CP unit and now a relatively successful independent contractor in Ithaca, New York. He also borrowed money from Morton Sobell:

> Julius called me at work and asked if I could lend him some money. He had to meet bills at the machine shop and was short of cash. He had never before come to me for financial help; I knew he must have felt very embarrassed. We met for lunch that afternoon. Our discussion about his predicament was uncomfortable for both of us; I had no idea that he was in desperate financial straits. After lunch I went to my bank and withdrew three hundred dollars, which I gave him without setting any time for repayment. I knew he would repay me as soon as he could.

Bernie and Dave had begun to voice their desire to pull out of Pitt. Bernie was particularly desperate since Gladys, his wife, had been diagnosed as having Hodgkin's Disease, at that time an incurable form of cancer. The couple had a young daughter, and without an income, Bernie probably felt that he could not idly sit by to see if the shop could provide him with a regular salary. Dave also felt pressured to leave. Aside from Dave's real need to support his family, Ruth constantly pushed him to do something about their declining financial situation. As early as 1946, she had begun complaining that he was not "being paid commensurate with the work done. . . ." Now that he literally was earning no money, she must have been outraged. Thus the three couples began to fight about leaving the business.

Julie did not want to be abandoned with a failing shop and no strategy for improving its prospects. Unlike his brothers-in-law, he had nowhere to turn for alternative sources of employment. Dave and Bernie had both served in the armed forces, received honorable discharges, and could account for their work histories. They did not have to conceal four and a half years of employment for which they were dismissed for Communist party membership. In the midst of the country's greatest anti-Communist hysteria, Julie's future rested more than ever with Pitt, and he fought Dave, Ruth, and Bernie to keep the partnership alive. Any arguments or hopes he offered, however, were overshadowed by the fact that month after month there continued to be too little work to provide them with incomes. In August 1949, Bernie resigned. A few weeks later, Dave followed his older brother's lead.

Alone, an inept engineer, an unsuccessful businessman, Julius Rosenberg attempted to restructure his failing company. He hired a new shop foreman, Charles Bozsick, to replace Dave and substituted new men for the cousins and friends of the Greenglass family who had worked on and off for the business. He warned his few employees that they would receive no vacations since the firm had not turned a profit in the past year and a half. With Dave and Bernie severed from Pitt, perhaps Julie's energies could now be focused on attracting work for the shop rather than spending countless hours in family arguments.

The conflict between Dave and Julie did not cease, however, when Dave resigned from the company. The issue remained of how to reimburse him for the stock he held in Pitt and for his initial investment. Julie had nothing to offer. "You can't get blood out of a stone," he argued. The fights continued, with Dave finally offering to accept a promissory note. Julie refused; he wanted Dave to simply relinquish his shares. In January 1950, Dave finally agreed to assign the shares to Julie but would not actually give him possession of them. "I kept telling him that the stock was in a safe deposit box and that I didn't have a chance to get it."

Then there was the issue of how much Dave should receive for his shares. Ruth insisted he accept nothing less than $2,000; Julie offered only $1,000. Dave was tired of fighting: "My wife wanted $2,000. I figured it's a headache, a note's a note whether he gives it to me or not it was lost money." The Greenglasses capitulated. According to Dave, "He finally agreed that he would give me $1,000 and when my wife made out the note to him to sign, he didn't want to sign the $1,000 note. He said his word is good enough and that he will pay me at such time when he will have the money available." That time never occurred, for in May 1950 Julie had to buy out David Schein as well. Schein was not someone whose wishes Julie could disregard as he did his younger brother-in-law's. On 1 May he agreed to pay Schein a $1,000 deposit on the purchase of his stock. He cashed in a bond he and Ethel had purchased during the war to come up with the deposit and obligated himself to pay Schein $160 per month for the remainder of his shares. Julie signed an agreement not permitting him to sell any of Pitt's assets until he had paid Schein in full.

Strapped for funds, heavily in debt, and without any business partners with whom to commiserate, the Rosenbergs were, perhaps, in the worst financial situation of their lives by the spring of 1950. Their relationship with the entire Greenglass family was at a nadir. Tessie firmly sided with Ruth and Dave, who now never saw Ethel and Julie except to fight about money. Although Bernie had played the role of ineffectual mediator in the struggles over Pitt and had less animosity toward Julie, he rarely saw the Rosenbergs since he, according to Julie, "was tied up with his wife dying in the hospital."

Against this backdrop of financial misfortune and alienation from her family, Ethel remained preoccupied with therapy and mothering. Now, in addition to her daily trips to her psychotherapists, she enrolled in a weekly guitar course taught by Oscar Brand. Michael was going to have every opportunity to study music that she was denied. Thus she intended to teach him guitar after she had mastered the instrument. By his seventh birthday, she also had him taking piano lessons on their second-hand piano. She and Julie might have to skimp on food and clothes, but her children were going to have the creative opportunities she had only longed for as a child.

Despite Julie's agonizing business problems, he still took enormous pride in being a father and deeply valued his home life with Ethel. Being a parent was far less conflictual and draining for him than for his wife, probably because he did not find his identity in being a father and was far more emotionally and psychologically removed from Mike and Robby than was Ethel. When he recalled the times he spent with his family, it was always with great fondness.

Both Ethel and Julie actively attempted to shield their children from the distress they were experiencing due to the machine shop's misfortunes and their conflict with the Greenglasses. In fact, Michael and Robby were protected from a number of their parents' troubles. Thus the events of Monday, 17 July 1950, astounded them.

The day had seemed normal enough. After supper, Robby was put to bed and Michael was allowed to stay up to listen to "The Lone Ranger." "The radio episode concerned bandits trying to frame the Lone Ranger by committing crimes with 'silver-looking' bullets." At around 7:30 P.M. there was a knock at the door. Julie answered it and asked someone to come in. Michael continued to listen to the radio. In the episode, "[j]ust as someone was exposing the fraud [against the Lone Ranger] by scraping the bullets to show they were softer than silver and only silver-colored," a strange man came up to the radio and turned it off. Michael turned it on again; the stranger turned it off. Michael defiantly turned it on; the stranger turned it off. Then suddenly Michael heard his mother scream, "I want a lawyer!" Within seconds, ten men dressed in suits swarmed into the apartment, opening closets, looking through bookshelves, examining furniture. Ethel was told to keep silent and move into the bedroom with the children. She did what she was told but not before demanding to see a search warrant and the right to call her attorney. Once huddled in the bedroom, it became clear that Julie had been taken away by the men who first knocked at the door. Michael asked his mother if his daddy would be home that night. "No, not tonight," she replied. And with that, Ethel Rosenberg's life entered history.

14

SOMETHING HAPPENED

What you have read thus far, has been as historically accurate and comprehensive as the rather limited sources permit. Yet it is a partial story, for it describes that aspect of Ethel Rosenberg's life least known to the public and least open to debate and controversy. It is, however, the majority of her life. For that reason, it needs to be understood on its own terms. Nevertheless we now must turn to the date, 17 July 1950, and the events that preceded it. Thus we temporarily leave the biographical narrative and its attempts at historical accuracy, and enter the world of fiction—the fiction of the Greenglasses, the FBI, and the purveyors of anti-Communism on the one hand, and the fiction of Ethel and Julius Rosenberg on the other.

"Fiction" is not meant to suggest that there are no objective events in the explanation of what led up to Julius Rosenberg's arrest in 1950. But these "events" are so few and so enveloped in stories that were suddenly "remembered" years after they occurred in order to prove a certain party guilty or innocent, that their historical authenticity is deeply problematic. Clearly, as we will see, the Greenglasses and the Rosenbergs lied in varying ways. It remains impossible for both of their accounts to demonstrate definitively where the lies end and the truth begins. This is so because their respective stories center on what occurred between them, alone, in the privacy of their homes. There were no objective witnesses to any of the acts they describe, no outside authority who can come forward and say, "Yes, this happened," or "No, he is lying." In the absence of such a voice, everyone involved in the controversy at the time, and in the years that followed, relied on circumstantial evidence to support either the Greenglass account or the Rosenberg account. The choice of which circumstantial evidence to reveal or highlight and the manner in which such evidence is presented allows one to weave a tale that often resembles fiction—a fiction built around the theme of spies, espionage, and devotion to the Soviet Union, or one constructed around the cold war, governmental deceit, and the actions of martyrs.

At present there is no definitive truth in the Rosenberg case. All we have at our disposal is the assertions of the actors, a large body of circumstantial evidence, and a knowledge of the historical period in which the events in question took place. How we view these elements is, of course, colored by our preconceptions and political prejudices—hardly the stuff of claims to definitive or objective truth.

What appears relatively immune to fictional representation, however, is the immediate political environment surrounding Julius Rosenberg's arrest. How much weight to assign this is a matter for the reader ultimately to decide.

After the atom bomb explosions at Hiroshima and Nagasaki in August 1945, the scientists who had designed the bomb quickly came before the American public to stress that there was no "secret" to developing the bomb and that other countries probably would be able to manufacture atomic bombs within three to five years. Therefore, they argued, international cooperation should govern control of this new force of human destruction. By 26 September 1945 the physicists, chemists, engineers, and biologists who had worked at the Oak Ridge, Tennessee, atomic bomb project formed an organization and issued a statement to the press:

> [N]o enduring monopoly of the atomic bomb by the Americans and British is possible and . . . an international authority for its control must be set up with adequate safeguards to prevent exploitation by one nation. . . . We can expect no enduring monopoly of the atomic bomb. Other

scientists can apply the fundamental principles, perhaps more successfully than we have. . . . Other countries know they can produce such bombs within a few years without any detailed technical information from us.

The "other country" Americans most feared manufacturing its own atom bomb was the USSR. The atomic scientists did nothing to allay these fears. One of the pivotal figures in the bomb's development, Dr. Harold Urey, told a Senate Special Committee on Atomic Energy in November 1945 that the Russians would not take more than about five years to detonate their own bomb. The Association of Oak Ridge Scientists issued their own statement on this matter in December: "In a few years, first Russia, then other nations will have atomic bombs."

The United States government seemed to confirm the idea that there were no atomic "secrets" it could prevent other countries from obtaining when it printed the *Official Report of the United States Government on Atomic Energy Developed for Military Purposes* by Henry De Wolf Smyth. Published in the fall of 1945, it described the process by which the United States had developed the atom bomb in some detail. This report contained a separate section outlining the principle of atomic bomb detonation, and included photographs of the buildings and installations where the component parts of the bomb had been manufactured. While much specific information was lacking, "it was fairly generally agreed" that trained scientists could get a clear idea of the bomb's structure. When the report was published as a book, *Atomic Energy for Military Purposes*, it had a first edition of 30,000 copies in the Soviet Union.

Despite the scientific community's assertions that no fundamental atomic secrets existed and that the USSR would design an atomic bomb on its own within five years, anti-Communists in government and in the press did not listen. They maintained that the Soviets could only develop an atomic bomb of their own by "stealing" America's "secrets." The Reds could only succeed through espionage and deceit.

The November 1946 elections ushered in the first Republican Congress since Herbert Hoover's presidency. After its inauguration, the newly chaired House Committee on Un-American Activities (HUAC) announced a program that included an investigation "of those groups and movements which are trying to dissipate our atomic bomb knowledge for the benefit of a foreign power." Armed only with ideology and short of facts, HUAC exacerbated a growing climate of fear and hostility over clandestine Soviet attempts to steal "our secrets." J. Parnell Thomas, the committee's chair, outlined his basic argument that "our atomic-energy secrets may be secrets no longer" in two articles that appeared in *American* magazine and *Liberty* magazine in the summer of 1947: "Russia Grabs Our Inventions," and "Reds in Our Atom-Bomb Plants."

Directly after these articles appeared, the FBI arrested two former U.S. Army sergeants who had worked at Los Alamos. Amid a flurry of "atom spy" headlines, the Justice Department announced that the GIs "had stolen vital atomic secrets from the heart of the atomic bomb project at Los Alamos." When brought to trial six weeks later, however, it was discovered that the sergeants had taken some classified documents as souvenirs and were given suspended sentences. Nonetheless the FBI continued undaunted in its search for atomic spies, arresting three more GIs who had served at Los Alamos in the ensuing months. Each arrest was accompanied by wide press coverage and each soldier was alleged to have stolen secret atomic data. When their cases finally reached courts of law, none were proven to be anything more than reckless souvenir hunters.

Just as the FBI's inability to convict any of its "atom spies" as espionage agents was becoming apparent, HUAC announced its intention to hold hearings into "how the atom bomb secret was handed over to the Reds," an apparent fait accompli based on literally no factual information. The press, however, seemed to have no need for evidence and relished the sensational information J. Parnell Thomas fed it from his hearings that were closed to the public and the media. For four weeks in September 1948, almost every responsible American newspaper had headlines based on Thomas's rendition of what occurred in his committee meetings: "ATOM BOMB LEAKS," "SPYING FOR RUSSIA BY ATOM SCIENTISTS," "RUSSIANS STOLE ATOMIC SECRETS." According to author William Reuben, it was in this period that HUAC "succeeded finally in kicking over the last of the traces of what had been a general public truth in 1945: that there were no atomic secrets. By the time the Committee finished its blitzkrieg assault on American credulity in that Summer of 1948, the 'Red atom bomb spy' had become firmly rooted in American folklore."

By the fall, HUAC had charged a list of at least eleven people with being part of an effective "Communist espionage apparatus in the United States . . . in connection with the development of the atom bomb." Furthermore, the committee accused the Democratic administration of indifference toward Soviet espionage "tantamount to a representation to the American people that espionage against the development of the atom bomb just did not exist. A representation such as this in a free country, where such representation is palpably at variance with the facts, is un-American." The "facts" would eventually show that none of the eleven charged had ever been espionage agents, but the equation of un-Americanism with failure to believe in Communist atomic espionage had been firmly planted in the public's mind.

———

I myself believed . . . they
would take about five years.
Well, they took four.
Philip Morrison,
coholder of the
patent on the bomb
dropped at Nagasaki

Since we were the only
ones who had it, they had
to have stolen it from us.
Richard Brennan,
former FBI agent

On 23 September 1949, President Truman announced that the Soviet Union had exploded its first atomic bomb the previous month. He calmly stated that "[e]ver since atomic energy was first released by man, the eventual development of this new force by other nations was to be expected. This probability has always been taken into account by us." His calm in the face of this shocking event was taken as further evidence of "un-Americanism" by Republicans in Congress. HUAC member Congressman Richard Nixon claimed that the Soviets' feat was contributed to by the "Truman Administration's failure to act against Red spies in the United States." "I feel the American people are . . . entitled to know the facts about the espionage ring which was responsible for turning over information on the atom bomb to agents of the Russian government."

Congressman Harold Velde responded to the President by releasing a press statement that read in part:

> *The Russians undoubtedly gained three to five years in producing the atomic bomb, solely because the American government for the last fifteen years has had the official attitude, from the White House down, of being highly tolerant of, and at times even sympathetic to, the views of Communists and fellow travellers, with the result that the Federal government has been infiltrated by a network of spies.*

Without a single piece of evidence to substantiate their claims, Republicans asserted without restraint that the Soviets had developed an atom bomb through espionage that had occurred because Democrats were indifferent toward and too tolerant of Communists. Within four years and without proof, Communism, espionage, and the theft of atom bomb "secrets" had become fundamentally associated with each other in American public discourse. The Communist party was, "in the national folklore, considered to have more interest in atomic espionage than socialism."

It came as little surprise to many, therefore, when a former German Communist party member and current atomic scientist was arrested in Britain on 2 February 1950 for passing information about the atom bomb's development to the Soviets. Klaus Fuchs, who lived in England, had worked at Los Alamos as a theoretical physicist and before that at Columbia University as a member of an Anglo-American team that attempted to devise a method for producing weapons-grade uranium. By his own confession, throughout this period of employment in the United States, he had given information to the Soviets through an American courier known to him only as "Raymond." It was to this man that Fuchs conveyed the progress of the Manhattan Project and his calculations of the atomic bomb's actual dimensions. Fuchs was tried and sentenced in Britain with lightning speed. Within a month and a half following his arrest, Klaus Fuchs was sentenced to fourteen years in prison, the maximum allowed under British law for espionage on behalf of a friendly country as opposed to a wartime enemy.

The reaction to the Fuchs conviction in the United States was sharp and immediate. Richard Nixon called for a full-scale congressional investigation into atomic espionage. Members of the Joint be extradited to the United States to be charged with a capital offense. A member of the Atomic Energy Commission told *Time* magazine that Fuchs's arrest "was one of the blackest days in the history . . . of the security of this country. We are treating this as the biggest problem we ever had."

More than anything, however, people wanted to know the identity of "Raymond." Armed with only a meager description of him from Fuchs, the FBI spent the spring desperately searching for Fuchs's courier. According to J. Edgar Hoover, in "all the history of the FBI there never was a more important problem than this one, never another case where we felt under such pressure. The unknown man simply had to be found."

On 23 May the FBI succeeded; a middle-aged, Jewish chemist from Philadelphia was arrested for being Klaus Fuchs's espionage conduit. Harry Gold had told FBI agents the previous day that he had been the man whom Klaus Fuchs had given material on the atomic bomb. In the course of his lengthy confession on 1 June 1950, Gold not only implicated Klaus Fuchs as a source of scientific information he passed along to the Soviets, but another man whom he could only describe to a Philadelphia FBI agent as follows: "A soldier, non-commissioned, married, no children (name not recalled). Gold stated that he contacted this individual at Albuquerque, New Mexico. . . . He picked up information from this soldier described by Gold as 'general information on installation.' He states that if supplied with a map of Albuquerque, New Mexico, he can show where this soldier lived. He paid the soldier $500 for the information obtained."

The following day, under intense pressure from the FBI to identify the unnamed soldier, Gold recalled that his Los Alamos source had been a draftsman, machinist, electrician, or worker in a physics laboratory, that he had been "not more than twenty-five years old, five feet seven inches, sturdily built, with dark brown or black curly hair, a snub nose and a wide mouth," and that his wife's "name may have been Ruth, although I am not sure." He further added that the soldier had a Bronx or Brooklyn accent, was probably Jewish, and recently had been married when he met him in 1945.

According to Ronald Radosh and Joyce Milton in *The Rosenberg File*, this information led the FBI to the name of David Greenglass. The FBI had contacted Greenglass in January 1950 because he had stolen a small amount of uranium from Los Alamos as a souvenir. Consequently, his name apparently appeared on a list in the FBI's possession that contained personal information on GIs who had been investigated. The details supplied by Gold coincided so greatly with the FBI's description of Greenglass that on 3 June agents showed Gold David's high school graduation picture and a recent surveillance photo. Gold, however, was only able to say that the photos "resembled" the man he had visited in New Mexico.

Such a response did not deter the FBI. A week later, agents secured a photo of David Greenglass taken in 1945 and immediately showed it to Gold. Suddenly, he was able to make an affirmative identification, claiming that Greenglass was the man he contacted in Albuquerque who had provided him with information on the atom bomb.

That afternoon FBI agents went to David Greenglass's Lower East Side apartment, searched it for five hours, and took their suspected espionage source to headquarters for questioning. There they confronted him for the first time with the information that confessed Soviet spy Harry Gold had identified him as a link in an espionage network. Apparently with little provocation, David Greenglass, the unambitious machinist, the unsuccessful, overweight Jew who was only able to provide his young family with a cold-water tenement flat, admitted that this was so. Little Doovey was a spy.

David thereupon signed a written statement asserting that when Ruth visited him in Albuquerque on their first wedding anniversary, she forwarded a request from Julius Rosenberg asking him to supply atom bomb information to the Soviets with which he subsequently complied. Upon signing the statement, David, in a rather typically unaware and boastful manner, told his interrogators: "I expect to have my day in court, at which time I will plead innocent, repudiate this statement, and claim I never saw you guys."

In a second statement on the morning of 16 June, after being in FBI custody less than twenty-four hours, David told of an incident in which Julius had introduced him to an unidentified man in a car who questioned him about high-explosive lens molds used in the atomic bomb. Having further incriminated his brother-in-law, David then boasted, according to an FBI agent present, that "under no circumstances would he testify against Rosenberg." Shortly thereafter he was interviewed by a representative of the attorney's office he had requested as counsel. When this lawyer asked David whether he intended to cooperate with the government and testify against

Julius, he replied emphatically, "Hell, no!" In fact, he wanted his brother-in-law informed of exactly what had transpired thus far.

Contrary to David's wishes, the FBI promptly went to see Julius Rosenberg, but with no intention of playing messenger on behalf of David Greenglass. Shortly after eight in the morning on Friday, 16 June, three FBI agents arrived at the Rosenbergs' apartment. According to Julius:

[They came] *before we had finished dressing the children and getting them ready for school; I didn't have my shirt on, I remember, I didn't finish my shave yet, and there was a knock on the door. I opened the door. They said, 'We are from the FBI. We would like to talk to you.' I said, 'Come in,' . . .*

I said, 'I will talk to you gentlemen.' And I finished dressing the children; my wife made some breakfast; I took my shave; and they looked around the apartment and said, 'We can't talk here. Would you like to come down to our office and we will drop in and have a cup of coffee?' And I went with the gentlemen of the FBI, about 9 o'clock.

Well, there was a Mr. Norton in the room sitting at a desk with a pad in front of him, and Mr. Harrington sat on the other side of the table. I sat down on the front side of the table and another member of the FBI came in and sat behind, and they started asking questions about what I knew about David Greenglass. First they tried to get my background, what relations I had with him. I gave them my school background, work background and I told them whatever I knew about David Greenglass's education and work background. . . .

They asked me questions concerning when David Greenglass came in on furlough. I didn't remember. Then they said, was it in the winter or the summer? And they tried to keep bringing me around to the point where they could try to get me to state that I could remember specifically when. I couldn't recall all the events of his furlough. . . . At one point in the discussion, I would say it was about two hours after I was there, they said to me, 'Do you know that your brother-in-law said you told him to supply information for Russia?'

So I says, 'That couldn't be so.' So I said, 'Where is David Greenglass?' I didn't know where he was because I knew he was taken in custody. They wouldn't tell me. I said, 'Will you bring him here and let him tell me that to my face?' And they said, 'What if we bring him here, what will you do?'

I will call him a liar to his face because that is not so.

And I said, 'Look, gentlemen, at first you asked me to come down and get some information concerning David Greenglass. Now you are trying to implicate me in something. I would like to see a lawyer.

Well, at this point Mr. Norton said, 'Oh, we are not accusing you of anything. We are just trying to help you.'

I said, 'I would like to get in touch with the lawyer for the Federation of Architects and Engineers. . . .

I finally remembered the name, Victor Rabinowitz, and I asked the FBI to please call him. Well, at this point Mr. Norton said, 'Have a smoke, have a piece of gum. Would you like something to eat?' . . .

Finally, some time after lunch, it was probably between 12 and 1, my wife reached me at the FBI office and I told her that the FBI is making some foolish accusations. . . .

[S]omewhere between two and three o'clock, Mr. Norton called up Mr. Rabinowitz's office and he told me that Mr. Rabinowitz was not in. I said I would like to talk to somebody there and Mr. Rabinowitz's partner got on the phone, another lawyer, and I told him I was down at the FBI, and he said, 'Are you under arrest?'

I said, 'I don't know.'

He says, 'Ask the FBI if you are under arrest.'

And I asked Mr. Norton, 'Am I under arrest?'

He says, 'No.'

Then he said, 'Pick yourself up and come down to our office,' and I said, 'Good bye, gentlemen,' and I left the FBI office. . . .

I remember that as I walked out of the building I saw a New York Post with the picture of David Greenglass, and I picked it up, because that is the first I realized he had been officially arrested . . .

Julius went at once to the law offices of Victor Rabinowitz and Leonard Boudin, with whom he had spoken on the phone. He wanted their firm to represent him, but since they were counsel for yet another alleged "atom spy," Judith Coplon, they suggested that it would be better—for them and for Julius—to find another attorney. They recommended Emanuel Bloch who frequently defended leftists

and, like Rabinowitz and Boudin, was friendly to the Communist
party.

That evening Julius and Bloch met for the first time near a subway stop close to Bloch's apartment on lower Fifth Avenue. They walked to a nearby coffee shop where Julius explained what had happened to him that day. According to Bloch, Julie "didn't appear too perturbed." He seemed to be "a rather soft, sweet, intellectual sort of fellow" who the attorney believed was "in the same boat with hundreds of other people" currently being harassed by the FBI for their Communist sympathies. "I told him I'd handle the case, that he should go on home and resume his normal life and work, and let me know if he got a summons to appear before a grand jury." Julie half-joked that he could not allow himself to worry about the FBI's charges since he had a wife and two children to support. The two shook hands and parted. As Bloch returned to his apartment he seemed genuinely unconcerned about representing Rosenberg, thinking that it would be "just another routine" Fifth Amendment case where the government would attempt to charge his new client with perjury before a grand jury. Even the suggestion of espionage did not unduly perturb the middle-aged attorney, since only a year before he had represented Communist party leader Steve Nelson on charges of being an "atom spy" before the House Committee on Un-American Activities. Thus we can be fairly certain that when Emanuel Bloch walked through the front door of his Greenwich Village apartment he resumed his normal life, relatively unaffected by the meeting with his new client. When Julius returned home on the night of 16 June 1950, however, there is little about which he thought or did that we can be certain.

––––––

Julius Rosenberg was to maintain until his death that prior to David Greenglass's arrest and subsequent confession, he had only known that his brother-in-law had been "in some serious trouble" but had little idea of what that trouble was. At most he thought it concerned David's theft of uranium from Los Alamos as a souvenir. David had "told me what happened to him in February [1950] when the FBI had come around to visit him and question him about some uranium. I thought maybe it had something to do with that or had something to do with a conversation Ruthie had with me many years back" about her husband's idea to "make some money and take some things from the Army." Therefore Julius claimed that whatever trouble David may have been in, it certainly had nothing to do with him. Thus when he was picked up by FBI agents for questioning on the morning of 16 June, he claimed to have little notion of why they were there and agreed to speak with them only because Ethel argued that "if Davey is in some sort of trouble, if you can help my brother, talk to them; maybe you can be of some assistance to them." It seems, however, that Julie may have known far more about his brother-in-law's "serious trouble" than he ever admitted and may have been well aware of his connection to it.

Shortly after Harry Gold was arrested on 23 May 1950, the FBI had announced that their newly captured spy was "cooperating to provide the authorities with a full account of his activities." From that point on, newspapers continually told their readers that Gold was in the process of supplying information that would lead to the arrest of more "atom spies." As early as 25 May, *The New York Herald Tribune*'s headline read "KEY RED ATOM SPY BEING HUNTED HERE, GOT GOLD'S SECRETS," and *The New York World Telegram* announced "FBI HUNTS SECOND AMERICAN A-SPY." On 27 May, the Associated Press reported that the FBI agents who were questioning Gold in his cell "are getting all the help he can give in their efforts to track down others of the Soviet atomic spy ring."

Once Gold had referred to a twenty-five-year-old Jewish soldier from Los Alamos, married to a woman named Ruth, who was part of his espionage network, the FBI put David Greenglass under sur-veillance. By the end of the first week in June, Ruth reported that she and her husband were "watched constantly." She informed her attorneys on 18 June that she and David "had been under surveil-lance by the FBI for several weeks." They had "noticed a car of the Acme Construction Company, 1400 First Avenue, Manhattan" parked outside their apartment house. When Ruth investigated, she "ascertained there was no such Company." On 17 June *The New York Daily Mirror* reported: "In the past three weeks, residents related, they noticed four men in a gray car watching the [Green-glass] house night and day, presumably FBI agents."

With newspaper headlines constantly referring to imminent ar-rests of "atom spies," and with David Greenglass clearly under FBI surveillance, it is interesting to note what the Rosenbergs did during the weeks between the announcement of Harry Gold's arrest and Julius's confrontation with the FBI on 16 June.

According to Pitt's shop foreman, Charlie Bozsik, Julie was absent from work on 28 May and from 4 to 8 June 1950. This may have been due to a strep throat Julie had sometime during this period but, if so, it did not prevent him from engaging in a fair amount of activity on Tuesday, 6 June.

On that day, the Rosenbergs closed the checking account they had maintained since 17 January 1942 at the Public National Bank and Trust Company at Delancey and Orchard streets on the Lower East Side. They redeemed $770.75 worth of Series E bonds they held, and most curiously, on that day Julius had the attorney who helped with matters relating to his business, Solomon H. Bauch, make Bernie Greenglass, still legally the vice president of Pitt, "certified as competent to sign checks." According to Bauch, this was done because the Rosenbergs "were contemplating a trip."

When Julie returned to work on 9 June 1950, he told Charlie that his brother-in-law Bernie had been given "power of attorney" because he, Julie, planned on "going on a vacation to Arizona or some such place." He also told his foreman that he had just sold some property he owned with a group in Westchester County for $2,500. This most likely was Julie's share in the Yorktown Development that he had purchased in 1944 along with Sigmund Diamond and Russell McNutt. Clearly, the Rosenbergs were liquidating their resources and telling some people they were planning a trip. The logical conclusion to be drawn from this is that they were intending to take an extended trip, requiring all the money they had at their disposal, including the savings they had previously refused to touch even while Pitt was providing almost nothing on which to live.

Why, then, were the Rosenbergs contemplating "going on a vacation" that would require all their financial resources at this point in time? One explanation rests in Morton Sobell's account of his own decision to leave for Mexico around this time. He explains why he and his wife, Helen, had "much to fear" in June 1950:

Helen and I had both committed perjury when we signed the 'loyalty oaths' at Reeves [their place of employment], and many of our relatives and friends had also been members of the Party. I had recently been granted 'secret' clearance with no apparent difficulty, but I was certain at some point to be the subject of an FBI inves-

tigation. Helen, of course, had long ago been officially accused of Communist Party membership when employed in Washington by the Bureau of Standards.

In addition to this realistic fear there were other apprehensions which pervaded the American Left in 1950, and which I shared. The belief was widespread that World War III was in the offing. It seemed to us that America was veering toward fascism, a fascism that would be much the same as that of Nazi Germany. We saw mass roundups, concentration camps, and death ovens, a la Hitler. . . .

The evening newspapers on Friday, June 16, carried headlines about a former army sergeant who had been arrested for the theft of the atom bomb. I saw it as more fuel for the rising temperature of the cold war. . . .

[H]ow should we respond to the menace I felt in the political situation? I knew I had to leave Reeves; but where to go; what alternative way of life?

I had been considering the possibility of our living abroad but it seemed an enormous step. Mexico seemed most practicable. We had talked of going there on vacation. It was close and living there was inexpensive. If we went, perhaps it would be merely a long summer vacation. We could go with an open mind, look around, and then decide our course of action. It was crazy, I knew, but I felt we had to get away to some place where the air would be cleaner, where we could relax—psychologically as well as physically. . . .

I went to work at Reeves that Monday and Tuesday. . . . On Wednesday I withdrew most of the money from our bank accounts, cashed our defense bonds, and obtained our tourist permits from the Mexican Consulate. . . . We started packing Wednesday evening. . . . We left from La Guardia Thursday, on an evening flight.

By his own account, Sobell made the decision to go to Mexico on Saturday, 17 June. By the following Thursday, he, Helen, their infant son Mark, and Helen's daughter, Sydney, were on a plane to Mexico City, having told none of their family they were leaving (despite the fact that Sobell's parents were long-time leftists).

Although Sobell's shockingly impulsive act to go to Mexico and live there under an assumed name does seem "crazy," given that he and his wife, according to his account, at most might have faced perjury charges for recently lying on their loyalty oaths, he perhaps was responding more to a climate of extreme apprehension and, for some, near panic as the American government and the majority of its citizens seemed determined to destroy anything and anyone associated with Communism. By June 1950, the fervor that had been growing since the end of World War II had turned into a national obsession, a hegemonic moral crusade. Alger Hiss had been convicted of perjury; Joe McCarthy was a national hero; the leaders of the Communist party had been found guilty of violating the Smith Act. Congress debated, and in September passed, a new Internal Security Act that required federal registration of what the government considered all "Communist-action" groups and their members, made political beliefs (and not actions) a standard for admission to and deportation from the United States, and provided for concentration camps to imprison anyone deemed to be subversive whenever the federal government believed the country to be in a state of "national emergency." This, however, was not enough for some. Republican Karl Mundt called for "vigilante action to combat Communism through . . . grass-roots committees, in every American town," and a Hearst syndicated columnist, Westbrook Pegler, declared in his 29 June 1950 column that reached some 30 million readers: "The only sensible and courageous way to deal with Communists in our midst is to make membership in Communist organizations or covert subsidies a capital offense and shoot or otherwise put to death all persons convicted of such."

World War III also seemed an imminent possibility, as Morton Sobell points out. Senator John McClellan argued that since war with Stalin was inevitable, "why not fire the first shot?", while the Secretary of the Navy, Francis Matthews, began echoing what many in less responsible positions had been clamoring for: a preventive atomic strike against the Soviet Union. "It would win for us a proud and popular title. We would become the first aggressors for peace," he proclaimed.

Unquestionably, this environment of repression and hostility must have weighed heavily on the Rosenbergs. Although they had little to fear in terms of perjury charges, the most common vehicle then used for imprisoning present and former Communists, the prospects of an atomic war with Russia and the vision of domestic concentration camps for people like themselves must have seemed very real and very threatening. Was this enough, however, for them to prepare to leave home for an extended period? Was it simply coincidence that they liquidated their savings and gave Bernie

Greenglass power of attorney on 6 June, following Harry Gold's arrest and the commencement of the FBI's surveillance of David Greenglass? Or is it possible that Julius Rosenberg knew far more than he ever admitted about why the FBI was following his brother-in-law's every move those first weeks of June 1950?

————

By midnight on 15 June, David Greenglass had been in the presence of FBI agents almost twelve hours, and at about 8:30 P.M. he had been confronted with the fact that Harry Gold had identified him as his Los Alamos espionage contact. When told that Gold claimed David had been given $500 for information he supplied, David apparently broke down and admitted that this was in fact the case but that he "did not furnish the information for the money but for the cause." His only concern was that his confession not be used in any way against his wife. If Ruth were implicated, he would commit suicide.

The confession that David Greenglass signed at approximately 1:30 A.M. was brief and to the point. On one occasion, in November 1944, Ruth came to visit David in New Mexico and brought with her a message from Julius Rosenberg requesting that David supply information about his work to the Soviets. She told him that a man would contact him later. According to David's confession, Harry Gold did visit and paid him $500 for the following pieces of information: the identity of a "world-famous scientist, who was working at Los Alamos under an assumed name"; the revelation that Oppenheimer and Kistiakowski were working at Los Alamos; a list of others who David thought could be approached for information; and "I think that I gave Gold a sketch of a high-explosive lens mold, or something of that type of thing, which was an experiment to study implosion effects on a steel tube. . . ." The means of identifying Gold as the man to whom he should pass this information was a torn card. David claimed he could not then recall whether it was presented to him by Ruth in February 1945, or by Julius Rosenberg while he was in New York City on furlough.

No secret of the atom bomb, no espionage rings, no prolonged period of spying, and, most interestingly, no mention of Ethel Rosenberg was included in this statement. It would be weeks before David essentially altered this initial confession and seriously implicated the Rosenbergs, weeks in which he was under pressure from his attorney and then his wife to cooperate with the govern- ment.

The reason David gave for his subsequent cooperation and further implication of the Rosenbergs in atomic espionage was that he feared Ruth would be prosecuted. In 1979 David explained the decision he made in 1950 as having been a rather simple one to reach:

> It was all in my mind. They didn't put pressure on me. I said I gotta make a choice. This [indicating Ruth who sat beside him] gotta stay with me. They [the Rosenbergs] gotta take care of themselves. In my mind, all they had to do was have a conversation, the same as I had a conversation.

David was under enormous strain; he envisioned a choice between his wife being arrested and perhaps harshly sentenced along with himself and thus orphaning their two small children, or implicating the Rosenbergs further. When he made his initial confession, however, he was under no such pressure, for Ruth was under no suspicion. She only came into danger of prosecution after David named her in his statement. He signed a confession that for the first time alerted the FBI to his wife's involvement in espionage and then threatened to commit suicide if the government used this confession against her. Similarly, he admitted to his brother-in-law's participation in spying and then wanted Julie informed of exactly what had happened, telling a representative of his attorney's office that under no circumstances would he testify against his brother-in-law.

These initial actions do not suggest a man coldly calculating how to deceive his interrogators or attempting to pin his guilt on an unsuspecting relative. Rather they reveal someone who most likely was extraordinarily naive and thoughtless. In answering questions about his background earlier in the evening of the 15th, David apparently thought nothing of admitting to FBI agents that he was a "leftwinger," informing them that he and Ruth had been members of the Young Communist League, gratuitously adding that he believed that "capitalism is not the best possible system." David Greenglass said this at the height of anti-Communist hysteria, in which thousands of people were perjuring themselves, going to jail, or refusing to reveal details of their past or present political beliefs and activities rather than admit any affinity for or with the Communist party. David, however, seemed blithely unaware that he was speaking to the agency most responsible for leading the anti-Communist crusade (along with HUAC) and for persecuting people who shared the kinds of backgrounds and espoused the sorts of beliefs he then was proudly claiming. While most people in his position would have experienced fear, contempt, or outrage, David Greenglass naively seemed to enjoy his interrogation. In an inter-office memo, the FBI reveals that throughout the search of his apartment and his interviews of 15 and 16 June, Greenglass maintained a "friendly attitude toward all of the FBI personnel and seemed to be in good spirits during the whole period."

Without the presence of his smarter, more practical, and calculating wife, David Greenglass was a foolish, trusting, and child-like "slob," as his own attorney referred to him, but he may not have been a liar—at least not yet. Before Ruth and their lawyer, O. John Rogge, convinced him to cooperate with the government, before he came to believe that lies and exaggerations were the means of saving his wife and avoiding a long jail term for himself, before he was imprisoned with Harry Gold to "reconcile discrepancies" in their respective stories, David sat alone at FBI headquarters and told the agents with whom he had spent the day the truth about his background, his political beliefs, and about his wife's role in espionage. David loved Ruth more than anyone in the world and vowed to commit suicide if anything happened to her, yet he revealed her involvement in spying, and he did so ignorant of the legal consequences. There is little evidence that his implication of Julius Rosenberg differed from his ill-advised revelations about his past, his beliefs, or Ruth's role.

This suggests that in 1944 Julius may have asked David to transmit information about the Los Alamos project to the Soviets through espionage channels he had contacted. This is in keeping with what we know about Julius's zealous idealization of the Soviet Union, his plans to leave New York after Harry Gold's arrest and David's subsequent surveillance, and the apparent candor of David's initial confession. There is also additional circumstantial evidence that lends support to this view.

Max Elitcher, a former classmate of Julius Rosenberg's from CCNY, was picked up for questioning by the FBI on 20 July 1950. At that time he told the agents present that when Julius had visited his apartment in Washington, while on assignment with the Signal

Corps in the summer of 1944, he spoke with Max about "the great   229
role Russia was playing in the war and the great sacrifice she was
making. [He said] some persons were contributing to the Russian
war effort by giving information concerning secret material and
developments to the Russians, which they would not ordinarily
receive. He asked me if I would contribute in this way."

Elitcher's initial story became somewhat elaborated after he
decided to cooperate with the government under the tutelage of his
attorney, the now omnipresent O. John Rogge. He, however, never
admitted to any espionage work or to witnessing Julius Rosenberg
engaged in any such work.

Another piece of corroborative circumstantial evidence comes
from a convict, turned government informer, who was in the same
jail as Julius Rosenberg for six months in 1950–1951. Jerome E.
Tartakow, with a record for pimping, armed robbery, and interstate
auto theft, became Julius's confidant and offered to inform on him
to the government in exchange for early parole and pay. Tartakow
supplied details about Julius Rosenberg's personal life to the FBI
that only someone who knew him intimately could be familiar. He
also mixed rather improbable material with some information that
could be corroborated elsewhere. Thus it is difficult to know what,
of the many things he reported to the FBI that Julius had told him,
are true or pure invention.

Tartakow reported to the FBI on 3 January 1951 that Julius had
admitted to him that "he played the game and lost, and would have
to take the results." Thereafter, for many months, Tartakow regaled
FBI agents with information about spy rings composed of many of
Julie's friends and their espionage exploits. The FBI was never able
to gather enough evidence to indict any of the people Tartakow
named (though certainly not through want of trying) and continued
to consider him an "informant of unknown reliability" as they ex-
haustively followed his leads.

An informant of indisputable reliability, however, recently came
forth with another small piece of circumstantial evidence. James
Weinstein, editor of the national weekly *In These Times* and a
widely respected historian of the American left, divulged for the
first time in 1978 that he had direct reason to believe Julius Rosenberg was involved in espionage. He reports that in 1949 a close
friend of his and classmate at Cornell, Max Finestone, told him that
he was quitting the Communist party, of which they were both
members, to engage in "secret work." In December of that year

Max moved into Weinstein's New York City apartment and the two became roommates. The following July, shortly after David Greenglass's arrest, Julius Rosenberg came to this apartment and asked to see Finestone. When Weinstein informed him that Max was not in, his visitor simply said, "Tell him Julius was here," and left. Later that evening, Weinstein told his roommate what had occurred. Max asked if he was sure it was Julius, and when Weinstein replied in the affirmative, "Max turned white as a sheet" and said, "he knows he's not supposed to come here."

Finally, it is interesting to note that during the summer of 1950, three of Julius Rosenberg's closest friends disappeared from their homes under suspicious circumstances. Morton Sobell, who had known Julius from the days of the Steinmetz Society, departed for Mexico on 22 June and upon settling there used a variety of assumed names while looking for means for him and his family to leave that country without valid passports. He was abducted on 16 August and returned to the United States against his will by Mexicans working at the request of the FBI. About a week earlier, Joel Barr, who had participated with Julius in the Steinmetz Society, FAECT, and the CP's Branch 16B, had disappeared from an apartment he rented in a Paris suburb. He eventually turned up in the Soviet Union where he apparently still resides under the name Joseph Berg. Al Sarant, also a former member of Julius and Joel's Party branch, left the country for Mexico on 9 August, leaving behind his wife and two young sons. He eventually surfaced in Czechoslovakia and then moved to the Soviet Union where he became a leading research scientist in the field of microelectronics. Filipp Georgievich Staros, aka Al Sarant, became the chief designer at a military research laboratory in Leningrad where his best friend and right-hand man was Joseph Berg.

Many have taken the actions of these three men as evidence of their mutual participation in a Soviet espionage ring that they feared would be exposed after the arrests of David Greenglass and Julius Rosenberg. Others have argued that, as former members of the Communist party and close friends of Julius Rosenberg, these men feared they would be unfairly harassed or arrested and their careers ruined because of their association with Rosenberg and the CP. According to this view, Barr and Sarant presumably chose the Soviet Union as a place to settle because they could pursue their chosen careers there free of political persecution.

If one believes that this circumstantial evidence suggests that

Julius Rosenberg was involved in spy work, does it imply that he
engineered the theft of the secret of the atom bomb, or that he was
a master spy, or the head of a Soviet espionage ring?

No. The only material David Greenglass ever admitted to "steal-ing" from Los Alamos was some uranium as a souvenir. What he confessed to giving Harry Gold were the names of scientists working at Los Alamos, a list of people who might be approached as espionage contacts, and a sketch of a lens mold drawn from memory. The names of scientists and possible spy recruits are obviously unrelated directly to the development of the atomic bomb, and a far more extensive and informed list of names probably was prepared by Klaus Fuchs. Furthermore, after the anti-Communist hysteria of the early nineteen-fifties abated, David Greenglass's rendition of a high-explosive lens mold was revealed not to be the secret of the atom bomb but rather a "ridiculous . . . baby drawing, it doesn't tell you anything," according to Victor Weisskopf, former deputy leader of the Theoretical Division at Los Alamos. George Kistiakowski, the chemist who directed the explosives division at Los Alamos and whom David Greenglass says he named in the information he transmitted to Harry Gold, describes the sketch as "uselessly crude," the value of which would be "absolutely nil" to the Soviets. Henry Linschitz, a physical chemist who was intimately involved in the development of the atomic bomb's implosion-type lens, concluded his assessment of Greenglass's material by stating: "It is not possible in any technologically useful way to condense the results of a two-billion-dollar development effort into a diagram, drawn by a high-school graduate machinist on a single sheet of paper." Finally, Philip Morrison, the physicist who is coholder of the patent on the Nagasaki implosion-type bomb, explains:

> They said this was the secret of the atom bomb, but I say it is far from that. There is no great secret of the atomic bomb. This is a crude caricature of the structure of one particular model, without enough detail to make it possible to reproduce or even to understand it as it was drawn, since it contains some errors. But what more could you expect from a man who has himself very little training, with a high school education and no direct contact at that time whatever with any but the simple mechanical parts that he might've seen if he'd worked in the shop or made the lens molds. . . . It's just too much to know. Too much for one

book to tell. Too much to write on any piece of paper. Volumes of technical skill. Laboratories full of people. Factories, machinists, machines, all sorts of things. That's what it takes. It's an industry, not a recipe.

The basic weakness of David Greenglass's sketch also was initially confirmed by Harry Gold. In a pretrial statement that Walter and Miriam Schneir obtained through Harry Gold's attorney, Gold described what purportedly occurred after he gave Greenglass's material to his Soviet espionage contact:

> *I turned the information over to John. John never mentioned anything about it, and on the one occasion that I did mention this man [Greenglass], sometime in the late fall of 1945, John said that we should forget all about him, that there wasn't much point in getting in touch with him. And I got from the manner in which he made the remark, that apparently the information received had not been of very much consequence at all.*

At most, the sketch David Greenglass confessed to transmitting may have confirmed a part of what Klaus Fuchs had already provided to the Soviet Union, albeit in a much less sophisticated and informed manner. Yet because of the political tenor of the period, the anti-Communist hysteria that gripped the nation, and the horror experienced by those in and out of government over the Soviet Union's possession of atomic weaponry, David Greenglass's "baby drawing" became the "secret of the atomic bomb" in the parlance of the FBI, government officials, reporters, newspaper editors, and subsequently, the American people.

That Julius Rosenberg may have asked David Greenglass for information about the Los Alamos project to pass on to the Soviets does not imply, however, that he was a master spy or the head of an espionage ring. Only after David decided to cooperate with the government did he begin to assert that his brother-in-law had been involved in spy work beyond the initial request David confessed to on the morning of 16 June. At that time he had stated unequivocally that since his discharge from the Army "he has not had any conversations with his brother-in-law, Julius Rosenberg, concerning Soviet espionage." Once he had decided to cooperate in exchange for Ruth's freedom and an anticipated lenient sentence for himself, however, David began to allege a series of conversations he had had with Julius from 1946 through 1949 that pertained to spying— all of which involved no other participants and could never be confirmed through any physical or circumstantial evidence.

Further, Julius' possible participation in espionage does not necessarily lend credence to the idea that the American Communist party was a recruiting ground for spies. It would have been politically and legally self-destructive for the American Party to encourage members or adherents to engage in espionage for the Soviets. Throughout the thirties and forties, the CPUSA was anxious to demonstrate its patriotism, its loyalty to America. After the war, which it had zealously supported, and as the tide of domestic and international anti-Communism spread, it certainly did not want to be identified with people who could be accused of divided loyalty or treasonous inclinations. In fact there has never been any solid evidence tying the Communist party in the United States to spying for the Soviet Union. Even Klaus Fuchs and Harry Gold, whose Communist sympathies were touted widely when they were arrested and sentenced, admired the Soviet Union but had never even been close to the CPUSA. Gold, who had been asked repeatedly by a friend in the ninteen-thirties to join the Party, consistently refused. In Gold's stated opinion, Communist party members were "a lot of whacked-up Bohemians;" in truth "a feeling of revulsion" came over him when a friend confessed he had become a Communist.

If, in fact, Julius Rosenberg spied for the Soviet Union, he was unlike the vast majority of those who have been indicted for this crime, in that he had been an active member of the American Communist party and remained loyal to it until his death. In her description of how her brother-in-law started spying, Ruth Greenglass claimed that the Party had been unable to satisfy his need to help the Soviet Union: "Julius said . . . that for two years he had been trying to get in touch with people who would assist him to be able to help the Russian people more directly other than just his membership in the Communist party." If the CP had been a recruiting ground for Soviet spies, or even if it merely encouraged such activity, it is doubtful that Julius, a Party member in good standing, would have had to spend two years of his life searching for someone who might connect him to Soviet espionage.

Of course none of this speaks to Ethel Rosenberg's involvement.

Because of the closeness of their relationship, because of Ethel's actions before and after her husband's arrest, there can be little question that Ethel was cognizant of whatever Julius may have been involved in and undoubtedly approved of it. Throughout the late forties, that is either during or after the time Julius may have engaged in espionage, Ethel continued to regard him as her "savior," on whom she had an "enormous dependence. . . . She thought he was absolutely wonderful; there was never any question about their relationship." From what we know of Ethel's history and her actions during the last three years of her life, there is literally nothing to suggest that she doubted or questioned her husband's activities during their marriage. Approval, however, is not participation.

According to Elizabeth Phillips, whom Ethel continued to see in therapy after her brother Dave was arrested, "before Julius was arrested there was some talk about maybe not continuing, maybe moving; there was a lot of uncertainty. Apparently they knew that they were closing in on Julius somehow; I mean it wasn't just a surprise." The Rosenbergs took action to leave the area; yet they remained. After David was arrested they were being watched and they knew it. Julie saw one of the agents who had questioned him on 16 June hanging around outside his shop. A neighbor of Ethel's recalls that "one day we were coming from the subway and I saw her and I was going to go up . . . ; she signaled me away as if to say don't come near me, and I thought it was a friendly thing to do because I'm sure she was being followed and she knew I'd have trouble." Ethel's old friend, Betty Birnbaum, with whom she had always enjoyed a warm relationship, ran into her outside Ohrbach's on Union Square around this time and recalls their interaction: " 'Ethel, how glad I am to see you. Why don't we try to keep in touch with each other. Come over to my house.' She couldn't wait to get away from me. She said 'no.' She was uneasy and I knew that I had better stop persisting. What was very clearly conveyed is that she was eager to get away from me." Shortly thereafter Betty read in the newspapers that Julius Rosenberg had been arrested.

In those last two weeks of June, as the Rosenbergs probably weighed their fears against their sense of reality, there were undoubtedly a number of considerations: Mr. Bloch's reassurances, their own ambivalence about leaving the Lower East Side for the unknown, dragging their two small sons with them into an uncertain future, that probably asserted a pull on them to stay and see what would happen. Conversely, they knew they were being watched by the FBI, and the political situation seemed to be deteriorating daily as the first salvos of the Korean War were fired on 25 June and talk of World War III—the all-out war against the Soviet Union—was on everyone's lips. But most of all during this time, Ethel and Julius must have wondered about David Greenglass and what he was doing and saying behind the walls of the West Street House of Detention.

At first, they must have been reassured by what they read in the press. At David's arraignment on 16 June, O. John Rogge, David's attorney, who was a former United States assistant attorney general and a former radical lawyer, announced that Greenglass was innocent and charged that he was a victim of the "hysteria of the Cold War." One week later, Rogge sought a preliminary hearing and had subpoenas issued for the FBI agents who had arrested his client. At the government's request the hearing was postponed until 13 July and Rogge was denied the right to subpoena the agents. As the *New York Journal-American* reported: "Today's hearing was acrimonious as Rogge . . . and Saypol clashed repeatedly. . . . Greenglass swore profusely as he was led in handcuffs back to the Federal House of Detention." For the following two weeks, however, there was a strange silence in the press about the Greenglass case.

Unbeknown to the Rosenbergs, during this period O. John Rogge was constructing the basis for Dave and Ruth's cooperation with the government. In fact, this process had started as early as Sunday, 18 June when Rogge held a meeting at the Greenglass apartment with Ruth, her brother-in-law Louis Abel, Bernie and Sam Greenglass and Issy Feit, Tessie's brother. According to Ronald Radosh, who interviewed O. John Rogge in 1978, at the beginning of the meeting Ruth expressed her fears "over the possibility that she would be arrested and separated from her children." She suggested that perhaps Rogge could use the argument "that her husband was emotionally unstable," which he discouraged, as he did her hope that "David's confession might be thrown out by the court." Rogge presented David's options to the assembled group, "stressing the possibility that the Greenglasses could plead guilty and become government witnesses—in his view the only chance for them both to escape heavy sentences. In trying to win Ruth over, Rogge mentioned several cases in which clients of his, having pleaded guilty, had gotten off with as little as three to five years for serious crimes." Ruth thereupon agreed to present Rogge's argument to her husband at her next visit, and the conference ended, ominously, with "a long discussion of J.R."

At this meeting it appears that the decision to further implicate Julius Rosenberg surfaced and was presumably accepted. What is astounding is that this occurred with the complicity of most of the Greenglass family. Here was Sam Greenglass, Ethel's estranged half-brother, who had severed his relationship with the Rosenbergs seven years earlier, presumably out of violent objection to their political beliefs. Here, too, was Bernie Greenglass, the peacekeeper in the business disputes between Dave and Julie. Apparently there was little question that he would sacrifice his brother-in-law and former business partner in order to spare his kid brother. Issy Feit was also present. He had lent Bernie the money that initially went into G and R Engineering and had lost most of it due to what we can be sure his sister, Tessie, and nephew, Dave, considered Julius Rosenberg's incompetence and ill-treatment of the Greenglass brothers.

The most positive comment that can be made about these family members' actions is that they probably could not foresee the horror that would be set in motion by their meeting of 18 June. It is not likely that any of them imagined that not only Julius, but Ethel would be arrested, that both would refuse to "confess," and that they would both be sent to their deaths after years in prison. They probably clung to the selfish, base point of view that Dave Greenglass would use years later in explaining his decision to cooperate: "This [indicating Ruth] gotta stay with me. They [the Rosenbergs] gotta take care of themselves."

An assessment that explains the Greenglasses' actions out of ignorance and self-interest rather than sheer malevolence, however, sidesteps the way that the assembled group imagined how Ethel, a member of their own family, would experience her husband's probable arrest, possible lengthy imprisonment, and the prospect of raising two fatherless sons on her own. More than any single event in Ethel's life about which we know, this meeting highlights the utter indifference with which Ethel Rosenberg was regarded by her own family. She was an outcast, not because she had physically deserted the family, but because she had dared to be different. She despised their lack of values, culture, and passion about anything outside their narrow self-interest. She had become a Communist

and married a man whom they had come to resent enormously   237
because he was contemptuous of Dave and Bernie. She fought
constantly with Tessie, unlike Ruth, and had to do everything her
own way. She had made her choice before, always defending her
husband in clashes over the family business, where Bernie and Dave
had lost everything they had put into it and Issy Feit was out a
considerable sum of money.

Was this reason enough for the family to completely turn their
backs on Ethel? The only way we can possibly make sense of the
Greenglasses' actions is to see them as a group of small-minded,
unsophisticated people overwhelmed by the events that surrounded
them. Having few experiences outside the enclosed Jewish ghetto
in which they lived, they sat in Ruth's apartment with a former
assistant attorney general of the United States of America, O. John
Rogge, who was telling them that cooperation was the "only chance"
Dave and Ruth had to avoid lengthy terms in prison. None of them
probably had ever met anyone as important or prestigious as Rogge,
and now he was sitting in Ruth's tenement, informing them how to
cope with the monumental crisis that had disrupted their lives only
three days before. Unused to thinking beyond individual self-interest, afraid, awed, and perhaps intimidated by Rogge, and deeply
resentful of the Rosenbergs, the Greenglass family set in motion a
plan not only for Ruth and Dave to cooperate with the government
by further implicating their brother-in-law, but for the family to keep
Ethel and Julie completely unaware of their intent.

The first indication the Rosenbergs probably received that Dave was
on the verge of cooperating came in reports of his second extradition
hearing of 12 July, which ended in a postponement. The New York
Daily Mirror of that date revealed: "The possibility that alleged
atomic spy David Greenglass has decided to tell what he knows
about the relay of secret information to Russia was evidenced yes-
terday when U.S. Commissioner McDonald granted the ex-Army
sergeant an adjournment of proceedings to move him to New Mexico for trial. . . . The court appearance followed the latest of a series
of conferences between Rogge and [U.S. Attorney Irving] Saypol."
The next day the *New York Journal-American* reported that Rogge
and Saypol had left the courtroom "practically arm in arm."

During this same week Ethel went to visit 64 Sheriff Street. She
described the incident as follows:

Well, I came to my mother's house because my sister-in-law, Gladys, was due home from the hospital that day. My children hadn't seen her for some time. I decided that when I picked the child up at 3 o'clock from school that I would take both youngsters down with me to my mother's house. . . .

Well, while I was there, my sister-in-law, Ruth, came in and at that time I asked . . . , 'Well, how is Davey?' And she said, 'All right,' and then she said to my mother, 'Ma, I have to pick up the baby; she is outside in the carriage near my mother's store. Goodbye,' and left very abruptly.

A few days later on Saturday, 15 July, Ethel again ran into Ruth.

I had come down [to 64 Sheriff] in the hopes that I would be able to go and visit my brother. I had gone to my mother's house and found nobody there. I went over to [Ruth's] mother's house and her mother told me that she had already left with my mother to . . . visit Davey.

And she said that my aunt [Tessie's sister] had been supposed to go along, too. Well, on my way . . . home I decided I would look in once more at my mother's house, and this time I found my aunt; she had not been permitted to go, for some reason, and so I stayed there and waited until my sister-in-law and my mother returned from visiting my brother; and when they came in I began to ply her with questions as to his health and how he was standing up under jail; and when I might get to see him: and my mother said, 'Well, look, Ruthie is very tired and very hungry. Suppose we sit down and eat and talk later.' So I did that. We sat down and had a bite to eat, and afterwards Ruth said that she was going to pick the child up, it was almost time for her bath, and when we got to her mother's house, to the store where everyone was, with the carriage, she said, 'You know, it is such a nice day, I think I will stay down with her another ten minutes. Then I will take her upstairs for her bath.' So we began to walk, she and I, with the carriage, around the block.

At this point Ruth claims that Ethel "said her counsel advised her to see me personally and get assurances from me that David would not talk. She said it would only be a matter of a couple of years,

and in the long run we would be better off; that Julius had been   **239**
picked up by the FBI for questioning. He said he was innocent and
that he had been released; that she had no doubt that he would
probably be picked up again. He would continue to say he was
innocent. That if David said he was innocent and Julius said he was
innocent, it would strengthen their position; everybody would stand
a better chance."

According to Ethel, she only innocently inquired at this point,
"Are you and Davey really mixed up in this horrible mess?"

Regardless of whose account one believes, Ruth, who according to Radosh and Milton was "acting on orders from Rogge,"
assured Ethel that "we have hired a lawyer and we are going to
fight this case." Ethel asserted in response: "Look, I really didn't
know what to think any more. There have been reports in the
newspapers about confessions and much as I believed, always believed in Davey, I really began to wonder. I had to hear it from
your own lips." Ruth tersely replied, "Well, now you have heard
it and it is the truth."

But it was a lie, for the day before, Dave and Ruth had begun
fully cooperating with the government, further implicating their
brother-in-law in espionage and setting the stage for Ethel's eventual
indictment. And, most likely, they did this with the knowledge and
acceptance of the Greenglass family, none of whom ever gave Ethel
any reason to doubt Ruth's reassurances.

Chief among those who kept Dave and Ruth's secret was undoubtedly Tessie Greenglass, who visited her favorite son in prison
a day after he had begun "remembering" incidents and events
linking Julius to a Soviet espionage ring. On Saturday, 15 July, she
had gone with Ruth to the West Street jail, and upon arriving home
deflected Ethel's questioning of how Dave was "standing up" and
when she would be able to see him with a reminder of how tired
and hungry Ruthie was, and that her daughter's questions could
wait until after they ate. Once they finished eating, however, Ruth
announced that she had to leave, and it is only because Ethel persisted by tagging along after her sister-in-law that she was able to
question her. Tessie had clearly not wanted Ethel to "ply Ruth with
questions" about Dave, at least not in her presence. Tessie's brother
and sons knew of Ruth and David's intentions and probably had
been warned by O. John Rogge not to mention anything to the
Rosenbergs, just as Ruth had been advised to lie to her sister-in-
law. It is extremely unlikely then that Tessie Greenglass, the family's
matriarch, knew less than those around her. Thus it was probably

of little surprise to her when Julius Rosenberg was arrested and taken from his home two days later on the basis of new information Ruth and Dave had provided the government.

On the evening of 17 July, Ethel had stood in her small apartment, her terrified children huddled around her as men from the FBI ransacked her closets, rifled through her drawers, tore through each one of her possessions, confiscating every family photograph, checkbook, tax form, birth certificate, letter, and bill. They also took her typewriter, the record she had made for Michael when Robby was born, a number of her books, and her notes on child rearing. Everything that was hers, that had her identity imprinted on it, was seized or examined and tossed aside. Alone, not wanting her children to sense the terror that undoubtedly filled her, Ethel only desired to go away to somewhere safe. She asked that an FBI agent take her to her mother's.

Sometime before nine o'clock on the evening of 17 July 1950, Ethel Rosenberg arrived at 64 Sheriff Street, her childhood home, with Michael and Robby in tow. Unbeknown to her, her mother was probably expecting her.

Saint Joan

1950–1953

15

"YOU'RE GONNA BURN WITH YOUR HUSBAND!"

The next morning, Tuesday, 18 July 1950, Ethel Rosenberg returned to her apartment and prepared for her greatest performance. Not since her theatrical ambitions waned in the late nineteen-thirties had she had the opportunity to play a role that so contradicted what she actually was experiencing. She and Julie apparently had devised a plan of how to present themselves to the public: they would show no fear or undue concern over what had occurred, for to do so would demonstrate guilty consciences. If they acted calm and un-ruffled, they seemed to have reasoned, their behavior would reflect their innocence. As Julie would later claim, "I wasn't concerned . . . because I wasn't guilty of any crime."

Although this strategy would thoroughly backfire, since the pub-lic interpreted it as evidence that these were two cold, unfeeling Stalinist spies, Ethel entered into her role with a certain amount of zeal. The stance of aloof indifference was one with which she was intimately acquainted. She had maintained it with her family, ad-olescent boys, and, most recently, her neighbors at Knickerbocker Village. She had assumed it when she felt vulnerable, anxious, rejected, and certainly with her husband suddenly behind bars, she never had more reason to experience such emotions. It was a lifetime psychological stance: don't show weakness and you won't be hurt.

Ethel chose to amplify this basic presentation of self by assuming the role of a typical nineteen-fifties American housewife—uninformed about politics and current events, focused on hearth and home, unaware of her husband's activities outside the family. Although the public was more disposed to accept this part of the performance, Ethel's seeming lack of concern about her husband's and then her own fate fundamentally contradicted what a typical housewife probably would experience under similar circumstances. Ethel's role was ill-conceived from the beginning, and its inherent problems were obvious from her first performance.

Less than twenty-four hours after her husband's arrest, Ethel Rosenberg invited the press into her apartment. This "typical" housewife wore a sleeveless, floral print housedress that exposed her fleshy arms and a slipping bra strap. Her stage was her tiny kitchen filled with drying clothes hanging from lines on the ceiling and a motley assortment of dishes in the drainer. The wall next to the sink was caked with dirt and grease, the garbage can was streaked with grime. Ethel went about showing the reporters how unconcerned she was over the previous night's events. She dried her dishes and cut up a chicken for the evening meal. Frequently, she posed for the camera with a wide grin and chicken carcass in hand. Although her husband was being described as an "atom spy" in the morning's newspapers, and imprisoned under $100,000 bail on the basis of charges her own brother made against him, Ethel Rosenberg was determined to show the world that she had nothing to fear or hide, and really knew very little about anything anyway.

> 'They came and got Julius the day after my brother was arrested,' Mrs. Rosenberg, a brunet, said. 'It was 8:15 in the morning. When he came back he merely said they had made crazy charges, but he didn't elaborate.'
>
> Mrs. Rosenberg appeared curiously unaware of her husband's activities.
>
> 'Did you ever have reason to think he was secretly sympathetic to subversive operators,' she was asked.
>
> 'Not in my 11 years of married life,' she replied. . . .
>
> 'Did you ever attend Communist meetings or sign Communist petitions?'
>
> 'Neither of us were ever Communists. We signed a

petition some years back to put somebody on a ballot—I don't remember which one.'

'Did you ever vote for Communist candidates?'

'No. But we did vote for American Labor Party candidates. . . .'

'Did you ever hear of Fuchs or Gold before?'

'No.'

Mrs. Rosenberg was calm and unemotional as she told of last night's visit by the FBI when her husband was arrested.

'We asked them for a search warrant but they never showed one,' she said. 'They searched the apartment thoroughly, examining my clothing and record books and going through closets and cupboards. They even went through those magazines page by page.'

She pointed to a stack of about three Parent magazines. . . .

In reply to what she thought of Americans accused of traitorous activity, she said the [sic] thought 'treason was very wrong.' She added quickly that she didn't think her husband or her brother was guilty.

Following her portrayal of the unaware and unperturbed housewife who did not know whose nominating petition she had signed nor showed the least bit of curiosity over her husband's interrogation by the FBI, Ethel took Michael for his regular therapy session with Mrs. Phillips, to whom she confessed that she was "terribly worried."

During the next week Ethel assumed control of Julie's business, informing the employees which jobs to complete, and urging Julie all the while to tell them the shop would have to be sold. She called the shop's accountant and asked him to visit Julie in jail to figure out Pitt's finances. He refused, stating that he "felt that his professional reputation would be affected." Ethel, therefore, had to meet with the accountant herself and delve into the world of business finances, a considerable undertaking since she had rarely even written a personal check.

The accountant's reaction was mirrored and amplified by almost everyone Ethel encountered. A neighbor from Knickerbocker Village recalls how "when Ethel was riding in the elevator from the basement and the elevator would stop on the first floor, none of the people who were waiting for the elevator would enter it when they saw Ethel. . . . Nobody would speak to Ethel after Julius was arrested."

The Cold War had turned hot, and association with someone who was married to a purported Communist "atom spy" was anathema to even the progressively minded people at Knickerbocker Village. The United States government had declared that the Kremlin was responsible for the Korean conflict, and on 19 July President Truman proposed a $10 billion rearmament program to enable the United States to halt Communist aggression in Korea and around the globe. He bluntly stated that the hostilities in Korea made "plain beyond all doubt that the international Communist movement is prepared to use armed invasion to conquer independent nations." With the United States preparing both for an international war on Communism and intensifying its domestic repression of almost anything or anyone left of center, Ethel Rosenberg, who was unliked by her neighbors to begin with, rode the elevator alone.

Although she continued to feign unconcern in public, when Ethel finally was able to visit her husband in jail the Sunday after his arrest, she spent most of the time crying. Here was her first chance to see her mainstay, her chief source of love and support, after their forced separation, and he spent most of their precious time together discussing Pitt and what needed to be done to sell the business, and she cried. This first jailhouse meeting presaged the pattern that would characterize their small amounts of time together over the next three years: Julie would use the meetings to work out the practical details of what to do with the business, or what strategy to use in court, or how to construct their legal appeals. Ethel's desperate need to talk about her anxieties, her unbearable loneliness, or her depression remained unfulfilled. Julie always felt tremendously guilty and repentant afterwards and would do his best to repair the situation through a letter.

The most important test of Ethel's fortitude and ability to perform her new role came on Monday, 7 August, when she was called before a grand jury at Foley Square, directly across from the park in which she often had eaten lunch while working at Bell Textile. Although she was called to offer information on the "atomic spy ring" in which her brother and husband were now implicated, the government also had more sinister designs. The Justice Department and FBI had spawned the idea of using Ethel as a "lever" against her husband to force him to cooperate. On the very day that Julie was arrested, Assistant Attorney General James McInerney requested that the FBI furnish "any additional information concerning Ethel Rosenberg" to the Justice Department, since he "was of the opinion that it might be possible to utilize her as a lever against her husband." The FBI investigations chief, A. H. Belmont, then passed this request onto his New York City agents: they "should consider every possible means to make him [Rosenberg] talk including . . . a careful study of the involvement of Ethel Rosenberg in order that charges be placed against her, if possible." J. Edgar Hoover warmly endorsed this idea, writing a letter to United States Attorney General J. Howard McGrath two days later: "There is no question but that if Julius Rosenberg would furnish the details of his extensive espionage activities it would be possible to proceed against other individuals. . . . [P]roceeding against his wife might serve as a lever in this matter." Irving Saypol, the government's prosecuting attorney handling the Greenglass-Rosenberg case, eagerly seized on this idea. He was so anxious to arrest Ethel in order to put pressure on her recalcitrant husband that he wanted to arrest her immediately. Therefore when Ethel appeared before the grand jury, Saypol's chief assistant, Myles Lane, did not question her in order to discover new information as much as to find a means for arresting her as a co-conspirator.

Ethel played her role on the witness stand with great composure. After consulting with Julie's attorney, Emanuel Bloch, she decided to take the Fifth Amendment in response to most questions. Since neither Bloch nor Ethel knew what David and Ruth had "confessed" to, nor what the government's intentions were, it probably seemed safer not to answer questions than be caught in a web of self-incrimination. She admitted signing a Communist party nominating petition (to which Julie had already testified during his Signal Corps loyalty hearing and about which Ethel had told reporters the day after Julie's arrest), but refused to answer all other questions on the basis that they would tend to incriminate her. Ethel "took the Fifth" in response to questions as benign as when did she first consult an attorney, whether she could recall her brother's furlough in the winter of 1944–1945, or had she ever met Harry Gold (which no one would ever claim she had). We have no record of what the grand jurors thought of Ethel's courtroom deportment, but Irving Saypol's assessment was clear: "she was not cooperative, . . . there were two or three times when she was almost in contempt of court, and . . . the Grand Jury was somewhat exercised over her conduct and were anxious to indict."

Ethel was allowed to leave the courtroom but was to return that Friday, 11 August, for yet another grand jury appearance. Clearly the line of questioning Myles Lane had pursued and the fact that she was summoned to the grand jury again suggested that the government was not interested in Ethel merely as a witness in the case but as a possible suspect.

With this possibility weighing on her, Ethel left Foley Square and immediately went to 64 Sheriff Street where her mother was baby-sitting Mike and Robby. As she entered her childhood home, she discerned the voices of her mother and Ruth talking in an animated fashion. When she came into the room where they were seated, they both immediately fell silent. Never one to show vulnerability, Ethel immediately turned to Ruth's infant daughter, Barbara, and commented on what a lovely baby she was. Ruth turned crimson. Tessie suddenly slammed her hand down on a table and screamed, "If you don't talk, you're gonna burn with your husband!" Ethel meekly replied, "But I've lived with him; I know he didn't do those things." She quickly left her mother's home, her two sons in tow. It must have seemed to her as if the entire world had abandoned her. Her major source of support was behind bars, depending on her to conduct herself in a noble manner while caring for their children, supervising his business, and withstanding FBI surveillance and the hostile questions from the government's prosecutor. Her best friend and confidante, Vivian Glassman, was now inaccessible too. On 3 August Vivian was descended upon by FBI agents. She spent the following day at FBI headquarters being grilled about the Rosenbergs and the circle of friends that radiated out from the CCNY school of engineering through the Communist party. Since the specter of the government's suspicion had now fallen on Vivian, Ethel could not risk implicating her friend further by visiting or even calling her on a phone that was probably tapped.

Ethel also had voluntarily shunned her one remaining confidant. After Julie was arrested, Ethel precipitously stopped seeing her psychiatrist. He read about the arrest in the papers and called her to offer his support. She responded in an embarrassed fashion by saying, "Oh, you don't have to see me anymore." He assured her that he was not concerned about being "tainted" or even "harassed."

At this, she broke down crying, saying only that she would be in
touch and then hung up the phone.

Looking back at why Ethel repelled his kind offer, Saul Miller
believed that she wanted to protect him. She had come to respect
him and the psychoanalytic endeavor enormously. In some ways,
she was humiliated by what had happened to her. She did not want
her psychiatrist, who seemed so far removed by reason of class,
profession, and sensibilities from the familial scandal that now enveloped her, to observe her in such a miserable and vulnerable
position. Conversely, when Elizabeth Phillips, the therapist she continued to see after Julie's arrest, was asked why Ethel terminated
her relationship with her psychiatrist and not with her, she responded simply, "Maybe she loved him more than she loved me."
It is also possible that since Mrs. Phillips was officially Michael's
therapist, Ethel may have felt more of an obligation to continue to
see that her son received as much help as possible during this ordeal.

Lacking most of her sources of support, Ethel persevered in her
relationship with her mother almost as though she could not believe
Tessie's increasingly obvious betrayal. Since Julie's arrest, Ethel frequently had left Michael and Robby with Tessie while she visited
her husband in jail, worked at Pitt, or met with Julie's attorney. But
after her mother's outburst on the afternoon of Ethel's first grand
jury appearance, Ethel began to realize she could no longer rely
on her mother for anything.

Alone, with the government closing in, and her apprehension
mounting, Ethel felt she had to do something about Mike and Robby.
Given the anxiety she experienced over being a good enough mother
prior to Julie's arrest, it is difficult to imagine what Ethel felt during
this second week of August, how she coped with her sons' fears
and distress in the midst of her own. Without having a single friend
or family member to whom she felt she could turn, Ethel called the
Jewish Community Homemakers Service and made an appointment
to "obtain assistance for [her] children and locate them in a home
while her husband was under arrest," according to Mrs. Helen
Turner with whom she had made the appointment. Ethel may have
told Mrs. Turner that she wanted to find a family to care for her
children because her husband was arrested, but it seems more likely
that she took this action in anticipation of her own arrest. In Ethel's
first letter from jail, she wrote to her husband that she deeply regretted not having made arrangements for the children in the event

she was arrested. Whatever her exact motivations, Ethel's appointment to place her children in a home was scheduled for Friday, 11 August.

On that day, she readied herself for her second grand jury appearance, which was scheduled at Foley Square that morning. She put on one of her nicest dresses, a short-sleeved, powder-blue taffeta with white polka dots. With some tastefulness, she put on white ankle-strapped sandles and carried a matching bag. But this simple, becoming effect was offset by a natural-colored straw hat with a six-inch flower on a stem sticking straight up from the crown. She had curled her hair, cut at midear length, so that small waves framed her face. On her pursed lips, she applied a dark red lipstick, her custom for important occasions.

Since her experience at her mother's house after her last grand jury appearance, Ethel had decided to find someone else to baby-sit Robby and Michael, who was off from school for summer vacation. A generous, nonconforming neighbor volunteered, later telling an interviewer, "I'm not such a hero—but if I have to be afraid of my own shadow, then what kind of America will I give my kids?"

When Ethel arrived at the courthouse, she was told to be seated in a waiting room. There, also scheduled to testify before the grand jury that morning, was Vivian Glassman. The two had not seen each other since their world had broken apart and Ethel had been forced to withstand the full weight of the government's inquisition on her own. Both of them sat there in stony silence, not once giving any sign that they had ever met, let alone been intimate friends. They undoubtedly recognized that openly acknowledging each other could hurt both of them at a time when mere acquaintance with an indicted or suspected "atomic spy" typically elicited FBI surveillance, harassment, loss of employment, rejection by friends, subpoenas to appear before the grand jury, and even arrest. Thus Ethel and Vivian sat only a few feet apart, yet remained perfectly silent in this, their last opportunity to speak before the two were permanently separated by forces over which they had no control.

When Ethel finally was called into the grand jury chamber, she was asked virtually the exact same questions that had been posed four days earlier, and she replied as she had on Monday. As one author notes, it is unclear who was more puzzled by this reproduction, Ethel or the grand jurors.

Ethel left the courthouse at a little past 1 P.M., anxious to make her appointment at the Jewish Community Homemakers Service.

As she headed for the subway, she was stopped by two FBI agents. Her upper arm suddenly was seized by one of the agents, and then she heard the words she must have been dreading: "You'll have to come with us—you're under arrest."

Ethel Rosenberg was directed to the twenty-ninth floor of the FBI's New York headquarters where both her husband and youngest brother had been taken before her. There she waited as an arrest warrant was obtained. She was permitted to call Julie's lawyer's office but found that Manny Bloch was on vacation in the Berkshires. His father, also an attorney, said he would come immediately in his son's place. Ethel was then escorted into another room where she was photographed and fingerprinted. FBI agents never left her side during these routine procedures and continually assaulted her with questions similar to those she had been asked in the grand jury chamber. Ethel steadfastly refused to answer any of their questions, "giving only information regarding her birth, education and employment."

A little before 4:00 P.M., she was led downstairs to the courtroom of U.S. Commissioner Edward W. McDonald. There she spoke briefly with Alexander Bloch, a man in his seventies who had very little experience in criminal cases. Members of the press filled the courtroom. Ethel was called to stand before the Commissioner. The now-familiar Myles Lane represented the government. For the first time, Ethel heard the charges against her. Lane accused her of "conspiracy to commit espionage," the same charge made against Julie. Lane claimed that there was "ample evidence that Mrs. Rosenberg and her husband have been affiliated with Communist activities for a long period of time," and that after Harry Gold was arrested the Rosenbergs attempted to persuade other undisclosed conspirators "to flee the United States and take refuge behind an Iron Curtain country." Specifically, Ethel was charged with two overt acts:

1. On or about the first day of November, 1944, the exact date being . . . unknown, at the Southern District of New York, the defendant Ethel Rosenberg had a discussion with Julius Rosenberg and others.
2. On or about the 10th day of January, 1945 . . . at the Southern District of New York, the defendant Ethel Rosenberg had a conversation with Julius Rosenberg, David Greenglass and others.

252   Such "crimes" would have been cause for incredulity and laughter had it not been for the fact that Lane then requested that Ethel be held under $100,000 bail. He explained to the Commissioner:

> [Her crime] by its very nature is one of the worst that could be committed, because it jeopardizes the lives of every man, woman and child in this country.
>
> If the crime with which she is charged had not occurred perhaps we would not have the present situation in Korea.

Alexander Bloch was clearly aghast at such shockingly unsubstantiated allegations. He argued to the Commissioner that the only specific charge against his client was "flimsy" since it merely stated she had talked with her husband and brother, something typically not considered a criminal act nor justification for bail of $100,000. He explained that Ethel had left her two small children with a babysitter because she had "no intimation that she was going to be apprehended." He then asked that his client be paroled into his custody just until Monday "so she could make arrangements for her children." The Commissioner replied that he "would not entertain any parole suggestion, even if it were made by the District Attorney." Bail was set at $100,000.

Ethel was then remanded into custody. She was permitted one telephone call. As she lifted the receiver and dialed the familiar CH2-8679, it is impossible to imagine her torment. When she heard the voice of her frightened, seven-year-old son, she said with forced calm, "Michael, you remember what happened to Daddy, dear?" Then it happened. Michael screamed, a long, agonized scream that would haunt his mother until she herself was silenced.

16

JUST ONE MORE BLOW

Ethel Rosenberg had become an important pawn in the government's attempts to make her husband talk and hence enlarge its pool of captured "Communist spies." In a country with no tradition or tolerance of physical torture in extracting confessions from prisoners, the United States government turned to far more subtle and acceptable means. It engineered the arrest of a housewife and mother and imprisoned her on $100,000 bail in order to put pressure on her uncooperative husband. Yet despite its best efforts, the "evidence" the government had mustered on her was benign, in no way justifying her arrest, let alone her extraordinary bail.

On 11 August what the government had in its possession was no different from what it held the day Julius Rosenberg was arrested, and the New York FBI office was instructed to conduct "a careful study of the involvement of Ethel Rosenberg." On that day, 17 July, Ruth Greenglass had made a lengthy statement to the FBI that contained the first mention of Ethel. In fact, she mentioned her sister-in-law thirteen times. David Greenglass also gave a statement that day, but, strangely, only mentioned Ethel once, and then merely to explain how he came to be acquainted with Julius Rosenberg. After reviewing this disparity, FBI agents met with David two days later to "reconcile discrepancies." The ever-pliant David Greenglass was unruffled. He quickly adopted Ruth's explanation as his own.

The most serious charge in Ruth's account against Ethel was that she had been present when Julius urged Ruth's involvement in espionage and had echoed her husband's suggestion. According to Ruth's 17 July 1950 statement about her visit to the Rosenbergs' apartment in November 1944, Julius requested that she obtain information from Dave, then stationed at Los Alamos, to help place the Soviet Union "on an equal plane with the other Allies as far as this atomic information was concerned." When Ruth appeared reluctant, Ethel said "she should at least ask her husband, David, if he would furnish this type of information."

Realizing the tenuousness of this "evidence," and unable to uncover anything linking Ethel more directly with espionage, the government became increasingly desperate. While FBI agents were grilling Ethel's best friend, Vivian Glassman, on 4 August, Myles Lane was trying to extract an admission from David Greenglass that his sister had a larger role in spying than he had previously confessed. David was uncharacteristically adamant in maintaining his position:

> Lane: Was Ethel present in any of these occasions [when David gave Julius information]?
>
> Greenglass: Never.
>
> Lane: Did Ethel talk to you about it?
>
> Greenglass: Never spoke about it to me and that's a fact. Aside from trying to protect my sister believe me that's a fact.

Unable to obtain anything more damning from David and without any prospects of unearthing further incriminating information, the government decided to arrest her anyway, cloaking its lack of evidence against her with the hyperbolic statement that she had jeopardized "the lives of every man, woman and child in this country." Thus Ethel Rosenberg was thrown into prison, never to know freedom again.

It had a swanky-sounding address, 10 Greenwich Avenue. A tall building, with fancy outside ornamentation, it could easily be mis-

taken for an apartment house, except for its long narrow heavily-screened windows. . . . **255**

There was a constant flow of traffic—buses, cars, trucks, and people passing on all sides, at all hours. The night noises of Greenwich Village, which apparently never goes to bed, deprived inmates of sleep. There was singing, shouting, fighting, musical instruments—what have you. Never was there a quiet moment. Whistles came up from the streets to attract the attention of a particular inmate. Others would call her. Families, friends, sweethearts, pimps, all arranged such contacts with the women on visiting days. . . .

Inside the building pandemonium reigned supreme. The noise was deafening, from the shrill incessant chatter of the inmates, the hysterical laughter, the screams of suffering addicts suddenly cut off from narcotics, and the weeping and cursing of forlorn and desperate women, crowded together in small quarters. The majority were awaiting trial or were there during their trials, because they could not secure bail. . . .

The cells were open, with a short curtain over the toilet as a concession to privacy. In each cell there was a narrow iron cot with a thin mattress, a covered toilet which also served as a seat before a small iron table, a washbowl, and a couple of stationary wooden hangers for clothing. The blankets were old and worn beyond all possibility of real cleanliness, though they were disinfected regularly. The food was indescribably revolting, unfit to eat. Watery spaghetti, half-cooked oatmeal, coffee that was hardly more than luke-warm water, wormy prunes, and soggy bread baked by the men on Welfare Island, very little meat and that usually an unsightly bologna. . . . There was never any fruit. Sugar and milk were scarce and both had to be bought in the commissary by inmates. . . .

The dehumanizing degradation of the House of Detention commences immediately. All your possessions are surrendered immediately, except glasses, and one gets a receipt upon entry. . . .

The second step after entering was to strip and leave all one's clothes in a side room where they were searched by an officer, while the prisoner was wrapped in a sheet and taken to the showers. Next we were ordered to take an enema and to climb on an examining table for an examination. All openings of the body were roughly searched for narcotics by 'a doctor'—a large woman who made insulting remarks about Communists who did not appreciate this country."

Elizabeth Gurley Flynn

New York City's Women's House of Detention was where Ethel spent her first night after being arrested and would remain for the next eight months. The majority of the inmates housed there were black and were charged with narcotics violations, prostitution, and a few with homicide for killing men who had beaten them and "in desperation would do things like take a kitchen knife or a can of lye and attack them to defend themselves." Most of the white prisoners were incarcerated because they were expensive call girls or had been involved in some kind of white-collar crime such as embezzlement.

Ethel was greeted by the residents of the House of Detention with suspicion and hostility. First, she was white and seemingly middle-class—characteristics that separated her from most of the prisoners. Second, as former fellow inmate Miriam Moskowitz recalls, "there was a certain amount of resentment toward . . . her because she was the focus of so much attention in the newspapers. Nobody got that kind of attention if you were a drug addict or a thief or a prostitute." Third, and worst of all, she was a purported Communist and spy. "These girls would get the *Daily News* every day or they would turn the radio on" and Ethel "was characterized in the worst terms possible." She was described as the "enemy of the world, of the free world, of democracy, their enemy."

Ignored and resented by her fellow prisoners, Ethel spent her many idle hours worrying about her sons. Without alternatives, she had had the neighbor who was minding Michael and Robby take the children to 64 Sheriff Street the day after her arrest. There the worst that Ethel had imagined began to unfold.

Immediately after receiving her grandchildren into her home, Tessie Greenglass telephoned Ethel's attorney and "complained that the boys were unruly, that she was old and not well, and that she would have to have help or would take them to a police station." Alexander Bloch was "shocked" by this, his first direct encounter with the self-serving Greenglass family.

Tessie then began routinely condemning Ethel and Julie in front of her grandchildren, informing Michael: "You're lucky they're born here or they'd be deported." The severity of the situation was conveyed in a letter to Ethel by Gladys Greenglass's sister, Jean:

> Your kids roam the streets and the only time I see anything done for them is when your Ma calls them in for feedings.

Your Ma reviles and rants about you and the situation you and Julie brought on her family and how much trouble the kids are and how bad they are and how bad you are, and why don't you do what Ruthie did so you too could be with your kids and why I don't go and tell you that. . . .

[W]hen I see your kids pushed around, screamed at, have to listen to your being spoken about badly and cursed and your Ma talking bad about your in-laws and poor Michael going into temper tantrums when your Ma curses you I want to hit her over the head. . . .

[C]all the proper authorities and get your kids out anywhere but with them [the Greenglasses], please.

As troubling as this "helpful" letter from Jean were Ethel's visits from members of her family. At the beginning of September, Sam Greenglass visited his sister and told her that "it was time that she thought of herself and the children." Although he pretended some degree of warmth and concern for his sister whom he had not seen in seven years, he did so in order to try to make her cooperate with the government. We know this because he conferred with the FBI shortly after his visit to the Women's House of Detention and informed its agents "that it is his opinion that a death penalty is too good for Julius and Ethel Rosenberg." After interviewing Sam, the FBI noted that he offered to "make further attempts by mail and in person to obtain the cooperation of his sister Ethel in instant case and that he would advise the New York office of his progress in this regard."

Sam was true to his word, as the letter he wrote his sister shows:

Dear Sis—
Today I visited Mom—I saw Robert and Michael. I told Michael that I had spoken to you. His first words to me were 'My mother is innocent'—'She would not do anything that was wrong'—Well, you certainly built up a lot of faith in this poor child.—How can you have the bitter thought on your conscience to let this child down in such a horrible way.

When a stranger walks into the house—his first question is 'Is she from the child welfare or is she an investiga-

tor—. I don't want to go to a foster home—I want to stay here.'

How can Mom keep those two children—They are wearing her away very quickly—I must say you have done and are still doing a very wonderful job—There is not much more disgrace you could bring to your family—but now your great problems seems [sic] to be—to get rid of them— one at a time—First Mom—Then Chuch [Tessie's sister]— The children in a foster home—your brother in jail—what an excellent job—. . . .

[G]ive up this wild ideology—come down to earth, give yourself a fighting chance (I may be able to help you) so that someday you may possibly be a mother to your two children—and not a number in some jail—rotting away your years.—I mention again that I may be able to help you but I must have your co-operation.

Worse yet were Ethel's visits with her mother, who was now in frequent contact with the FBI. Normally when family members visited inmates at the House of Detention, prisoners were led into one large room where they stood in stalls behind a wall of thick plate glass and shouted to make themselves heard. When Tessie visited, however, she was placed in a separate room to confer with Ethel alone, even though her daughter never requested such privilege.

Tessie used these occasions to urge Ethel to "behave like Dave and Ruth." She screamed at her daughter, "What are you doing to Davey?" and then pleaded with her "to save Davey" by cooperating with the government. Tessie proudly reported to the FBI that she told her daughter, "You are a dirty Communist, but you should never have harmed your own country." She then related that Ethel "held her throat so as she would not break down." At one point she suggested that Ethel divorce her husband, and at this Ethel finally erupted, telling her mother she should never visit again.

Ethel responded to her family's unremitting and unbridled bitterness and wrath "with sadness—but what sadness!" remembers fellow inmate Miriam Moskowitz. Each one of her family's actions was "just one more blow" in a life that already had experienced many. "She felt wronged and sad more than angry" Elizabeth Phillips recalls.

Ethel did everything she could to conceal her feelings from her fellow inmates and the omnipresent prison matrons. She never cried

outside her jail cell and continually made an effort to get to know
her prisonmates and immerse herself in their problems. This began
to win her the respect and friendship of many of the women. Yet
from her very first week in jail, Ethel was beset by migraines, severe
back pain, and crying jags that went on for hours. She confessed
these sufferings to Julie, but always attempted to make light of them
in some way.

What sustained Ethel in prison was her husband's love and the
example that he set. Almost whenever she received a new blow
from her family, she gained solace and strength from her husband's
latest avowal of love and admiration. Julius Rosenberg originally
had "saved" Ethel from the coldness of the Greenglass family when
he fell in love with her during the winter of 1936–1937. Now he
rescued her emotionally over and over again in small ways each
time Ethel was hurt by one of her family while in prison. Not since
she was a child had she been so vulnerable to her family's meanness
and therefore so hurt by their incomprehensible cruelty. Yet Julie
was always there, reminding her of his deep love and respect, of
how beautiful she was, and of how she must continue to endure
her imprisonment with courage.

Ethel clearly idealized her husband. The memory of how he
handled himself in court could ameliorate the pain Ethel felt from
being separated from him and her children. His determination to
withstand the government's pressure without cooperating humbled
Ethel and gave her strength to calm her rising sense of desperation.
A former inmate of the Women's House of Detention recalls how
Ethel never tired of talking about Julie. "Nothing she said was phony,
but I just couldn't believe that any marriage was all she said hers
was." Miriam Moskowitz remembers that "I didn't think any man
could be as perfect and as smart as she thought Julie was."

Ethel's problem then became getting enough of Julie's support,
having sufficient time with him to counteract the pain she experienced daily. His letters filled some of this need, since they were
consistently models of love, compassion, and admiration. But they
were infrequent and written with the knowledge that the prison
authorities read every word they contained. The legal consultations
that she began to attend with Julie and attorney Manny Bloch were
another way she had contact with her husband. But she felt inhibited
from expressing herself around Bloch, and Julie usually was too
preoccupied with legal matters to give Ethel the support and tenderness for which she yearned. The only other times Ethel saw her

husband were during their court appearances and their rides to and from court. While the former offered no opportunity to talk, the latter allowed for a few precious moments of closeness. A large prison van would pick up male inmates from the Federal House of Detention and then stop at the women's jail to transport them all to the courthouse at Foley Square. As a former inmate reports:

> Julie had the seat I learned later the men always reserved for him—next to the grating which separated men from women. It was a pretty large open steel mesh screen.
>
> The women who were going to court that day held back and let Ethel take her seat. I sat down opposite her. It was dark in the van. I didn't even know at the time where Julie was, for you couldn't see any faces. Then I struck a match to light a cigarette.
>
> I'll never forget what that match lit up. Julie and Ethel, kissing each other through that darned screen. I didn't even wait to get a light, I blew it out.

None of these opportunities, however, were sufficient to quell Ethel's numbing loneliness or soothe her bouts of panic for long periods of time. She therefore was forced to look to others for the additional help she needed.

Immediately upon hearing of Ethel's arrest, Elizabeth Phillips had called the Women's House of Detention to make arrangements to see Ethel on a regular basis. Their first meeting took place during Ethel's second week in jail in a small room just like the one in which she visited with her mother. Although it was wonderful to meet in private and not be encumbered by a screen or other device to keep them apart, Ethel feared the room was bugged. It seems likely that she withheld discussion of anything she did not want the government to hear. Mrs. Phillips also explicitly discouraged any talk of Ethel's legal case and its attendant issues, exhorting Ethel to "save for your lawyer things that belong to your lawyer and we'll talk about things that belong to the family." Nonetheless, Ethel used these weekly sessions to confide her fears about the children, her pain over her family's rejection of her, and the difficulty she was experiencing adjusting to prison life.

Increasingly, Ethel began telling Mrs. Phillips of how much she longed to see her psychiatrist. Having rejected his efforts to meet with her before her arrest, she now longed to see the man with

whom she had shared her most deeply guarded fears and needs
over the previous year. Her concerns about protecting him and
preventing him from seeing her in such a humiliating position seem
to have disappeared in the face of her overwhelming anguish. Yet
there were now other obstacles to their meeting. Manny Bloch had
expressed some concern over what the government might make of
Ethel's psychiatric treatment. Apparently he said nothing about Ethel's therapy with Mrs. Phillips, presumably because Michael was
the identified patient, and Mrs. Phillips was only a social worker.
Bloch, however, seems to have taken the view that participation in
psychiatric therapy could be used against Ethel when she was put
on trial. In fact, he later would try to impugn the testimony of a
key witness against the Rosenbergs on the basis of his treatment
with a psychiatrist.

Because Ethel felt that her personal problems were not subjects
to discuss with her attorney, she was unable to ask Bloch what he
thought about her seeing her psychiatrist in prison. She also did not
know if Miller would be willing to see her under these circumstances. The House of Detention was considerably different from
the serene privacy of his Upper West Side office. Ethel's imprisonment also precluded the possibility of continuing in psychoanalytic psychotherapy, which demanded some disengagement from
the world in order to focus on the repressed contents of unconscious
mental life. Would he meet with her under such unorthodox and
unpleasant circumstances?

Ethel entertained the hope that if Miller knew the details of her
family's betrayal and what she had been made to withstand, he
would rush to her side. Therefore she begged Mrs. Phillips, an
objective and professional witness to Ethel's unhappiness, to explain
her situation to her psychiatrist, something Ethel apparently was too
embarrassed to do herself. Elizabeth Phillips refused, however, believing that no actions should be taken without Ethel's lawyer's
cognizance and approval. She urged Ethel to stand up for herself
with Manny Bloch and make her valid emotional needs known.

Sensing the correctness of this proposal, Ethel raised the issue
of her seeing Dr. Miller at the next consultation she had with Julie
and her attorney. Bloch said that he would be willing to speak with
her psychiatrist, thus giving Ethel hope that she might soon be able
to see him herself. Ultimately, however, Manny Bloch decided that
it would be unwise. He seems to have concluded that unless Ethel
would collapse without Miller's presence, of which she gave little

indication, prison visits by her psychiatrist would only be used by the prosecution to Ethel's disadvantage.

In hindsight, Bloch's decision may have been ill-advised. According to the released FBI records in the Rosenberg case, the government was doing almost nothing to investigate Ethel Rosenberg's background and showed no interest in her psychiatric treatment. While the FBI was spending literally thousands of man-hours and dollars interviewing every one of Julius Rosenberg's acquaintances, business contacts, and childhood friends, it spent little time or effort on Ethel. Since she had been seeing a psychiatrist three times a week for a year, one would imagine that the FBI would have interviewed him to see if he would divulge any information about his purported "atom spy" patient. Yet Saul Miller was never contacted by any government agency in connection with his famous patient.

Certainly the FBI knew his identity, since Ethel's letters and most likely "bugged" sessions with Mrs. Phillips often mentioned Miller by name. And certainly, given the tenor of the times, it is unlikely that respect for doctor-patient confidentiality would have frightened away the FBI. But the government never approached Miller, presumably for the same reasons it failed to investigate most aspects of Ethel's background. She had not been arrested as a supposed espionage agent, but as a "lever" to put pressure on her husband, the real "atom spy" suspect. Prison visits by a psychiatrist might have made copy for news-hungry reporters anxious to defame Ethel and unaware that the government possessed almost nothing linking her to espionage. And, for this reason, Bloch's decision may have made sense. But the government never mentioned Ethel's psychiatric treatment—at the Rosenberg trial or elsewhere—nor suggested that she suffered from any emotional problems.

Bloch's decision left Ethel with Julie and Mrs. Phillips as her sole sources of emotional support. Aside from the increasingly infrequent and typically unpleasant visits from members of the Greenglass family, Ethel's only other visitors were Julie's sisters, Ethel and Lena, and his mother, Sophie. Although they were enormously kind women, they were deeply ashamed, overwhelmed by what had happened to Julie and Ethel, and prone to break down into helpless tears during their jailhouse visits. Thus, Ethel often had to reassure them and pacify their fears rather than look to them for support.

Ethel's relationship with her sisters-in-law also became somewhat strained by their refusal to help Michael and Robby. It had become very clear very quickly that the children were suffering enormously living with Tessie Greenglass. Michael had started talking of suicide and was not eating; Robby, only three, was compulsively grinding his teeth. Tessie was doing everything to turn her grandchildren against their parents. Julie and Ethel's first thought was that Julie's family should take them in. His mother, however, was ill and frail so they never suggested that she look after them. His brother Dave, Michael's godfather, refused to help. Lena and Ethel also declined. Thirty-five years after her decision, Ethel Rosenberg Appel explains:

> See Julie wanted me to take over the children. I would have never have hesitated but we were in Maspeth, which was a Bircher area, and it was all Gentile. If I brought the kids into my home, they would have stoned our store, and this was our livelihood. We were afraid. . . . I kept my mouth shut. . . . Even with my mah-jongg group I didn't let them know. I had a group of high-class [friends] . . . doctors' wives and some were lawyers' wives and I was playing with them . . . and I had this tragedy and I still kept my game going . . . Communist was a dirty word, right?

Lacking any alternative, Ethel sought to place Robby and Michael in a foster home or shelter. Mrs. Phillips put Ethel in touch with a social service worker with whom she began to discuss her children's future. By the beginning of October 1950, she had settled on the Hebrew Children's Home in the Bronx as a suitable place. Because Ethel had so much faith in child-rearing experts, she believed the care that Michael and Robby would soon receive would not only be beneficial but might very well surpass what she had been able to offer as a mother. Her experience with Mrs. Phillips and the social service workers she encountered in jail encouraged her to believe that the Hebrew Children's Home would be a model of enlightened, scientific child-rearing techniques since it had nurses and social workers connected to it.

During the first week of November 1950, Tessie and a social worker drove Michael and Robby to their new home in the Bronx. Instead of a model shelter straight out of *Parents' Magazine*, however, they discovered a cold, decaying institution "with poor food, cold, drafty dormitory rooms, a setting worthy of a Charles Dickens novel." Instead of highly trained professionals, the children were cared for by underpaid, young black women, who treated their charges with a callousness bordering on abuse. Michael and Robby were immediately separated, allowed to see each other only at bedtime. Robby felt incomprehensibly abandoned; Michael believed he was being punished: "I felt I must have done something wrong; being there was my punishment. My voice breaking, I pleaded with anyone—an older kid, a worker—who would listen: 'I've been here a whole week, don't you think that's enough and that they'll let me go home now?' "

Soon after the children had left 64 Sheriff Street, Tessie Greenglass, who essentially had forced Michael and Robby out of her home, sent a telegram to her daughter in jail on 9 November:

DEAR ETHEL WENT TO SEE CHILDREN LAST SUNDAY AND SAW THEM TWICE DURING THE WEEK BUT THEY DIDN'T SEE ME. THEY WERE CRYING STEADILY. WOULD COME TO SEE YOU BUT WOULD NOT BE ABLE TO TAKE IT. ALL BROKEN UP WITH HEARTACHE. LET ME HEAR FROM YOU—MOTHER

Why Tessie Greenglass, who had so desperately wanted to be rid of her grandchildren, suddenly was "all broken up with heartache" at their plight is curious. Perhaps she was genuinely despondent over the crisis she had created and simply wanted to apprise Ethel of the situation. More likely, her telegram probably was directly or indirectly suggested by the government in order to put pressure on her uncooperative daughter. Although she was frequently overwhelmed by depression, anxiety, fear, loneliness, and a plethora of psychosomatic symptoms, Ethel had been steadfast in her resolve to remain true to her husband and her principles. Tessie believed that cooperation with governmental authority, which she both feared and respected, was the only safe path to follow. If making Ethel feel guilty over what had happened to her children provoked her recalcitrant daughter into cooperation with the government, Tessie probably felt justified in using any means available to her. Not only might her actions save her daughter by compelling her to "confess," but they would also prove that she, Tessie Greenglass, was a law-abiding, loyal American, who was more than willing to do the government's bidding.

Unfortunately, from Tessie's point of view, Ethel's arrest and imprisonment had only seemed to strengthen both her and Julius's resolve to stand up to the government, no matter what the consequences. Ethel's unceasing and profound admiration for the way her husband handled himself and analyzed their situation, and Ju-

lie's self-conscious and loving attempts to maintain Ethel's determination and self-esteem, mutually reinforced their resolve to never
have anyone "use the name . . . Rosenberg to make the word
'Communist' mean 'spy' and 'spy' mean 'Communist.' "

As a result, the government's strategy was failing. Instead of
compelling Julius Rosenberg to confess to espionage and name other
members of his "spy ring," Ethel's arrest only seemed to confirm
his belief that the government was conducting a witch-hunt and
arresting people on trumped-up charges. Therefore, by the beginning of 1951, the government found itself in a difficult position.
With the Rosenbergs set to be put on trial at the beginning of March,
and with no indication that either of them had any intention of
"confessing," it had to come up with something that seriously linked
Ethel Rosenberg with the charge against her: "conspiracy to commit
espionage." Without any objective witnesses or material or circumstantial evidence to develop a case against her, the government
turned to the one source it knew could be trusted to manufacture
some new "evidence."

On 8 February 1951, Myles Lane met with the Joint Committee on
Atomic Energy in Washington, D.C., to explain the Justice Department's plans for the upcoming Rosenberg spy trial. In it the
government was planning to have David Greenglass reveal the details of the lens mold diagrams he purportedly passed to the Russians, and Lane wanted to apprise the Committee of the need to
"temporarily" declassify the information about which Greenglass
would testify. Lane made clear that it was necessary to bring this
technical information out in open court in order to obtain a death
sentence for Julius Rosenberg. He informed the congressmen,

> I seriously doubt from my own experience, that any judge
> would impose a death penalty merely because a man tes-
> tified there was an agreement and they passed out infor-
> mation respecting the number of people that were working
> there [at Los Alamos] or the names of the scientists who
> were working there.

And why was it necessary to send Rosenberg to his death?

> [T]he only thing that will break this man Rosenberg is the
> prospect of a death penalty or getting the chair, plus that

*if we can convict his wife, too, and give her a stiff sentence
of 25 or 30 years, that combination may serve to make this
fellow disgorge and give us the information on those other
individuals. . . .*

*It is about the only thing you can use as a lever on
these people.*

The government's "lever" strategy had taken a new and lethal turn.
Having recognized that his wife's arrest and imprisonment did nothing to loosen Julius Rosenberg's tongue, it now raised the stakes.
That the trial court judge should determine sentence or that punishment should bear a relationship to the actual crime committed
were mere legal technicalities the Justice Department, and now the
collaborating congressional committee, could easily ignore. This
was the McCarthy era and these men's duty, as national leaders,
was to rid their country of Communists and spies.

Since the rationale for Ethel Rosenberg's conviction had diminished as her value as a "lever" declined, the government found
it necessary to establish new justification for its planned "stiff sentence." In reply to questions regarding David Greenglass's testifying
against his own sister, Myles Lane explained the Justice Department's new rationale: "[T]he case is not too strong against Mrs.
Rosenberg. But for the purpose of acting as a deterrent, I think it is
very important that she be convicted too, and given a strong sentence."

The meaning of Ethel's arrest and imprisonment had changed
without her knowledge. Instead of being a "lever," she was now
a "deterrent," but to whom—potential Communists, spies, or devoted wives—was not clear. What was evident, however, was that
in the government's shifting and private rationale, Ethel Rosenberg
was not yet a spy, a conspirator, or even much of an accomplice.
By Lane's own admission, the case against her was "not too strong,"
and this was only one month before she was to be put on trial for
her life.

It was quite fortuitous then that two weeks before the trial date,
Ruth and Dave Greenglass suddenly "remembered" some incriminating information about Ethel they previously had "forgotten" to
tell the FBI. On 23 and 24 February, Ruth related in detail a conversation she had with Ethel in January 1945, which, according to
the FBI's summation, began with Ruth stating to her sister-in-law
that

[she] looked rather tired and Ethel replied that she had been up late the night before typing the material that David had given to Julius and typing other material that Julius had received. She told Ruth that she always typed Julius' material that he received and occasionally had to stay up late at night to do this. Ethel told Ruth that Julius was full [sic] engrossed in the work he was doing and all he talked about was his work. She stated that he was away from home many times and stayed out late at night and that this was okay with her because she was satisfied with what Julius was doing.

Then, according to Ruth's newly refreshed memory, in September 1945 David gave Julius some handwritten notes and sketches in the Rosenbergs' apartment as Ruth and Ethel looked on:

Julius took the info into the bathroom and read it and when he came out he called Ethel and told her she had to type this info immediately. . . . Ethel then sat down at the typewriter which she had placed on a bridge table in the living room and proceeded to type the info which David had given to Julius. . . . [A]t times Ethel was unable to decipher David's handwriting and David would look over her shoulder and tell her what he had written. . . . [A]t other times Ethel would read a sentence aloud and comment that it was not correct grammatically and that [Ruth] and Ethel assisted by Julius would correct the sentence grammatically.

Following a familiar pattern, David Greenglass was interviewed two days later and confirmed Ruth's statement.

It is noteworthy to compare these newly "remembered" scenarios of February 1951 with David's earlier confessions. In David's signed statement of 17 July 1950, he clearly recalled giving Julius information on "the atomic bomb, as well as a couple of sketches of the molds which make up the bomb" in September 1945. But Ethel was not present since Dave met Julius "on the street somewhere in the city." When asked specifically if Ethel were present on *any* occasion when Dave gave his brother-in-law information, Greenglass had replied "never" on 4 August 1950.

When asked in a 1979 interview how the subject of Ethel's typing initially had been raised in February 1951, Ruth Greenglass replied: "It was almost as if we threw that in to involve her and I began to think of why that occurred. And I realized that I had no typewriter and that the information David had brought home [from Los Alamos] had been handwritten. . . ."

David then added, "Well, I recall at one point—it's in my mind—that one of the FBI men said to me, 'You came to Julius's apartment and you discussed all this stuff. Where was Ethel?' So at that point I said, 'Yeah, she must have been around.' "

David's suggestibility and Ruth's readiness to "involve" her sister-in-law became the basis of the government's case against Ethel Rosenberg. As the government's prosecutor, Irving Saypol, later explained to the jury at her trial: "This description of the atom bomb, destined for delivery to the Soviet Union, was typed up by the defendant Ethel Rosenberg. . . . Just so had she on countless other occasions sat at that typewriter and struck the keys, blow by blow, against her own country in the interests of the Soviets."

David and Ruth had spent so much of the previous seven months conferring with the government, "remembering" new incidents that implicated Julius Rosenberg in espionage, and "reconciling discrepancies" both between their accounts and with those of Harry Gold and other government witnesses, that this additional "memory" of Ethel's involvement must have come rather easily. As Ruth revealed in 1979, "I don't remember when I told them [the FBI] a particular thing. . . . At a certain point the agents became your friends. They can elicit whatever they want from you." The Greenglasses believed, for reasons that can only be surmised, that others had implicated Ethel in spying and that their "recollections" augmented but did not create the evidence against her.

It had been eight months that Dave had been in prison, eight months in which Ruth and Dave had been continuously supported in their cooperation with the government by their families, friends, attorneys, and the "friendly" agents of the FBI. There was no going back. The anti-Communist *Jewish Daily Forward* had run a series of articles on the Greenglass-Rosenberg case based on interviews with Ruth. The paper had dined her at Luchows, an expensive Manhattan restaurant, and made her a small-time celebrity among its Lower East Side readers with such articles as, "Mrs. Greenglass Tells How Her Husband Was Misled by His Brother-in-Law," and "My Husband Was Misled, But He Is Not a Traitor, Says Ruth Greenglass." Ruth and Dave saw that complete cooperation with the government not only had already saved Ruth from indictment, as promised, but had provided them with more attention, and in some quarters, respect than they had ever imagined or received in their lives.

Cooperation with the government in HUAC hearings, McCarthy hearings, loyalty investigations, and trials of Communists was touted by every organ of the mass media as the only honorable alternative because the United States faced the "imminent peril" of being "swallowed by the Communist world." The "Informer Principle," as Victor Navasky terms it, became Cold War America's new moral code. Naming names, turning on former friends and associates, cooperating with the government at whatever cost became "the litmus test, the ultimate evidence, the guarantor of patriotism."

Dave and Ruth, who had long felt excluded from the American dream by their inability to move beyond the poverty of the Lower East Side, who had come perilously close to feeling the full brunt of the government's anti-Communist persecution, were at last doing something fully American. They seemed completely unencumbered by conscience, so they could adapt to the new morality governed by the "Informer Principle" without guilt. The Greenglass family ethic of self-interest, against which Ethel Rosenberg had so thoroughly rebelled, left a lasting imprint on its youngest member and was echoed by his wife. By providing the government with the "evidence" it sought against Ethel, David and Ruth Greenglass not only protected their self-interest, but lived up to America's new standard of patriotism.

17

"COURAGE, CONFIDENCE, AND PERSPECTIVE"

Ethel and Julius Rosenberg adhered to an entirely different code of ethics than the Greenglasses. In their legal consultations with Manny Bloch leading up to their trial, the Rosenbergs discouraged the idea of calling witnesses on their behalf. Since the only incriminating material they knew the government possessed was based on what occurred between them and the Greenglasses in private, no one could be called to confirm or deny Dave and Ruth's description of events. Character witnesses, however, could be subpoenaed to testify generally in the Rosenbergs' support. "But," according to Manny Bloch, "Ethel wouldn't have it. Said it would injure them [potential witnesses] in their professions." In an interview that author John Wexley conducted with Bloch, the Rosenbergs' attorney further explained this decision:

> For one thing, such character witnesses could swear only that they had known the Rosenbergs as a decent, moral, and hard-working couple. But Saypol [the chief prosecutor] would hardly trouble to contest this. In fact . . . their very virtues might be presented as a 'front' behind which the 'spy ring' operated.

For another thing, suppose Saypol threw the question, 'Do you know for a fact that your friends the Rosenbergs were not spies?' What could the friend reply but a feeble, 'Well, I don't know—but I am sure they couldn't have been.' . . .

Finally, there was the danger that such friends would be asked about their own political beliefs and associations. How many could afford to risk perjury prosecutions by truthful denials or contempt citations by refusal to name other friends? And again, if they took the privilege [against self-incrimination], would not their character endorsements be considered worthless as coming from 'Fifth Amendment Communists?'

The Rosenbergs' principled position, however, cloaked the sad fact that it was doubtful they could have called any character witnesses, even had they wished to do so. It was obvious that any of their friends or acquaintances who were followers or members of the American Communist party were ineligible. If these people's backgrounds were investigated by the prosecution and then revealed in court, their testimony would hurt rather than help the Rosenbergs. Julie and Ethel's families could not be called upon either. The Greenglasses would never have considered the possibility of doing anything that might harm Davey, and the Rosenbergs were so ashamed by the whole affair that they would not even attend the trial, much less testify. Further, their neighbors would have nothing to do with them. An older woman who had lived near the Rosenbergs when they occupied a furnished room on Avenue A in the early nineteen-forties reports that she was shocked when she heard of their arrest:

Then when I read that Michael and Robby were put in a city shelter, I got on a train and traveled to New York. I looked up their attorney, Mr. Bloch. What could I do, I asked, and why weren't people moving heaven and earth to get those children out of that shelter?

He looked at me. Tears came to his eyes. 'You're the first person who's come near me to offer help,' he said. 'They're so little known, you see'. . . .

I went around knocking on doors of other old neighbors of theirs. I guess some believed the lie [that they were spies].

Others admitted they were too frightened to move. Finally I went back home.

The second and perhaps most important issue the Rosenbergs had to decide before their trial was how they would respond to the inevitable questions about their participation in the Communist party. Julie and Ethel's first inclination was to stand behind the Fifth Amendment, and Manny Bloch agreed. But Bloch's father, Alexander, who was Ethel's attorney of record from the day she was arrested, objected. According to John Wexley, he argued as follows:

> *Since the prevailing public attitude was hostile toward anyone 'hiding behind the Fifth Amendment,' perhaps it would be best to come right out and frankly admit his student membership in YCL. And since Julius's dismissal from the Signal Corps . . . was bound to come up in any case, perhaps a stout admission of what was after all guaranteed under the First Amendment—the freedom of association and political beliefs—would forestall the prosecution's political onslaught and force it to stick to the evidence.*

Alexander Bloch had had no experience defending alleged Communists and was less interested in adhering to political principles than were the Rosenbergs. He focused on how the jury would interpret his clients' refusal either to deny or admit Communist affiliation. The judge would, of course, give the jury instructions that taking the Fifth did not imply an affirmative or negative response. Yet there was no legal way to prevent the jury from concluding that the Rosenbergs were taking the Fifth because they had something to hide, perhaps something so horrible that they were unwilling to admit it in open court.

Manny Bloch felt differently. He had seen how a defendant's admission of Communist affiliation could elicit a labyrinthine series of questions regarding friends and acquaintances that resulted in contempt of court charges, perjury charges, or the inadvertent implication of others. Nevertheless, the younger Bloch took his father's perspective seriously and decided to let the Rosenbergs determine the defense strategy. On Monday, 5 March, the day before the trial was to begin, the Blochs interviewed their clients separately in their respective jails. Ethel and Julie were of one mind: they would take the Fifth because their political beliefs should not be on trial; to do anything else could be used "only to turn us into informers or to create the idea all Communists are spies."

Throughout this discussion of how to approach the question of Communism, it is entirely possible that Alexander and Emanuel Bloch really did not know how involved Ethel and Julie had been in the Party. Membership in the CP was an intensely private matter. Close friends frequently remained unaware of each other's status. Ethel and Julie consistently maintained to Julie's family that they had never been members of the Communist party, and they never publicly admitted Party membership. For Ethel this may have been formally true, but certainly her activities in the past were identical with those of a rank-and-file member. Julie's denial was a blatant lie.

According to historian Paul Lyons, many lawyers actively discouraged their clients from telling them about their involvement in the Party. One lawyer reported that he "fought against loose tongues. I never asked a soul whether they were Communists or not." "Several left-wing attorneys stress that they did not want to be in a position to betray anyone or risk a perjury charge if questioned about their own affiliations and associations."

The possibility that the Blochs did not know about their clients' Party affiliations is also suggested by the case of Carl Marzani. After he left the East Side Defense Council to serve in World War II, Marzani obtained an important position in the Office of Strategic Services. After the war ended, he became the first individual to be indicted during the burgeoning wave of anti-Communism for having been in the Communist party. His became an important test case, and Marzani retained one of the best-known civil liberties lawyers to defend him.

> I was determined that before he took the case he should know where I stood. I didn't say I was a member of the Communist Party because I couldn't tell him that. Because it would be wrong. But I did everything else but. I even said to him, 'Look, if there are any questions in your mind of any kind I'll answer them truthfully, but there are some questions I don't think you should ask.' That's as close as I could get to telling him [about my CP membership].

Marzani's lawyer was not sympathetic to the Communist party as Manny Bloch was, but he agreed to take the case regardless of his client's status in the CP because he believed his client's civil liberties had been violated. Nevertheless, for Marzani, a leading Communist intellectual, a frank discussion of Party membership, even with his own attorney, "would be wrong."

The Rosenbergs, who looked up to people like Marzani, never revealed their association with the Party in any letter, statement or, apparently, private conversation that was bugged by the government during their three years in prison. Their position that their political beliefs and associations were their own private matter was a principled one. Unfortunately, it would prove to be neither practical nor convincing.

> One would hardly have thought that he
> and his wife were on trial for their lives.
> Morton Sobell

On the morning of Tuesday, 6 March 1951, Ethel Rosenberg prepared for the first day of her trial. The charges against her were no more specific than those given on the day she was arrested. As far as she was aware, she faced the possibility of life imprisonment or death by electrocution for "conferring with" her husband, brother, and sister-in-law on two separate occasions.

Ethel dressed that morning in a simple white blouse and dark skirt. Some of her fellow inmates, with whom she had become quite friendly over the past seven months, gave her a scarlet bodice to improve her drab appearance. To this she added a monstrous hat—wide-brimmed with a mass of netting that gathered at the crown and tied under her double chin. Miriam Moskowitz lamented that the "clothes Ethel wore to trial broke my heart. . . . So long as Julie thought she looked pretty she didn't seem to care. But we girls used to worry—particularly those of us who had been before juries."

Ethel had made many friends at the House of Detention. After the initial shock of being a prisoner among women completely dissimilar to herself, Ethel became quite comfortable. Unlike her experience at Knickerbocker Village, in jail she had nothing for which to be ashamed or defensive. With the prostitutes, drug addicts, and embezzlers, Ethel could be herself—warm, empathic, motherly. After years of learning about the horrors of racial discrimination from the Communist party, Ethel was unusually open and caring with the black inmates. She continually extended herself to others—always asking about their children and families, offering items of food she had purchased from commissary, attending every religious service provided, and joining happily into any game of ping-pong or softball that took place during the prisoners' brief exercise periods. For this she was accepted and respected by the women she affectionately called her "buddies."

When she left the supportive environment she had constructed for herself in jail, however, Ethel Rosenberg underwent an abrupt transformation. Suddenly thrust into a world of belligerent and vulturous reporters, unfeeling matrons and courtroom officials, she assumed the aloof posture to which she always seemed to gravitate when she felt vulnerable and anxious. She would throw back her head, arch her eyebrows and set her face into a visage of stony imperiousness. She radiated disdain. This appearance was clearly a defensive posture. Given the uniformly hostile environment she faced outside jail, she probably clung to any psychological maneuver that would enable her simply to endure her public appearances. In addition to this external environment, which was not of her making, there were the demands placed on her by the roles she and Julie seem to have chosen for themselves. They had explicitly adopted as their "motto" the words "courage, confidence, and perspective," and their correspondence frequently reveals this litany as a standard of behavior they set for themselves. To this they added "dignity" and "calm" as norms for themselves. They seem to have taken the position that if they demonstrated how dignified and unperturbed they were in the face of the government's accusations against them, the jury, the courtroom spectators and reporters, the public at large would view them as fine people, unintimidated by the government's "lies," and thereby honest and innocent. As it would turn out, Ethel played her role well, too well in fact.

The courtroom at Foley Square to which Ethel was ushered that cold, gray morning of 6 March 1951, was an imposing one with marbled- and wood-paneled walls, twenty-four-foot-high ceilings, and dark wood furniture. When she entered, the room was already filled with reporters and spectators eager to witness what many thought would be one of the most sensational trials of the century. The "dramatic potentialities," as *The New York Times* put it, were many. At long last, the details of how the Reds "stole" the "secret" of the atom bomb would be revealed. Top atomic scientists such as Robert Oppenheimer and Harold Urey were to be called as government witnesses. The well-known former Communist-turned-professional informer Elizabeth Bentley also was to be called. U.S. Attorney Irving Saypol, "the nation's Number One legal hunter of top Communists," as *Time* magazine described him, would prosecute the case. Saypol had become an important symbol of anti-Communism for his prosecution of Alger Hiss and of the leaders of the Communist party under the Smith Act. Another interesting twist to this already interesting case was that Saypol, presiding Judge Irving Kaufman, and the defendants in the case were all Jews, leading to much speculation—none of it ever evidenced in the trial, FBI records, or any other source—that the Rosenbergs' religion was a factor in their arrest and prosecution. But the greatest drama of the trial was the "prospect of Mrs. Rosenberg being faced by her brother, former United States Army Sgt. David Greenglass, who has pleaded guilty in the case and is now listed as a Government witness."

Ethel took her seat near the end of the long defense table. For reasons that remained unclear to all those seated at the table, Morton Sobell, Julie's old friend, had been arrested and charged under the same indictment as the Rosenbergs for "having conspired with Julius Rosenberg and others" to commit espionage. The charges never really became any more specific than that, despite his attorneys' attempts to force the government to outline its allegations. Thus Morton Sobell sat at one end of the table separated from the Rosenbergs by his two attorneys and Manny and Alexander Bloch. The "lawyers could confer, but we defendants were as separated as we had been all along," Sobell remembers. "I saw very little of Julius and Ethel during the courtroom appearances, nodding and smiling to each other. . . . The authorities never let us occupy the same holding cell, before or after going to the courtroom."

Ethel must have felt very alone in the cathedral-like courtroom, the only woman participant on the stage of this legal drama, her scarlet bodice the "brightest dab of color in the great chestnut-paneled chamber." Her sense of isolation probably had escalated since the previous day when she and the Blochs had first been shown the list of witnesses the prosecution intended to call on its behalf. On it were many of the Rosenbergs' friends and acquaintances: Mark and Stella Page, formerly Pogarsky, Ann and Mike Sidorovich, Vivian Glassman, Max and Helene Elitcher, Julie's old friends from college Bill Danziger and William Perl (né Mutterperl), their doctors, George Bernhardt and Max Hart, even their former maid, Evelyn Cox. Although Vivian Glassman's or Ann Sidorovich's betrayal seemed unlikely, Ethel had been completely isolated from her friends for months and had little idea of what kind of pressure the government had been applying. In the case of the Pages, from whom she and Julie were estranged, or the Elitchers, whom Ethel barely knew, their testifying against the Rosenbergs must have seemed quite possible.

As the clerk of the court read aloud the names of 102 witnesses the prosecution intended to call, no one at the defense table knew that the majority were listed only to frighten the defendants into making confessions. As an FBI agent writing at the time to J. Edgar Hoover revealed, "It is unlikely all of these witnesses will be called. . . . [T]he names of some individuals appear, whom it is quite evident would be hostile, because of their attitude when questioned by Bureau agents and their appearance before the Federal Grand Jury but their names are included by the US Attorney as part of his over-all strategy in the prosecution of this case."

If this psychological provocation were not sufficient, Irving Saypol, in an unusual aside at the beginning of the trial, informed Manny Bloch that "if your clients don't confess they are doomed."

The remaining source of potential sympathy in this otherwise hostile courtroom was the judge. If he at least presumed innocence and conducted a fair trial, the Rosenbergs might stand a chance. As he questioned prospective jurors, however, hopes of sympathy must have vaporized at the defense table. He demonstrated his intention to dismiss any potential juror who harbored "any prejudice against the atomic bomb," who opposed "the use of atomic weapons in time of war," or who believed that "developments and information concerning atomic energy should be revealed to Russia." If anyone held "prejudice or bias against the House Committee on Un-American Activities," belonged to any left-wing organization, read any leftist publication, or objected to capital punishment, Judge Kaufman showed his readiness to dismiss them. The one prospective juror who showed any left-wing sympathy, through his admission that he occasionally read the publication *In Fact*, was challenged by Kaufman and excused.

After a day and a half, Kaufman had found his jury. Out of New York City's heterogeneous population, the judge had impaneled a strikingly uniform group: eleven men and no Jews. Of the ten white men, three were auditors, two accountants, and there was one estimator, a sales manager, a caterer, a restauranteur, and a retired civil servant. The one black man was an electrician for Consolidated

Edison, and the one woman was a housewife. None of these twelve read very widely, since that was a trait discouraged by the judge's questions. In fact, they were a group of average Americans: they approved of atomic warfare, capital punishment, the HUAC investigations, and measures preventing the Russians from having access to America's "secrets." They had no association with left-wing politics and they admitted to holding no strong opinions.

The government's case began on Wednesday, at 3:35 P.M. Irving Saypol began his opening statement by explaining the legal basis of conspiracy:

> [A] conspiracy is very simply an agreement and understanding between two or more people to violate some law of the United States. . . . When any one of the persons who have entered into the agreement . . . does any overt act, that is, any physical act to help along the conspiracy . . . then all those other persons who had entered into this agreement and understanding with him become guilty of the crime of conspiracy.

In low tones that forced the defendants to sit "semi-rigid, edged a little forward on their chairs to catch the prosecutor's softly spoken but carefully measured words," Saypol then launched into the substance of the government's case. "The evidence will show that the loyalty and the allegiance of the Rosenbergs and Sobell were not to our country, but that it was to Communism, Communism in this country and Communism throughout the world." Despite Manny Bloch's objection that "Communism is not on trial here," the judge allowed Saypol to continue. The prosecutor stated:

> The evidence will show . . . these defendants joined with their coconspirators in a deliberate, carefully planned conspiracy to deliver to the Soviet Union, the information and the weapons which the Soviet Union could use to destroy us. . . .
>
> We will prove that the Rosenbergs devised and put into operation . . . an elaborate scheme which enabled them to steal through David Greenglass this one weapon, that might well hold the key to the survival of this nation and means the peace of the world, the atomic bomb. . . .
>
> The evidence will prove to you, not only beyond a

reasonable doubt, but beyond any doubt, that all three of
these defendants have committed the most serious crime
which can be committed against the people of this country.

Throughout all of Saypol's inflammatory and hyperbolic remarks, Ethel "seemed calmer and more placid than the two men. Her husband kept drumming the counsel table with long nervous fingers. Sobell's hands moved over his jaw, and he was twitchy. . . ." Despite the fact that all eyes in the courtroom "had shifted toward the defendants," Saypol's accusations "brought no outward sign of emotional reaction" from Ethel. Her gaze remained "fixed on the jury box."

Ethel's success in following her self-prescribed role continued throughout the next day and a half of the trial. During that time Max Elitcher, an acquaintance of Julie's from CCNY, testified to how Julie had unsuccessfully attempted to recruit him to do espionage work. No mention was made of Ethel; she barely knew Elitcher and was not present when her husband allegedly queried him about spying.

On Friday, 9 March, however, Ethel's feigned calm was seriously challenged. At about 2:30 P.M. David Greenglass, whom Ethel had not seen since before he was arrested the previous June, took the witness stand. The younger brother whom she had cared for as a child, encouraged into left-wing politics as an adolescent, and with whom she had formed what she thought was an adult friendship, now was sworn in for the sole purpose of testifying against her and her husband on a capital offense.

Ethel's strategy was the same as it had been during the previous three days. She would sit erect, her face emotionless, averting her eyes from the witness stand only to stare directly at the jury box whenever one of the prosecuting attorneys was speaking. She was well aware that this had to be her most effective performance. Everyone would be scrutinizing her to see how she would react to her brother's accusations. To demonstrate her innocence, she was determined never to flinch, never to take her eyes off him, for to do so, Ethel seems to have reasoned, would make it seem that her younger brother was speaking the truth.

Those at the defense table really had no idea what David Greenglass was about to claim. Thus when he began to answer questions in a low, toneless voice, attorneys and defendants sat on the edge of their seats, straining to hear his responses.

Greenglass kept his eyes fixed on the prosecuting attorney. Saypol had given the weighty responsibility of examining the government's prize witness to his most promising assistant, Roy Cohn, "a dark-haired boyish official with a ringing voice," as the *Times* described him, and also a Jew. David looked to Cohn, who had coached him earlier on how the line of questioning would develop, probably for reassurance and probably in order to avoid his older sister's steady glare.

David's initial comments were unsurprising. He testified to his background, his Army service, his assignment to Los Alamos. Then he dropped his first bombshell: Julius Rosenberg had known the purpose of the project at Los Alamos before David did. Then another half hour of testimony ensued describing his life and work at Los Alamos. Suddenly Cohn's direction shifted: "Now did you have any discussion with Ethel and Julius concerning the relative merits of our form of government and that of the Soviet Union?"

Manny Bloch, who was obviously suffering from a cold, immediately objected, fearful that Cohn was about to start a line of questioning that would lead to testimony "concerning political affiliations, like affiliations with the Communist Party." Although Cohn had not yet mentioned the Communist party, Bloch's readiness to object at the mere suggestion of it, combined with the obvious nervousness he revealed in his objection, must have made those in attendance wonder what he had to hide regarding the subject.

Cohn rephrased the question and David replied that the Rosenbergs "preferred Socialism to capitalism . . . Russian Socialism." As David spoke these words his face broke into a broad grin. Then each time he told of his sister's and brother-in-law's beliefs or activities, he smiled. This seemed to be involuntary and irrepressible, since under questioning from Manny Bloch he admitted that he was "not very" aware that he was smiling while continuing to smile.

After establishing the Rosenbergs' preference for Russian socialism, David then testified that his sister had told his wife in November 1944 that "Julius has finally gotten to a point where he is doing what he wanted to do all along, which was that he was giving information to the Soviet Union." He then related how both the Rosenbergs had requested Ruth to ask him to engage in espionage at Los Alamos.

Hearing this, Ethel "went deathly pale. . . . At one point she pressed tight fingers against her eyeballs, her head lowered to her bosom. . . . Mrs. Rosenberg's features were almost snow pale."

Shortly after these revelations, the trial was adjourned to Monday and Ethel was escorted from the courtroom. Her face was still pale but she managed to hold her head high and imperiously avoid the eyes of those around her.

The ensuing weekend allowed Ethel to regain her composure and to absorb the latest blow from her family. During the next week of testimony, Ethel never allowed herself to show the pain she had displayed during her brother's first day on the witness stand. She sat impassively as he told of her typing his notes to make them easier for the Russians to read and expressing her happiness that he had "come in with them on this espionage work." She even was able to keep her gaze riveted on him as he responded to Manny Bloch's cross-examination:

Q. *Do you bear any affection for your sister Ethel?*

A. *I do.*

Q. *You realize, do you not, that Ethel is being tried here on a charge of conspiracy to commit espionage?*

A. *I do.*

Q. *And you realize the grave implications of that charge?*

A. *I do.*

Q. *And you realize the possible death penalty, in the event that Ethel is convicted by this jury, do you not?*

A. *I do. . . .*

Q. *And you bear affection for her?*

A. *I do.*

Q. *This moment?*

A. *At this moment.*

When David surrendered the witness stand to his wife on the morning of 14 March after three days of testifying, the tenor in the courtroom changed. Dave had been a soft-spoken, seemingly earnest witness who spoke in short declarative sentences and did not elaborate without prodding from the examining attorney. From the moment Ruth assumed the stand, reporters noted how self-possessed and forthcoming this "buxom brunette" appeared to be. She spoke clearly and articulately, repeating portions of her testimony in almost the exact words as she had initially presented them upon demand. She never allowed herself to be intimidated by the defense attorney, often forcefully responding to his questions with a punctuated, "Well, Mr. Bloch . . ."

In her testimony, Ruth confirmed the essentials of what her husband had claimed under oath, but added detailed descriptions of her own. Ruth precisely recalled a January 1945 conversation she had with Ethel while Dave and Julie "were talking about technical things":

> *Well, Ethel said that she was tired, and I asked her what she had been doing. She said she had been typing. . . . Then she said that Julie, too, was tired: that he was very busy; he ran around a good deal; that all his time and his energies were used in this thing; that was the most important thing to him; that he was away a good deal and spent time with his friends; that he had to make a good impression; that it sometimes cost him as much as $50 to $75 an evening to entertain his friends.*

Later she spoke of Julie's offer to send the Greenglasses to the Soviet Union once Klaus Fuchs and Harry Gold were arrested. She recalled a conversation she had with Julie on 24 May 1950:

> *I asked him what he was doing. He said he was going too, that he would not leave at the same time, and he would meet us in Mexico. We would see him there, and I asked him what Ethel thought about it and he said Ethel didn't like the idea of it herself but she realized it was necessary and they were going to go.*

Neither Manny nor Alexander Bloch was able to do much to challenge David or Ruth's testimony. The defense strategy had been to accept the fact that David and Ruth had been involved in espionage and that David actually had stolen vital atomic secrets, but that the Rosenbergs had nothing to do with this. There was little the Blochs could do to prove their clients were not involved, other than to find some substantive inconsistency in the Greenglasses' testimony, and this they were unable to do.

Thus when a series of witnesses followed Ruth onto the stand confirming various aspects of what the Greenglasses had said, the

case against the Rosenbergs began to solidify. On Thursday, 15
March, convicted spy Harry Gold testified that his Soviet espionage
superior requested that he meet a contact stationed at the Los Alamos project in 1945. To this end, the Soviet "gave me a sheet of
paper: it was onionskin paper, and on it was typed the following:
First, the name 'Greenglass.' . . . Then a number [on] 'High Street'
. . . and then underneath that was 'Albuquerque, New Mexico.'
The last thing that was on the paper was 'Recognition signal. I come
from Julius.' "

The following day, Friday, 16 March, the physician who cared
for Michael, Robby, and Julius testified that Julius had called him
in late May wanting "to know what injections one needs to go to
Mexico. . . . [I]t is not for me; it's for a friend of mine." Thus "Dr.
Bernie," as Robby and Michael affectionately referred to Dr. George
Bernhardt, seemed to confirm the Greenglasses' assertion that Julius
was trying to get Ruth and Dave out of the country after Gold's
arrest.

Ruth's sister, brother-in-law, and Bill Danziger also testified to
minor incidents that confirmed small parts of the Greenglasses' or
Max Elitcher's testimony. Then on Wednesday, 21 March, professional informer Elizabeth Bentley took the stand for the prosecution.
Known as the "Red Spy Queen," Bentley had become something
of a celebrity in the period following World War II as a former
Communist who could be trusted to "remember" names of Party
members, spies, and clandestine Communist activity years after she
supposedly had revealed all to the FBI. Bentley was trotted out at
the Rosenberg-Sobell trial largely to expound on the evils of the
American CP: "The Communist Party being part of the Communist
International only served the interests of Moscow, whether it be
propaganda or espionage or sabotage." But she also presented some
vague circumstantial "evidence" about a "Julius" whom she had
heard of and who had called her on the phone requesting to be put
in touch with her boss, a spy for the Soviets. This was by far the
weakest testimony yet presented, but it provided the crucial link
between Communism and espionage that the prosecution sought
to demonstrate, and served to suggest that Julius Rosenberg was
involved in spying sanctioned by the Party. Shortly after the appearance of Elizabeth Bentley, the prosecution rested its case.

Saypol's ending took the defense by surprise. Where were all
the Rosenbergs' friends listed as prosecution witnesses? Where were
the famous atomic scientists who were going to testify? And where

was a single witness, outside of Dave and Ruth Greenglass, who would offer one word linking Ethel Rosenberg to any conspiracy or crime? Having had very little time to prepare, Manny Bloch was forced to call his first witness. Julius Rosenberg took the stand.

Handsomely dressed in a gray suit, white shirt, and silver and maroon tie, Julie sat back in the witness chair, his legs crossed, his hands calmly folded in his lap. As Bloch led him through a description of his background and a point-by-point denial of the Greenglasses' accusations against him, Julius spoke in a firm, self-confident fashion, clearly eager to make a good impression on the jury. He seemed earnest and respectful, addressing his attorney and the judge as "sir." By the close of his first afternoon on the stand, he had acquitted himself well.

The next morning Bloch's questions continued in a similar vein, when suddenly the judge questioned Julius as to whether he ever discussed "the respective preferences of economic systems between Russia and the United States." The response he received was forthright:

> First of all, I am not an expert on matters on different economic systems, but in my normal social intercourse with my friends we discussed matters like that. And I believe there are merits in both systems, I mean from what I have been able to read and ascertain. . . . I heartily approve our [sic] system of justice as performed in this country, Anglo-Saxon jurisprudence. I am in favor, heartily in favor of our Constitution and Bill of Rights and I owe my allegiance to my country at all times.

To voice the belief that there was merit in the Soviet system was a bold and sincere statement to make in the midst of this clearly anti-Communist courtroom. Instead of nervously objecting to the mere mention of the Soviet Union, Julius had faced the issue honestly and in a manner that obviously delighted his attorney, for Bloch quickly sought to pursue the subject:

Q. *Do you owe allegiance to any other country?*

A. *No, I do not. . . .*

Q. *Would you fight for this country—*

A. *Yes, I will.*

A. Yes, I will, and in discussing the merits of other forms of governments, I discussed that with my friends on the basis of the performance of what they accomplished, and I felt that the Soviet government has improved a lot of [sic] the underdog there, has made a lot of progress in eliminating illiteracy, has done a lot of reconstruction work and built up a lot of resources, and at the same time I felt that they contributed a major share in destroying the Hitler beast who killed six million of my co-religionists, and I feel emotional about that thing.

This was clearly amazing. Julius Rosenberg was lecturing the court on the accomplishments of the Soviet Union. Instead of something that was so horrible, incriminating, and inflammatory that it should not be alluded to openly—as Manny Bloch's persistent and ineffectual objections suggested—Communism's deeds were being publicly extolled by the major defendant in the case.

This moment passed quickly, however, for Julius immediately proclaimed his constitutional privilege. Judge Kaufman asked:

Q. Well, did you ever belong to any group that discussed the system of Russia?

A. Well, your Honor, if you are referring to political groups— is that what you are referring to?

Q. Any group.

A. Well, your Honor, I feel at this time that I refuse to answer a question that might tend to incriminate me.

It was as though Julius had just been waiting for the first opportunity to unleash the Fifth Amendment. It was the one weapon he had in his legal arsenal and he defiantly invoked it again and again, as if the words "I refuse to answer on the ground that it might tend to incriminate me" meant what they said and no more. Julie always had taken words at face value. Truth was immutable, scientific, pure. If he were guaranteed protection against self-incrimination by the Constitution, then he literally would be so protected whenever he chose to claim it. Something as nuanced as the psychological effect on the jury of "taking the Fifth" did not seem to enter into his preparations for the stand.

Of course he had the legal right to claim the privilege, and given the context of the trial one can argue that it was wise to do so. But he did it so often, with such apparent self-satisfaction, and even when it was totally uncalled for, that it undoubtedly caused a negative reaction in the jury box. As attorney Louis Nizer has concluded:

> *Instead of forthrightness, there was furtiveness. Instead of uninhibited truth, there was legalism. Instead of courage which he had exhibited by praising what he liked in Russia, there was fear. He was entitled to his constitutional right not to give an answer which might help prove him guilty of a crime, but what effect would his concern have on the jury, despite the instruction that no adverse inference be drawn from the exercise of his privilege? The jury system is susceptible of psychological forces which beat upon it, and they cannot be ignored.*

That afternoon Julius Rosenberg's fortunes as a witness seriously deteriorated. Irving Saypol began his cross-examination, and his very first question revealed what was really on trial that day at Foley Square and it had little to do with the atom bomb:

> *Q. Mr. Rosenberg, tell us a little bit about your associates when you were at City College. Who were they?*

("It was a corollary of the Informer Principle that the act of informing was more important than the information imparted.")

Julie dutifully began to name men whom he knew the FBI was aware of because of the appearance of their names on the list of prosecution witnesses. He then was asked if he had participated in any "activities" in college. His response demonstrated the stance he would take throughout his cross-examination: he pretended he did not understand the question, forced the prosecutor and the judge to explain, and then suddenly and inappropriately seized on his constitutional privilege against self-incrimination:

> *A. I don't understand what you mean, Mr. Saypol.*

The Court. *He wants to know whether you belonged to anything . . .; did you have any club or anything like that?*

The Witness: *What kind of a club?*

Q. *You tell me.*

A. *I don't understand the question. . . .*

Q. *Well, is there a Boy Scout troop up there?*

A. *Not to my knowledge. . . .*

Q. *Was there a Hillel Society up there at City College?*

A. *Yes, I believe there was.*

Q. *Were you all active in that?*

A. *No, I was not. . . .*

Q. *Now, tell us what groups you were active in. . . .*

The Witness: *Can I state something, sir?*

The Court. *Yes.*

Mr. Saypol. *You will in a minute.*

The Court. *Let him state.*

The Witness: *I would like to state, on any answer I made on this question, I don't intend to waive any part of my right of self-incrimination, and if Mr. Saypol is referring to the Young Communist League or the Communist Party, I will not answer any question on it.*

This sort of sparring continued throughout the afternoon and for most of the next session. It was not until the afternoon of Monday, 26 March, that Ethel Rosenberg was called to follow her husband onto the witness stand.

There was a certain dignity or imperiousness about her as she walked slowly to the stand. Dressed in a simple pink blouse and black skirt, Ethel appeared somewhat heavier than she had at the beginning of the trial. As she confided to Helen Sobell the following day, "She would just eat everything. She had said she had gained maybe ten pounds during the time of the trial because of this gnawing inside of her."

The questioning by Alexander Bloch began simply enough. He

merely guided her through a description of her background—her education, her marriage, her life as a housewife and mother. Although she spoke with great composure and assuredness as Bloch addressed her, when the judge interposed his own questions, she "knotted her fingers and wrinkled her forehead," and her voice faded.

Her typing quickly became a centerpiece of her testimony. She had to explain how she had acquired her typewriter—from a member of the Clark Players in the early nineteen-thirties—and the nature of what she typed—Julie's engineering reports for college, his business letters, and "his letters in regard to reinstatement after he was dismissed by the government." This last remark provoked Judge Kaufman:

> Q. *Did you know anything about the charges that had been leveled against your husband by the Government in '45? . . .*
>
> A. *Well, it was alleged that he was a member of the Communist Party.*
>
> Q. *And he was dismissed for that reason?*
>
> A. *I refuse to answer on the ground that this might be incriminating.*

Following her husband's lead, Ethel Rosenberg rushed to take the Fifth Amendment even when it was thoroughly uncalled for. Kaufman merely was asking if Julius was dismissed because the government *alleged* he was a CP member, not if he *was* a member in fact. Alexander Bloch thus was forced to "advise the witness to answer that question."

This interchange initiated a pattern. The elderly Bloch would guide his client through a recitation of events or read long excerpts of the Greenglasses' testimony and then ask Ethel if the testimony was true, and she would simply respond "No," or "No, I did not." Then the court would intervene by asking questions about Communism, or the Soviet Union, or aspects of previous testimony and Ethel would refuse to answer on the ground of self-incrimination. If she did not take the Fifth, she would utilize the other strategy she had initiated the day after Julie's arrest—playing the somewhat inept housewife.

The Court. *Well, what were your own views about the subject matter of the United States having any weapon that Russia didn't have at that time? That is, in 1944 and 1945? . . .*

The Witness. *I don't recall having any views at all about it.*

Q. *Your mind was a blank on the subject?*

A. *Absolutely.*

And:

Q. *Did you hear your husband testify here that the console table was kept against the northerly wall of the living room?*

A. *Well, I am very poor when it comes to directions. I simply couldn't say north, south, east or west.*

And:

Q. *And you or your husband owed Davey a thousand dollars for his stock?*

A. *I am afraid I am a little hazy when it comes to business, the business matters, the financial arrangements. I really know very little about them.*

Unfortunately the "dumb housewife" simply did not conform with Ethel's other persona, that of the utterly calm, composed, aloof witness who understood every question, was keenly protective of her constitutional rights, and never demonstrated the least emotion, even when asked the following:

Q. *And you were six years older than he was; and what was the relationship between him and you throughout the period of your living together in the same household, until you married and after you married?*

A. *Well, he was my baby brother. . . .*

Q. *Did you love him?*

A. *Yes, I loved him very much.*

If Ethel had shown the least sadness or hurt at the mention of this, the jury and press might have sympathized with this woman, so clearly betrayed by the younger brother she had loved "very much." But Ethel refused, probably for both conscious and unconscious reasons, to play the victim and thereby suggest vulnerability. She was unwilling or perhaps unable to obey the rules of what constituted correct female behavior in this setting. The same sort of assumptions that would have inclined the jury and press to pity a woman betrayed by her own family, were used in this case to fault a woman who did not respond with the proper amount of anguish and remorse. It is because of her performance in court and the media's reaction to it that many people began to assume that Ethel Rosenberg, and not her husband, was the moving spirit behind the theft of the atomic bomb.

If the members of the jury were struck by Ethel's stoicism during her examination by Alexander Bloch, her behavior under cross-examination by Irving Saypol must have been cause for wonder. Saypol's intention was to demonstrate that the testimony Ethel had given to the grand jury in August 1950—largely consisting of refusals to testify on the ground of self-incrimination—contradicted what she had just testified to under oath.

> Q. *Now, you came before the grand jury on August 7th; do you remember that?*
>
> A. *Yes, about that time.*
>
> Q. *And everything you told the grand jury was the truth?*
>
> A. *Right.*
>
> Q. *Do you remember having been asked this question and giving this answer:*
>
> > '*Q. When did you consult with your attorney for the first time in connection with this matter?*'
> >
> > '*A. I refuse to answer on the ground that this may tend to incriminate me.*'
>
> Q. *Do you remember having been asked that and having given that answer?*
>
> A. *That's right.*
>
> Q. *Was that the truth?*

Manny Bloch adamantly objected. Ethel had asserted the Fifth because at the time of her grand jury appearance neither she nor Bloch

knew what the government was attempting to prove, who they were
trying to implicate, or what "evidence" they might have against
her or Julie. They probably had chosen the strategy of refusing to
testify on the ground of self-incrimination, believing that the less
Ethel said, the less ammunition the government would have to use
against her or others. Now, however, her refusal to admit when she
first consulted her attorney must have seemed suspicious. Saypol,
with the judge's approval, continued.

Q. *Was that the truth?* . . .

A. *Was what the truth? That I answered the question that
way?*

Q. *That you answered that to disclose whether you had
consulted with your lawyer about this matter would incriminate you?*

A. *All I can say, Mr. Saypol, at this time, is that I don't
remember what reason I may or may not have had at that
time for giving such an answer.*

Q. *Might it have been an untruthful reason?*

A. *No.*

Kaufman readily took up the prosecution's line of questioning:

The Court. *The fact of the matter is that you have no objection to giving the answer to that?*

A. *That's right.* . . .

Q. *And today you feel there is nothing incriminating about
that answer?*

A. *No.*

Q. *But at that time, before the grand jury, you did?*

A. *I must have had some reason for feeling that way.*

Q. *Now, what was the reason?*

A. *I couldn't say at this time.*

The Court. *In your own interest, I think you ought to think
about it and see if you can give us some reason.*

The Witness. *I really couldn't say.*

In 1957 the United States Supreme Court would rule that what Ethel was being subjected to was illegal. It held in *Grunewald v. United States* that grand jury testimony was not allowable at a trial for purposes of showing inconsistency. It argued that a witness could take the Fifth for a variety of reasons before a grand jury, and that these reasons were not necessarily inconsistent with a subsequent decision to testify at a trial. But that was six years away, and Ethel had to continue to endure what Morton Sobell called the "one-two combination of judge and prosecutor, working in tandem":

> Q. *Do you remember having been asked this question before the grand jury and giving this answer:*
>
> > '*Q. Did you discuss this case with your brother, David Greenglass?*'
> >
> > '*A. I refuse to answer on the ground that this might tend to incriminate me.*'
>
> Q. *Was that question asked and did you give that answer?*
>
> A. *Yes.*
>
> Q. *Was that answer true? . . .*
>
> A. *It was true, because my brother David was under arrest.*
>
> Q. *How would that incriminate you, if you are innocent? . . .*
>
> A. *It wouldn't necessarily incriminate me, but it might—*
>
> Q. *You mean—*
>
> A. *—and as long as I had any idea that there might be some chance for me to be incriminated I had the right to use that privilege . . .*
>
> Q. *As a matter of fact, at that time you didn't know how much the FBI knew about you and so you weren't taking any chances; isn't that it?*
>
> Mr. E.H. Bloch. *I object to the form of the question . . .*
>
> The Court. *Overruled. . . .*
>
> The Witness. *I didn't know what the FBI knew or didn't know.*
>
> Q. *Of course you didn't so you weren't taking any chance in implicating yourself or your husband.*

On and on this went for another hour as Saypol carefully went
through each of Ethel's refusals to answer questions put to her at
the grand jury and then crisply demanded if her answers were true.
Kaufman overruled almost every one of Bloch's objections. The
judge explained that "when a witness freely answers questions at
a trial, . . . the answers to the very same questions to which the
witness had refused to answer previously upon a ground assigned
by that witness, I ask you, is that not a question then for the jury
to consider on the question of credibility."

Throughout all of this, Ethel remained thoroughly composed.
She stood up to the prosecutor and judge repeatedly and steadfastly
stated her position.

> A. *My husband had been arrested on July 17 and I had
> been subpoenaed to come before the grand jury. It was not
> for me to state what I thought or didn't think the Govern-
> ment might or might not have in the way of accusation
> against me. I didn't have to state my reason, but I did feel
> that in answering certain questions I might be incriminating
> myself until I exercised my privilege.*

And:

> A. *When one uses the right of self-incrimination one does
> not mean that the answer is yes and one does not mean
> that the answer is no. . . . I simply refused to answer on
> the ground that that answer might incriminate me.*

And:

> A. *It is not necessary to explain the use of self-incrimination.*

Helen Sobell, the only supporter among the courtroom spectators,
recalls:

> [W]hen she was on the stand, she was just horribly badg-
> ered. She was incredibly strong. It was a most, most difficult
> situation, and the government attorney was extremely pro-
> voking and irritating in every kind of way and nasty, and
> to all of this she remained a thinking person. It would have
> been so easy just to have become completely numb. . . .
> You could see she would be almost provoked into some-

thing and would pull back. She was manifesting sheer will-power . . . , and when the same questions were reiterated again and again . . . she would again consider the question, again answer the question, again try to see where she was being led. I was tremendously impressed.

Morton Sobell, who witnessed the proceedings from the defense table, called her cross-examination "the crucifixion of Ethel":

> *It was a wonder that through it all Ethel remained calm and collected, never once becoming emotional. The cross-examination of Ethel in that courtroom was the most dramatic episode I had ever seen—on stage or off . . . rather like a modern Greek tragedy.*
> *I wouldn't have believed that she was capable of that behavior. I wouldn't have been able to do it; I would have blown-up, I know. I don't know how she kept her cool.*

The witness was able to "keep her cool" because she had spent much of her life concealing her vulnerability and refusing to reveal fright or anxiety to those who tormented or intimidated her. She may have been a second-class amateur actress in the Clark Players, but her composure, dignity, and vigorous defense of her position on the witness stand on 27 March 1951, in view of "the gnawing inside her," bore out Seward Park High School's "Class Prophecy" of 1931—that in the year 1950 Ethel Greenglass would be "America's leading actress."

18

THE VERDICT
AND SENTENCE

The day after Ethel stepped down from the witness stand, Wednesday, 28 March 1951, Manny Bloch presented his summation to a packed courtroom. He opened in a manner that had become familiar; he was obsequious in his praise of the court, probably hoping that this would curry favor with the jury and demonstrate how upstanding and honest the defense was:

> I would like to say to the Court on behalf of all defense counsel that we feel that you have treated us with the utmost courtesy, that you have extended to us the privileges that we expect as lawyers, and despite any disagreements we may have had with the Court on questions of law, we feel that the trial has been conducted and we hope we have contributed our share, with that dignity and that decorum that befits an American trial.
>
> I would like to also say to the members of Mr. Saypol's staff that we are appreciative of the courtesies extended to us.

Bloch then launched into the substance of his summary argument: David and Ruth Greenglass, confessed espionage agents, had "fooled" the FBI and now were trying to fool the jury. It was not a tremendously complex or inspiring explanation, but Bloch spared no emotion or hyperbole in his presentation:

> But one thing I think you do know, that any man who will testify against his own blood and flesh, his own sister, is repulsive, is revolting, who violates every code that any civilization has ever lived by. He is the lowest of the lowest animals that I have ever seen, and if you are honest with yourself you will admit that he is lowest [sic] than the lowest animal that you have ever seen . . .
>
> Maybe some of you are more acute in sizing up women than others, but if Ruth Greenglass is not the embodiment of evil, I would like to know what person is? . . .
>
> Well, if she can fool the FBI, I do hope that she won't be able to fool you.

Irving Saypol began his summation that afternoon on a different note. He took the offensive, as he had throughout the trial, and matched, and perhaps surpassed, Emanuel Bloch's capacity for vilification. The first object of his invective was Ethel's performance on the witness stand:

> If there has been any fooling, you will remember that one of the defendants made blanket negatives, blanket answers, in denial as to whether she knew Harry Gold, as to whether she had ever talked to David Greenglass about his work at Los Alamos, as to whether she or her husband ever talked about atomic bombs, and yet I showed you that in the grand jury, on the advice of her counsel, she refused to answer those questions on the ground that to answer them would be self-incriminating. . . . I leave it to you as to who may have been fooled.

After reviewing the material presented at the trial, Saypol turned to an assessment of the Rosenbergs as people:

> Rosenberg and his wife have added the supreme touch to their betrayal of this country by taking the stand before you, by taking advantage of every legal opportunity that is afforded defendants, and then, by lying and lying and lying

here, brazenly in an attempt to deceive you, to lie their way out of what they did. . . .

The issue in this case, we are all agreed, transcends any family consideration; but clearly the breach of family loyalty is that of an older sister and brother-in-law dragging an American soldier into the sordid business of betraying his country for the benefit of the Soviet Union. The difference between the Greenglasses and the Rosenbergs? The Greenglasses have told the truth. They have tried to make amends for the hurt which has been done to our nation and to the world.

The Rosenbergs, on the other hand, have magnified their sins by lying.

Saypol then concluded:

The crime charged here is one of the most serious that could be committed against the United States of America. These defendants before you are parties to an agreement to spy and steal from their own country, to serve the interests of a foreign power which today seeks to wipe us off the face of the earth. It would use the produce of these defendants, the information received through them, from these traitors, to destroy Americans and the people of the United Nations. . . .

No defendants ever stood before the bar of American justice less deserving of sympathy than these.

With these words ringing in their ears, the members of the jury were instructed in the law and evidence of the case by Judge Kaufman, who then told them to decide the fate of Julius and Ethel Rosenberg and their codefendant Morton Sobell. At 4:53 P.M., the jury retired.

The defendants were led down to the basement of the courthouse to await the verdict in separate holding cells. An hour and a half passed and then suddenly they were escorted upstairs to resume their seats at the defense table only to hear that the jury was requesting a copy of the indictment and a list of witnesses. The defendants immediately were returned to the basement. This pattern of waiting and then returning to the courtroom, only to hear of some minor request by the jury, continued throughout the evening. At one point, Helen Sobell was allowed to join her husband, and the

Rosenbergs were permitted to wait together. Upon seeing each other, Ethel and Julie immediately embraced and Julie fell into Ethel's arms as she caressed his head. After their third appearance in the courtroom that evening, the defendants were allowed to remain together in an upstairs "bullpen." Manny Bloch joined them and they talked about their families, clearly avoiding any discussion of the trial.

After their fourth appearance, they were returned to the basement holding cells a little before 10:00 P.M. Suddenly Ethel began to sing. Helen Sobell remembers: "In that environment it was very strange to hear the sweetness of her voice. . . . To me at that time it sounded celestial, as if it were coming from a different world—very sweet, strong, clear, and precise."

Ethel plainly loved the sound of her voice and knew that Julie loved it. Undoubtedly, she considered it her greatest asset and had never been shy about displaying it. From her first week in the Women's House of Detention, Ethel had serenaded her fellow inmates after the lights were turned out. Alone in her jail cell, she sang operatic arias or lullabies. "It was her way of saying good night, and no officer seemed to want to stop her—it was too beautiful," recalled Miriam Moskowitz. Ethel relished the praise she received for her singing as much in prison as she had at Loew's amateur nights. In her second letter from prison to her husband, Ethel delighted in reporting that she received nightly requests from her prison mates to hear their favorite songs.

As she probably knew quite well from her experience in political activities, singing could be a source of inspiration, pulling people out of their immediate circumstances, and helping them feel a sense of community with others. Although nothing she sang that night was overtly political—an operatic aria and the then-popular "Goodnight Irene"—Ronnie Gilbert, the singer who made "Goodnight Irene" one of the most popular in the immediate postwar period has said, "Sometimes at a time of war and horror, a love song just comes out like the most political thing you can do, because it speaks of basic human values."

Suddenly, at 11:00 P.M., the defendants were led upstairs into the courtroom again. Judge Kaufman announced: "I have a communication from the jury which reads as follows: 'one of the jurors has some doubt in his mind as to whether or not he can recommend leniency for one of the defendants. He is interested in knowing your mind on the matter.' " Most people immediately assumed the reference was to Ethel. "After all," Morton Sobell remembers thinking, "the evidence against her had been so minimal."

Judge Kaufman crisply reminded the jury that the "duty of imposing sentence rests exclusively upon the Court. You cannot allow a consideration of a punishment which may be inflicted upon the defendants to influence your verdict in any way." The jury was then excused and the defendants were led away once more. Finally, at 12:22 A.M., the jury returned to ask that the judge make arrangements for them to retire to a hotel for the night since there was still one "dissident vote amongst us." Kaufman bristled: if the jury had reached a verdict on any one of the defendants, why not have that verdict rendered at once?

> Mr. A. Bloch. *Tonight?*
>
> The Court. *Yes.*
>
> Mr. A. Bloch. *That is cruelty to us.*
>
> The Court. *Why prolong the agony? If they have it, they have it.*

Kaufman put the question to the jury, and its response was immediate: "We have reached our verdict on two of the defendants and we prefer to reserve rendering our verdict on all these defendants until we have complete unanimity." The jury retired to a hotel for the night.

The following morning, after virtually no sleep, the defendants were returned to the courtroom. At 11:01 A.M., the clerk of the court addressed the jury foreman:

> The Clerk: *Mr. Foreman, have you agreed upon a verdict?*
>
> The Foreman: *Yes, your Honor, we have.*
>
> The Clerk: *How say you?*
>
> The Foreman: *We the jury find Julius Rosenberg guilty as charged. We the jury find Ethel Rosenberg guilty as charged. We the jury find Morton Sobell guilty as charged.*

According to *The New York Times*, Ethel "took the verdict stoically without changing expression." She then remained utterly still, her face a mask, as the press and spectators gawked at her while Judge Kaufman addressed the jury:

*My own opinion is that your verdict is a correct verdict.
. . . I must say that as an individual I cannot be happy
because it is a sad day for America. The thought that citizens
of our country would lend themselves to the destruction of
their own country by the most destructive weapon known
to man is so shocking that I can't find words to describe
this loathsome offense.*

Irving Saypol, however, was able to find words, which he offered
after Kaufman had concluded:

*It is not possible for a great nation to be free from traitors,
but this case shows that it is possible to reach them and
ultimately bring them to the bar for punishment. Lord Acton
said, 'Eternal vigilance is the price of freedom'. . . . This
case has merely adapted that saying to the atomic age.*

*The jury's verdict is a ringing answer of our democratic
society to those who would destroy it. . . . The case itself
has implications so wide in their ramifications that they
involve the very question of whether or when the devas-
tation of atomic war may fall upon the world.*

After hearing these words that bore so little relation to the clients
he had just defended, Manny Bloch also felt moved to speak:

*I would like to restate what I said when I opened to the
jury. I want to extend my appreciation to the Court for its
courtesies, and again I repeat I want to extend my appreciation for the courtesies extended to me by Mr. Saypol and
the members of his staff, as well as the members of the FBI,
and I would like to say to the jury that a lawyer does not
always win a case; all that a lawyer expects is a jury to
decide a case on the evidence with mature deliberation.*

*I feel satisfied by reason of the length of time that you
took for your deliberations, as well as the questions asked
during the course of your deliberations, that you examined
carefully the evidence and came to a certain conclusion.*

What the defendants may have been thinking at this point was
expressed by Morton Sobell:

Afterwards everyone began congratulating everyone else—
while the defendants looked on helplessly. . . . It was all a
part of the game theory under which our legal system op-
erates. The trial was a game, and the officers of the court
the contestants. In this case the lives of the defendants were
the stakes.

Sentencing was set for 5 April, one week away, and then the defendants were led to the basement once again. This time, however,
they were ushered into a conference room, where they were soon
joined by their lawyers and Helen Sobell. The implication of the
jury's verdict was so horrific, it remained unspeakable:

We talked about Kaufman's raw rulings and ridiculing Say-
pol's uncouth behavior. There were no recriminations—not
even for the performance the lawyers had just before put
on. Lunch arrived and each of the attorneys fumbled in his
pocket. Manny Bloch finally won the race. . . . But in spite
of the good fellowship, it was apparent that the lawyers
were depressed, and so we, the convicted, made a valiant
effort to cheer them up.

One of Morton Sobell's attorneys "passed around a recent newspaper clipping which referred to his chess triumphs at the turn of
the century. Manny told us how much weight he had lost during
the trial, and we all joined in a discussion of hot pastrami vs. corned
beef." And then suddenly it was over. At 2:00 P.M. the lawyers and
Helen Sobell were forced to leave and the convicts were readied
for their ride back to jail. Ethel and Julie donned their winter coats
and Ethel put on a small crocheted hat one of her friends in jail had
made for her. Julie's wrists were locked into handcuffs. Ethel slipped
her hand through his arm and the Rosenbergs walked out into the
cold, overcast March air. Dozens of reporters, flashbulbs, and motion picture cameras greeted them. Ethel held her body rigid, her
expression disdainful, refusing to look at any of the cameras. Then
abruptly Julie was pulled away from her by a United States marshal
and, for one moment, Ethel glanced at her husband with frightened
eyes, her hand extended in midair.

When Ethel returned to the Women's House of Detention, she
was immediately transferred from the ninth floor, where she had

been imprisoned since her arrest, to the fifth. Here she was placed in a cell directly across from the guard's station so she could be watched at all times. The prison officials were afraid their newly convicted atom spy would try to commit suicide. Nothing, however, could have been further from the truth. The conviction seemed to have increased Ethel's determination to play the role of the stoic, only now with greater drama, and greater dignity.

This intention was successfully displayed the following day, the appointed time for Jewish services at the Women's House of Detention. Because there were so few Jewish prisoners, typically only one or two women attended. But on this day some eight to ten inmates gathered in hopes of seeing Ethel. "As they sat there in the solemn hush of the chapel, the little group spoke in whispers of one subject—her conviction. . . . Then Ethel appeared in the doorway and began the walk down the long aisle, her face composed, her head thrown back a little, her step measured and poised, as if she were the focus of a thousand pairs of eyes instead of eight or ten, and trying to assure them all that she was quite all right."

Throughout the next week Ethel continued to feign calm and play her self-appointed role as though she were the object of a thousand pair of eyes. She faced the daily drama of her life within the Women's House of Detention unaware that her fate had become the object of much debate within the government. Assistant prosecutor Roy Cohn apparently had come to believe that all three defendants should receive the death penalty, but argued to Judge Kaufman that "if Mrs. Rosenberg were sentenced to a prison term there was a possibility that she would talk and that additional criminal prosecutions could be had on the basis of her evidence." Cohn's boss, Irving Saypol, thought differently. In a meeting with Kaufman in the judge's office, he recommended that both the Rosenbergs be sent to their deaths. Kaufman, in turn, wanted to know what Saypol's superiors suggested. At the judge's bidding, Saypol discovered that Deputy Attorney General Peyton Ford did not wish to see a woman sent to the electric chair. J. Edgar Hoover also had qualms. He recommended that both Julius and Morton Sobell receive death sentences, but that Ethel be given thirty years because she was the mother of two small children and was "presumed to be acting under the influence of her husband." He harbored no illusions that Ethel would confess under the pressure of a long prison sentence, but worried about the "psychological reaction of the public" to sending a woman and mother to her death. In none of this was there any consideration given to the idea that the impending sentence should be related to Ethel's purported "crime." Saypol dutifully reported these opinions to Kaufman, who then requested that Saypol make no recommendation in court regarding sentencing.

> *It is too bad that drawing and*
> *quartering has been abolished.*
> William H. Rehnquist,
> memo written in regard
> to the Rosenbergs

Thursday, 5 April, was a clear spring day. When the prison van arrived at the Women's House of Detention, Ethel took her "reserved" seat next to her husband and immediately placed her fingers through the mesh screen to clasp his handcuffed hand. They rode to Foley Square believing that Julie would receive the death penalty and that Ethel would be given a much lighter sentence, perhaps even a suspended one.

When they reached the defense table at 10:30 A.M., the courtroom was filled to capacity and the corridors were packed with reporters and spectators. For the past week gossip columnists had regaled their readers with "scoops" from "inside sources . . . that the three atom spies will get the death penalty so that they will crack and talk." The public was eager to see the ultimate punishment meted out to these despised Communist traitors.

After a number of motions, Julius and Ethel Rosenberg were asked to approach the bench. Realizing that attorneys for both sides would have much to say before he actually pronounced sentence, Judge Kaufman requested that chairs be set up for the Rosenbergs. Irving Saypol then began his remarks. He reminded the Court that the maximum penalty for conspiracy to commit espionage during time of war was death, and that the statute under which the Rosenbergs were convicted did not differentiate between wartime allies and enemies. Although he formally honored Kaufman's request not to recommend sentence, he proceeded to make his general opinion of the defendants clear:

> *In terms of human life, these defendants have affected the*
> *lives, and perhaps the freedom, of whole generations of*
> *mankind. Any consideration for their personal interests nec-*

essarily involves a hardening of the heart toward the fate and suffering of countless other human beings.

After Saypol concluded, Emanuel Bloch rose to speak:

> I would be remiss in my duty if I were not to tell the Court and the entire world that my clients, Julius Rosenberg and Ethel Rosenberg, have always maintained their innocence; they still maintain their innocence. And they have informed me no matter what, they will always maintain their innocence.

Bloch then went on to argue that the overt acts of which his clients were accused and convicted occurred in 1944 and 1945, a time during which

> [T]he greatest statesmen in the world . . . remarked that the Soviet Union was to be helped, was to be trusted, and was to be taken as a full-fledged ally . . .
>
> Assuming that the United States Government had found out in 1945 what they found out years later and which impelled them to bring these charges; one, would these defendants find themselves in a criminal court? And if, two, they found themselves as defendants, would there be the hullaballoo and hysteria which has accompanied the progress of this criminal procedure?

Bloch then tried yet another angle that might moderate the judge's sentence:

> I didn't want to say this, but I am going to say it—I hope that any sentence of this Court will not exacerbate [tensions] that exist in the world today. I believe that we can be more hopeful at this moment in the arena of international relations than ever before. We find strenuous efforts on the part of the greatest statesmen throughout the world to bring the Soviet Union and the United States into some orbit of understanding. . . .
>
> Now, certainly that is not my business in this case to talk about too much, except as it impinges upon how your sentence may affect relations, precisely because this case

is a celebrated case, and any sentence that your Honor imposes will be radioed throughout the world within three minutes.

Finally, Bloch asked the Court to compare the Rosenbergs to other "traitors" and criminals:

I say to the Court that we have had situations in the United States within the last few years, where people like Tokyo Rose and Axis Sally, who were convicted of treason and who were aiding our enemy, Germany, during our war against Germany, I find that these people received terms of 10 to 15 years. . . .

Your Honor, I know you haven't been on the bench very long, but I know you have had a lot of experience in criminal law. . . . I am going to ask you to say yourself, in your own conscience, your Honor, whether or not these people are the type of people that ordinarily come before you in a criminal case?

This rather simple-minded plea constituted Manny Bloch's last words in defense of his clients in the courtroom proceedings. Ethel and Julius Rosenberg then came before the bench. Judge Irving Kaufman began his sentencing speech with a bold-faced lie:

Because of the seriousness of this case and the lack of precedence [sic], I have refrained from asking the Government for a recommendation. The responsibility is so great that I believe that the Court alone should assume this responsibility.

In a hoarse, faint voice, the forty-year-old judge then made his intentions evident:

Citizens of this country who betray their fellow-countrymen can be under none of the delusions about the benignity of Soviet power that they might have been prior to World War II. The nature of Russian terrorism is now self-evident. . . .

It is so difficult to make people realize that this country is engaged in a life and death struggle with a completely different system. . . . I believe that never at any time in our history were we ever confronted to the same degree that we are today with such a challenge to our very existence.

Then, dramatically, the church bell at nearby St. Anthony's began to toll the noon hour in sonorous tones that reverberated throughout the hushed courtroom. Julie began to sway slowly back and forth on the balls of his feet; Ethel remained perfectly still. Kaufman raised his voice to be heard over the clamor:

> *I consider your crime worse than murder. Plain deliberate contemplated murder is dwarfed in magnitude by comparison with the crime you have committed. In committing the act of murder, the criminal kills only his victim. The immediate family is brought to grief and when justice is meted out the chapter is closed. But in your case, I believe your conduct in putting into the hands of the Russians the A-bomb years before our best scientists predicted Russia would perfect the bomb has already caused, in my opinion, the Communist aggression in Korea, with the resultant casualties exceeding 50,000 and who knows but that millions more of innocent people may pay the price of your treason. Indeed, by your betrayal you undoubtedly have altered the course of history to the disadvantage of our country. . . . We have evidence of your treachery all around us every day—for the civilian defense activities throughout the nation are aimed at preparing us for an atom bomb attack.*
>
> *The evidence indicated quite clearly that Julius Rosenberg was the prime mover in this conspiracy. However, let no mistake be made about the role which his wife, Ethel Rosenberg, played in this conspiracy. Instead of deterring him from pursuing his ignoble cause, she encouraged and assisted the cause. She was a mature woman,—almost three years older than her husband and almost seven years older than her younger brother. She was a full-fledged partner in this crime.*

At this, Ethel clamped her right hand in a white-knuckled grip on a chair before her.

> *Indeed the defendants Julius and Ethel Rosenberg placed their devotion to their cause above their own personal safety*

and were conscious that they were sacrificing their own children, should their misdeeds be detected—all of which did not deter them from pursuing their course. Love for their cause dominated their lives—it was even greater than their love for their children. . . .

The sentence of the Court upon Julius and Ethel Rosenberg is, for the crime for which you have been convicted, you are hereby sentenced to the punishment of death.

Julius "gave a short imperative nod to his wife, signaling her to leave." As the couple turned to exit, four United States marshals quickly flanked them and escorted them through a side door.

When the Rosenbergs were led into the courthouse basement, a fellow inmate from the House of Detention waiting in one of the holding cells caught Julie's eye. He recalls that Julie's "face was livid. He was trying to say something. But the words stuck. All he could do was to hold up two fingers. I thought, he must mean both him and Sobell. Finally the words came: 'Ethel, too.' "

The basement fell silent as Julie and then Ethel were locked into separate holding cells. For many minutes none of the other prisoners dared to move or speak. Then suddenly, as if to relieve the growing tension, Julie shouted out to his fellow inmates whom he could neither see nor hear: "Hey, what do they use, DC or AC?" In relief, another prisoner quickly hollered: "What's the difference, Julie? You'll never get it."

Ethel also wanted to join in this show of strength, this demonstration of "courage, confidence, and perspective," but was neither as composed nor clever as her husband. "Julie," she cried. "Julie, I don't think I'd like to be electrocuted. I think I'd rather be shot."

The painfulness of this remark stunned the basement inhabitants once more into silence. Within moments, however, marshals arrived to take the Rosenbergs into a conference room for one last meeting with their counsel. A sense of relief washed over the inmates as they no longer were forced to be party to the Rosenbergs' tortured attempts at self-control and bravado.

As Ethel was led down the corridor, she met Alexander Bloch who was openly crying. This lawyer, whom Ethel had affectionately begun to call "Pop," had played little more than a role subsidiary to his son's in the Rosenbergs' defense. Yet he was still Ethel's attorney of record and felt a deep sense of responsibility for the sentence that had just been handed down. Ethel tenderly embraced the old man and bravely reassured him that he had done everything he could. The two then entered the conference room together.

After seating himself at the head of the table, Julie was quick to tell his attorneys that there was nothing they could have done to alter the sentence. There would be no room for tears or self-reproach, for Julius Rosenberg, the political analyst, would allow the situation to be seen only in its political and historic terms. According to Manny Bloch,

> He explained that the verdict was inevitable, part of the government's plan to intensify hatred against the Soviet Union and terrorize left-progressives and those for peace in this country. This plan, he said, called for a native atom spy case. He pointed out that only nine days after Greenglass was arrested the Korean war was started.

Julius referred to the Alger Hiss case and the trial of the Communist party leaders under the Smith Act as part of the government's plan. The "pinnacle" of the plan, however, was the "Rosenberg case," which Julie now referred to as though it had little to do with himself: "In the Rosenberg case," Julie continued, "the government hoped to sell the people finally the concept that an espionage agent must be a Communist, and a Communist an espionage agent."

Manny Bloch briefly talked about his intention to appeal and then the conference was over. The Rosenbergs were ushered back into holding cells. Before Julie was placed in a large pen with other male inmates, a U.S. marshal informed him that the marshal's office was awaiting instructions from Washington as to whether the Rosenbergs would be transferred to Sing Sing Prison that very day. As soon as Julie was locked in, he yelled to his wife, "Ethel, don't be scared if some clown tells you we may be taken to the Death House tonight—everything will be all right, they won't do it." He then turned to the other prisoners, most of whom he knew, and in hushed tones began "discussing the case as impersonally as if he were not involved at all. He began saying that the public was bound to move before long, and outlining steps in a post-trial campaign. That their case must evoke a sense of outrage in time he had no doubt at all."

Ethel, alone in her cell, could not hear her husband's words. To her, the basement must have seemed silent, just as it was when she and Julie first entered from the courtroom. Perhaps she imagined that the inmates were waiting once again for her or Julie to speak; perhaps she assumed that her husband was sitting in gloomy silence; she may have been filled with insufferable longing for Julie, or maybe she felt that her new role as the deeply wronged stoic required a dramatic gesture. Whatever the motivation, clearly and without a trace of quaver or tremor, Ethel began singing Puccini's impassioned "Un bel di, vedremo," an aria that Madame had taught her so many years before. When she finally finished this moving lament of lost love, which ends with the brave words, "Banish your idle fears, for he will return, I know it," Julie excitedly called out, "Ethel, the other one!" At this, she immediately burst into Puccini's "Ah, doce notte! Quante stelle!" This went on for more than an hour as Ethel sang "Goodnight Irene" and other nonoperatic tunes, and Julie occasionally joining in with a rendition of "The Battle Hymn of the Republic."

After Ethel had finished her second aria by Puccini, a U.S. marshal reportedly came to Julie's holding pen and unselfconsciously blurted out: "[Y]ou're a low-down son of a bitch. But you're the luckiest man in the world because no man ever had a woman who loved him that much."

Julie, cool and quick-thinking, reportedly replied: "No, think of it this way. I just got the death sentence because I'm a big shot in an espionage ring. Yeah, I pass out $1,000 here, $1,500 there, toss $5,000 to my brother-in-law—but I never had the money to train that voice; I never had the money to do anything for her. Think of that." And then Ethel once more began to sing.

19

SACRIFICE

On the evening of April 5th Ethel was returned to the Women's House of Detention. The threat to transfer the Rosenbergs immediately to the death house at Sing Sing had been just that, a threat without substance.

As she walked back to her cellblock, Ethel appeared dazed. Her face was ashen; the lipstick she customarily wore to court had long since faded. When she was warmly greeted by her fellow inmates, she could speak of only one thing—the comment Judge Kaufman had made about her and Julie "sacrificing their own children." This seemingly had affected her more than his sentence of death. Given the distraught manner in which she spoke and her haggard appearance, a prison matron approached, offering her a sedative. Ethel immediately corrected her posture, threw back her head, refused the matron's offer, and walked stiffly to her cell. Despite her distraction and exhaustion, Ethel still could summon up the attributes of the self-controlled stoic.

Kaufman's stinging indictment of Ethel loving her "cause" more than her children probably inflamed Ethel's already enormous sense of guilt. Although the suggestion that she loved her children less than Communism or "espionage work" was pure fiction, the charge that she sacrificed her children to a larger "cause" in some ways was not. Robby and Michael were extremely unhappy at the Hebrew Children's Home; they had not seen their mother or father in eight months. If Ethel had "confessed," she might have avoided prosecution entirely or at least received a minimal sentence and been able to resume the care of her children. Yet she fully shared in Julie's analysis of why they were convicted and why it was critical for them to never allow people to believe that "an espionage agent must be a Communist, and a Communist an espionage agent." Wasn't this a principle, an ethic, a "cause"? Her family, her upbringing, the culture around her, the books and magazines she read, the psychoanalytic perspective she revered, all repeatedly stated, confirmed, described, extolled a woman's role as mother. Hadn't she abandoned this role, and abandoned her sons?

In the Women's House of Detention Ethel continually talked about her children and talked to other women about theirs. The inmates on her cellblock noticed that whenever Ethel felt "restless she'd visit other prisoners on her corridor and bring the talk around to children." When it was clear to her prisonmates that she had not slept well, she would explain "Oh, no, nothing's wrong. I just heard that scream again last night," referring to Michael's response to her arrest. She constantly called in social workers recommended by Mrs. Phillips or connected to the Hebrew Children's Home to discuss Robby and Michael's needs. According to Ethel's confidante at the House of Detention, during the trial Ethel was more concerned with the children than with her own defense.

Nothing she did, however, could obviate the fact that she had chosen to stand with her husband against the government and thus effectively had abandoned Michael and Robby. The justifications were obvious. First, to "confess" would violate her moral and political beliefs and would have disastrous and widespread ramifications. Julie and Manny increasingly talked of the worldwide implications of their case. Manny had argued in court that the outcome of the Rosenberg trial would affect U.S.-Soviet relations and would be "radioed throughout the world within three minutes." Julie believed their courage and refusal to submit to the government's persecution would make their case a cause célèbre.

Second, Ethel believed herself to be an inadequate mother. She understood herself to be developing into a more mature person because of her psychotherapy, but that had been abruptly curtailed and she had not yet become the person, or the mother, she wanted to be. She therefore harbored the idea that others—experts—could care for her children better than she. Did she perhaps think that Michael and Robby were better off without her? Could she have used this to ameliorate her guilt?

Although Ethel acted like "a fierce mother wolf" in arranging for her children's care while she was at the Women's House of Detention, and constantly worried about their welfare, she was adamantly opposed to letting Michael and Robby visit her and wrote them very little. She argued initially that since she might be acquitted, it was cruel to subject two small boys to the sight of their mother in jail. Once she was found guilty and sentenced to death, she maintained that it was wrong for her sons to see her and Julie separately. This then became the criterion for allowing her sons to visit: unless she and Julie could meet with them in a "natural" setting, she insisted that they not visit at all.

She also communicated with them very little. In April Julie began to urge her to write her sons. This was a request that Julie was to make from time to time throughout the next two years.

Why did Ethel, who described herself as having a desperate need to be with her children, in reality demonstrate such reluctance to see and communicate with them while in jail? Elizabeth Phillips, who continued her prison visits until shortly before the trial, when she moved out of the area, speculates that Ethel's unwillingness may have been related to her preoccupation with doing the "right thing." From her reading of child-rearing literature and child psychology, and her numerous conferences with social workers in the Women's House of Detention, Ethel had developed definite ideas about what was best for the children. She may have been told directly or inferred from her reading and conversations that the "right thing" was to allow the children to visit only under specific circumstances, and until those circumstances could be arranged, no meeting was preferable to one that was fundamentally flawed. Ethel was so enamored of expert advice that it is quite possible she would allow it, or her interpretation of it, to override her "desperate need." Yet Phillips's analysis is speculative, for she ultimately asks "who knows what happens in prison to people who begin to perceive themselves as maybe some use to the world forever as martyrs? . . . Who knows what changes psychologically for a person in prison, cut off from virtually everyone but her husband and thinking that you're doing something, making a mark?"

These questions were taken up by Ethel's psychiatrist who began to visit her shortly after she was sentenced and continued to see her until her death. He maintains that while Ethel was in prison "the children really didn't exist for her." She was more and more preoccupied by the role she had constructed for herself. Her sons and anyone extraneous to "the immediate experience of her situation" became more abstract than real.

Alternatively, Ethel's reluctance to see her children in prison may have stemmed from her ambivalent feelings about motherhood, at least in terms of how she understood motherhood—as a full-time, isolated, all-consuming occupation that demanded perfection, a thorough knowledge of the most modern advice literature, and complete emotional equilibrium. As she spent more time in prison, Ethel began to move away from the maternal role, and was probably both excited by and guilty about this movement.

Ethel's growing identity as a stoic heroine stood in diametric opposition to what her psychiatrist confirms was one of the fundamental images Ethel had of herself—that of an inadequate and contemptible mother. From this perspective, Robby and Michael were reminders of a previous life that was not heroic or exemplary in any way. This is not to say that Ethel did not love them, miss them, or feel enormous guilt over their plight. These feelings undoubtedly coexisted with any others she may have had. But the prospect of seeing her sons, their plaintive faces a reminder of her previous failings and her current abandonment of them, may have been too awful for her to contemplate. She admitted to her husband that due to her overwhelming guilt she was having difficulty knowing how she really felt about Michael and Robby. This ambivalence seems to have haunted Ethel throughout her imprisonment and made her particularly sensitive to any charge that she was an uncaring or unloving mother. Thus Judge Kaufman's words about "sacrificing" her children during his sentencing speech apparently stung like no other words he uttered that day.

———

During the week following her sentencing, Ethel spent most of the time outside her cell with her friend and fellow inmate, Miriam Moskowitz. Perhaps more than anyone, Miriam could empathize with Ethel's situation. Almost the same age, of Jewish background and left-wing political sympathies, Miriam had been arrested as an "atom spy" two weeks earlier than Ethel and charged with conspiracy to obstruct justice. The specific charge against her was that she had been present during conversations between her lover and business partner, Abraham Brothman, and confessed spy Harry Gold as they purportedly planned to lie to a grand jury. She was tried before Judge Irving Kaufman by government prosecutor Irving Saypol and his assistant, Roy Cohn. Only one witness, Harry Gold, cited her presence at the meetings between himself and Brothman. In the same courtroom in which Ethel would be tried and convicted, and in legal proceedings that could be viewed as a "warm-up" for the Rosenberg-Sobell trial, Miriam Moskowitz was sentenced on 29 November 1950 to the maximum term permissible under the law— two years and a $10,000 fine. Although even the prosecution admitted that there was "no evidence that she engaged in espionage," the press continued to refer to Moskowitz as an "atom spy" and a member of the "Fuchs-Gold spy ring."

During most of Ethel's stay at the Women's House of Detention, the two "atom spies" were incarcerated on separate floors. Although they had never met, they recognized each other from newspaper photos and would wave if they happened to see each other at a distance. Once Ethel was convicted, however, she was brought down to the fifth floor where Miriam was imprisoned. Miriam was allowed to visit Ethel in her cell, and the two immediately embraced. Miriam cried, "They can't get away with this." Ethel quickly replied, "Oh yes they can." From that moment on they spent all the time they could with each other; they took their meals, commissary, and exercise periods together.

> There would be commissary every afternoon around 3:00. Commissary would clank down the elevator with a great big urn of coffee and a variety of sandwiches and cake. This is what we called "free world" food; it was not from the institution; it was brought in from the outside. Each day we would buy a cup of coffee and a slab of cake and we would sit together and we would blot out the environment. We were in a fancy restaurant having a great cup of coffee. We talked about a lot of things that had nothing to do with ourselves so that our conversation took flight and we with it. Sooner or later one of the officers would come by and say, 'you're not in the Waldorf; finish up and get back.' We would come back to earth with a thud. . . .
>
> We were two people who shared values. There was no one else with whom we could share those values within that institution. We were . . . somewhat intellectual. . . .

We used to stand up on the roof together, looking out toward the west, imagining that we could see the flagpole flying over the men's House of Detention [where Julie and Abe Brothman were housed]. . . . I'm sure we couldn't see it, but we would spend our recreation time standing on the bench to see if we could see the flagpole. We talked one time about how we would celebrate with one big blast of a party when we got out. Of course she was never ebullient about these discussions. It was I who would say, 'oh, what a party we're gonna have,' and I could get carried away planning it. She would nod and say 'yeah, we'll do it,' but she never got carried away.

The two women did not only fantasize about life outside the Women's House of Detention however. One of the more serious topics they discussed was the Communist party's lack of support for the Rosenbergs. This was something Miriam felt very strongly about: "It was incorrect for them not to take part; it was incorrect for them not to be immediately screaming that these were frame-ups!"

The Party that both Ethel and Julius were trying so hard to shield from attack, for which they were offering their lives so that espionage and Communism would not be equated, had been silent in regard to their case. The CP could have offered legal assistance and money for the defense to hire investigators and assistants. It could have formed a defense committee, mobilized thousands in the New York area to demonstrate for the Rosenbergs, fought against the biased reporting of the case that appeared in the media, written daily analyses of the trial for the *Daily Worker* that exposed how anti-Communism pervaded the courtroom, and more. Yet it did nothing.

Max Gordon, a senior editor of the *Daily Worker*, reports that Manny Bloch approached him many times, pleading with him to write about the Rosenberg case. Gordon notes, however, that he was prevented from writing anything until the CP leadership "gave the signal," which it refused to do. David Alman, a resident of Knickerbocker Village who had never met the Rosenbergs but was interested in forming a defense committee, visited the Party's headquarters to solicit support. His wife reports that the response he received was that the Rosenbergs were "expendable."

The Party, however, did speak out against the death penalty the Rosenbergs received. In an article in the *Daily Worker* of 6 April

1951 and an editorial in the *People's World*, the West Coast CP paper, of 11 April 1951, the Party called the sentence "cruel and barbaric." It argued that the verdict was "designed to shock the American people into a sense of emergency and of danger from the Soviet Union." It then proceeded to an analysis not unlike that which Julie had been making:

> *According to Judge Kaufman, espionage somehow rises out of Marxism and socialism. . . . But it is a myth that socialism has anything to do with espionage. . . . It is an ugly and calculated lie that the Communist Party provides the 'motives' for espionage. On the contrary, those who fight for peace and believe in socialism stand for the highest loyalty to their country when they seek to save it from war and preserve it from monopoly-made depression. . . .*
>
> *The savagery of the death sentence against the Rosenbergs will not succeed in crushing the will for peace or in curbing activities to achieve it.*

Although this was the strongest indictment of the Rosenberg case that appeared in the United States, it left unquestioned the Rosenbergs' guilt, the veracity of the charges made against them, and the fairness of the trial itself. Although it condemned the "savagery" of their death sentence, it did not call for a protest against it.

The question of why the Communist party did not come to the support of Ethel and Julius Rosenberg has been debated as much as any aspect of the Rosenberg case. The explanation, however, is probably no more complicated than the one Ethel provided herself. She responded to Miriam Moskowitz's outrage at the Party's lack of involvement by stating simply that it "shouldn't get contaminated by these [atom spy] cases." This, according to Ethel, was the "politically correct" position. It seems quite possible that Party leaders wanted to avoid any connection to a case where it could be shown that CP followers were traitors to their country. Elizabeth Gurley Flynn, a member of the CP's National Board, is reported to have asked a friend rhetorically in 1951, "What do spy trials have to do with politics?" In other words, the Party did not believe the Rosenberg case to be "political" in the same way that the Smith Act trials had been or as were the HUAC investigations which were then further reducing its ranks.

In truth, the Party in which the Rosenbergs had placed their

faith and devotion had become a pitiful shadow of the organization
that Ethel and Julie had been active in the late thirties and early
forties. From 1948 on, according to Joseph Starobin, "the American
Communist Party became at least a case in civil liberties, at best
an object of sympathy, but no longer a power." It had been deci-
mated by both external and internal witch-hunts. By the time the
Rosenbergs were placed on trial, the Party's top leaders had been
convicted under the Smith Act of conspiring to advocate the overthrow of the government by force and violence; the Justice Department and J. Edgar Hoover publicly referred to the "15,000
potential Smith Act defendants" yet to be arrested, and the Internal
Security Act that equated dissent with treason had been passed by
a rabidly anti-Communist Congress over the veto of President Truman. According to Starobin, then a Party member:

> [A]n atmosphere of near-panic gripped the American Com-
> munists. Offices had been closed down. Public activity had
> diminished and in some areas ceased. Important cadres had
> disappeared. . . . The Party's chairman believed that war
> between America and Russia was inevitable. He also be-
> lieved that the Party would inevitably be declared illegal.
> . . . With this authoritative judgment, the Communists went
> forward with the project to build an operational structure
> capable of withstanding quasi-fascist repression.

The structure that the Party was constructing in March and April
1951 was an underground apparatus for its leaders and an above-
ground "cadre-organization," or "skeletal force" that could "withstand further repression." Thus, at the time of the Rosenberg trial,
the American Communist party was on the verge of returning to
being the small, sectarian, apocalyptic organization that it had been
in the nineteen-twenties and early nineteen-thirties.

Leaders who were poised to go underground or who lived in
fear of being placed in one of the concentration camps that the
Internal Security Act provided for in cases of "national emergency,"
did not seem eager to come to the aid of two obscure rank-and-
filers who very well could have been guilty of espionage. What end
would be achieved by committing the Party's overtaxed resources
to the defense of the Rosenbergs? Would not such action only further
connect organized Communism with the charge of treason in the
government's and the public's eyes? The Party's leaders (who knew

of Manny Bloch's pleas for help and David Alman's request for support) seemed to have reasoned that Ethel and Julius Rosenberg were worth sacrificing to spare the Party from the taint of treason and spying.

Ethel appears to have agreed with this perspective. "I thought she was bending over backwards," Miriam Moskowitz asserts in recollecting Ethel's acceptance of the CP's stance in regard to her case:

> She was not a rebel. She was a good soldier. She followed the Party line uncritically, unquestionably, and aggressively. It wasn't only that she followed the line, but she argued for it and justified it with a lot of voluminous verbosity. She was totally uncritical. . . .
>
> If I had met her outside of prison, I probably would not have liked her, because I never liked doctrinaire people and she was doctrinaire. . . . I never liked people who said, "Miriam, you should be on the picket line, you should be out selling the Sunday Worker, you should be collecting signatures on a petition," and I think that's what she was.

By Monday, 9 April, Ethel seemed closer than ever to losing her courage, confidence and perspective. Over the weekend she learned that her mother had had a private conference with Judge Kaufman the day before she was sentenced, and had pleaded for leniency for her son and not her daughter. Ethel may have been misinformed, since *The New York Times* reported that Tessie pleaded "for mercy for her *children*." Nonetheless Ethel had every reason to believe that her mother would gladly sacrifice her if it assisted Davey in any way, and never questioned the information she received. It follows that it must have been particularly distressing to her when her mother tried to visit the Women's House of Detention over the weekend. With her husband's and lawyer's encouragement, Ethel refused to see her. Tessie immediately reported this to the FBI. Ethel became increasingly depressed.

On the evening of the ninth, a prison matron "overheard" Ethel saying to another inmate that she "would rather commit suicide than be executed." The warden conveyed this information to the FBI and explained further that "Mrs. Rosenberg is attempting to give an outward appearance of calm, but actually is considerably wor-

ried about her forthcoming execution." The warden then requested
that Ethel be transferred out of the Women's House of Detention.

Whether it was due to this request, the requirement that prisoners sentenced to death be isolated from the rest of the inmate population, or the attempt to pressure her into talking, the government decided to remove Ethel at once from the House of Detention and transfer her to the death house at Sing Sing Prison.

On the morning of Wednesday, 11 April, Ethel was summoned to the first-floor prison administration offices presumably to answer some routine questions. As soon as she was escorted into an elevator, two guards stormed out of another elevator and into her cell. They stripped it, gathered up her possessions, and left within minutes. Word spread throughout the fifth and ninth floors that Ethel was being transferred. Inmates who had known Ethel over the eight months of her incarceration rushed to the barred windows in an attempt to catch a last glimpse of her and yell their farewells.

While the inmates waited, Manny Bloch hurried to the jail after being tipped off by a newspaperman that Ethel was being taken to Sing Sing without notice. Although he obviously had had no time to prepare any legal motion, he put up an argument with United States Marshal William Carroll that removing Ethel to Sing Sing while appeals were pending was "unnecessary and vindictive." He argued for an hour, but to no avail. According to Bloch, when it was clear she would have to leave, Ethel was calm and analytic. She told him: "They expect me to break under the strain because I am a woman. They think that in the Death House I will be haunted by images, alone, and without Julie I'll collapse. But I won't."

The inmates who had been waiting for over an hour to say goodbye to Ethel, now got their chance. Miriam Moskowitz who was sitting patiently by a fifth-floor window remembers:

> We couldn't get our heads out [of the windows], so we were determined she'd hear us. . . . Then, when we saw that unmistakable bustle and movement, and the cameramen ready to shoot, we knew she was coming out. Then we motioned to others behind us, and we filled those windows and we yelled . . . 'Goodbye, good luck, Ethel!' and 'We love you!' And I mean we screamed . . .
>
> We didn't see her. But we felt sure she heard us, because one of the papers carried a picture of her turning, and looking up and smiling and waving. Maybe she thought

we could see. But all we could see was the car moving away . . . So her smile was for us.

This then would be Ethel's last performance before an audience until the day of her death. She played it wonderfully, never letting on for a moment that she felt any fear or anxiety. To look at the smiling face captured in the press photograph, one cannot imagine that this woman was being sent to the death house. She looks joyous, as if she had just won a prize or was being whisked away on her honeymoon. It is virtually impossible to reconcile that happy countenance with the caption above it: "Mrs. Rosenberg, Condemned Atom Spy, Taken to Sing Sing." Yet, Ethel probably was genuinely pleased. The cries of affection and good wishes from the windows above told her that she had been a success, that she was loved and respected by the women with whom she had lived for the past eight months. The scene in the courtyard of the Women's House of Detention that day was not unlike being on stage and receiving an ovation from an appreciative audience. Ethel glowed.

As the car in which she was seated pulled away from the jail, the public got its last glimpse of Ethel Rosenberg. Before she was forever sequestered behind the massive walls of Sing Sing Prison, she had wanted to let the world know she was not afraid. And she succeeded.

20

THE VALIANT*

At 1:50 P.M. on 11 April 1951, the sedan carrying Ethel Rosenberg arrived at Sing Sing. The fortress-like walls with machine guns built into turrets was considerably different from the Women's House of Detention, which fit unobtrusively into the urban landscape of Greenwich Village. Ethel was escorted through a number of metal doors into an office where she was handed a routine questionnaire. When asked what led her to commit her crime, she wrote, "I deny guilt." She then signed a waiver that permitted her to receive mail inspected by the prison administration. She was asked to forfeit the $15 she had in her possession and was assigned prison number 110,510. She was then led through another metal door and out into a yard where a van was waiting to drive her to the "death house"

---

* The following chapter has effectively been censored by Michael and Robert Meeropol. They hold the copyright on Ethel and Julius Rosenbergs' prison correspondence, and have denied me not only the right to excerpt from this correspondence but the right to paraphrase it as well. This correspondence had originally formed the backbone of this chapter. Although the Meeropols were supportive of this book initially (e.g., allowing me to read all of their parents' unpublished letters, giving me the names and addresses of people to interview), once they read the manuscript they became quite distressed. They have refused to specify their criticisms, saying only that their "problems" with the book are so "basic . . . that nothing constructive would come of citing a few examples of those problems." (Personal communication

or "condemned cells" about a half mile away. Once she entered this prison within a prison, and the steel door closed behind her, Ethel Rosenberg never walked outside it again.

After being escorted through more doors, each of which had to be unlocked with a large key, Ethel entered the women's wing—three cells on a single corridor. Each cell was identical. They were about twelve feet long and six feet wide and contained a cot, a straight-back chair, a small metal table, a toilet, and a wash basin. Everything was painted gray. A fourth cell contained a stall shower. Adjoining the corridor was an exercise yard, about fifty feet wide and fifty to sixty feet long. The entire yard was enclosed by a twenty-foot-high wall so that it was impossible to see anything but the sky above. This completely barren environment would constitute Ethel's entire world for the next twenty-six months.

Ethel was the only prisoner in the women's death house. She was alone twenty-four hours a day except for a matron who sat guard outside her cell. Ethel, like all condemned prisoners, was not permitted to work in the prison.

After her cell door was shut and the excitement of her ovation at the Women's House of Detention had faded, Ethel was forced to look soberly around her. Except for its institutional furniture, her cell was entirely empty. She had been transferred with only the clothes she wore. The remainder of her clothes and all her toiletries had been sent to Mrs. Sophie Rosenberg, whom Ethel had previously designated as her "next of kin." Manny had arranged to have the administrators at the House of Detention give him the photos and letters that Ethel had in her cell, but he was not able to visit until Saturday, three days away. Ethel sank into a deep depression.

When Bloch finally arrived at the appointed time on Saturday, he found Ethel already seated in the counsel room on the second floor of the condemned cells. She sat there listlessly, without lipstick, her hair unkempt, wearing a prison housecoat and slippers.

---

from Robert Meeropol, 7/20/87.) Through their attorney, they repeatedly tried to pressure my publisher into not publishing this book, threatening a legal suit on unspecified grounds. Because of their refusal to describe their "problems" with the book, their reasons for denying me permission to quote or paraphrase, or their motivation for attempting to prevent this book from being published, I can only conclude that they do not want anything to appear in print about the Rosenbergs that does not conform to their own idealized portrait of their parents. Although they have long charged the government with covering up the truth about their parents' case, it seems that they are all too willing to "cover up" material they do not wish the public to see.

Although she was able, as always, to hold back tears, she described the horrors of her solitary confinement in morose detail. In response, Bloch did everything he could to boost her morale. He spoke of her heroic mission, how the government was coming down hardest on her, and how she should aspire to be a person whose spirit could never be extinguished. He assured her that he had already begun writing an appeal to have her returned to New York City on the ground that she was being subjected to cruel and unusual punishment. He asked her to write an affidavit in support of this writ of habeas corpus, to describe her confinement in the same detail she had just recited. She, in turn, requested that he phone her psychiatrist. She wanted desperately to see him, and Manny could no longer object that such a meeting might hurt her chances with a jury.

By the time Manny departed, Ethel's spirits had lifted. This human contact seemed to have reminded her of the historic role she believed she had been given, and of how important it was for her to withstand the government's cruelty. The prospect of seeing Dr. Miller, the possibility that she would be returned to the Women's House of Detention, and the receipt of many of her old possessions from Manny seem to have made her feel that life was worth living.

The companionship of one of her guards, Bessie Irving, also began to enter into how Ethel experienced her situation. Mrs. Irving was an older Irish woman who had a keen sense of humor and much sympathy for Ethel's plight. She loved to spend her shift talking with her charge, so the two would sit for hours discussing life outside the prison walls, much as Ethel and Miriam Moskowitz had for brief moments at the Women's House of Detention.

By the end of the month, Ethel was reunited with her psychiatrist. After being contacted by Manny Bloch, Saul Miller made arrangements with the warden at Sing Sing to visit Ethel once every two weeks. With a matron close by, he was allowed to sit in the corridor outside Ethel's cell and talk with her for an hour or more. Certainly these were not therapy sessions, but rather opportunities for Ethel to discuss whatever was on her mind. She described how she was coping, or asked for advice on how to contend with the children, her family, an unfriendly matron or her attorney.

These meetings soon became pivotal for Ethel's emotional stability. Each one was greatly anticipated. Before Miller arrived Ethel waited anxiously, unable to concentrate on anything but Miller's anticipated arrival. After he departed, she broke down into mournful tears over their separation. He became the major authority figure, expert, and audience she strove to please and impress. In front of her psychiatrist, she never cried or acted depressed. She wanted him to see her as a heroine, and, by his own report, because he "continually came to see her, this reflected back to her that she *was* a heroine." Why else would such a busy, distinguished professional drive all the way to Sing Sing Prison only to sit inside the morgue-like death house for no fee? Dr. Miller asserts that he would have done this for any one of his patients, that he simply "wanted to be there for her." But Ethel seems to have taken his visits as an indication of how exceptional and praiseworthy she had become in his eyes. He did nothing to dissuade her of this notion so that their meetings became a forum not only for discussion of her coping behavior and her children's welfare, but also for a lot of "forced bravado" that she must have believed reinforced her laudability.

After he left and Ethel recovered from the sadness of his departure, she typically felt enormously strengthened. He was always supportive of her, letting her know that he was consistently on her side. This stance and the unfailing regularity of his visits sustained Ethel throughout her incarceration, raised her morale, and encouraged her in her self-concept as a heroine.

Ethel's good spirits lasted throughout the week of Miller's first visit—her fourth in the death house. On Saturday, 5 May, she wrote Julie about the other person who had become critically important to her, Bessie Irving. This older woman with an Irish brogue spent hours talking with Ethel, who, in turn, entertained her only friend in prison with jokes and a feigned Irish accent. On this day Ethel delighted in regaling her husband with transcriptions of funny little tunes she had just devised to greet Mrs. Irving the following day. As she wrote Julie she was giddy, almost hysterical, consumed with her thoughts of how the cherished matron would react to her cleverness.

By the evening, however, Ethel's mood had abruptly changed. She began to cry, could not stop, and felt as though she could not continue on.

This sudden alternation between light-heartedness and near hysteria, or overwhelming depression, characterized Ethel's first spring and summer in the death house. Often within a single day, such as on May 5th, she traversed an emotional landscape replete with both irreverent jokes about the electric chair and irrepressible tears over the hopelessness of her situation. Her depression could be triggered by a negative external event—a slanderous article in the newspapers, the cancellation of a visit she was expecting—but typically was induced by some internal voice only Ethel could hear.

———

Despite Manny Bloch's continued attempts to have Ethel removed to the Women's House of Detention, it seemed unlikely the government would suddenly reverse itself. Nevertheless, Manny retained the services of a Dr. Frederic Wertham, a psychiatrist sympathetic to the CP, to provide expert testimony on the effects of Ethel's incarceration at Sing Sing. Wertham was not permitted to visit Ethel or to communicate with her in any way, yet he testified at a court hearing on 7 May that a prolonged confinement would "lead to a nervous breakdown and in all probability drive her insane." From talking to Manny, he developed the analysis, to which he testified under oath, that if Ethel were unable to confer with her husband, she most likely would develop a prison psychosis. Apparently the government was not interested in a psychotic prisoner—in such a condition she would never reliably confess and name names—so one week later, rather than return Ethel to New York, it transferred Julius Rosenberg to the men's wing of the death house.

Sing Sing had little precedent for accommodating the needs of a husband and wife housed within its walls, so Ethel and Julie were forced to wait for a conference with their attorney to see each other. On 16 May, Bloch arrived. In the death house counsel room, the Rosenbergs embraced and kissed for the first time in over a month. It was their last embrace, however, for they were quickly separated and henceforth never permitted to touch when they attended conferences with their attorney.

Ethel and Julie's cells were separated by only some thirty feet, but massive concrete walls, metal doors, and iron bars vitiated their physical proximity. On Friday, 25 May they were finally permitted to visit outside the presence of their attorney, and Ethel was ecstatic. Her life began to revolve around these all too infrequent meetings with her "savior."

Their visits together, which they were soon allowed every Wednesday morning with Julie seated in a cage outside his wife's cell, excited Ethel and stimulated her erotic desires. She began to write her husband about how madly in love she was with him, how much she wanted him, and how her needs to satisfy her carnal desires sometimes overcame her.

Julie, however, was embarrassed by his wife's openness and cautioned her to be more circumspect in what she wrote, all of which was read by prison officials. He urged her to try sublimation. Ethel's response was to the point: She suggested that Irving Saypol and Judge Kaufman try sublimation; she would only be satisfied with the real thing!

Ethel's thoughts and expressions of sexual desire continued throughout the warm summer months at Sing Sing, untempered by her husband's admonitions. But then her interest in sex, or at least her eagerness to express it in writing, dissipated. As the summer passed she became increasingly depressed; her periods of depression began to overtake those happier days in which her mind feasted on sexual fantasies, conjured up pleasant memories, or focused on a book she was reading or a conversation she had had with Manny Bloch or Saul Miller. The summer had brought with it a host of bad news. First, after much work from behind bars, Ethel had arranged for Robby and Michael to be cared for by her mother-in-law. She had been forced to acknowledge that the home in which her sons were housed was not a model out of *Parents' Magazine*. After her conviction, she began to arrange for a new situation for them, but since the home's policy was to release its charges only to relatives, Ethel was severely limited in what she could devise. With the Rosenberg family's financial assistance, Ethel eventually arranged for Sophie Rosenberg to move into her own apartment in June—she had been living with her daughter Lena—and for her to take in Robby and Michael.

Ethel initially was overjoyed that her sons were now in a real home, but she soon learned that they were faring poorly in this, their third living situation since their mother's arrest. Michael resisted his grandmother's every attempt to control him; he incurred the wrath of neighbors for the noise he created at night, and he antagonized the registered nurse hired by the Rosenberg family to assist Julie's ailing mother. Once Ethel's sisters-in-law started visiting Sing Sing in July, they brought continual reports of how "disturbed" Michael and Robby were. By August, it was clear that Sophie's health was deteriorating due to the strain she was experiencing at home. Once again Ethel's failings as a mother had come back to haunt her: her sons were deeply troubled; her mother-in-law's health was in jeopardy as a result; her sisters-in-law were overwrought by the burden under which their mother was suffering.

Second, matron Bessie Irving suddenly died of a cerebral hemorrhage at the beginning of July. Ethel was informed of this on the evening of 2 July and immediately broke down into hysterical tears over the loss of the one friend she had made at Sing Sing. She cried on and off for the next week, exquisitely aware of how silent the women's wing was without the familiar Irish lilt that had filled the concrete tomb in which she lived.

Equally disturbing that summer were Bernie Greenglass's visits to his sister. Ethel had had no contact with her family since her mother's unsuccessful attempt to see her in the House of Detention shortly after she was sentenced. At the end of June, however, her brother came to Sing Sing without notice. Although she initially reported to Julie that the visit had gone well, by her Wednesday conference with her husband four days later, Ethel had worked herself into an anxious frenzy over her brother's visit and took up their precious hour together unable to speak of anything but her family's betrayal. She instantly felt guilty over her uncontrolled ruminations and wrote Julie that she regretted her behavior.

Fourth, and perhaps most significantly for her deteriorating state of mind, Ethel saw Robby and Michael for the first time in almost a year on 1 August. Shortly after Julie was transferred to Sing Sing, Ethel seriously began to consider allowing her sons to visit, but only if it could be accomplished under the "right" circumstances, with expert approval. She asked her attorney to solicit Dr. Miller's opinion on whether the children should visit her in the death house, and if they did, how she should handle their anticipated questions about the death penalty. For Ethel, nothing could be decided regarding her sons without the expert advice on which she had become so thoroughly dependent.

Apparently the counsel she received—or her interpretation of it—was that the children should be allowed to visit, but should not be permitted to see their parents behind bars. Thus, for the next two months, Ethel negotiated with the prison administration so that she and Julie could visit with their sons outside their cells, something typically forbidden condemned prisoners. In July, however, the warden consented, and it was arranged that Manny would bring the boys to Sing Sing on 1 August.

Initially, Ethel experienced indifference over the anticipated visit. But then, three days before their arrival, she reported a re-emergence of maternal feelings. The warden would not permit Ethel and Julie to visit with their sons simultaneously, so Ethel was to see them first, followed by her husband.

On the morning of 1 August, Ethel, wearing a gray housecoat and prison slippers, entered the condemned cells' counsel room to find two little boys who had grown dramatically since the last time she had seen them. She hugged and kissed them as Manny and a guard looked on. Both the boys immediately said, "You look shorter, mama," and everyone, including Manny, joined in a discussion of why this might be so. Ethel then unveiled an envelope of insects she had been collecting for them, candy bars purchased from the commissary, and a *Fireside Song Book* with children's songs marked. The hour passed quickly and ended with Ethel leading her two sons in songs she had taught them long before her family had been touched by the shadow of the death house. After the guard nodded, Ethel announced, "Mommy has to go somewhere now," and departed. A few moments later Julie entered the room. He tried to play with the children but was moved to near tears when Robby asked why he would not come home and why he had not visited them at the Hebrew Children's Home on Sundays. Mike could hardly look at his father, and blurted out toward the end of the visit that it would be better if *he* were in prison rather than Julie.

After this visit, the children began to go to Sing Sing regularly, coming about every month or month and a half. Ethel tried to make each one of these visits as pleasant and comforting to the children as possible, but after each she became deeply depressed and overwhelmed with a sense of personal failure. In letter after letter to her husband she spoke of an increasing lack of confidence as a mother. Each visit was a test that Ethel privately designed for herself, a test of her perfection as a mother. And she failed each test for reasons known only to her. Certainly the children were deeply troubled, and their very appearance at Sing Sing was a reminder of her abandonment of them. Yet, Michael remembers their time together in a very positive light, recalling only an environment of "warmth and love," the memory of which both he and Robby cherish to this day.

_____

The background against which the events of the summer of 1951 unfolded was probably as painful for Ethel as any single incident that had occurred. Since the day of their sentencing, Julie and, to a lesser degree, Manny Bloch had spoken repeatedly of an avalanche of protest that would be forthcoming on the Rosenbergs' behalf. In his Sing Sing conferences with his clients—all of which were bugged, summarized by prison officials, and transmitted to the FBI—Manny Bloch encouraged this perspective by telling Ethel and Julie that their case would become a national political issue and would be discussed at the highest levels of government. Still, Ethel saw no evidence of an avalanche of protest or heard of any people trying to help her or her husband. It was as though she had been excluded from the world of the living, entombed and forgotten.

When she was most depressed, Ethel fell into crying jags that would last for hours. The matron who now guarded her in the mornings, Mrs. Evans, would attempt to comfort her. Mrs. Jackson, the guard who took over at 2:30 P.M., however, consistently ignored her charge during her eight-hour shift, leaving Ethel painfully alone throughout the afternoon and evening. Ethel also developed severe headaches and nausea when she was particularly upset. When she was feeling better, however, chronic anxiety led her to eat compulsively. She constantly supplemented the starchy prison fare with purchases from the commissary—cream cheese, candy bars, cake. On top of the weight she had already gained during the trial and through her lack of exercise, Ethel became quite heavy at Sing Sing. By the beginning of the summer, Julie was already cautioning her to watch her weight. A year later Ethel needed some undergarments and wrote her sister-in-law to look for extra-large sizes to accommodate her thirty-six-inch waist and forty-two-inch hips.

Ethel increasingly hungered for her husband's reassurance and approval to lift her out of the doldrums. As always, Julie was there for her, coaxing, praising, admiring, expressing his love. He suggested that his wife read, practice singing, and engage in a program of self-study on music, psychiatry, or both to overcome her depression. None of these suggestions, however, had the effect that his encouragement of her writing evoked.

Beginning in October 1950, while Ethel was awaiting trial at the Women's House of Detention, Julie had begun to praise his wife's talents as a writer. He encouraged her to pour her thoughts and emotions into the letters she wrote and suggested that she consider writing her life's history. Ethel immediately responded. In school, writing had been her academic forte and had provided a means of gaining esteem long before she discovered acting. Holed up in her room at 64 Sheriff Street, Ethel had spent hours writing and rewriting compositions for her English class, which typically were then praised and read aloud by the teacher who was impressed by her student's use of sophisticated vocabulary. Although this talent had lain dormant since high school, the circumstances of her imprisonment and Julie's ever-present encouragement reawakened Ethel's interest in writing.

More and more, the Rosenbergs' correspondence became their only way of communicating to the world. As both Ethel and Julius began to see their case in world historic terms, their letters took on even greater meaning. From relatively early on, Julie wanted the public to know what had happened to him and his wife; he wanted their plight to be cause for public outcry, their bravery and dignity a source of inspiration and hope in a society that he believed was moving toward fascism. In the absence of alternatives, writing was the only means to alert the world to the Rosenbergs' situation, their courage, confidence, and perspective, their stature as historic figures. Once they both had been sentenced to death, Julie's eagerness to reach the public dramatically increased; he needed its support; he wanted its attention and respect for what he was withstanding. He decided that all of his and Ethel's letters should be preserved with the hope that they eventually would be published and presumably ignite the long-awaited avalanche of protest. On 24 April 1951, Julie announced this decision to his attorney and requested that Bloch keep copies of each of his and Ethel's letters. Thereafter, whenever the Rosenbergs penned, or more accurately, penciled, a letter, they copied it exactly and had one of their visitors, usually Julie's sister Ethel, take a bundle of similarly copied letters to Manny Bloch.

The Rosenbergs' correspondence always had been intended for public consumption, given the prison administration's review of every letter they sent or received. But after their verdict and sentencing, Julie and Ethel wrote letters to one another that were strange amalgams of personal reflection and revelation coupled with direct statements and appeals to the American people. Because they chose to make these appeals under the guise of personal communication between husband and wife, their correspondence assumed an artificial, disingenuous quality.

Julius wrote letters to his wife which informed her that he had been one of five children, that his parents had been Orthodox Jews, that his father had been an ardent trade unionist—hardly news to his wife of thirteen years. Frequently the facade of personal communication was often abdicated altogether, and Julie and Ethel spoke directly to their intended audience or referred to themselves in the third person. Julius wrote letters to Ethel that referred to his wife and children. Ethel wrote Julie to inform him that she had received

a birthday card from her husband. In the midst of one letter to Ethel,
Julie suddenly pleads with the American people to bring an end to his imprisonment. In another, addressed to Julie, Ethel asks the women of America to break their silence in regard to the Rosenberg case.

For Ethel the ability to write did not come easily. It was a studied, painstaking effort to find the most dramatic and evocative words that would impress the reader. Ethel kept a notebook in which she wrote down her ideas for letters and auditioned phrases and sentences before she committed them to prison stationery. At the time of her death, this notebook contained some two hundred pages of rough draft. She also constantly consulted a dictionary, looking for words that sounded dramatic and sophisticated—her use of sophisticated vocabulary had impressed her English teacher in school, why not the American public?

Increasingly, Ethel used Manny Bloch as an informal literary agent or editor. As she became more impressed with her abilities as a writer, more self-conscious and painstaking in her choice of vocabulary, she demanded more of Manny's assistance on the letters he was collecting for her. In regard to a previous letter she had spent much time composing, she told her attorney that she was extremely annoyed with herself for her ignorant use of a word. She had discovered its true meaning in the dictionary, believed her reputation as an author had been compromised because of this misuse, and demanded that Manny change it for her. A week later she again asked him to change another letter's wording. A few days later she requested that he omit something she had written since it ruined the sentence's rhythm for her.

The solace and self-esteem Ethel derived from writing was buoyed enormously in August. Following Manny Bloch's repeatedly unsuccessful attempts to interest the *Daily Worker* in his clients' plight, he had turned to two nonsectarian, left-wing periodicals to take up the Rosenberg's case in their pages. The *Compass* was not interested. Its editor, I.F. Stone, believed the Rosenbergs were guilty. The *National Guardian*, however, was intrigued. Its editors, Cedric Belfrage and James Aronson, were persuaded by Bloch's arguments that the conviction and sentence of his clients was politically motivated. They assigned one of their best reporters, William Reuben, to investigate.

The *National Guardian* had been founded as a weekly newspaper in 1948 as the organ of the newly formed Progressive party

332 that was built around the presidential candidacy of Henry Wallace. Although the Communist party avidly campaigned for Wallace, Roosevelt's former vice-president, and was the object of much respect and sympathy at the *Guardian*, the newsweekly was independent of the Party, explicitly defining its politics as "progressive" rather than socialist or communist. The Wallace campaign suffered a resounding defeat at the polls in 1948, but the *Guardian* continued, garnering support from liberals and former Party members who were increasingly repelled by the Party's sectarianism and the *Daily Worker's* irrelevance.

On 15 August 1951, the *National Guardian* announced on its front page: "THE ROSENBERG CONVICTION—IS THIS THE DREYFUS CASE OF COLD WAR AMERICA?" Under this headline, the editors boldly stated that "We are convinced of the overwhelming probability that the Rosenbergs are completely innocent," and pledged to lead a campaign to vindicate the convicted couple. In another front page editorial on 22 August, the editors set forth their perspective on the case, one which would provide the framework of support for the Rosenbergs during the next decade:

> After careful analysis of the entire trial record, the Guardian contends:
>
> That the very best that can be said for the government case against the Rosenbergs is that it leaves such reasonable doubt as to entitle them, by all American legal standards, to acquittal;
>
> That there are strong grounds for suspecting they are victims of an out-and-out political frame-up, in a period of build-up for war when victims are needed by the government to silence the opposition at any cost to the United States Constitution. . . .
>
> The conviction and sentencing to death of the Rosenbergs appears to conflict with the constitutional safeguards against civil [sic] and inhuman punishment. Even assuming that the sentence may technically come within the constitutional power, it nevertheless appears cruel and inhuman to the point of barbarity.
>
> The Rosenbergs have from the start maintained their complete innocence of any knowledge or part of the plot of which they are accused.

The individuals produced as witnesses to their alleged 'overt acts' were confessed spies, whose testimony was flimsy, rehearsed and entirely unsupported by documentary evidence. . . .

The Rosenberg Case reeks of frame-up. That the government should have connived in demanding death sentences for these two particular individuals, while consenting to freedom and clemency for confessed participants in the same alleged plot, leads to the conclusion that there was a special, political objective in making a supreme example of the Rosenbergs, because of their left-wing politics.

Over the course of the next six weeks, William Reuben proceeded carefully to dissect the trial transcript and to suggest possible explanations for the testimony presented against the Rosenbergs. Apparently, however, Ethel and Julie had been unaware of the *Guardian* or, at least, had never read it, probably due to the narrowness of their political vision, which focused solely on the *Daily Worker*. Thus when Manny Bloch came to Sing Sing with clippings from Reuben's exposés, the Rosenbergs were surprised to find this previously unknown paper so completely championing their cause, something which the Communist party still refused to do.

It was not until the end of September, however, that the Rosenbergs actually saw copies of all the *National Guardians* in which they were featured. At this point what had been restrained enthusiasm gave way to unbridled relief and optimism as they saw how the *Guardian* resembled the *Daily Worker* during its Popular Front incarnation, and how the editorials and Reuben's articles presented an analysis of their case virtually identical to their own.

In October it seemed as though the avalanche of protest that Julie had long been anticipating might finally be realized. First, in an attempt to highlight "the human side of this young New York couple," the *Guardian* printed the first two letters Ethel and Julie had written to each other after Ethel was transferred to Sing Sing. By way of introduction, the paper claimed that the letters "round out the picture of two Americans whose strength, tenderness and conviction should be a source of rare pride to the progressive movement in which they have for years been modestly active." Second, alongside the Rosenbergs' letters, the *Guardian* announced the formation of the National Committee to Secure Justice for the Rosenbergs with William Reuben as its provisional chairman:

As the single group of Americans now best informed about the case, all Guardian readers are invited to join this committee. Support on a nationwide scale—which our readers can provide—is needed NOW for the cause of securing justice in this supremely important case. By joining the committee you can, wherever you are, help in the tasks of bringing the facts to the general public in reprint and digest form, and of assuring that funds are available to carry on the appeals of Ethel and Julius Rosenberg against their conviction and sentence of death.

By the end of the month, Reuben could report:

The Guardian announcement of formation of a National Committee to Secure Justice for the Rosenbergs has brought an unprecedented response from all over the land. . . . Here are a few excerpts from letters received: . . .

Nan Pendrell, New York City (with check for $20): 'Though I am a writer and the words should come easily, I cannot set down my reverence for the fortitude and integrity of Ethel and Julius Rosenberg—I cannot phrase my love for their children. But I can ask you to be good enough to let me know how I can give these youngsters a little of the parental love now denied them with such cynical cruelty. Would Michael like to go to a football game some Saturday or Sunday?' . . .

A physician in New Jersey (who sent in a large check . . .): 'My wife and I are willing to take the Rosenberg children in our home and take care of them as long as necessary.' . . .

Sam Sergel of North Hollywood, Calif.: . . . 'I have been following your exposé of the unbelievable farce of justice, the Rosenberg story. Their letters to each other are the products of the minds of two wonderful people. Even if one did not know the true story of their framed conviction, these letters alone would be proof of two souls entirely incapable of the deeds for which they have been convicted.' . . .

Michael A. Terman, Chicago, Ill., professional man (with $10): '. . . Tell the Rosenbergs there are tens of thousands

in our beloved country who would do as I am doing if they
only knew the facts.' . . .

    A member of the New York Bar (with $5): 'I have been
a bedridden patient for four years and this left me without
funds. Or else there would be no limit to what I would
contribute.' . . .

    A Bronx, N.Y. graduate student (with $5): 'Julius and
Ethel Rosenberg will be free because we will never stop
fighting until they are free . . . The names of Julius and Ethel
Rosenberg will live forever as a shining beacon of truth and
justice, of humility and compassion, of understanding and
sacrifice, and of love of freedom and their fellow man.'

Two days after this outpouring of support appeared, Manny Bloch
spent three hours at Sing Sing reading the *Guardian* letters to his
clients and informed them that the first meeting of the Committee
to Secure Justice was planned for 8 November. The *Guardian* asked
Bloch to get his clients' reaction. On 7 November, the paper printed
Julie and Ethel's remarks, which Bloch had dutifully copied down.
Presumably, Ethel extemporaneously said:

> *All of a sudden my drab and wretched surroundings are*
> *touched with radiance and color. The expressions of sup-*
> *port from my new-found brothers and sisters are unutterably*
> *touching. I am speechless with gratitude and admiration*
> *for all the precious human beings who have offered their*
> *love and assistance to our dear children and have at the*
> *same time tendered such a beautiful tribute to us, their*
> *parents. In all humility, I pledge myself anew to the un-*
> *ceasing war against man's inhumanity to man in whatever*
> *form it may rear its brutal head. I shall never sell short the*
> *faith and trust that the Guardian readers have reposed in*
> *my husband and me. Else shall our lives have gone for*
> *naught.*

Surely this pronouncement was as studied and rehearsed as any
letter Ethel wrote, yet even with its self-conscious and florid style,
it spoke with a dignity and eloquence rarely heard from those in-
terred behind prison walls. Individuals imprisoned for overtly political reasons—such as the Communist party leaders convicted un-

der the Smith Act—were far more likely to speak of "filthy lies," "Hitlerite sentences," and the "fascistization of the country," than "man's inhumanity to man."

The committee that began to coalesce out of the *Guardian's* appeals recognized Ethel's writing abilities and started to run advertisements in newspapers and magazines that led with "A MOTHER WRITES FROM THE DEATH HOUSE," followed by a quote from "Mrs. Ethel Rosenberg," an explanation of the Committee's activities, and then a solicitation for funds. Ethel's impassioned literary style clearly was seen as a means of garnering support for the Rosenberg case.

Whenever Ethel was called upon to write, by the Committee or by her husband, she typically was able to rise to the occasion, grandiloquently expressing her courage, confidence, and perspective. Yet, at precisely the moment she was gaining national recognition as a heroine, poised to receive the acclaim for which she had been thirsting since her earliest ambitions to perform on stage, Ethel Rosenberg was sinking into a depression over which she had little control. The *Guardian* articles, the formation of the support committee, the first publication of her writing, all encouraged her and gave her moments of peace and self-satisfaction. But these apparently were not enough to penetrate the thick wall of depression that had settled around her. As winter settled in and snow covered Sing Sing, Ethel became so depressed that she could rarely bring herself to write. She wanted so much for her letters to be perfect, beautiful, inspiring, but mostly now when she wrote she could only reflect on the monotonous passage of time. In October she had sent eleven letters to her husband; in November, six; in December and January, five a month and, in February, three. She wrote only the most perfunctory letters to her in-laws, and to her sons she had long been unable to communicate.

By the last week of February, Julie had not received a letter from his wife in two-and-a-half weeks. When he saw her at their weekly meetings, she often remained in tears during the entire hour. Throughout the month, he repeatedly wrote her of how much he admired and loved her, but nothing helped to rouse her from her depression—nothing except a critical defeat.

On Monday, 25 February 1952, the U.S. Circuit Court of Appeals affirmed the conviction of Ethel and Julius Rosenberg. Judge Jerome Frank, one of the most liberal and distinguished jurists in the nation, wrote the opinion. In response to Manny Bloch's argument that the testimony of confessed spies Ruth and David Greenglass was unreliable, Frank agreed that if the Greenglass testimony were disregarded "the conviction could not stand." "But," he continued, "where trial is by jury, this court is not allowed to consider the credibility of witnesses or the reliability of testimony. Particularly in the federal judicial system, that is the jury's province." To Bloch's argument "that the trial judge behaved himself so improperly as to deprive the Rosenbergs of a fair trial," Frank recalled that Bloch, "summing up for the jury, stated that 'we feel that the trial has been conducted . . . with that dignity and decorum that befits an American trial.' Still later, the same counsel said that 'the court conducted itself as an American judge.' These remarks, by a highly competent and experienced lawyer, are not compatible with the complaints now made." Frank went on to argue that Judge Kaufman had acted properly, that the issue of the Rosenbergs' Communist affiliation was relevant evidence that presented a motive for spying, and that, ultimately, there was no precedent for the Appeals Court to rule on the issue of whether the punishment handed down was fair: "If there is one rule in the federal criminal practice which is firmly established, it is that the Appellate Court has no control over a sentence which is within the limits allowed by a statute." The only hope that Frank offered was a precise outline of how the Rosenbergs' counsel could appeal to the Supreme Court for a reduction of sentence.

This was a severe blow. Manny and his assistant, Gloria Agrin, had worked tirelessly over the past nine months writing an appellate brief that raised no less than twenty-five points of alleged error in the Rosenberg trial and 210 specific instances of Judge Kaufman's prejudicial conduct. Ethel and Julie believed Manny to be a legal genius and saw Jerome Frank, a known opponent of capital punishment, to be their best chance for sympathetic judicial review. When the news came that Frank had written the opinion upholding their conviction, Ethel could have been expected to collapse and perhaps develop the prison psychosis Frederic Wertham had previously predicted. But somehow Ethel rallied, temporarily warded off her depression and suddenly was in a position to embolden her husband. Within days of the court's decision she was planning a birthday party for Michael and finally writing her sons a letter.

Ethel's response to the Appeals Court decision indicated a pattern that she would demonstrate each time the Rosenbergs experienced a legal defeat or a challenge from the outside world over the course of the next sixteen months. She would emerge from an enveloping depression, experience anger or outrage, and write letters that reflected great courage and strength. For a period of time afterward, she would face her imprisonment and increasingly remote chances for reprieve with calm and forbearance, and then gradually slide once again into a depression that prevented her from putting pencil to paper, from doing much more than breaking into helpless tears whenever she saw her husband.

No matter how tortured she was however, Ethel never allowed her attorney, her psychiatrist, her sons, or her relatives see her cry or witness the extreme depression she experienced. These few people were her audience; to them she was a heroine, a martyr. She only allowed her misery to show with Julie and in the confines of her own cell. In the face of external stimuli, such as the denial of a legal appeal or a meeting with her attorney or psychiatrist, Ethel was alive—responsive, combative, heroic, using her intellect, her skills as a writer or an actress to convince her audience that she was fine. When she was alone in her cell for hours on end, days punctuated by nothing more than the changing of the guard or the arrival of meals, she was deadened to all but her internal pain.

Aside from her visits with her husband, Ethel's only other form of emotional support was her meetings with Saul Miller. According to her psychiatrist, his visits to Sing Sing were something he would do for any one of his patients under similar circumstances. He "never thought of her as anything but a young person"; her "neediness and anxiety" caused him to regard her as "a grown child." Yet, for Ethel, her relationship to Miller had become something far more than the straightforward, formal relationship between therapist and patient that he has described some thirty-three years after the fact.

Ethel began writing Miller what could easily be characterized as love letters. She addressed him by his first name and called him "darling." She wrote of the excruciating pain she experienced when he left her, the extremity of her need for him, and the love that she felt.

Dr. Miller says only that he "was very fond of her"—nothing more. It is impossible to know what he said to her during their meetings at Sing Sing, however; if he encouraged her to call him by his first name; if he approved or returned her expressions of love; if he did nothing to stem the intensity of her need for him. Transference and counter-transference often are subjects so loaded, so prone to conscious denial that they are impossible to make sense of by the participants themselves or by outside observers. It is clear, however, that Ethel and her psychiatrist were never alone at Sing Sing; a matron always sat nearby. His visits also were conditional upon the approval of the warden. If anything improper occurred, the warden would promptly be informed by the matron or through the same means the prison used to monitor Ethel's meetings with her attorney. This is not to say, however, that Miller could not have encouraged Ethel's infatuation or romantic fantasies subtly, in a manner that would have gone unnoticed by prison officials and been quite innocent on his part.

Throughout her imprisonment in the death house, Saul Miller was the one visitor toward whom Ethel never experienced anger or frustration. At one time or another, Ethel found fault with her in-laws—for their naiveté and timidity; with her lawyer—for his disregard of issues concerning the children; and with her brother Bernie. Her psychiatrist remained idealized. Even when he left on vacations and could not see her for months, Ethel seems to have experienced only longing rather than impatience. He was the only visitor who was autonomously hers. She shared everyone else with her husband, except for her brother who she probably would have been only too happy to share. Her psychiatrist came to Sing Sing exclusively to see her; he was not obligated by blood or money, but only concern and caring. Ethel also knew relatively little about him. His psychoanalytic stance did not permit discussion of his personal life, so that Ethel was free to fantasize about his life and her meaning to him. Alone in her cell with little more than her imagination to console and entertain her, Ethel could dwell endlessly on thoughts and desires about the distinguished, authoritative man who had become the most exciting feature on her pitifully limited horizon.

Dr. Miller's attentiveness, constancy, and support allowed Ethel to feel valued and loved. In light of so many others' betrayal, the interest of this professional man, this venerated "expert," proved crucial to Ethel's ability to withstand her incarceration. Because she was always able to be heroic in his presence and because she believed he approved and admired her heroic stance, her resolve was strengthened. The man she had come to idealize and love sanctioned her role as the death house's sole heroine; therefore she was determined to justify the faith that she believed he placed in her.

In October 1952 Ethel was confronted with yet another herculean test of her heroism, since it was in that month that the Rosenbergs awaited the outcome of what seemed to be the last legal effort to save their lives. The Supreme Court of the United States was slated to rule on whether or not it would grant a review of the Appeals Court's findings, legally referred to as "certiorari." It could not review disputes of facts, but only determine whether or not the Appeals Court decision contained any legal error.

On Friday, 10 October, Ethel and Julie released a statement through their attorney to the public. It was printed in the *National Guardian* of 16 October:

> *Our pleas to the Supreme Court have been restricted by legal protocol, but before the bar of public opinion we cannot reassert often or emphatically enough our complete innocence of the charge.*
>
> *One matter should be made unequivocally clear. No matter what the result, we will continue in our determination to expose the political frame-up perpetuated against us by those who would silence by death, through spurious espionage accusations, opposition to the conspiracy to impose war abroad and a police state at home.*
>
> *We do not want to die. We are young and yearn for a long life of accomplishment. Yet, if the only alternative to death is the purchase of life at the cost of standards, there is no future for us or any legacy we can leave our children or those who survive and follow us.*
>
> *For what is life without the right to live it? Death holds no horror as great as the horror of a sterile existence devoid of social responsibility and the courage of one's convictions.*
>
> *We believe that our fellow Americans share these sentiments. We believe they will save us—and themselves—from this conspiracy to put to death innocent Americans.*

Three days later Ethel and Julie's belief that their fellow Americans would have to save them was confirmed. The Supreme Court, with only Justice Hugo Black dissenting, refused to grant the Rosenbergs certiorari. Manny Bloch immediately appealed the Supreme Court's ruling, but on 17 November 1952 the Court announced its refusal to reconsider. Judge Irving Kaufman set 12 January 1953 as the Rosenbergs' execution date. Uncharacteristically, Ethel was unable to respond to this seemingly lethal set-back. She became so depressed that she was not able to write a single letter during the month of December.

In the face of their impending deaths, Julie had decided to write his life story, anticipating that it eventually would be published. Directly after the Supreme Court's initial denial of certiorari, he wrote Ethel suggesting that she write an autobiographical account of her background, education, home life and experience since she was arrested. Ethel did not respond, but Julie proceeded anyway, becoming thoroughly absorbed in his writing. By the beginning of December, he was busy writing throughout the day and evening. Ethel, however, languished. On 7 November she had confessed that she could no longer focus her thoughts to write him, and with that, she never wrote her husband again.

This may have been due in part to the fact that in November Ethel was allowed to visit more frequently with Julie. In addition to their regular Wednesday meetings, they were now permitted to see each other each Friday. Thus she could communicate with him in person more frequently. But her inability to write her husband probably also reflected her deepening depression. As an explanation for why she hadn't written more, she enjoined her attorney to recognize that for her to simply function at all consumed all her energy. She usually did not need to offer explanations to Julie, as she always allowed him to see the pain and depression that prevented her from writing. Nevertheless, even he was alarmed at her complete silence.

Writing had gradually taken on new meaning for Ethel. As her letters were increasingly excerpted in the *National Guardian*, used by the Committee to Secure Justice in leaflets, pamphlets, and advertisements, and slated for publication in book form, Ethel apparently believed they should only reflect her heroism and literary prowess. Therefore, by 1953, after yet another stay of execution had been granted, her writing was directed almost exclusively to Manny Bloch with the anticipation that it would be used publicly. With Julie, however, she could not be heroic; with him she wanted only to indulge her misery. Julie was the only person to whom she could reveal her misery, and she did this frequently. Their relationship was the one enclave in which Ethel could indulge her feelings and remain confident that she would continue to be loved and esteemed. With no other person did she believe she was loved or respected without qualification. Thus with others—her psychiatrist, her attorney, the thousands of her unseen supporters and admirers described by the *Guardian*, Manny Bloch and her sisters-in-law—she had to be something more than she was with Julie; she had to live up to the expectations she believed they had of her. With Julie she would be Ethel Rosenberg, with all her fears, neuroses, and pain; for everyone else she would be Joan of Arc.

———

On Sunday, 21 December 1952, nearly 1,000 supporters of the Rosenbergs gathered outside Sing Sing Prison to bring season's greetings to Ethel and Julius. Although the police barricaded the street leading to the prison, the crowd stood for two hours in a heavy rain to sing songs and listen to speeches by William Patterson of the Civil Rights Congress and Howard Fast, internationally acclaimed novelist. The next day Ethel and Julie were served copies of their death sentences. They were scheduled to be put to death in three weeks. As these events unfolded Ethel sat in her cell reading George Bernard Shaw's *Saint Joan*.

If they did not wholly believe it before, it now seemed undeniable that the Rosenbergs' only hope rested with "the people." If enough of them made their voices heard, the soon-to-be-inaugurated Dwight D. Eisenhower might be persuaded to grant executive clemency—the Rosenbergs' last recourse. Each one of Manny Bloch's legal efforts had failed; the Rosenbergs now saw the entire judicial system as subject to a growing movement toward fascism. As the judiciary continued to "transform . . . the constitutional petitions of decent citizens for redress of grievances . . . into vilification and abuse," the avalanche of protest seemed to have materialized. Branches of the Committee to Secure Justice had spread throughout the United States. London announced the formation of a committee on 27 November 1952, Paris on 3 December. By the end of the year the major countries of Western and Eastern Europe and Israel had indigenous committees in support of Julius and Ethel Rosenberg.

Undoubtedly, this sudden and dramatic upsurge in international concern was generated by the Communist party, which finally endorsed the formation of committees in the Rosenbergs' defense. Why this unexpected endorsement occurred remains unclear and has been a matter of strenuous debate along ideological lines. Did the CP act when it did because it was now clear that the Rosenbergs were never going to confess to espionage and thus the Party would not be embarrassed by their disclosures? Or, was the Party attempting to divert international attention from the staged trial and executions of prominent, and largely Jewish, former leaders of the Czechoslovakian Communist party that occurred in Prague in November and December 1952? Or, was the Party simply opportunistic?—once the Committee to Secure Justice began enlisting thousands of people in its cause, the CP saw a progressive, popular movement to address, control, and win over to Communism. Although the actual reasons for the Party's November change of heart may never be known, its endorsement caused a torrent of activity, especially in those countries, such as France and Italy, where it still wielded political power.

With Jean-Paul Sartre, Marc Chagall, Pablo Picasso, and Harold Urey coming to the defense of the Rosenbergs; with literally tens of thousands beginning to demonstrate throughout the world for clemency; with unions, ministries, and major foreign newspapers demanding mercy, and with her execution imminent, Ethel began to see herself in mythic terms. She consciously appropriated Joan of Arc as a model with whom to compare herself.

On 30 December 1952, Manny Bloch pleaded with Judge Kaufman for a reduction of sentence for his clients, arguing that "once the current passes through the bodies of the Rosenbergs, nothing in the world can ever be done to correct the wrong done to them, to their children and to American justice." In his ruling of 2 January, Kaufman stayed the Rosenbergs' execution, previously set to occur in two weeks, so that Bloch could file a clemency petition with the White House, but denied the Rosenbergs' request for an alteration of sentence. Quoting George Eliot, he argued that: "There is a mercy which is weakness, and even treason against the common good," and went on to explain:

> Neither defendant has seen fit to follow the course of David Greenglass and Harry Gold. Their lips have been sealed and they prefer the glory which they believe will be theirs by the martyrdom which will be bestowed upon them by those who enlisted them in this diabolical conspiracy (and who, indeed, desire them to remain silent) . . . I still feel that their crime was worse than murder. . . . The application is denied.

Ethel responded to this ruling theatrically, effusively, and with direct quotes from *Saint Joan* in a letter of 9 January 1953. Although it ostensibly was addressed to Manny Bloch, she anticipated its publication for a wider audience, particularly since the Committee to Secure Justice had decided toward the end of 1952 to publish the Rosenbergs' prison correspondence in book form. Ethel quoted long sections from Shaw's *Saint Joan* and compared herself directly to the martyred Maid of Orleans. She warned those responsible for her imminent execution that they would forever live in hell, in the same manner Bernard Shaw predicted that the ecclesiastical court at Rouen would for executing Joan of heresy and witchcraft.

Although the analogy with Joan of Arc was obviously imprecise, perhaps nothing differentiated Ethel from the maid of Orleans more than the role of her own family in her downfall. Her family's betrayal was her unique fate and it was one that seriously tested her courage. After almost two years in the death house at Sing Sing, Ethel had only seen her brother Bernie; no other member of Ethel's family had tried to visit her. Then, suddenly, on 5 January, Tessie Greenglass appeared in the condemned cells to visit her daughter. She sat down outside Ethel's cell and said that she wanted to help. What could she do to save her daughter? The two spoke for an hour and a half. Ethel was calm, even when she asked her mother why she took Davey's side and not her own. While Tessie's response to this question remains unknown, she did agree to ask President Eisenhower for clemency for her daughter. Ethel was elated; at last it seemed that her mother was about to help, to give her the support that she had craved for so long. After Tessie left, Ethel immediately sent a telegram to her attorney instructing him to contact her mother at once as she was willing to do anything to help their case.

Ethel, however, was mistaken. After returning home from Sing Sing, Tessie Greenglass contacted the FBI. She informed an agent that she intended to visit O. John Rogge's office and work out a plan to make Ethel confess. She assured the agency that there was no doubt that her daughter and son-in-law were guilty, and that she planned to see Manny Bloch to "pretend" she wanted to help. She added that before she visited Ethel she had made her "heart like a stone," presumably so that she would be unmoved by her daughter's plight. Tessie may have genuinely wanted to save her daughter's life and worked toward this end through the only means she could accept—cooperation with those in authority whom she both feared and respected. Yet, as in virtually everything she had done, Tessie's actions were anathema to her daughter.

Two weeks later Tessie visited Ethel again. She had gone to see Bloch in the interim, and had "wanted to bust out at him but kept my mouth shut." Although she told Manny that she wanted to help, she made plain both her desire to see her daughter confess and her continued and unqualified support of David, then serving the second of his fifteen-year sentence at Lewisburg Penitentiary. Bloch apparently relayed details of this meeting to Ethel so that she had steeled herself for her mother's next visit. Ethel reportedly "told her off," later informing Manny, "I'm not sorry I did. And I'm not going to think any more about it." Yet the courageous heroine then confided, "But, Manny—I know it's foolish—but I'd still give anything in the world for one kind word from her."

Ethel was to see her mother only once more before she was executed. On Saturday, 14 March, Tessie and Bernie arrived to try yet again to make Ethel confess. According to the prison official who listened in on their conversation, Ethel was enraged: she called her mother a "witch" and "yelled and raved to such an extent, that she was cautioned by the guard that the interview would be terminated unless she quieted down." After this Tessie vowed to the FBI that she would never see her daughter again, "since," as an agent summarized, "no matter what she tried to do she was accused of doing wrong."

Cowards die many times before their death;
The valiant never taste of death but once.
The Valiant
(a play which Ethel
performed with the Clark Players
in the early thirties)

On Wednesday, 11 February 1953, President Dwight D. Eisenhower denied clemency to Ethel and Julius Rosenberg. In reasoning reminiscent of Judge Irving Kaufman's, the President asserted:

The nature of the crime for which they have been found guilty and sentenced far exceeds that of the taking of the life of another citizen: it involves the deliberate betrayal of the entire nation and could very well result in the death of many, many thousands of innocent citizens. By their act these two individuals have in fact betrayed the cause of freedom for which free men are fighting and dying at this very hour.

In private, Eisenhower responded to a friend's suggestion that the execution of a young mother might seem inhuman to some of America's foreign allies by claiming that Ethel was "the more strong-minded and the apparent leader of the two." Later in a letter to his son, John, he wrote, "in this instance it is the woman who is the strong and recalcitrant character, the man who is the weak one. She has obviously been the leader in everything they did in the spy ring." Thus Ethel was to perish because Dwight Eisenhower apparently had been exposed to rumors and idle speculation that he took as fact. The Rosenberg case was of such little weight, their lives so inconsequential that the President was quite willing to allow mere speculation to inform his decision about whether Ethel should live or die.

The media generally assumed that Ethel and Julius were now "doomed." *Time* magazine's conclusion was typical: "Dwight Eisenhower's answer all but closed the door of doom on the Rosenbergs. There are still a few desperate delaying actions to be made—and Lawyer Emanuel Bloch might succeed in winning more borrowed time—but the only real opportunity of escape lay with the Rosenbergs themselves. If they broke their long silence—if they confessed the secrets of their spy ring—then the President might consider a new appeal for clemency. But up to now the Rosenbergs have clung to their dark secrets, have shown no flicker of regret."

Although the *Guardian*, the Committee, and the tens of thousands of the Rosenbergs' supporters throughout the world rejected this doomfulness, believing that if enough people were mobilized in defense of clemency the Rosenbergs could be saved, the mainstream media essentially was correct. Manny Bloch did obtain another stay of execution on 17 February to appeal once more to the Supreme Court, but the Court again denied certiorari on 25 May.

Throughout the spring, Ethel remained silent. The letters she had been writing Manny Bloch stopped. On 24 February, she told her attorney that her solitary confinement had become impossible to tolerate, and then put down her newly acquired pen until the middle of May.

The children's welfare—the subject that had preoccupied her in the past—was now largely forgotten. The previous year she had arranged for her friends, Ben and Sonia Bach, to take Robby and Michael into their home near Toms River, New Jersey. Once people had started writing in to the *Guardian*, offering to care for the Rosenbergs' sons, Ethel saw a means for at last relieving both her mother-in-law of a responsibility she could not shoulder, and her sons of a situation in which they were languishing. At first, the boys were sent for a trial weekend with the doctor from New Jersey who had been one of the first to offer his home through the pages of the *Guardian*. Another trial weekend at another supporter's house followed. But then Ben and Sonia offered to take in Robby and Michael, just as they had welcomed Ethel and Michael into their home during the summer of 1945, when the cottage the Rosenbergs had rented turned out to be uninhabitable.

Ben and Sonia were loving, thoughtful, progressively minded people. Ethel could feel secure about entrusting her children to them. This undoubtedly was an enormous relief after two years of almost constant anxiety about their welfare. But, it was more likely Ethel's profound depression, her two-year entombment in the death house separated from the world of the living, that caused her to think less and less about the children. Significantly, she forgot Michael's tenth birthday, despite Julie's gentle urging that she send her son a birthday greeting. The one letter she did manage to write her children that spring began with an admission that she had forgotten Robby's birthday as well. In what followed Ethel did not address herself to her sons but spoke only of the birds she had been watching, a flower that had blossomed in her yard, and the birth of a child in Holland who had been named "Ethel Julia" in honor of the Rosenbergs. There was nothing to or about her sons.

Throughout this period Julie was able to sustain himself through reading and writing. In addition to the eight newspapers he read daily, he read books on a variety of subjects but particularly favored history. He also read plays and novels, and continued to write long letters to his wife and attorney. When he was not so engaged, he played chess with the prisoner in the cell next to his. With a chessboard in front of him, he would call his moves to the other inmate who had his own chessboard. In this fashion he was able to pass the endless hours in the condemned cells.

Ethel's experience, of course, was quite different. She did not write. She subscribed only to the *Guardian*, *Parents' Magazine*, *Ebony*, and probably no more than one daily newspaper. She read books intermittently, and clearly had no one with whom to play chess. Earlier in her imprisonment at Sing Sing, she had spent time singing alone in her cell. Without an audience, however, she had come to sing less and less. One of her only means of escape was through chatting with Helen Evans, the matron who guarded her during the weekday mornings and early afternoons. This was all she had, aside from her visits with her in-laws, psychiatrist, and lawyer. Compared to the resources her husband was able to summon up, it seemed little indeed.

On 25 May the Supreme Court again refused to review the Rosenbergs' case. Their execution was then scheduled for Thursday, 18 June, at 11 P.M.—Ethel and Julie's fourteenth wedding anniversary. On 2 June the Rosenbergs received an unprecedented visit from John V. Bennett, Director of the Bureau of Prisons. He offered Ethel and Julie what appeared to be their last official opportunity to confess and name names. They adamantly refused. On Monday, 15 June, the Supreme Court ruled against Manny's appeal for another stay of execution. As the Justices adjourned for the summer, the Rosenbergs' last opportunity rested with a second clemency plea to President Eisenhower.

On Tuesday, 16 June, Robby, Michael, and Ben Bach were driven to New York City to meet Manny. From there, the four drove to Sing Sing. Although no one articulated the words, Michael, age ten, understood this to be his last meeting with his parents. Bloch left the children with Bach in the administration building and entered the condemned cells alone. He met with his clients in the counsel room, reading the latest petition for clemency he had written. He then escorted the children in to see their parents. After many hugs and kisses, Ethel surprised Manny with a letter she had written directly to the President pleading for mercy. As the children wandered aimlessly around the room, Ethel read aloud her letter asking for compassion for her small Jewish family.

After she finished reading, both she and Julie tried to play with Michael and Robby as though this were just an ordinary visit. It was Ethel's belief to the very last moment with her sons that if she could evidence calm so would they. As with so many of her beliefs about child rearing, she was wrong again, for Michael could not tolerate what seemed to be his parents' indifference over this, their last visit together. It appeared that he alone was the only one suffering. He started to cry "One more day to live, one more day to live" repeatedly in an attempt to move his parents, to force them to acknowledge that this was their last meeting, not just an ordinary visit. Ethel was unprepared for this reaction and was about to burst into tears. Rather than allow her sons to see her cry, she quickly kissed them, promised she would write, and ran from the room.

On Wednesday, 17 June, Ethel and Julie had their last visits with Julie's mother, his sister Ethel, and his brother Dave. Julie's sister, Lena, had suffered a "nervous breakdown" and was unable to travel to Sing Sing. That morning as Sophie and Ethel visited with Ethel, and Dave and Julie met, the 11:30 news was broadcast over the prison loudspeaker. Suddenly it was announced that Supreme Court Justice William O. Douglas had independently granted a stay of execution to the Rosenbergs on the grounds that they were improperly tried under the General Espionage Act of 1917 rather than Section 10 of the Atomic Energy Act of 1946 that superseded it. The 1946 act provides that "the death penalty or imprisonment for life may be imposed only upon recommendation of the jury." If this later act were applicable, Douglas reasoned, the District Court was without power to impose the death penalty. Therefore the Justice ordered that a stay be granted until the lower courts had an opportunity to determine the applicability of the Atomic Energy Act to the Rosenbergs' case.

Briefly, Ethel and Julie had triumphed. In their almost three years behind prison walls, this was their first major victory. It was a fleeting victory, however. At 6:00 P.M., over the same prison loudspeaker, it was announced that at the request of the Attorney General, Chief Justice Fred Vinson had ordered the Supreme Court to convene a special session the following day to reaffirm its previous ruling refusing to stay the death penalty.

On Thursday, 18 June, knowing very well the meaning of Vinson's announcement, Ethel and Julie prepared to die. On this, their fourteenth wedding anniversary, they met together in the morning and afternoon, and held a joint meeting with the prison's Jewish chaplain. The day passed without word from the reconvened Supreme Court.

On Friday, 19 June, Judge Vinson announced that the Court had vacated Douglas's stay on a six-to-three vote. Less than an hour later, President Eisenhower refused executive clemency for the second time. In order to avoid executing the couple on the Jewish sabbath, which would begin at sundown, Attorney General Herbert Brownell ordered that the Rosenbergs be put to death at 8:00 P.M. instead of the scheduled time of 11:00 P.M., that very day.

The nineteenth was humid and hot, with temperatures reaching the eighties. Outside Sing Sing Prison, sixty New York State troopers, night sticks in hand, gathered to augment the prison guard force and local police in case any demonstration occurred. They erected wooden barricades across all roads leading to the prison, and allowed only those with the proper credentials to pass.

Inside the prison walls, over thirty reporters gathered in the stifling visitors' room to await word from the death house. In the warden's garage, the FBI had set up a secret command post with a direct line to FBI headquarters. A second line was installed in a room on the second floor of the condemned cells, readied for the interrogation of the Rosenbergs, if either one or both of them broke down and confessed.

In the morning Ethel wrote a brief note to her attorney requesting that Saul Miller look after Robby and Michael. She insisted that he help her children receive professional help if needed. She assured Manny that she believed he had done everything possible in their case.

In the afternoon Ethel and Julie met. They both signed their names to a letter that Ethel wrote to Robby and Michael enjoining them to always remember that their parents were innocent. Ethel then attached a postscript to Manny. She asked that her only two pieces of jewelry be given to her sons. The first was her wedding ring, a simple gold band. The second was a blue enameled religious medallion that she had worn around her neck. This pendant was a present from Miriam Moskowitz, who had been given it by her mother. Miriam had worn it throughout her own incarceration. When she was released from prison, she immediately had visited Manny Bloch and presented him with the pendant. "Give this to Ethel—it represents some mother's love," she told him.

Below this postscript was yet another addressed to Manny asking him to give Saul Miller her love.

After spending the afternoon and early evening in his familiar place outside Ethel's cell, Julie was forced to depart at 7:20 P.M. He was taken into a cell where his head and leg were partially shaved so that electrodes could be applied easily. His pant leg was slit to accommodate the wire. The Jewish chaplain, Irving Koslowe, appeared and asked Julie to follow him. The rabbi began to intone the Twenty-third Psalm, "The Lord is my shepherd, I shall not want," as Julie followed slowly behind escorted by two guards. At 8:00 Julius Rosenberg walked into the execution chamber. At 8:06 he was pronounced dead.

Ethel had been readied in the same manner. The two matrons she had requested, Helen Evans and Lucy Many, were with her.

She wore a dark green dress with white polka dots and cloth slippers.
As the execution chamber was being readied anew, the rabbi came to Ethel and implored her to talk for her children's sake. She simply answered him in the negative and indicated her readiness to proceed. He began chanting the Thirty-first Psalm, "In thee, O Lord, do I put my trust; let me never be ashamed. . . . For I have heard the slander of many; fear was on every side: While they took counsel together against me, they devised to take away my life."

As she entered the glaringly lighted, white-walled execution chamber, Ethel was faced with a room full of impassive, tight-lipped men. There was the United States marshal and his chief deputy, the warden, the executioner, two doctors, and three wire-service correspondents chosen to represent the media that had been arguing so long and so loudly for her death. Confronted with these unfriendly faces, Ethel turned impulsively to the women at her side. Mrs. Evans instinctively grasped her outstretched hand and Ethel drew her near, kissed her lightly on the cheek and with great feeling whispered, "Oh, Mrs. Evans, you're such a wonderful woman." The matron was so overcome by this that she dashed from the room. Ethel then shook the other woman's hand and watched her depart. She then mounted the oak chair. As the electrodes were attached to her body and the straps bound her limbs, she stared directly into the faces of the men in front of her "with the most composed look you ever saw," according to a witness. She winced when an electrode was applied to her head, but her arms remained relaxed under the thick straps that shackled her. A leather mask was then placed over her face.

At 8:11, Ethel was given the standard three electric shocks. The doctors then applied their stethoscopes to discover, incredulously, that she was still alive. Ethel Rosenberg had defied her executioners. After two more shocks she was pronounced dead at 8:16 P.M.

Bob Considine, one of the reporters who witnessed the execution, quickly left the execution chamber to brief the waiting members of the press:

They died differently, gave off different sounds, different grotesque manners. Uh—he died quickly, there didn't seem to be too much life left in him when he entered behind the rabbi. He seemed to be walking in a cadence of steps of just keeping in time with the muttering of the Twenty-third Psalm. Never said a word. Never looked like he wanted to say a word. She died a lot harder. When it appeared that she had received enough electricity to kill an ordinary person and had received the exact amount that killed her husband, the doctors went over and placed the stethoscope to her and looked to each other rather dumbfounded and seemed surprised that she was not dead. And she was given more electricity which started again the kind of ghastly plume of smoke that rose from her head. After two more little jolts, Ethel Rosenberg was dead.

Michael Rosenberg had been playing ball with his friend Steve outside the home of Ben and Sonia Bach. When night fell the two boys went back to the house.

I asked what had happened. They didn't answer directly, 'We listened to every station; they all said the same thing.' I couldn't react. I was not to cry emotionally for six years. Steve piped up, 'You're taking it just like a man, Mike.' Sonia cried and hugged me. She said, 'You'll stay here with us.' Yes, I thought, I guess I will. They suggested I not tell Robby, who was probably asleep already. He pretended ignorance about the execution, which relieved everyone. In fact, he understood very well—

Judge Irving R. Kaufman heard about the execution in his chambers at Foley Square. He then left the courthouse for his country home escorted by two FBI agents.

Emanuel Bloch eulogized his "brother and sister":

This is not a time to grieve. They would not have wanted it that way. They were hurt—but they didn't cry; tortured—but they didn't yield. Their courage has been an inspiration to tens of millions to stand up boldly and fight oppression and tyranny.

The American people should know, as the rest of the world knows, that America today, by virtue of the execution of the Rosenbergs, is living under the heel of a military dictatorship garbed in civilian attire. The men who are running our country have no hearts. They have stones for hearts. They have the souls of murderers. This was an act of cold, deliberate murder. When I requested in Washington that these executions be put off so that they would not occur on the Jewish Sabbath, the request was granted by a barbarian who instead of postponing the hour of death, pushed it up so they could be done away with before the beginning of the Sabbath. . . .

I place the murder of the Rosenbergs at the door of President Eisenhower, Atty. Gen. Brownell and J. Edgar Hoover. This was not the American tradition, not American justice and not American fair play. . . .

Tens of millions are in sorrow—but they are in anger. We must be angry today to resist Nazism—for this is the face of Nazism. They have killed two of us, but the people are still here. Let us never forget that it was Nazism that killed the Rosenbergs—for if we do, we will cringe, we will be on our knees and be afraid. Insanity, irrationality, barbarism and murder seem to be part of the feeling of those who rule us.

Ethel and Julius had faith in you that they would not be let down. They knew full well that if they died, the people would understand why they died—and that their death would provide an opportunity to fight the terror that made them its victims.

Bernie Greenglass felt compelled to write his brother Dave two days after their sister and brother-in-law were killed. He began by saying that he was writing "a few lines representing the views of the family . . . Mom in particular. . . .

To begin with we feel you did the proper thing, whereas Eth and Julie did not. They not only did a disservice to the country but from a more personal viewpoint they put their children in a most horrible situation.

Then too, they were willing to trade yours' and your family's lives for their stinking principals [sic] . . . Believe me Dave, I spent hours eating my heart out with Eth, but to no avail. According to her, Mom, Chuch [Tessie's sister], everyone connected with the case, and your counsel all lied—and when I questioned her concerning some of the points of contention, she countered with the stock phrase, 'Were you there' or 'its [sic] a dirty lie.' I got the impression

354

*that they wanted everything on their terms—and easygoing
as I am, I did not relish the idea of being used, and thats'
[sic] exactly what they were doing, even as they did with
you and Ruthie. Don't lose any sleep over them—for although I don't think they deserved what they got, nevertheless they were the masters of their fate and could have
saved themselves, to say nothing of the heartaches they
could have spared all their families and friends through the
last 2½ years.*

*Keep well 'Duo,' take care of yourself and don't worry
about your family—for I look in as do many, many friends
you have—believe me! May it pass quickly—so you'll be
back where you belong, among all of us.*

Love, Bernie

Tessie Greenglass, who had asked President Eisenhower for clemency for her daughter, collapsed after she learned of Ethel's execution. Ruth, who was staying with her, called a doctor who came
to 64 Sheriff Street and gave Tessie a sedative. Five days later Tessie
called the FBI. She spoke with agent John Harrington, chief field
officer in the Rosenberg investigation. She informed him that she
had not gone into mourning for her daughter, since Ethel did not
love her or any other members of her family and had no love for
her children, Michael and Robert. Tessie asserted that Ethel and
Julius wanted only to be "soldiers of Stalin" and offered the opinion
that they "were with him [Stalin who had died three months earlier]
wherever he might be." She asserted that she had no feeling for her
daughter except that she could not understand how Ethel could hurt
the United States of America in the manner that she did. Tessie
believed that Ethel hated this country and deserved to pay for the
crime she committed. From her perspective, Ethel had committed
"suicide," and the only person who should have her death on his
conscience was Manny Bloch for preventing her daughter from
confessing. Finally, in explaining why she didn't attend her daughter's funeral, she said, "Mr. Harrington, you should know that I do
not attend political rallies."

The Federal Bureau of Investigation devoted itself to tracking
down leads in the Rosenberg "spy network," although its supposed
leader was now dead. That the agency was not sure that Ethel was
involved in any espionage work was indicated by a memorandum
the FBI had prepared on 17 June in the eventuality Julius decided

to confess. On the long list of questions to ask the "atom spy" was number nine: "Was your wife cognizant of your activities?" Thus, as Ethel Rosenberg awaited her electrocution, denied clemency because Dwight Eisenhower believed she had "been the leader in everything they did in the spy ring," the FBI was still questioning her husband as to whether she had any role.

Eugene Dennis, leader of the American Communist party then imprisoned in the Atlanta Federal Penitentiary for violating the Smith Act, released a statement:

> Millions of people the world over will long remember Ethel and Julius Rosenberg. And June 19, 1953 will go down in history as a day of infamy when a barbaric crime was committed against humanity. . . .
>
> Not a few Americans will ask in hopelessness, why was it not possible to prevent this ghoulish Hitlerite execution? The answer lies partly in the advanced process of fascistization that has developed in our country as part of the cold war program. . . . The other part of the answer lies in the dangerous and costly fact that the weakest link in the worldwide movement of the peoples for clemency and human rights, for democracy and peace is here in the USA. . . . Too many people and mass organizations, including many opponents of McCarthyism and atomic warfare, as well as numerous adversaries of capital punishment, remained aloof from the struggle. The objective and subjective factors responsible for this heartrending defeat must be examined searchingly.

Critic Leslie Fiedler concluded:

> [E]ven at the end the Rosenbergs were not able to think of themselves as real people, only as 'cases,' very like the other for which they had helped fight, Scottsboro and Harry Bridges and Trenton Ten, replaceable puppets in a manifestation that never ends. There is something touching in their own accounts of reading each issue of the National Guardian to share in the ritualistic exploitation of themselves. . . .
>
> Reading the 'death-house letters' of the Rosenbergs, one has the sense that not only the Marxist dream of social

justice but the very possibilities of any heroism and martyrdom are being blasphemed. It is a parody of martyrdom they give us, too absurd to be truly tragic, too grim to be the joke it is always threatening to become. . . .

The Defense of the Soviet Union—here is the sole principle and criterion of all value—and to this principle the Rosenbergs felt that they had been true; in this sense, they genuinely believed themselves innocent, more innocent than if they had never committed espionage.

The final pity was that they could not say even so much aloud—except in certain symbolic outcries of frame-up and persecution, and only through the most palpable lies. It is for this reason that they failed in the end to become martyrs or heroes, or even men.

The *National Guardian* printed an editorial:

The National Guardian *stands in horror and shame before the crime committed by the United States government—a crime which stains America's name before the world; which writes the date 'June 19, 1953' in mourning black for future generations—mourning for the hope and the glory that America once meant for humanity.*

The hope and the glory will come again. The heroism of the two who have gone to their death is the testimony of that . . .

We salute the memory of Ethel and Julius, two of the noblest Americans who ever walked this land. . . .

Ethel and Julius were able to die as heroes because they had lived—and because they knew what they were dying for. Because they died as heroes, they live on—and they have work for us to do: to them, and to their children, we owe a solemn debt.

And so began the myths known as Ethel Rosenberg.

NOTES

INTRODUCTION

1 "the lives of every man . . . in this country.": Cited in William Reuben, *The Atom Spy Hoax*, Action Books, New York; 1955; p. 433.

1 "may have condemned . . . all over the world.": Quoted in *New York Times*, 6/20/53.

1 "crime worse than murder . . . to the disadvantage of our country.": Transcript of Record, *Julius Rosenberg and Ethel Rosenberg, vs. The United States of America*; Supreme Court of the United States, October Term, 1951 [hereafter "Trial Transcript"]; pp. 1614–1615.

2 "lifted the hearts . . . of the earth.": Cedric Belfrage, *National Guardian*, 6/15/53.

2 "America will enshrine . . . in the cause of truth.": *The Worker*, 9/20/53.

2 "the defense of the Soviet Union . . . of all value.": Leslie Fiedler, "Afterthoughts on the Rosenbergs," in Fiedler's *An End to Innocence*; Beacon Press, Boston; 1955; p. 45.

2 "saved America's name": Cedric Belfrage, op cit.

2 "noblest Americans who ever walked this land": *National Guardian* editorial, 6/22/53.

2 "thought and felt . . . and to feel": Robert Warshow, "The 'Idealism' of Julius and Ethel Rosenberg," in Warshow's *The Immediate Experience*; Doubleday, Garden City, New York; 1962; p. 80.

2 "in this instance . . . the spy ring.": Quoted in Ronald Radosh and Joyce Milton, *The Rosenberg File*; Holt, Rinehart and Winston, New York; 1983; p. 379.

3 "placed her duty . . . above her two children.": Max Lerner in the *New York Post*, quoted in William Reuben, op cit; p. 437.

4 "Saint on Earth;": *The Worker*, 11/1/53.

358   5   The anti-Communist and neoconservative ideologues: I am not speaking here of the many people who believe one or both of the Rosenbergs were guilty as charged, but who feel that the death penalty was not justified.

6   "trace the growth . . . martyrs to world peace.": *The Testament of Ethel and Julius Rosenberg*; Cameron and Kahn, New York; 1954; title page.

6   "words have already become . . . eloquence and inspiration.": ibid; untitled front page.

7   "incapable of telling treason . . . from honesty" and that her . . . was false: Leslie Fiedler, op cit, pp. 41–42.

7   "no eloquence . . . from truth and experience.": Robert Warshow, op cit, p. 81.

7   Louis Nizer, *The Implosion Conspiracy*; Doubleday, Garden City, New York; 1973.

7   Walter and Miriam Schneir, *Invitation to An Inquest*; Pantheon, New York; 1983.

8   "I'm afraid . . . they led unexceptional lives.": Quoted in Virginia Gardner, *The Rosenberg Story*; Masses and Mainstream, New York; 1954; p. 7.

9   Robert and Michael Meeropol did visit their parents regularly but less frequently than Mrs. Appel. They were, however, only six and ten years old respectively when their parents were killed, so their recollections are quite limited.

10   "a psychological intersection . . . of his subject.": Quoted in James L. Clifford, *From Puzzles to Portraits: Problems of a Literary Biographer*; University of North Carolina Press, Chapel Hill; 1970; p. 12.

CHAPTER ONE

17   "I can never forget . . . A beggar sang.": Michael Gold, *Jews Without Money*; Carroll and Graf, New York; 1984 [1930]; p. 13.

18   "the one hopeless form of tenement construction.": Quoted in Irving Howe, *World of Our Fathers*; Simon and Schuster, New York; 1976; p. 152.

20   Ethel spoke of her early life as one of "penury": Interview with Saul Miller, 1/19/85.

20   "Not only tradition . . . their sexuality drained out.": Irving Howe, op cit, p. 174.

21   Most have characterized him as . . . a *nebechel*: Ethel Appel, interview of 4/2/85, uses this term meaning literally a nothing, a pitiful person.

22   "The Jews who came . . . their 'fix.' ": Irving Howe and Kenneth Libo, *How We Lived*; Plume Books, New York; 1979; p. 17.

22   "was always on . . . side of practicality.": Quoted in Virginia Gardner, op cit, p. 14.

22   "an adorable little man with high red cheeks.": ibid, p. 23.

23   "a bitter woman . . . in the family.": ibid, p. 14.

23   "Woe to the father whose children are girls.": Quoted in Charlotte Baum, Paula Hyman and Sonya Michel, *The Jewish Woman in America*; Plume Books, New York; 1976; p. 10.

23   "with gratifications postponed, the culture of the East Side became a culture utterly devoted to its sons.": Irving Howe, *World of Our Fathers*, op cit, p. 251.

23   "many daughters . . . many honors.": Quoted in Charlotte Baum et al, op cit, p. 11.

24   As an adult, Ethel confided: Interview with Saul Miller, 1/19/85.

24   "The tales . . . of New York today.": Quoted in Milton Hindus (ed), *The Old East Side*; The Jewish Publication Society of America, Philadelphia; 1969; pp. 88–89.

26 "The kids ran in . . . to like their chatter.": Quoted in Virginia Gardner, op cit, p. 23.

CHAPTER TWO

27 Tessie was a strict parent: Interview with Saul Miller, 1/19/85.
28 "Only one girl . . . in her approach to scholarship.": Interview with Ethel Rosenberg's childhood friend who chose to remain anonymous.
29 "faculty comprised . . . the requirements.": Dr. Bessie Stolzenberg, *Fiftieth Anniversary Program, Seward Park High*, 1980.
31 "For second-generation . . . to its feminine realization.": Stuart and Elizabeth Ewen, *Channels of Desire*; McGraw-Hill, New York; 1982; p. 102.
31 "was the star . . . in assembly.": Quoted in Virginia Gardner, op cit, p. 16.
31 "sitting rather stiffly . . . for the curvature.": Interview with Ethel Rosenberg's childhood friend who chose to remain anonymous.
32 "She did have talent . . . 'angel face.' ": Quoted in Virginia Gardner, op cit, pp. 11–12.
33 "our wonderful little actress, Ethel.": ibid, p. 13.
33 According to one source . . .: Louis Nizer, op cit, p. 18.
33 "success on the stage . . . by the infant.": Otto Fenichel, "On Acting," *Psychoanalytic Quarterly*, Vol. 15 (1946); p. 148.
34 "despite her yearning . . . from self-erected barriers.": Quoted in Virginia Gardner, op cit, p. 16.
34 "[n]ot through some piddling . . . like her dad.": ibid.
35 "If God had meant for . . . music lessons.": ibid, p. 14.
36 "Ethel's family . . . make up for the rest.": ibid, p. 70.
36 "Actually I think . . . on corners selling apples.": ibid, pp. 13–14, 17.

CHAPTER THREE

39 The Depression had hit New York: See Dixon Wecter, *The Age of the Great Depression 1929–1941*; Macmillan, New York; 1952; and Robert Goldston, *The Great Depression*; Bobbs-Merrill, New York; 1968.
39 "[m]any persons left . . . of selling apples.": Cited in Robert Goldston, op cit, p. 49.
41 "who had responsible positions": Studs Terkel, *Hard Times*; Pantheon, New York; 1970; p. 391.
41 "It's funny . . . the world around us.": Quoted in *The Worker*, 9/27/53; p. 9.
42 "a home away from home . . . find me at home.": Interview with Paula Berger, 4/17/87.
42 "She had a passion . . . She worked very hard.": Interview with Maurice Blond, 4/17/87.
43 "Cowards die . . . of death but once.": Holworthy Hall and Robert Middlemass, *The Valiant*; copyright Harold E. Porter, New York; 1924.
43 "she wasn't even a liberal.": Quoted in *The Worker*, 9/27/53; p. 8.
44 "was about true artists . . . her family did.": ibid, p. 9.
45 "I think I know . . . than Lily Pons.": Quoted in *The Worker*, 10/4/53, p. 9.
45 "that she was not . . . to be different.": Quoted in Virginia Gardner, op cit, p. 21.
46 "very tough . . . they can handle it.": Quoted in *New York Times*, 2/22/80.
48 He would occasionally put them "under stop watch": Interview with Morris Fleissig, 3/23/85.
48 "for the men . . . arms almost dropped off.": Quoted in Virginia Gardner, op cit, p. 31–32.

48   an "air of comradery" existed among the workers.: Interview with Morris Fleissig, 3/23/85.

49   The Communist party, on the other hand: This figure reflects both the membership of the Communist party and its youth affiliate, the Young Communist League.

50   "Fewer High-Falutin . . . strikes, demonstrations, etc.": Quoted in Harvey Klehr, *The Heyday of American Communism*; Basic Books, New York; 1984; pp. 86, 87, 32.

50   "take their followers away from them": ibid, p. 100.

50   "For A Revolutionary . . . and The Peasants.": One of its common slogans of the period, quoted in Melech Epstein, *The Jew and Communism*; Trade Union Sponsoring Committee, New York; 1959; p. 263.

51   Communists and their "fellow travelers": Although "fellow traveler" became a term of derision used primarily by anti-Communists, in the early thirties it was used by Party members in a positive way. Joseph Freeman, editor of the CP affiliated *New Masses*, explained that the term was "coined in literary criticism to describe artists and writers who are not members of the Communist Party but who sympathize with the revolution and assist in their capacity as artists and writers." Quoted in Harvey Klehr, op cit, p. 76.

51   "the Jewish bourgeoisie . . . is our brother.": Quoted in Melech Epstein, op cit, p. 66.

52   "a pro-Jewish . . . in another country.": ibid, p. 171.

52   Great disillusionment and disaffection appeared . . .: ibid, p. 172.

52   Nationally, by the thirties . . .: See Paul Lyons, *Philadelphia Communists: 1936–1956*; Temple University Press, Philadelphia; 1982; p. 71, and Harvey Klehr, op cit, p. 163.

53   "Of course Ethel knew . . . no limit to her ambitions": Quoted in Virginia Gardner, op cit, p. 13.

CHAPTER FOUR

55   Although many of the politicized workers: Interview with Morris Fleissig, 3/23/85.

57   "[y]ou couldn't forget Ethel . . . in all she did.": Quoted in Virginia Gardner, op cit, p. 31.

58   Philip Gosseen charged . . .: *New York Times*, 8/31/35, p. 6.

58   The sense of comradery . . .: *The Worker*, 11/15/53, p. 7.

58   "started her speaking up against injustice.": ibid.

59   "You have a child . . . butt in any more.": Quoted in the *Herald Tribune*, 6/17/50.

59   "My parents objected . . . They felt lost.": Irving Howe, *A Margin of Hope*; Harcourt Brace Jovanovich, New York; 1982; pp. 13–14.

60   David Dubinsky, president of the ILGWU . . .: Quoted in the *New York Times*, 9/12/35.

61   Ethel "addressed the meeting . . . the right points.": Quoted in Virginia Gardner, op cit, p. 33.

63   "had no less than . . . out of personal friendship.": *The Worker*, 11/15/53.

63   "There is no allegation . . . membership and activities.": *Decisions and Order of the NLRB*, Vol. 1; 7 December 1935–1 July 1936; U.S. Government Printing Office, Washington, DC; 1936; p. 1016.

CHAPTER FIVE

66   "This meant a very heavy . . . I was sort of mad.": Quoted in Virginia Gardner, op cit, pp. 24–25.

67   "We were living in New York . . . could be openly expressed.": Irving Howe, **361**
A Margin of Hope, op cit, pp. 25–26.

67   "all not for us . . . are for us.": Paul Lyons, op cit; p. 23.

69   "Fascism is definitely . . . for the prevention of communism.": Quoted in
Raymond Gram Swing, Forerunners of American Fascism; Julian Messner,
New York; 1935; p. 148.

69   "about one-third of all Americans . . . 'Don't know.' ": Seymour Martin Lipset
and Earl Raab, The Politics of Unreason; Harper and Row, New York; 1970;
pp. 188, 189.

70   While most Jewish organizations refused to demonstrate: See Melech Epstein,
op cit, p. 294.

70   "Across the galleries, . . . twentieth-century Americanism.": New Masses,
7/7/36.

71   "a strong and consistent fight . . . a socialist path.": Quoted in James Weinstein, Ambiguous Legacy: The Left in American Politics; New Viewpoints,
New York; 1975; p. 74.

71   "That was the tremendous thing . . . Because I was a Communist.": "Selma
Gardinsky," quoted in Vivian Gornick, The Romance of American Communism; Basic Books, New York; 1977; p. 42 (emphasis in original).

72   "A city within a city . . . were the New Dealers . . .": Quoted in Vivian
Gornick, op cit, p. 119.

72   "[I]t was a total world . . . we had community.": "Norma Raymond" quoted
in Vivian Gornick, op cit, pp. 115–116.

73   By October 1936, the Party . . .: See Harvey Klehr, op cit, p. 297.

74   "to support the Spanish people . . . to the Spanish people.": Resolution of
the CPUSA, quoted in the New York Times, 8/11/36.

75   "Because you're suffering through the night . . . Arditi's "Il Bacio.": Interview
with Betty Birnbaum, 1/16/85.

75   But she had withdrawn from the Schola Cantorum . . .: Louis Nizer, op cit,
p. 20.

76   "never went out with boys . . . Ethel kept aloof.": Quoted in Virginia Gardner,
op cit, p. 16.

76   "We were very immature . . . it was about like going to the Astor roof": ibid,
pp. 19–20.

77   "simply had no interest . . . bigger and better things": Quoted in The Worker,
9/27/53, p. 9.

77   "One's mother spoke English . . . the tastes of the world.": Irving Howe,
World of Our Fathers, op cit, p. 262.

78   "Ciribiribin . . . kiss me again.": Copyright, The Boston Music Company,
1934.

CHAPTER SIX

80   "I remember . . . divide one among us.": Quoted in Virginia Gardner, op cit,
p. 40.

81   "In Europe we had to pay . . . you learn to cook.": ibid, p. 35.

82   "He had blond curls . . . a heart of stone.": ibid, p. 37.

83   "He loved it . . . 'you are overdoing it.' ": ibid, p. 46.

84   "She screamed and shouted . . . treated by others.": Interview with Ethel
Appel, 4/2/85.

84   "My father lost his head . . . she was very disturbing.": ibid.

85   "We started to get mad . . . be that religious.": Quoted in Virginia Gardner,
op cit, p. 44.

85   "I can see Julie's face . . . more than I liked.": ibid, pp. 48, 50.

85   "too gullible, too sincere": ibid.

362   86   "What is a belch? . . . explode into laughter.: Interview with Ethel Appel, 4/2/85.

86   "to make yet another . . . the leadership of the Communist Parties.": From the Comintern's "Open Letter to Social Democrats," 3/18/33; and *Theses and Decisions: Thirteenth Plenum of the E.C.C.I.*, 1934, cited in Harvey Klehr, op cit, pp. 98, 99.

86   Their aim was to free the West Coast labor leader . . .: Tom Mooney had been convicted of exploding a bomb that killed nine people in a Preparedness Day Parade in 1916.

87   According to Milty, his best friend . . .: FBI JR-HQ 1108, 5/27/51. In citing information from the FBI files on the Rosenberg case I use the same notation employed by Walter and Miriam Schneir in the second edition of their book *Invitation to An Inquest* (Pantheon, New York; 1983). I do this so there will be some consistency among various works that use the FBI records released under the Freedom of Information Act on the Rosenberg case. JR-HQ refers to the Julius and Ethel Rosenberg file from the FBI headquarters. The number following that notation refers to the FBI Serial Number, and the date following that refers to the date of the file.

87   "you can kiss . . . but for pennies.": Interview with Carl Marzani, 1/12/85.

87   As in the Mooney case . . .: In 1931 nine black men (the "boys") were convicted in Scottsboro, Alabama of raping two white women. Eight of the nine were sentenced to death, and one to life in prison.

88   "I suppose he chose engineering . . . than it did in mine.": Morton Sobell, *On Doing Time*; Charles Scribner's Sons, New York; 1974; pp. 32–33.

88   Furthermore, City probably had . . .: See Arthur Liebman, *Jews and the Left*; John Wiley and Sons, New York; 1979; pp. 371, 436.

89   "Jewish students from CCNY . . . in New York City.": ibid, pp. 367–368.

89   "significantly higher than at any other campus in America.": ibid.

89   "one of the largest . . . perhaps a dozen party members.": ibid, p. 436; Irving Howe, *A Margin of Hope*, op cit, p. 64.

89   "You could walk . . . entirely fresh cast of characters.": Irving Howe, *A Margin of Hope*, op cit, pp. 64–65.

90   "disinterested or incompetent.": Morton Sobell, op cit, p. 28.

90   Carl Marzani has termed "Communist territory": Interview with Carl Marzani, 1/12/85.

90   "Who could bother to study when next month the world was going to blow up?": Irving Howe, *A Margin of Hope*, op cit, p. 62.

92   He gave an alias . . .: FBI JR-HQ 730, 2/20/51 from Jerome Tartakow; and HR-HQ 1108, 5/27/51 from Milton Manes.

93   "Before he gave an opinion he would read his *Daily Worker*.": Interview with Harry Steingart, 11/23/84.

93   Julie loved to talk . . . his singleness of purpose which marked him.": Quoted in Virginia Gardner, op cit, pp. 54, 55.

94   Julie "could be hard . . . with complete firmness.": ibid, p. 54.

94   Morton Sobell remembers . . . with the Trotskyites there.": Interview with Morton Sobell, 1/15/85.

95   "Julie had that sense of history . . . when others were full of gloom.": Quoted in Virginia Gardner, op cit, p. 53.

96   "Never before . . . day and night from commonplace boredom.": Irving Howe, *A Margin of Hope*, op cit, p. 42.

CHAPTER SEVEN

98   "was a tall, good-looking boy . . . arm in arm.": Quoted in Virginia Gardner, op cit, p. 62.

99   "savior" . . . in her own right.": Interview with Saul Miller, 1/19/85.

99   "every time I went . . . I sort of lost interest.": Quoted in Virginia Gardner, op cit, p. 19.

100   "was very much involved with Julius to the exclusion of others.": Interview with Betty Birnbaum, 1/16/85.

100   "former intimate association with him diminished rapidly . . .": FBI JR-HQ 637, 1/31/51.

100   "Communist morality . . . decidedly wary of hedonism.": Paul Lyons, op cit, p. 98.

100   They "had a solution to all the world's problems" and vied: Interview with Betty Birnbaum, 1/16/85.

101   "withhold personal feelings . . . for privacy was the rule.": Paul Lyons, op cit, pp. 65–66.

101   "people were so involved . . . much about personal matters": Interview with Sylvia Steingart, 11/23/84.

101   "the less you knew, the less trouble you could make for somebody.": Interview with Betty Birnbaum, 1/16/85.

101   "contemporary life . . . in a way that mainstream culture did not.: Paul Lyons, op cit, p. 65.

101   "suppressed and despised . . . as frivolous as my *feelings*.": "Diane Vinson" quoted in Vivian Gornick, op cit, p. 231 (emphasis in original).

102   In 1950, Sam Greenglass . . .: FBI JR-HQ 493, 9/12/50. Further evidence of Sam's hostility to his sister is provided by Ethel's psychiatrist, other information cited in the FBI files, and the fact that Sam cut off relations with Ethel when she was 26 years old.

103   "as alike as two drops of water.": Interview with Betty Birnbaum, 1/16/85.

103   "*free and legal information* . . . not only for the rich.": *Working Woman*, 2/28/34, p. 15 (emphasis in original).

104   "Communist support for the family . . . characterizes capitalist society.": Quoted in the *Daily Worker*, 10/11/37.

104   In a national survey of 1,400 college students . . .: Cited in Dixon Wecter, op cit, p. 197.

104   Conversely, the Jewish culture in which all of Ethel and Julie's friends . . .: See Charlotte Baum, et al, op cit, pp. 7–8.

105   "the flush of radicalism . . . for most young Communists.": Paul Lyons, op cit, p. 112.

106   "They wanted to be married . . . They waited.": Quoted in Virginia Gardner, op cit, pp. 37–38.

107   "Going to school in the Thirties . . . this was redundant).": Morton Sobell, *On Doing Time*, op cit, p. 31.

107   "the rounds of the employment agencies . . . no Jews were wanted.": ibid, p. 33.

108   According to one Yiddish "memoirist": Cited in Irving Howe, *World of Our Fathers*, op cit, p. 221.

108   "would come and announce . . . a fuss over it.": Interview with Betty Birnbaum, 1/16/85.

108   On Sunday, 18 June 1939 . . .: In her courtroom testimony, Ethel responds to a question about who married her with, "I believe it was Rabbi Zin." The FBI files record that the rabbi's name was Saron Dyue and that his address was 258 East Fourth Street (FBI JR-HQ 107, 7/20/50). Louis Nizer reports, without citing any reference, that "[f]or the sake of their relatives, the ceremony was in a synagogue on the corner of Sheriff Street. Ethel's brother Bernard was best man, but her favorite younger brother, David was at her side" (*The Implosion Conspiracy*, op cit, p. 23).

364 108 The event was either so brief or so unimpressive . . .: Interview with Dave Roberts, 4/2/85; interview with Ethel Appel, 4/2/85.

108 "Always they were touching each other": Quoted in Virginia Gardner, op cit, p. 37.

108 "they couldn't wait to . . . in love they were.": Interview with Ethel Appel, 1/13/85.

CHAPTER EIGHT

113 "few liberal organizations . . . in the trade union movement.": Harvey Klehr, op cit, p. 386.

113 "the nation's press . . . campaign without hindrance.": ibid, p. 196.

113 "There were never more . . . followed the Party's direction.": ibid, p. 373.

114 "These younger Communists . . . for reforms took precedence.": ibid, pp. 217–218.

114 This semantic transformation signaled the Party's intention: Gene Dennis, "Some Questions Concerning the Democratic Front;" the *Communist*, June 1938.

114 "With fascism wiped off the face . . . rather rapid and painless.": Earl Browder, "Twenty Years of Soviet Power;" the *Communist*, November 1938.

115 "[t]here is as much chance . . . of the Chamber of Commerce": Quoted in Maurice Isserman, *Which Side Were You On?*; Wesleyan University Press, Middletown, CT; 1982; p. 18.

115 "chewing the dirty . . . this is a lie.": Quoted in Melech Epstein, op cit, p. 347.

115 "matter of taste . . . system of political views.": *Izvestia* editorial of 10/9/39, quoted in Melech Epstein, op cit, p. 355.

115 "The British empire . . . of the entire capitalist system.": William Foster, "World Socialism and the War," the *Communist*, June 1940.

115 "the same direction which Hitler gave for Germany in 1933.": Earl Browder, "The Domestic Reactionary Counterpart of the War Policy of the Bourgeoisie," the *Communist*, July 1940.

116 "between rival imperialisms . . . are equally guilty . . .": *Daily Worker*, 9/19/39.

116 Much of the liberal and socialist Jewish community . . .: See Melech Epstein, op cit, pp. 351–363.

117 "thing that stood out . . . their own solidarity.": Quoted in Maurice Isserman, op cit, p. 36.

117 "there are times when . . . seemingly compromising situations.": Paul Lyons, op cit, pp. 140–141.

117 "tended to live . . . prepared for that step.": Maurice Isserman, op cit, p. 36.

118 In addition to discussing what was taking place . . .: See Morton Sobell, *On Doing Time*, op cit, pp. 31–32.

119 "I first knew Julius . . . they were part of the working staff.": Interview with a former FAECT member who chooses to remain anonymous.

120 "stenographers, shipping clerks . . . and pool rooms.": *New York Post*, 6/20/38.

121 "a blend of radio-play . . . relatively mediocre actors.": Dixon Wecter, op cit, p. 263.

121 although there is no evidence that she . . .: See the *Worker*, 10/4/53.

122 "I dreamed a dream last night . . . this pressure loose ourselves.' ": Elsa Dixler, "The Woman Question: Women and the American Communist Party, 1929–1941," Ph.D. dissertation, Yale University; 1974; pp. 219, 221–222.

122 "Jewish women were expected . . . even in the home.": Quoted in Irving Howe, *World of Our Fathers*, op cit, p. 265.

123   "all the best radicals come out of the Yeshiva.": Interview with Betty Birnbaum, 1/16/85.

123   "this was rather unusual.": Interview with Sylvia Steingart, 11/13/84.

123   "He accepted the classical idea of democratic centralism": Interview with Harry Steingart, 11/23/84.

123   "Ethel accepted it . . . giving him good reasons and convincing him.": ibid.

123   "heartily supported it . . . were the Party's positions.": ibid.

124   "the CP . . . where girls were not educated and boys were.": Interview with Elizabeth Phillips, 1/26/85.

124   Although she would never be as politically active as her husband . . .: The FBI files state: "We have no information that she is a member of the Communist Party, although she definitely adheres to this philosophy." FBI JR-HQ 450X, 8/2/50.

125   "Marxist discussion group . . . of federal civil service employees.": Sol Tannenbaum quoted in FBI JR-HQ 951, 3/28/51.

125   We know this because a Miss S. Liggetts . . .: FBI JR-HQ 78, 6/20/50; and JR-HQ unrecorded after 469, 8/9/41.

125   "It is hard for those . . . the inner precincts from doubt . . .": Irving Howe, *A Margin of Hope*, op cit, pp. 71–72.

CHAPTER NINE

126   "a fantastic salary for any of us": Morton Sobell, *On Doing Time*, op cit, p. 33.

127   "[m]any employers . . . would be able to support them": Elsa Dixler, op cit, p. 204.

127   . . . the American people seemed to agree, as reflected in Gallup polls of the time.: In 1936 a Gallup poll indicated that 82% of all Americans believed that a wife should not work if her husband held a job. Cited in Elsa Dixler, ibid.

128   "who stated she was a distant relative . . . an employee of the Census Bureau.": FBI JR-HQ x, 5/25/40.

128   Although Milty had never been attracted to the Party . . .: FBI JR-HQ 89, 7/18/50.

129   "model American town of the future.": *Life* magazine, 11/15/37.

130   "urging the United States to . . . arsenal of democracy.": Maurice Isserman, op cit, p. 87.

131   "He was not always cautious . . . of his fellow workers.": Interview with former FAECT member who chooses to remain anonymous.

131   He "shot off his mouth.": Interview with another former FAECT member who chooses to remain anonymous.

131   "was very, very outspoken . . . whoever you were working for.": Interview with Philip Salaff, 4/8/85.

131   "[e]ven if [Ethel] did sign a petition . . . her views are similar to mine [sic] own.": FBI JR-HQ unrecorded after 76, 4/11/41.

132   "I never took part in . . . distribution of Communist literature.": ibid.

132   "I asked my wife . . . I know that she is no Communist.": ibid.

133   "I . . . talked it over with my wife . . . they have not sent me away on any work.": ibid.

134   "the poorest housekeeper . . . was a complete mess": FBI JR-HQ unrecorded after 2307, 3/20/57.

134   "thumbing through birthday cards . . . in all honesty send that one.' ": Quoted in Virginia Gardner, op cit, p. 68.

134   "He was very much in love . . . would always look to one another.": Interview with Harry Steingart, 11/23/84.

134 "All was harmony . . . both of them doing work.": Interview with former FAECT member who chooses to remain anonymous.

135 "Julie and Ethel were so truly united . . . with an added vitality.": Quoted in Virginia Gardner, op cit, p. 65.

135 Julie was a "sensitive" man . . . his love for people was overwhelming.": ibid.

135 "He was always worrying . . . if there were children involved.": Interview with former neighbor of the Rosenbergs who chooses to remain anonymous.

135 His reaction to a black prisoner's unjust execution . . .: The prisoner was Willie McGee.

135 Harry Steingart was impressed . . . for her empathic understanding of her husband.: Interview with Harry Steingart, 11/23/84.

135 "She was a warm human being . . . your problems are and so on.": ibid.

135 "Ethel radiated a warmth one didn't find in many people.": Morton Sobell, *On Doing Time*, op cit, p. 45.

135 She was "very solicitous . . . that sort of thing.": Interview with Carl Marzani, 1/12/85.

135 Ethel "was amazingly soft and warm . . . so thoughtful, very solicitous.": Interview with Betty Birnbaum, 1/16/85.

135 "She was quite a dame . . . you felt she meant it.": Interview with former FAECT member who chooses to remain anonymous.

136 "They didn't have any money . . . They were young and carefree then.": Quoted in Virginia Gardner, op cit, p. 63.

136 McNutt apparently had been a member of the YCL . . .: See Harvey Klehr, op cit, pp. 320–321.

137 "the Communists responded as if . . . the war would attract considerable public support.": Maurice Isserman, op cit, pp. 103, 111.

137 "I assume the Party sent her . . . You never ask if someone's in the CP.": Interview with Carl Marzani, 1/12/85.

138 The Conference was supposedly composed of some 296 organizations, groups, societies and clubs: See *Daily Worker*, 10/27/41.

138 "a shovelful of earth over the grave which Hitler and his crowd dug for themselves": Maurice Isserman, op cit, p. 124.

139 "100,000 East Siders cheered . . . to Hitler and his appeaser pals.": *Daily Worker*, 9/26/41.

139 "she mothered me to death": Interview with Carl Marzani, 1/12/85.

139 "very cheerful, very competent . . . what are women for?": ibid.

139 "When I tell you that I had no idea . . . he never mentioned it.": ibid.

140 One of her closest friends from this period . . .: Interview with Sylvia Steingart, 11/13/84.

140 "Ethel was always worrying . . . she just had an ordinary American childhood.": Quoted in Virginia Gardner, op cit, p. 63.

140 "beautiful coloratura soprano.": Interview with Sylvia Steingart, 11/13/84.

140 "loved to sing . . . a few operatic airs.": Interview with former FAECT member who chooses to remain anonymous.

140 "I am sure she felt no regret . . . simply a joy to her.": Quoted in Virginia Gardner, op cit, p. 64.

141 "Ethel was working night and day at the Defense Council.": ibid, p. 65.

142 "the one book above all to read on Russia": Quoted in Maurice Isserman, op cit, p. 128.

144 "a big event for them . . . walking on the clouds.": Interview with former neighbor of the Rosenbergs who chooses to remain anonymous.

144 "I would let you use my furniture . . . have the use of the furniture.": Trial Transcript, op cit, p. 1054.

CHAPTER TEN

146 His new job consisted in: FBI JR-HQ 371, 10/18/44.
148 Julie and Mark had had a rather serious disagreement, the cause of which
remains unclear.: The FBI records are of little help in understanding the nature
of this quarrel. Page (aka Pogarsky) was to have "obtained some equipment
for Julius Rosenberg at one time several years ago [this in 1950], and there
had been a fight over that matter, the result of which was that he [Page]
discontinued his relationship with Julius Rosenberg." FBI JR-HQ unrecorded
after 603, 12/6/50. When I personally tried to contact the Pages, they would
not answer my letters and hung up on me when I telephoned.
148 the Rosenbergs refrained from discussing politics with their families: Interview
with Ethel Appel, 1/13/85.
149 "wasn't the usual thing . . . every week in and week out.": Trial Transcript,
op cit, p. 1326.
149 "twenty-four hours a day . . . I couldn't stand it.": Interview with Ethel Appel,
1/13/85.
150 "Michael was sleeping . . . she seemed quite harried then.": Interview with
Betty Birnbaum, 1/16/85.
150 "A woman took a leave . . . did not mean anything to anyone.' ": Robert
Shaffer, "Women and the Communist Party, USA, 1930–1940"; Socialist
Review, Vol. 9, No. 3 (1976); p. 111.
151 For all her rebelliousness, Ethel in many ways longed for her mother's approval
and love.: This interpretation was confirmed through interview with Saul Miller,
1/19/85.
152 "Ethel couldn't stand to . . . suffer in any way.' ": Quoted in Virginia Gardner,
op cit, p. 69.
152 "He was such a disturbing child . . . But Ethel was different.": Interview with
Ethel Appel, 1/13/85.
152 "was ubiquitous . . . 'the child's best interest.' ": Terry Strathman, "From the
Quotidian to the Utopian: Child Rearing Literature in America, 1926–1946,"
Berkeley Journal of Sociology, Vol. 29 (1984), p. 2.
152 "failure on the part of the parent . . . than the child's.": Parents' Magazine,
1947, quoted in Strathman, op cit, p. 10.
153 According to Morton Sobell, it was Gesell's book . . .: Interview with Morton
Sobell, 1/15/85.
153 "the summaries then become standards of reference . . . the simple method
of best fit.": Arnold Gesell, The First Five Years of Life; Harper and Row, New
York; 1940; p. 17.
153 Like most new mothers searching for help . . .: That Ethel continued to sub-
scribe to Parents' Magazine even throughout her imprisonment at Sing Sing
testifies to the fact that she must have found it helpful.
154 Some have suggested that this was Ethel's relationship to the Communist party.:
cf Leslie Fiedler, op cit; Robert Warshow, op cit; author's interview with
Miriam Moskowitz, 4/9/85.
154 According to Elizabeth Phillips . . . "It was kind of the misrepresentation of
Spock," Phillips notes.: Interview with Elizabeth Phillips, 1/26/85.
154 "child raising from a problem . . . to be defended against theirs.": Daniel
Beekman, The Mechanical Baby; Lawrence Hill and Company, Westport, CT;
1977; p. 173.
154 "The spirit and organization of the family . . . through guidance and understanding.": Quoted in ibid, p. 174.

368   155   "She tried to get on a 'baby-sitter' . . . to make the evening good": Interview with Elizabeth Phillips, 1/26/85.

155   "One day—the boys . . . So she was a very peculiar girl.": Interview with Annette Kardon, 5/23/85.

156   "felt she was raised . . . differently than she had been raised.": Interview with Elizabeth Phillips, 1/26/85.

156   In many ways, Ethel continued to see her mother as a "witch": Interview with Saul Miller, 1/19/85.

156   "she had enormously high standards" by which she judged her success as a parent.: Interview with Elizabeth Phillips, 1/26/85.

156   "never did I see such patience . . . 'play with us like Ethel does.' ": Quoted in Virginia Gardner, op cit, pp. 68–69.

156   "I had a tremendous sense of being . . . a very tense child.": Michael Meeropol quoted in Robert and Michael Meeropol, *We Are Your Sons*; University of Illinois Press, Urbana and Chicago; 1986; pp. 91–92, 94–95.

156   Nonetheless, Julie referred repeatedly to her seething anger . . .: cf interview with Saul Miller, 1/19/85; and Michael Meeropol, op cit, p. 95.

158   "In every nursery there are ghosts . . . with another set of characters.": Selma Fraiberg, Edna Adelson, and Vivian Shapiro, "Ghosts in the Nursery: A Psychoanalytic Approach to the Problems of Impaired Infant-Mother Relationships"; *Journal of the American Academy of Child Psychiatry*, Vol. 14, No. 3 (1975); p. 287. I am grateful to Mary Margaret McClure for bringing this to my attention.

158   "the Industrial Division headquarters of the Party issued transfer cards to neighborhood units": Cited in Ronald Radosh and Joyce Milton, *The Rosenberg File*; Holt, Rinehart and Winston, New York; 1983; p. 496.

159   She continued to read and follow the *Daily Worker* . . .: See, for example, Ruth Greenglass's letter of 1/10/44 to David Greenglass, cited in Radosh and Milton, op cit, p. 63.

160   Ethel adamantly believed that "children were more important than the house": Neighbor at Knickerbocker Village, quoted in Virginia Gardner, op cit, p. 68.

160   "took no care of their home . . . [it] was very upset and untidy.": FBI JR-HQ 1258, 2/29/52.

160   "was literally a mother 24 hours out of every 24.": Neighbor at Knickerbocker Village, quoted in Virginia Gardner, op cit, p. 67.

161   she "suffered in quiet.": Interview with Ethel Appel, 1/13/85.

161   He cried "24 hours a day.": ibid.

161   "He would throw things around . . . because of Michael's behavior.": ibid.

161   "He came to Budd Lake once . . . She was a good daughter.": ibid.

162   "originated in a series of lectures . . . from the New School of Social Research in New York.": Edith Buxbaum, *Your Child Makes Sense*; International Universities Press, New York; 1949; p. xi.

162   "the Vienna Institute of Psychoanalysis . . . in which I participated.": ibid.

163   "Although we tend to think . . . of the errors brought on by irrational fears.": ibid, pp. 99, 63, 201.

164   "[u]nfortunately, misinterpreting these theories . . . to be more anxious rather than less.": Daniel Beekman, op cit, p. 190.

164   A. Well, it so happens that I have had . . . the winter between the time he was a year and a half to two.: Trial Transcript, op cit, pp. 1324–1326.

166   "emphasis on party members living like 'ordinary workers' . . .: James Weinstein, *Ambiguous Legacy*; New Viewpoints, New York; 1975; p. 163.

CHAPTER ELEVEN

167   Julie invested between $1,000 and $1,500 in the Yorktown Development.: FBI JR-HQ 922, 3/14/51.

169 "I am not now, and never have been . . . the slightest basis in fact.": Trial **369**
Transcript, op cit, p. 1185.

169 "consequence of the CP's wartime shortage of experienced cadres . . . who
show possibilities for development.' ": Maurice Isserman, op cit, pp. 148–
149.

169 According to Ronald Radosh and Joyce Milton . . .: Radosh and Milton, op
cit, p. 498.

170 in April, Julie took the train to Washington to see Samuel Dickstein in person
. . .: For a description of this experience in Julie's own words, see the Trial
Transcript, op cit, pp. 1154–1156.

171 Eleven months earlier, Earl Browder had orchestrated this metamorphosis
. . .: Earl Browder, *Teheran and America, Perspectives and Tasks*; Workers
Library, New York; 1944; pp. 5–41 passim.

171 "conspires or acts to subvert, undermine, weaken or overthrow any or all
institutions of American democracy.": Quoted in Maurice Isserman, op cit,
p. 204.

171 "traditions of Washington, Jefferson, Paine, Jackson and Lincoln.": ibid,
p. 205.

171 "tried for a year to drum up activity . . . was put up on it.": Quoted in Virginia
Gardner, op cit, p. 59.

174 "[f]or some, service in the armed forces . . . in abstract or romantic terms.":
Maurice Isserman, op cit, p. 152.

175 "despite our recognition of these changing cultural patterns . . . of community
life and consumption.": Steve Nelson, James R. Barrett, Rob Ruck, *Steve
Nelson, American Radical*; University of Pittsburgh Press, Pittsburgh, PA; 1981;
pp. 284–285.

175 Between mid-1944 and the beginning of 1946, 50,000 members had left the
Communist Party, USA.: Joseph R. Starobin, *American Communism in Crisis,
1943–1957*; Harvard University Press, Cambridge, MA; 1972; p. 113.

176 He was not beyond exaggerating his abilities . . .: FBI JR-HQ 1259, 3/18/52.

176 "wherever he went there was a cloud over him, a shadow over him . . . he
could not get employment.": Interview with Philip Salaff, 4/8/85.

177 Neither Dave nor Ruth evidenced much understanding of Marxism . . .: For
excellent evidence of this, see the correspondence of David and Ruth Greenglass excerpted in Radosh and Milton, op cit, pp. 58–66.

177 "Please don't delay in sending me the Browder speech . . . Find out from
Ethel what she and Julie think about it.": Cited in Radosh and Milton, op cit,
p. 63.

177 "a classified top secrecy project . . . except maybe Julie.": Cited in Radosh
and Milton, op cit, p. 66.

177 "I'll raise the red flag yet so don't worry about the future.": Cited in Radosh
and Milton, op cit, p. 60.

178 "I most certainly will be glad . . . Count me in . . .": Cited in Radosh and
Milton, op cit, p. 66. It is interesting to note that Radosh and Milton mistakenly
assert that David's reference to "the community project that Julius and his
friends have in mind" is espionage.

179 "The axe must be applied . . . must be systematically weakened and eventually
broken.": Quoted in Joseph Starobin, op cit, p. 126.

180 "It happened that in 1946 or '47, I was in a job . . . She pleaded with him
to "do what you can to help Julie in the business.": Interview with a former
member of FAECT who chooses to remain anonymous.

180 "The few times we did see him . . . from the business at that time.": Interview
with another former member of FAECT who chooses to remain anonymous.

181 Ethel "appeared to have less than the majority of them.": FBI JR-HQ 1258,
2/29/52.

181 The Rosenbergs were forced to start asking for credit from the Village Grocery . . .: FBI JR-HQ 503, 9/8/50.

181 Mrs. Berger and another neighbor report that Ethel occasionally borrowed . . .: FBI JR-HQ 1258, 2/29/52.

181 "just moved over to the hospital . . . that is where you must be.' ": Quoted in Virginia Gardner, op cit, p. 39.

182 Shortly before she went into the hospital, for example, she went to the expense of actually recording her voice . . .: The FBI confiscated this recording disc on 17 July 1950. That agency has never released it, although it is the only known recording of Ethel's voice.

CHAPTER TWELVE

183 "bright, fragile child . . . ten or fifteen pages.": Interview with a former member of FAECT who chooses to remain anonymous.

183 "Ethel would stop and talk . . . Ethel would permit Michael to light a fire.": FBI JR-HQ 1258, 2/29/52.

184 "that Michael was allowed to do anything that he cared to.": ibid.

184 "could do anything he pleased . . . discipline over him.": ibid.

184 "would play the phonograph as late . . . as little to do with them as possible.": FBI JR-HQ 922, 3/14/51.

184 "It was not easy to be friendly . . . with her neighbors.": FBI JR-HQ 1258, 2/29/52.

184 Ethel "wasn't a person who . . . deign to talk to us.": Interview with Annette Kardon, 5/23/85.

184 "nice but withdrawn . . . through a barrier there.": Interview with Ray Malikin, 3/30/85.

185 "Steel yourself to family and friends . . . to their comments.": Dorothy V. Whipple, "Self-Demand Babies," Parents' Magazine; December 1946; p. 125.

185 "was a contented child.": Interview with Ethel Appel, 1/13/85.

185 "very emotionally disturbed for quite a number of years.": Trial Transcript, op cit, p. 1195.

185 "One of the three times that I was over . . . on the question of raising children.": Interview with Helen Sobell, 9/12/84.

186 "was more than normal preoccupation . . . about whether she was bringing them up right.": Interview with Morton Sobell, 1/15/85.

186 "Party culture always eschewed . . . the rational, the material, or the political.": Paul Lyons, op cit, p. 66.

187 Reputed by the FBI to be a Party leader: FBI JR-HQ 351, 8/15/50.

188 so much so that she had begun to think of giving him up to foster care.: Ethel admitted this to her psychiatrist when she first went to see him in 1949. Interview with Saul Miller, 1/19/85.

188 Ethel declared on her application to the clinic . . .: FBI JR-HQ 503, 9/8/50.

189 "I saw him for the first treatment session . . . became enormously tense and not communicate.": Interview with Elizabeth Phillips, 1/26/85.

189 "very easy to relate to and . . . was looking for parental approval.": ibid.

190 "set no boundaries . . . I can't remember her talking about much that was autonomously hers.": ibid.

191 "[M]aterialism cannot conceive and does not accept . . . to the instinct theory . . .": Joseph Wortis, Soviet Psychiatry; Williams and Wilkins, New York; 1950; p. 71.

191 "It must be stated directly that the only true evaluation . . . to wholesome psychological development.": Quoted in ibid, pp. 76, 71.

191 "a generation taught by the Party . . . as a 'bourgeois' phenomenon.": Paul Lyons, op cit, p. 179.

192   "in the pages of the *Daily Worker* . . . thought except Pavlov's.": Joseph   **371**
Starobin, op cit, p. 203.

192   "never discussed anything . . . you felt guilty, confused, trivial.": Quoted in
Vivian Gornick, op cit, p. 58.

193   The psychiatrist Ethel went to see . . .: Although he took notes on their therapy
sessions, Miller destroyed every record pertaining to her treatment after she
was arrested so he would have nothing to give the FBI. The following then is
based on his recollection of their treatment together.

193   "She couldn't control him . . . she felt guilty about this.": Interview with Saul
Miller, 1/19/85.

193   "She blamed herself for not being a good mother; she believed she handled
Michael nastily,": ibid.

193   From the start, Ethel was a "good patient." . . . As with Mrs. Phillips, Ethel
never spoke to Dr. Miller about politics or anything having to do with the
Communist party. According to him, "she knew he knew she was in the CP.":
All of the above quotations are from ibid.

194   "she had a lot of faith in psychiatry,": Interview with Elizabeth Phillips,
1/26/85.

194   [These] times made more of an impression on me . . . you couldn't get through
a barrier there.: Interview with Ray Malikin, 3/30/85. This mysterious behavior
was later taken by some of Ethel's neighbors as evidence that she was involved
in espionage.

195   Yet there is no evidence that she confided this news to any of her family or
friends either.: Interview with Saul Miller, 1/19/85; interview with Ethel Appel,
1/13/85.

CHAPTER THIRTEEN

196   "Red Fascism . . . fraternal orders, and the government itself.": David M.
Oshinsky, *A Conspiracy So Immense*; The Free Press, New York; 1983;
p. 96.

197   the Attorney General asserted that there were "many Communists in America
. . . the germs of death for society.": Quoted in ibid, p. 97.

198   J. Edgar Hoover announced in May 1947 . . .: See ibid, p. 96.

198   "dramatic round-up of dozens of Communist leaders and fellow-travellers.":
Quoted in Joseph Starobin, op cit, p. 172.

199   "Those members who remained . . . *they went through agony from within*.":
ibid, pp. 197–198 (emphasis in original).

200   Thousands more were pushed out . . .: See ibid, p. 203.

200   "A Party member who visited her sister . . . suspicion had become the mark
of Cain.": Vivian Gornick, op cit, p. 170.

200   It does seem, however, that they agreed with the Party's line . . .: This is
reflected in both their published and unpublished prison correspondence and
interviews conducted by the author.

201   "I wasn't reading the *Worker* regularly . . . carrying a possible five year
sentence.": Morton Sobell, *On Doing Time*, op cit, p. 53.

203   "[E]nvied Ethel's modern apartment . . . in a house which had an elevator.":
John Wexley, *The Judgment of Julius and Ethel Rosenberg*; Ballantine Books,
New York; 1977; p. 109.

203   "most of the hard work," . . . "handed out orders instead of obtaining any.":
ibid.

203   "David decided to go to night school . . . and finally David quit school because
of that.": Trial Transcript, op cit, p. 1105.

203   "You are taking advantage of my husband . . . You should let him go to
school.": ibid, p. 1106.

204 He took a superior attitude toward his wife's youngest brother . . .: See ibid, p. 1101 for evidence of this.

204 she would evince "patient indulgence" toward what he did . . .: Interview with Helen Sobell, 9/12/84.

204 "were not paying attention to the shop . . . and he was tired of the whole business.": Trial Transcript, op cit, p. 764.

205 "it was common knowledge that Ruthie always nagged Davey about money.": ibid, p. 1369.

206 The family's income for 1948 was . . .: FBI JR-HQ 438, 8/16/50.

206 "be King Tut or nothing.": Bernard Greenglass quoted in Radosh and Milton, op cit, p. 95.

206 "She said I was taking advantage of him . . . we will never make a living.": Trial Transcript, op cit, pp. 1244–1245.

206 "[t]here were quarrels of every type . . . over the way the outside was run.": ibid, p. 664.

207 "Julius called me at work . . . he would repay me as soon as he could.": Morton Sobell, On Doing Time, op cit, pp. 57–58.

207 "being paid commensurate with the work done . . .": Trial Transcript, op cit, p. 774.

208 He warned his few employees that they would receive no vacations . . .: See Walter and Miriam Schneir, Invitation To an Inquest; Pantheon, New York; 1983; p. 79.

208 "You can't get blood out of a stone," he argued.: Trial Transcript, op cit, p. 1119.

208 "I kept telling him that . . . a chance to get it.": ibid, p. 673.

208 "My wife wanted $2000 . . . it was lost money.": FBI JR-HQ 328, 8/7/50.

208 "he finally agreed that he would give me $1000 . . . when he will have the money available.": Trial Transcript, op cit, p. 670.

209 "was tied up with his wife dying in the hospital.": ibid, p. 1264.

209 "The radio episode concerned bandits . . . "I want a lawyer!": Michael Meeropol, We Are Your Sons, op cit, p. 5.

210 She did what she was told but . . .: The FBI termed this "a typical Communist remonstrance." FBI JR-HQ 97, 7/17/50.

210 "No, not tonight.": Michael Meeropol, We Are Your Sons, op cit, p. 5.

CHAPTER FOURTEEN

212 "[N]o enduring monopoly of the atomic bomb. . . . any detailed technical information from us.": Quoted in William Reuben, The Atom Spy Hoax; op cit, p. 2.

213 One of the pivotal figures in the bomb's development . . .: See ibid, p. 4.

213 The Association of Oak Ridge Scientists issued their own statement . . .: Cited in ibid, p. 14.

213 While much specific information was lacking . . .: See ibid, p. 3.

213 "of those groups and movements . . . for the benefit of a foreign power.": House Committee on Un-American Activities Annual Report; Government Printing Office, Washington, DC; 12/31/48; pp. 2–3.

214 J. Parnell Thomas, the committee's chair . . .: J. Parnell Thomas, "Russia Grabs Our Inventions," American, June 1947; and J. Parnell Thomas, "Reds in Our Atom-Bomb Plants," Liberty, 6/21/47.

214 "had stolen vital atomic secrets from the heart of the atomic bomb project at Los Alamos.": Quoted in William Reuben, The Atom Spy Hoax; op cit, p. 125.

214 "how the atom bomb secret was handed over to the Reds,": New York Sun, 8/18/48.

214 "succeeded finally in kicking over . . . rooted in American folklore.": William **373**
   Reuben, *The Atom Spy Hoax*, op cit, pp. 140–141.

214 By the fall, HUAC had charged . . . such representation is palpably at variance
   with the facts, is un-American.": House Committee on Un-American Activities
   Report on Soviet Espionage Activities in Connection with the Atom Bomb;
   Government Printing Office, Washington, D.C.; 9/28/48.

215 "I myself believed . . . to have stolen it from us.": Both Morrison's and
   Brennan's quotes are from Alvin H. Goldstein, *The Unquiet Death of Julius
   and Ethel Rosenberg*; Lawrence Hill and Co., New York; 1975; unpaginated.

215 "[e]ver since atomic energy . . . into account by us.": Quoted in the *New
   York Times*, 9/24/49.

215 HUAC member Congressman Richard Nixon claimed . . . agents of the Russian
   government.": Quoted in New York *Journal-American*, 9/24/49.

216 "The Russians undoubtedly gained . . . a network of spies . . .": Quoted in
   William Reuben, *The Atom Spy Hoax*; op cit, p. 151.

216 "in the national folklore, considered to have more interest in atomic espionage
   than socialism.": William Reuben, *The Atom Spy Hoax*, op cit, p. 156.

217 "was one of the blackest days . . . we ever had.": *Time*, 2/13/50.

217 According to J. Edgar Hoover . . . simply had to be found.": J. Edgar Hoover,
   "The Crime of the Century," *Reader's Digest*, May 1951, p. 159.

217 "A soldier, non-commissioned, . . . $500 for the information obtained.": This
   is from the FBI's file on Harry Gold's Philadelphia interrogation, 6/1/50.

217 Gold recalled that his Los Alamos source had been . . .: ibid.

218 "I expect to have my day in court . . . I never saw you guys.": FBI DG-HQ
   179, 6/15/50.

218 "under no circumstances would he testify against Rosenberg.": Quoted in
   Walter and Miriam Schneir, op cit, p. 453.

219 "Hell, no!": Quoted in Radosh and Milton, op cit, p. 85.

219 "[They came] before we had finished dressing the children . . . because that
   is the first I realized he had been officially arrested . . .": Trial Transcript, op
   cit, pp. 1137–1141.

221 According to Bloch . . . before a grand jury.": Cited in Virginia Gardner, op
   cit, pp. 95, 96.

221 As Bloch returned to his apartment . . .: Cited in John Wexley, op cit, p. 135.

221 Julius Rosenberg was to maintain until his death . . . take some things from
   the Army.": Trial Transcript, op cit, pp. 1266, 1253, 1219.

222 Ethel argued that "if Davey is in some . . . assistance to them.": Trial Transcript,
   op cit, p. 1137.

222 "cooperating to provide the authorities with a full account of his activities.":
   Quoted in William Reuben, *The Atom Spy Hoax*, op cit, p. 252.

222 She informed her attorneys on 18 June that . . . ascertained there was no such
   Company.": Quoted in John Wexley, op cit, p. 540.

223 According to Pitt's shop foreman . . .: FBI JR-HQ 176, 7/26/50.

223 On that day, the Rosenbergs closed the checking account . . .: FBI JR-HQ
   107, 7/20/50.

223 They redeemed $770.75 worth of Series E bonds they held: ibid.

223 Julius had the attorney who helped with matters relating to his business . . .
   "were contemplating a trip.": FBI JR-HQ 503, 9/8/50.

223 When Julius returned to work . . . he owned with a group in Westchester
   County for $2,500.: ibid.

224 "Helen and I had both committed perjury when we signed the 'loyalty oaths'
   . . . We left from La Guardia Thursday, on an evening flight.": Morton Sobell,
   On Doing Time, op cit, pp. 59–62.

225 "vigilante action to combat Communism through . . . grass-roots committees,
   in every American town,": Quoted in David M. Oshinsky, op cit, p. 104.

225   "The only sensible and courageous way . . . to death all persons convicted of such.": Quoted from New York *Journal-American*, 6/29/50.

225   Senator John McClellan argued that . . . We would become the first aggressors for peace," he proclaimed.: Quoted in David M. Oshinsky, op cit, p. 172.

226   When told that Gold claimed David had been given $500 . . . he would commit suicide.: Cited in Radosh and Milton, op cit, p. 81.

226   The confession that David Greenglass signed at approximately 1:30 A.M. was brief and to the point . . . by Julius Rosenberg while he was in New York City on furlough.: See Walter and Miriam Schneir, op cit, pp. 452–453.

227   "It was all in my mind . . . the same as I had a conversation.": Quoted in Radosh and Milton, op cit, p. 88.

227   When he made his initial confession, however, he was under no such pressure, for Ruth was under no suspicion.: We probably will never know, however, exactly what sort of pressure the FBI placed on David Greenglass before he signed his confession, for, as Michael Meeropol has pointed out, "the most important way to get at [the truth] is the issue of the very first time the FBI interviews anybody . . . [yet] all the agents' handwritten logged notes of the twelve hour grilling they gave David Greenglass before they got him to sign that first statement that implicated my father . . . were destroyed." *Were the Rosenbergs Framed?*, a transcript of a public debate held 10/20/83 at Town Hall, New York City; available through The Nation Institute, New York; p. 82.

227   In answering questions about his background . . . "capitalism is not the best possible system.": Cited in Walter and Miriam Schneir, op cit, p. 451.

228   In an interoffice memo . . . in good spirits during the whole period.": Cited in ibid, p. 453.

228   "slob," as his own attorney referred to him: Cited in ibid, p. 456.

229   "the great role Russia was playing . . . if I would contribute in this way.": Quoted in the FBI's Max Elitcher headquarters file no. 75, 7/20/50.

229   Tartakow supplied details about Julius Rosenberg's personal life to the FBI with which only someone who knew him intimately could be familiar.: For example he knew when and where Julie and Ethel met; some of Julie's political activity as a teenager; how Ethel and her mother had an extremely strained relationship, etc. See FBI JR-HQ 639, 1/3/51; 730, 2/20/51; 901, 3/16/51.

229   "he played the game and lost, and would have to take the results.": FBI JR-HQ 639, 1/3/51.

229   An informant of indisputable reliability, however, recently came forth . . . "he knows he's not suppose to come here.": When Ronald Radosh interviewed Finestone in 1978 he responded to Weinstein's recollection by saying: "I think Jim is fantasizing. I never said to Jim, 'I told him never to come here.' That is pure fantasy." Weinstein, he added, was simply "remembering things I just don't remember." Both Weinstein and Finestone are quoted in Radosh and Milton, op cit, p. 313. Since Weinstein has no imaginable motive for "fantasizing" this incident, whereas Finestone has ample reason for denying it ever took place, and since even the Rosenbergs' most ardent supporters have never questioned Weinstein's recollection due, I imagine, to his stature in intellectual and left political circles, I am convinced James Weinstein is telling the truth.

231   "ridiculous . . . baby drawing, it doesn't tell you anything," according to Victor Weisskopf: Quoted in Alvin H. Goldstein, op cit, unpaginated.

231   "uselessly crude," the value of which would be "absolutely nil" to the Soviets.: Quoted in ibid.

231   "It is not possible in any technologically useful way . . . on a single sheet of paper.": Quoted in Walter and Miriam Schneir, op cit, p. 464.

231   "They said this was the secret of the atom bomb . . . It's an industry, not a recipe.": Quoted in Alvin H. Goldstein, op cit, unpaginated.

232 "I turned the information over to John . . . had not been of very much consequence at all.": Quoted in ibid.

232 "he has not had any conversations with his brother-in-law, Julius Rosenberg, concerning Soviet espionage.": Quoted in Walter and Miriam Schneir, op cit, p. 470.

233 In Gold's stated opinion . . .: See William Reuben, *The Atom Spy Hoax*, op cit, p. 259; and Radosh and Milton, op cit, p. 25.

233 "Julius said . . . other than just his membership in the Communisty Party . . .": Trial Transcript, op cit, p. 679.

234 "enormous dependence . . . about their relationship.": Interview with Elizabeth Phillips, 1/26/85.

234 "before Julius was arrested . . . I mean it wasn't just a surprise.": ibid.

234 "one day we were coming from the subway . . . and she knew I'd have trouble.": Interview with Annette Kardon, 5/23/85.

234 " 'Ethel, how glad I am to see you . . . Shortly thereafter Betty read in the newspapers that Julius Rosenberg had been arrested.: Interview with Betty Birnbaum, 1/16/85.

235 he was a victim of the "hysteria of the Cold War.": Quoted in William Reuben, *The Atom Spy Hoax*, op cit, p. 346.

235 As the *New York Journal-American* reported . . .: In in its issue of 6/23/50.

235 According to Ronald Radosh . . . with a "long discussion of J.R.": Radosh and Milton, op cit, p. 86.

238 Well, I came to my mother's house . . . So we began to walk, she and I, with the carriage, around the block . . .": Trial Transcript, op cit, pp. 1338–1339.

238 At this point Ruth claims . . .: ibid, p. 714.

239 everybody would stand a better chance . . .": ibid, p. 714.

239 "Are you and Davey really mixed up in this horrible mess?" ibid, p. 1339.

239 according to Radosh and Milton was "acting on orders from Rogge": Radosh and Milton, op cit, p. 96.

239 "we have hired a lawyer . . . "Well, now you have heard it and it is the truth." Trial Transcript, op cit, pp. 1339–1340.

CHAPTER FIFTEEN

243 "I wasn't concerned . . . because I wasn't guilty of any crime.": Trial Transcript, op cit, p. 1203.

244 "They came and got Julius the day after my brother" . . . she didn't think her husband or her brother was guilty: "Doubts FBI Charge: Wife Defends A Spy Suspect," *New York Journal-American*, 7/17/50.

245 to whom she confessed that she was "terribly worried.": Interview with Elizabeth Phillips, 1/26/85.

245 "he felt that his professional reputation would be affected.": FBI JR-HQ 438, 8/16/50.

246 "when Ethel was riding in the elevator . . . Nobody would speak to Ethel after Julius was arrested.": FBI JR-HQ 1258, 2/29/52.

246 "plain beyond all doubt . . . to conquer independent nations.": Quoted in *New York Times*, 7/20/50.

247 On the very day that Julie was arrested, Assistant Attorney General James McInerney requested . . .: FBI JR-HQ 188, 7/17/50.

247 "should consider every possible means . . . in order that charges be placed against her, if possible.": ibid.

247 "There is no question but that . . . his wife might serve as a lever in this matter.": FBI JR-HQ 97, 7/19/50.

247 "she was not cooperative . . . over her conduct and were anxious to indict.": FBI JR-HQ 433X1, 8/8/50.

248 "If you don't talk, you're gonna burn . . . I know he didn't do those things.":
Interview with Ethel Appel, 1/13/85.

248 Ethel precipitously stopped seeing her psychiatrist . . . be in touch and then
hung up the phone.: Interview with Saul Miller, 1/19/85.

249 "maybe she loved him more than she loved me.": Interview with Elizabeth
Phillips, 1/26/85.

249 "obtain assistance for [her] children . . . with whom she had made the appointment.: FBI JR-HQ 922, 3/14/51.

250 "I'm not such a hero . . . what kind of America will I give my kids?": Quoted
in John Wexley, op cit, p. 151.

250 Thus Ethel and Vivian sat only a few feet apart . . .: It is this author's firm
belief that Vivian Glassman, now Pataki, is one of the very few people still
living who has intimate knowledge of the Rosenbergs' lives between 1945
and 1950. I believe she is the one person, aside from Dave and Ruth Greenglass, who could shed light on the question of Julius Rosenberg's involvement
in espionage. But she steadfastly has refused to speak in public. When I wrote
to her in 1985 requesting an interview, she sent back a typed envelope with
no return address and a brief letter with no signature, clearly not wanting me
to have any sample of her handwriting, for reasons known only to her. She
declined to be interviewed. Her reluctance to speak remains a mystery and
legitimately raises the possibility that she has something to hide. This stance
is extremely unfortunate for when Ms. Pataki, who is now in her seventies,
dies, an invaluable source of information about the Rosenberg case will be
lost forever.

250 As one author notes, . . . Ethel or the grand jurors.: See Radosh and Milton,
op cit, p. 101.

251 "You'll have to come with us—you're under arrest.": Cited in John Wexley,
op cit, p. 151.

251 Ethel steadfastly refused to answer any of their questions . . .: FBI JR-HQ 536X,
9/1/50.

251 Lane accused her of "conspiracy to commit espionage," . . . "to flee the
United States and take refuge behind an Iron Curtain country.": Quoted in
the New York Times, 8/12/50.

252 [Her crime] by its very nature . . . the present situation in Korea.: Quoted in
the New York Times, 8/12/50.

252 He argued to the Commissioner that the only specific charge . . . Bail was set
at $100,000.: ibid.

252 When she heard the voice of her frightened, seven-year-old son . . . that would
haunt his mother until she herself was silenced.: Reported in Virginia Gardner,
op cit, p. 74.

CHAPTER SIXTEEN

253 On 11 August what the government had in its possession . . .: See Walter and
Miriam Schneir, op cit, p. 459.

254 "on an equal plane with the . . . furnish this type of information.": FBI JR-
HQ 130, 7/17/50.

254 Lane: "Was Ethel present . . . to protect my sister believe me that's a fact.":
FBI JR-HQ 813, 2/26/51.

254 It had a swanky-sounding address . . . who did not appreciate this country.:
Elizabeth Gurley Flynn, The Anderson Story; International Publishers, New
York; 1963; pp. 15–17, 20–21. Flynn arrived at the Women's House of De-
tention shortly after Ethel was transferred to Sing Sing in 1951.

256 "in desperation would do things . . . to defend themselves.": Interview with
Miriam Moskowitz, 4/9/85.

256 "there was a certain amount of resentment . . . of democracy, their enemy.": ibid.

256 "complained that the boys . . . encounter with the self-serving Greenglass family.: Quoted in Virginia Gardner, op cit, pp. 97–98.

256 "You're lucky they're born here or they'd be deported.": Quoted in Robert and Michael Meeropol, *We Are Your Sons*, op cit, p. 22.

257 "Your kids roam the streets . . . anywhere but with them [the Greenglasses], please.": Letter of "Jean" to Ethel Rosenberg, 10/25/50.

257 "it was time that she thought of herself and the children.": FBI JR-HQ 482, 9/18/50.

257 "that it is his opinion . . . of his progress in this regard.": FBI JR-HQ 493, 9/15/50.

257 "Dear Sis—. . . but I must have your co-operation.": Letter of Sam Greenglass to Ethel Rosenberg, undated.

258 Tessie used these occasions to urge Ethel . . . telling her mother she should never visit again.: FBI JR-HQ 482, 9/18/50; JR-HQ 1364, 12/10/52; cited in Virginia Gardner, op cit, pp. 82–3.

258 "with sadness . . . just one more blow": Interview with Miriam Moskowitz, 4/9/85.

258 "She felt wronged and sad more than angry": Interview with Elizabeth Phillips, 1/26/85.

259 "Nothing she said was phony . . . all she said hers was.": Quoted in Virginia Gardner, op cit, p. 78.

259 "I didn't think any man could be as perfect and as smart as she thought Julie was.": ibid, p. 83.

260 "Julie had the seat . . . I blew it out.": ibid, p. 78.

260 "save for your lawyer things that belong to your lawyer and we'll talk about things that belong to the family.": Interview with Elizabeth Phillips, 1/26/85.

261 In fact, he later would try . . . his treatment with a psychiatrist.: See Emanuel Bloch's cross-examination of Max Elitcher, Trial Transcript, op cit, pp. 348–350.

263 "See Julie wanted me to take over the children . . . Communist was a dirty word, right?": Interview with Ethel Appel, 1/13/85.

263 "with poor food, cold, drafty dormitory rooms . . . and that they'll let me go home now?": Michael Meeropol, *We Are Your Sons*, op cit, p. 26.

264 DEAR ETHEL WENT TO SEE CHILDREN . . . LET ME HEAR FROM YOU—MOTHER: Telegram of Tessie Greenglass to Ethel Rosenberg, 11/9/50.

265 "use the name . . . and 'spy' mean 'Communist.' " Julius Rosenberg quoted in Virginia Gardner, op cit, p. 94.

265 If it was a choice between . . . I thought I had.: Quoted in Radosh and Milton, op cit, p. 168.

265 I seriously doubt from my own experience . . . is about the only thing you can use as a lever on these people.: Joint Committee on Atomic Energy, *Proceedings*; Atomic Energy Commission, File No. 403, 2/8/51.

266 "[T]he case is not too strong . . . given a strong sentence.": ibid.

267 [She] looked rather tired . . . and Ethel assisted by Julius would correct the sentence grammatically.: FBI JR-HQ 812, 3/2/51.

268 "It was almost as if we threw that in to involve her . . . So at that point I said, 'Yeah, she must have been around.' ": Quoted in Radosh and Milton, op cit, pp. 164, 165.

268 "This description of the atom bomb . . . in the interests of the Soviets.": Trial Transcript, op cit, p. 1523.

268 "I don't remember when I told them . . . they want from you.": Quoted in Radosh and Milton, op cit, p. 165.

268 The paper had dined her at Luchows . . .: *Jewish Daily Forward*, 8/30/50 and 9/2/50.

269 the United States faced the "imminent peril" of being "swallowed by the Communist world.": Governor Thomas Dewey quoted in the *New York Times*, 8/1/50.

269 the "Informer Principle," . . . the ultimate evidence, the guarantor of patriotism.": Victor Navasky, *Naming Names*; Penguin Books, New York; 1982, p. 28.

CHAPTER SEVENTEEN

270 "But," according to Manny Bloch . . . in their professions.": Quoted in Virginia Gardner, op cit, p. 98.

270 For one thing, such character witnesses . . . be considered worthless as coming from "Fifth Amendment Communists?": Quoted in John Wexley, op cit, p. 226.

271 "Then when I read that . . . Finally I went back home.": Quoted in Virginia Gardner, op cit, p. 66.

272 Since the prevailing public attitude . . . and force it to stick to the evidence.: John Wexley, op cit, p. 225.

273 "only to turn us into informers or to create the idea all Communists are spies.": This is Emanuel Bloch's paraphrasing of the Rosenbergs' position, quoted in Virginia Gardner, op cit, p. 98.

273 "fought against loose tongues . . . about their own affiliations and associations.": Paul Lyons, op cit, pp. 134–135.

273 I was determined that before . . . I could get to telling him [about my CP membership].": Interview with Carl Marzani, 1/12/85.

274 One would hardly have thought that he and his wife were on trial for their lives.: Morton Sobell, *On Doing Time*, op cit, p. 213.

274 As far as she was aware, she faced the possibility of life imprisonment . . .: Ruth Greenglass's name had been added to the conspiracy in which Ethel purportedly was involved in the indictment of 17 August 1950.

274 "clothes Ethel wore to trial broke my heart . . . particularly those of us who had been before juries.": Quoted in Virginia Gardner, op cit, p. 77.

276 "prospect of Mrs. Rosenberg being faced . . . and is now listed as a Government witness.": *New York Times*, 3/7/51.

276 "lawyers could confer, but we defendants . . . before or after going to the courtroom.": Morton Sobell, *On Doing Time*, op cit, p. 124, 123.

276 "brightest dab of color in the great chestnut-paneled chamber.": *New York Times*, 3/7/51.

277 "it is unlikely all of these witnesses . . . strategy in the prosecution of this case.": FBI JR-HQ 795, 3/5/51.

277 "if your clients don't confess they are doomed.": Quoted in Radosh and Milton, op cit, p. 171.

277 He demonstrated his intention to dismiss . . . was challenged by Kaufman and excused.: Trial Transcript, op cit, pp. 59, 74.

278 [A] conspiracy is very simply . . . guilty of the crime of conspiracy.: Trial Transcript, op cit, p. 179.

278 "semi-rigid, edged a little forward . . . carefully measured words,": *New York Times*, 3/8/51.

278 "The evidence will show that the loyalty and the allegiance . . . can be committed against the people of this country.": Trial Transcript, op cit, pp. 180–184, passim.

279 Throughout all of Saypol's inflammatory . . . "fixed on the jury box.": *New York Times*, 3/8/51.

280 "a dark-haired boyish official with ringing voice,": *New York Times*, 3/10/51.

280 "Now did you have any discussion with Ethel and Julius . . . aware that he was smiling while continuing to smile.: Trial Transcript, op cit, pp. 399, 414, 420, 540.

280 "Julius has finally gotten to a point . . . to engage in espionage at Los Alamos.: ibid, p. 424.

280 "went deathly pale . . . features were almost snow pale.": *New York Times*, 3/10/51.

281 "come in with them on this espionage work.": Trial Transcript, op cit, p. 489.

281 Q. Do you bear any affection for your sister . . . A. At this moment.: ibid, p. 558.

282 Well, Ethel said that she was tired . . . to entertain his friends . . .: ibid, p. 691.

282 I asked him what he was doing . . . it was necessary and they were going to go.: ibid, p. 713.

283 "gave me a sheet of paper: . . . I come from Julius'.": ibid, p. 822.

283 "to know what injections . . . for a friend of mine.": ibid, p. 851.

283 "The Communist Party being part of . . . propaganda or espionage or sabotage.": ibid, p. 978.

284 First of all, I am not an expert on matters on different economic systems . . . A. Well, your Honor, I feel at this time that I refuse to answer a question that might tend to incriminate me.: ibid, pp. 1078–1080.

286 Instead of forthrightness, there was furtiveness . . . and they cannot be ignored . . .: Louis Nizer, *The Implosion Conspiracy*; Fawcett Publications, Greenwich, Conn.; 1973; p. 237.

286 Q. 'Mr. Rosenberg, tell us . . . Who were they?': Trial Transcript, op cit, p. 1159.

286 ("It was a corollary of the Informer Principle that the act of informing was more important than the information imparted."): Victor Navasky, op cit, pp. 28–29.

286 A. I don't understand what you mean, Mr. Saypol . . . I will not answer any question on it.: Trial Transcript, op cit, pp. 1159–1165, passim.

287 "she would just eat everything . . . because of this gnawing inside of her.": Interview with Helen Sobell, 9/12/84.

288 "knotted her fingers and wrinkled her forehead," and her voice faded.: *New York Times*, 3/27/51.

288 Her typing quickly became a centerpiece of her testimony.: For all quotations from Ethel's direct and cross-examination, see Trial Transcript, op cit, pp. 1293–1402.

292 "one-two combination of judge and prosecutor, working in tandem.": Morton Sobell, *On Doing Time*, op cit, p. 224.

293 [W]hen she was on the stand, she was just horribly badgered . . . I was tremendously impressed.: Interview with Helen Sobell, 9/12/84.

294 It was a wonder that through it all . . . rather like a modern Greek tragedy.: Morton Sobell, *On Doing Time*, op cit, p. 229.

294 I wouldn't have believed that she was capable . . . I don't know how she kept her cool.: Interview with Morton Sobell, 1/15/85.

CHAPTER EIGHTEEN

295 "I would like to say to the Court . . . we are appreciative of the courtesies extended to us . . .": Trial Transcript, op cit, pp. 1452–1453.

296 But one thing I think you do know, . . . that you have ever seen . . .: ibid, p. 1467.

380

296 Maybe some of you are more acute . . . she won't be able to fool you.: ibid, pp. 1475–1477, passim.

296 If there has been any fooling . . . leave it to you as to who may have been fooled.: ibid, p. 1509.

296 Rosenberg and his wife have added . . . their sins by lying.: ibid, pp. 1519, 1520.

297 The crime charged here is one of the most serious . . . less deserving of sympathy than these.: ibid, p. 1535.

298 "In that environment it was . . . very sweet, strong, clear, and precise.": Interview with Helen Sobell, 9/12/84.

298 "It was her way of saying good night . . . recalled Miriam Moskowitz.: Quoted in Virginia Gardner, op cit, p. 76.

298 "sometimes at a time of war and horror . . . it speaks of basic human values.": Interview with Ronnie Gilbert, published in "Singing for Their Lives," *Socialist Review*, Vol. 14, No. 1 (Jan–Feb 1984); p. 87.

298 "I have a communication from the jury . . . upon the defendants to influence your verdict in any way.": Trial Transcript, op cit, p. 1574.

299 "After all . . . the evidence against her had been so minimal.": Morton Sobell, *On Doing Time*, op cit, p. 248.

299 *Mr. A. Bloch:* Tonight? . . . our verdict on all these defendants until we have complete unanimity.": ibid, pp. 1575–1578, passim.

299 *The Clerk:* Mr. Foreman, . . . We the jury find Morton Sobell guilty as charged.: ibid, p. 1579.

299 Ethel "took the verdict stoically without changing expression.": *New York Times*, 3/30/51.

300 My own opinion is that your verdict is a correct verdict . . . that you examined carefully the evidence and came to a certain conclusion.: Trial Transcript, op cit, pp. 1580–1583.

301 Afterwards everyone began congratulating everyone else . . . In this case the lives of the defendants were the stakes.: Morton Sobell, *On Doing Time*, op cit, pp. 249–250.

301 "We talked about Kaufman's raw rulings . . . and we all joined in a discussion of hot pastrami vs. corned beef.": ibid, p. 250.

302 "As they sat there in the solemn hush . . . trying to assure them all that she was quite all right.": Quoted in Virginia Gardner, op cit, p. 80.

302 "if Mrs. Rosenberg were sentenced to a prison . . . on the basis of her evidence.": FBI JR-HQ 945, 4/3/51.

302 J. Edgar Hoover also had qualms . . . to sending a woman and mother to her death.: FBI JR-HQ 944, and unrecorded before 945, 4/2/51.

303 "It is too bad that drawing and quartering has been abolished.": As law clerk to Supreme Court Justice Robert Jackson, Rehnquist wrote this in a memo to Jackson in 1953. Quoted in *New York Times*, 7/27/86.

303 They rode to Foley Square believing . . .: See FBI JR-HQ 730, 2/10/51 and 961, 4/5/51.

303 "inside sources . . . that they will crack and talk.": Hy Gardner, New York *Herald Tribune*, 4/12/51.

303 "In terms of human life, . . . suffering of countless other human beings.": Trial Transcript, op cit, pp. 1602–1603.

304 After Saypol concluded, Emanuel Bloch rose to speak . . . these people are the type of people that ordinarily come before you in a criminal case?: ibid, pp. 1604–1612.

305 Judge Kaufman began his sentencing speech with a bold-faced lie . . . you are hereby sentenced to the punishment of death . . .: ibid, pp. 1612–1616.

307 Julius "gave a short imperative nod to his wife, signaling her to leave.": *New York Times*, 4/6/51.

307 Julie's "face was livid . . . Finally the words came: 'Ethel, too.' ": Quoted in Virginia Gardner, op cit, p. 91.

307 Then suddenly, as if to relieve the growing tension . . . I think I'd rather be shot.": Quoted in ibid.

308 He explained that the verdict was inevitable . . . and a Communist an espionage agent.": Quoted in ibid, pp. 96–97.

308 "Ethel, don't be scared if some clown . . . must evoke a sense of outrage in time he had no doubt at all.": Quoted in ibid, p. 92.

309 "Ethel, the other one!": Quoted in ibid, p. 93.

309 "[Y]ou're a low-down son of a bitch . . . I never had the money to do anything for her. Think of that.": Quoted in ibid.

CHAPTER NINETEEN

311 "Oh, no, nothing's wrong. I just heard that scream again last night,": Quoted in Virginia Gardner, op cit, p. 74.

311 According to Ethel's confidante . . .: Interview with Miriam Moskowitz, 4/9/85.

312 Although Ethel acted like "a fierce mother wolf": Interview with Miriam Moskowitz, 4/9/85.

312 "who knows what happens in prison . . . thinking that you're doing something, making a mark?": Interview with Elizabeth Phillips, 1/26/85.

313 He maintains that while Ethel was in prison "the children . . . became more abstract than real.: Interview with Saul Miller, 1/19/85.

314 Miriam cried, "They can't get away with this;" . . . to be immediately screaming that these were frame-ups!": Interview with Miriam Moskowitz, 4/9/85.

315 Gordon notes, however, that he was prevented from writing anything until the Party leadership "gave the signal," which it refused to do.: Cited in Radosh and Milton, op cit, p. 328.

315 His wife reports that the response he received was that the Rosenbergs were "expendable.": ibid, p. 327.

316 it "shouldn't get contaminated by these [atom spy] cases . . . was the "politically correct" position.: Interview with Miriam Moskowitz, 4/9/85.

316 "what do spy trials have to do with politics?": Interview with William Reuben, 1/30/85.

317 "the American Communist Party became . . . but no longer a power.": Joseph Starobin, op cit, p. 191.

317 the Justice Department and J. Edgar Hoover publicly referred to the "15,000 potential Smith Act defendants" yet to be arrested: Cited in Victor Navasky, op cit, p. 27.

317 [A]n atmosphere of near-panic gripped the American Communists . . . capable of withstanding quasi-fascist repression.: Joseph Starobin, op cit, pp. 419–420.

317 The structure that the Party was constructing in March and April 1951 . . .: ibid, p. 421.

318 She was not a rebel . . . and I think that's what she was.: Interview with Miriam Moskowitz, 4/9/85.

318 The New York Times reported that Tessie pleaded "for mercy for her children.": New York Times, 4/5/51 (emphasis added).

318 On the evening of the ninth, . . . Ethel be transferred out of the Women's House of Detention.: FBI JR-HQ 1001, 4/9/51.

319 "They expect me to break under the strain . . . But I won't.": Quoted in Virginia Gardner, op cit, p. 99.

319 We couldn't get our heads out [of the windows], . . . So her smile was for us . . .: Quoted in the Worker, 10/25/53, and Virginia Gardner, op cit, p. 72.

320   "Mrs. Rosenberg, Condemned Atom Spy, Taken to Sing Sing.": *New York Times*, 4/12/51.

CHAPTER TWENTY

324   he "continually came to see her, this reflected back to her that she *was* a heroine.": Interview with Saul Miller, 1/19/85.

324   Dr. Miller asserts that he would have done this for any one . . . that she must have believed reinforced her laudability.: ibid.

325   "lead to a nervous breakdown and in all probability drive her insane.": Quoted in the *New York Times*, 5/8/51.

328   Both the boys immediately said . . . why this might be so.: Michael Meeropol, *We Are Your Sons*, op cit, p. 85.

328   After the guard nodded, Ethel announced "Mommy has to go somewhere now" and departed.: *National Guardian*, 8/8/51.

328   Yet, Michael remembers their time together in a very positive light . . .: See Michael Meeropol, *We Are Your Sons*, op cit, p. 86.

328   In his Sing Sing conferences with his clients—all of which were bugged, summarized by prison officials, and transmitted to the FBI: See FBI JR-HQ 1139, 8/8/51; and JR-HQ 1150, 8/14/51.

329   Manny Bloch encouraged this perspective by telling Ethel and Julie . . .: FBI JR-HQ 1185, 11/2/51; and JR-HQ 1689, 6/3/53.

331   At the time of her death, this notebook contained some 200 pages of rough draft.: FBI JR-HQ 1996, 6/29/53.

331   Its editor, I. F. Stone, believed the Rosenbergs were guilty.: Interview with William Reuben, 1/30/85.

333   In October it seemed as though the avalanche of protest . . . on the appeals of Ethel and Julius Rosenberg against their conviction and sentence to death.: *National Guardian*, 10/10/51.

334   By the end of the month, Reuben could report . . . and of love of freedom and their fellow man.: ibid, 10/31/51.

336   On Monday, 25 February, the United States Circuit Court of Appeals . . . to the Supreme Court for a reduction of sentence.: Louis Nizer, *The Implosion Conspiracy*, Fawcett Crest, New York; 1973; pp. 421–439, passim.

338   He "never thought of her . . . as "a grown child.": Interview with Saul Miller, 1/19/85.

342   "transform . . . the constitutional petitions of decent citizens for redress of grievances . . . into vilification and abuse,": Statement of Ethel and Julius Rosenberg, *National Guardian*, 1/8/53.

343   "once the current passes through the bodies . . . to their children and to American justice . . .": Quoted in the *National Guardian*, 1/8/53.

343   "There is mercy which is weakness . . . The application is denied.": Ruling on judicial clemency, 1/2/53, on file at Foley Square.

344   After returning home from Sing Sing, Tessie Greenglass . . . she would be unmoved by her daughter's plight.: FBI JR-HQ 1410, 1/9/53, and JR-HQ, 1/9/53.

344   "wanted to bust out at him but kept my mouth shut.": FBI JR-HQ 1410, 1/9/53.

345   Ethel reportedly "told her off," . . . one kind word from her.": As told by Emanuel Bloch in Virginia Gardner, op cit, p. 101.

345   According to the prison official who listened . . . "no matter what she tried to do she was accused of doing wrong.": FBI JR-HQ 1570, 3/17/53, and JR-HQ 1578, 3/25/53.

345   "Cowards die many times . . . taste of death but once.": Holworthy Hall and Robert Middlemass, *The Valiant*; Harold E. Porter, New York; 1924; p. 25.

345 The nature of the crime . . . are fighting and dying at this very hour.: Quoted in *New York Times*, 2/12/53.

346 "the more strong-minded and the apparent leader of the two.": Quoted in Radosh and Milton, op cit, p. 378.

346 "in this instance it is the woman . . . in everything they did in the spy ring.": Quoted in Stephen E. Ambrose with Richard H. Immerman, *Ike's Spies*; Doubleday, New York; 1981; pp. 182–183.

346 "Dwight Eisenhower's answer all but closed the door . . . have shown no flicker of regret.": *Time*, 2/23/53.

348 As the children wandered aimlessly around the room, Ethel read aloud her letter . . .: Quoted in Louis Nizer, *The Implosion Conspiracy*; Fawcett Crest, Greenwich, Ct; 1973; pp. 490–491.

348 Michael could not tolerate what seemed to be his parents' indifference . . .: See Michael Meeropol, *We Are Your Sons*, op cit, p.226.

350 "Give this to Ethel—it represents some mother's love": Interview with Miriam Moskowitz, 4/9/85.

351 "Oh, Mrs. Evans, you're such a wonderful woman.": Quoted in Virginia Gardner, "Ethel's Last Hours—Never Forgotten," *The Daily People's World*, 6/16/59.

351 "with the most composed look you ever saw": *New York Times*, 6/20/53.

351 "They died differently . . . Ethel Rosenberg was dead.": Quoted in Alvin H. Goldstein, op cit, unpaginated.

352 "I asked what had happened . . . In fact, he understood very well—": Michael Meeropol, *We Are Your Sons*, op cit, p. 238.

352 "[T]his is not a time to grieve . . . the terror that made them its victims.": Quoted in *National Guardian*, 6/29/53.

353 "a few lines representing the view of the family . . . so you'll be back where you belong, among all of us. Love, Bernie.": FBI JR-HQ 1995, 6/21/53.

354 Five days later Tessie called the FBI . . . "Mr. Harrington, you should know that I do not attend political rallies.": FBI JR-HQ 2043, 6/24/53.

355 "Was your wife cognizant of your activities?": FBI JR-HQ 1935, 6/17/53.

355 Millions of people the world over will long remember . . . this heartrending defeat must be examined searchingly.: Quoted in Peggy Dennis, *The Autobiography of an American Communist*; Lawrence Hill and Co., Westport, CT; 1977; p. 210.

355 "[E]ven at the end the Rosenbergs were not able to think . . . in the end to become martyrs or heroes, or even men.": Leslie Fiedler, "Afterthoughts on the Rosenbergs," in his *An End to Innocence*; Beacon Press, Boston; 1955; pp. 38, 45.

356 "The *National Guardian* stands in horror and shame . . . and to their children, we owe a solemn debt.": *National Guardian*, 6/22/53.

ACKNOWLEDGMENTS

In working on this book I have learned how the legacy of McCarthyism and Stalinism linger in the 1980's. The number of people who declined to be interviewed for this book—out of fear or recalcitrance—the threatened legal action by the Rosenbergs' sons, the reluctance of some of those I interviewed to have controversial or "incorrect" statements appear in print, has taught me far more than any book I've read or research I've conducted. In this light, my greatest appreciation must go to those people who spoke openly and honestly with me about their memories of Ethel Rosenberg. Their names appear throughout this book and it is to them that I owe my greatest debt. I have also benefitted enormously from two books, long out of print, that provided much information and background: Virginia Gardner's *The Rosenberg Story* and William Reuben's *The Atom Spy Hoax*. Although they draw different conclusions from the material they present than is found in this book, their work was invaluable.

Throughout this entire project Michael Bader has been a constant source of support, encouragement and stability. I could not have written this without him. Because of Elliott Currie's enthusiasm and assistance, a biography of Ethel Rosenberg was transformed from an idea into a book. As a critical and compassionate writer, he remains a role model. I also would like to thank Richard Corey, Barbara Epstein, Jeffrey Escoffier, Linda Goettina, Alice Hamers, and Zeese Papanikolas for their help. And to the many friends and colleagues who have supported me in maintaining that historical inquiry should not be fettered by political or ideological claims, I owe an enormous debt.

INDEX